The Brotherhood of the Common Life and Its Influence

SUNY Series in Western Esoteric Traditions
Edited by David Appelbaum

D1594783

The Brotherhood
of the Common Life
and Its Influence

by
ROSS FULLER

STATE UNIVERSITY OF NEW YORK PRESS

All illustrations reprinted by permission of the British Library.

Published by
State University of New York Press, Albany

© 1995   Ross Fuller

For information, address State University of New York Press,
State University Plaza, Albany, N.Y., 12246

Production by Cathleen Collins
Marketing by Bernadette LaManna

Library of Congress Cataloging-in-Publication Data

Fuller, Ross, 1946–
    The Brotherhood of the Common Life and its influence / Ross
Fuller
        p.   cm. — (SUNY series in Western esoteric traditions)
    Includes bibliographical references and index.
    ISBN 0–7914–2243–7 — ISBN 0–7914–2244–5
    1. Brothers of the Common Life. 2. Devotio moderna—Influence.
3. Laity—Catholic Church—Religious life. 4. Spiritual life—
Catholic Church. 5. Reformation—Early movements.   I. Title.
II. Series.
BX3070.F85   1995
267'.242—dc20   94–545
                                                                                  CIP

10 9 8 7 6 5 4 3 2 1

Contents

Illustrations

A Personal Preface

'Who am I?' Drawn naturally to the horizon between my worlds, as a young research student I stumbled across material so uncomfortably close to home that I have been troubled by it ever since.

> Man will consider himself master of his lower self as long as he has not sensed the lack of faith, hope and love in his mind.

Material for thought, indeed! How passionately it was sought, how assiduously gathered, and, the process slowing and deflecting, how reluctantly digested! If it is true that we listen only to our own thought while learning and thus hear nothing new, it is also true that, realising this, a hunger develops, as if our thought had an inner form, a proper food. But as a dutiful student I was rapidly learning to convert the true coin of my ignorance into something easier to live with, only at moments suspecting uneasily that, within academic circles, a genuine hunger threatening to enter evoked its opposite, setting in motion a passive process of substitution, of which a mere "knowing about" ideas could be the only residue. If the price of an active mental enquiry was freedom from all the subtle forms of emotional interference and the rediscovery of the intelligence of the heart, where then was the paymaster?

I had already discerned in the Gothic cathedral, on Mount Athos, in Ravenna, in ancient liturgy and art, the imprint of a forgotten Christian culture, an immeasurable depth and simplicity of feeling. It seems to me now that this gave birth to a wordless question about its source, and that *I* was somehow included, therefore at stake, in these finer impressions just because they had been received. Whether or not this was a rite of passage, the promise and threat of being answerable has been with me ever since. If the categories of sacred meaning had reached the present day only in name, what was the question? And if not now, when? The experience of these contradictions, poverty and wealth touching, alerted something not entirely subjective, or perhaps truly subjective.

The material that I subsequently found, or was found by, although hypnotic for me, concerned de-hypnosis: the possibility that moments of awakening to oneself could so permeate daily life that it could be radically reorientated.

> I pray Him to take heed to me & soothly I myself take neither heed to myself nor to Him . . . and yet for all that He cries to us, saying: "O ye sinners, turn again & remember yourself. Take heed & see, for I am God."

This material pointed to nothing less than a lost tradition of spiritual work, a 'way in life' for 'the householder,' known by our ancestors six hundred years ago—and perhaps time out of mind, for the Brethren of The Common Life believed this to have been the teaching received by the Apostles.

The Brethren gathered around Gerard Groote, whose words on faith, hope and love were cited above, at the end of the fourteenth century in the Low Countries. They lived and worked together voluntarily, but without taking 'vows' and without separating themselves from the life of their time. From a hidden reservoir of living Christian spirituality, a practical way of freeing and interiorising the power of attention was conducted through Gerard and his helpers to touch just those whom it touched in a society increasingly hidebound by its external separation of the sacred and profane. The balance to which they were called, a 'mixed life' reconciling action and contemplation, included a third term, a devotion which was 'new' in the sense of needing to be found and refound, yet understood already in those monastic circles by whom Gerard was guided:

> Thou hast one cell without, another within. The outward cell is the house wherein thy soul and thy body dwell together; the inward is thy conscience, which ought to be dwelt in by God (who is more inward than all thine inward parts) and by thy spirit. . . . Wherefore love thou thine inward cell, and love the outward; and give unto each its proper service . . . and get for thyself the lordship therein.

I must state here that, during my researches and now, the birth of a more conscious influence lies beyond my field of vision. Although the question of levels of consciousness was always with me while writing, and indeed runs through this book like a red thread, the word 'esoteric' occurs nowhere in the text. I do not claim to have demonstrated that this late medieval brotherhood was an esoteric school, but I have traced a transmission of spiritual exercises supported by a powerful psychological critique, which, being perennial, is strangely familiar in the climate of today's search for meaning. I have consistently attempted to put into words more than I understand, in order to bring it closer.

Whatever questions one may entertain about the duality of human nature and the presence of two streams in the history of mankind, common sense urges that such conscious influences, however elusive, equivocal or distorted in the accidentally surviving historical record, must have been borne by people in order to have entered our world. In questioning them personally, as it were, I have tried to penetrate upstream, in the direction of a source, by every means open to me. Because, in my view, the intellectual formulae of modern thought are singularly unsuited to embrace the essential quality of this material, serving an understanding at best vicarious, at worst voyeuristic, I have endeavoured to consider it on its own terms, in the context of traditional thought and, as it could only be, in the light of my own experience.

In doing so, I came to feel that this relatively short-lived movement came from 'somewhere more intelligent,' bearing a corresponding influence, an influence so appropriate that it seems in retrospect inevitable, and was able to carry it into the life of its time for a certain period, while assuming the necessary cultural subjectivity in matters of outer organisation. While studying the Brotherhood I persistently felt it to have been a kind of experiment, realising uneasily that I was far from understanding such an implied scale of meaning. Altogether, there is something here 'in the depths too deep and in the shallows too swift' to be easily netted.

The material I am presenting hovers around the inherent human possibility to awaken impartially to 'what is,' just that state of 'remembering oneself' in the total absence of which 'the common Life' remains a fantasy, then as now.

I have coined the name 'New Devotionalist,' to denote those who were demonstrably touched by these questions, however it was expressed in their life work. I have tried to focus on an inner movement at the point of entering the stream of 'history,' rather than a 'historical movement' in the conventional sense. In the course of writing the subject has moved, with the deepening of my interest, to a point somewhere between psychology, philosophy and spirituality.

For about two hundred years an echo of the influence which the Brethren in their turn transmitted—'the New Devotion'—can be detected in the attitude of the new religious orders of the Counter Reformation, and especially in the crescendo of manuals of all doctrinal persuasions dealing with the ordering of daily life, from within and without. It was this literature, incidentally—or perhaps not so incidentally, which fortified the first settlers in 'the New World.' This influence coincided, providentially, with a landslide in European culture, in which much of the centuries-old understanding of man and his place in the world disappeared or was denatured out of recognition.

Standing at this moment in a wide circle of indebtedness, I wish to acknowledge those who have supported this work: Professor Jacob Needleman, Alexandra Dobbs, Jenny Koralek, James Watson, the late Christopher Kenney O.B.E., Dr. Louis and Nancy Brenner, Father Robert Bell, Brian and the late Jackie Painter, Lesley Croome, Hannah Bensley, John Beadle, George Rayer, Robin Allard, the late Neil Olley, Julian Keable, Ben Pearce-Higgins, Peter Nott, David Jongeward, Michael Hackett, Stella Marsden, Dick Temple, Philippe Clément and Dr. Christopher Solomon, for reading and making suggestions on the manuscript; the sterling help of Brian and Robert Painter with the mysteries of the computer;

Jeffrey Somers, Dick Keane, Walter Nelson, Roy Ashwell and Robin Waterfield for legal and publishing advice; Tony Hare for a quotation from Meister Eckhart; Georgina and Eric Poole for their translations from the Latin; Professor John Varey for the use of his fax machine; Mike Barker, Connie Walker, Nan Ashcroft, Edward and Marie-Claire Siegel and Richard and Susan Toub for their kindness. The generosity of Sally Hornby enabled me to edit the text on a word-processor. Without the support of Virginia Walker, Renee Elsner, Anne Israel, Eleanor Hudson and Nesta Brooking, the final stages would have foundered. Mrs. Anny Juer was the midwife. The limitations are mine.

This book is dedicated to my Father and Mother, and to Dr. and Mrs. Juer with love and gratitude.

Introduction

Brother Body is our cell, and the body sits therein like a hermit
and thinks on God and prays to Him.

Francis of Assisi, 1217

Christ knows how needful the true Christian man be in this
world.

The Original and sprynge of all sectes and orders, 1537

This book examines the transition between the human laboratory of the early
medieval monastery and the Reformation's revelation of "the true Christian
man in this world." It focuses on the emergence, amidst the decay of medieval
culture, of 'the mixed life'—the reconciliation of action and contemplation—as
the essential link in the passage from medieval spirituality to Protestantism, in
harmony with the traditional Monastic Way but not requiring formal withdrawal
from the world. This is an element in the spiritual inheritance of modern man
that has hardly reached him, except perhaps as a vague idea.

At the heart of the enquiry lies the spiritual and psychological understanding
on which the daily life of the Brethren was based, and the transmission of their
work to laymen seeking the interior dimension to their lives, in the form of hitherto 'monastic' spiritual exercises for strengthening attention. Together with its
reflection in the eleventh hour 'Observant' monastic reform movement, the totality of this influence came to be known as 'The New Devotion.'

I am trying, in other words, to follow a movement between the inner life and
the outer 'historical' manifestation, which is reflected in the two quotations heading this introduction. It is my view that Christianity, in common with all traditional teachings, is essentially concerned with wholeness, the healing of division
on every level. During the period in question, this aspiration was still being supported by a comprehensive Christian knowledge of the human condition, which
the Brethren, contrary to our ideas about 'the age of faith,' were encouraged to
verify for themselves. This knowledge recognised, for example, the crucial signifi-

cance of the force of attention in the recollection of oneself and God. The emphasis I have placed on the search for, and the development of, this force in the individual is confirmed everywhere in the material presented, yet is virtually ignored in present-day accounts of the Christian tradition. Such questions are clearly experiential rather than academic: my intention has been to bring these two, usually mutually exclusive approaches closer to each other, in the belief that both might benefit. The poor vestiges of our spiritual tradition are too important to become the exclusive preserve of the intellectual academic or partisan religious. There is much more practicality in the Christian legacy than we have been led to believe.

The word 'religion,' which occurs constantly in this book, signifies both the historical monastic condition and the act of reuniting, literally binding-together-again (re-ligare). The history with which we will be concerned turns on this ambiguity. Both these meanings of religion open worlds of enquiry, and the second bears a profound question which, even if it cannot be answered, must yet be remembered, for it lies close to the very ground of human experience. When these two meanings—the outer and the inner—have met in the being of one person, the tradition has been sustained.

There are signs today of a renewed interest in the Christian tradition, for Christianity remains, in a sense, an unknown religion. Everything I have studied and experienced has reinforced the dual impression that, buried in the historical record are fragments of a teaching the most significant part of which has been lost, and that something needs to be rediscovered and reanimated in the individual before a viable relationship with the meaning of the tradition can be reestablished. The unique familiarity of the words and phrases conventionally used to describe Christianity maintains a sense of a common 'objective' understanding which is reassuring but false, because each person unwittingly associates with these terms subjectively.

An idea cannot be understood unless it is lived: in the absence of this attempt understanding is assumed. How, then, can one begin to think authoritatively about the greater reality of a teaching? Research brings the realisation that the increase of knowledge does not automatically increase understanding. The accumulation of information on the same level can extinguish even the interest I had. That active, useful learning begins with a painful awareness of ignorance, underlying which is the ignorance of ourselves, can link us with these remote historical figures, our brothers indeed, who well understood this.

At all times and in all places human beings have recorded the fleeting sense of realising and then forgetting that they were being called to experience their lives more consciously: to awaken. This movement has been described in religious and philosophical traditions as the struggle between light and darkness, good and evil, joy and sorrow. The innumerable forms it has taken—and still takes—truly constitute the drama of the lives of men and of man, that is, of history at all levels.

Monasticism had been one of the fundamental Ways by which this awakening to higher truth and meaning, to what is called God, had been sought. This book is simply about the means adopted at a certain period for intensifying this struggle. The mixed life, uniting action and contemplation in the midst of daily activity, could become such a preparation for the whole commitment to religion as monasticism itself had been. In order to understand better what had to be transmitted, we must first enquire more deeply into the original reality of the medieval monastery, while carrying the question of what a man's effort in this direction might entail.

In all religious traditions there have been special communities of more intensive practice and intentional organisation, set apart on principle from the influences and values 'of the world,' as places of probation and preparation. Benedict of Nursia (c. 480–547), 'the father of Western Monasticism,' a man "knowingly ignorant and wisely unlearned," gathered such a community in southern Italy during a temporary lull in the continual warfare, in which the fabric of 'civilised' life, as it had been known for over five hundred years, was being dissolved. This 'invisible' event was a turning point. His foundation went unnoticed in the slender chronicles of the time, and within thirty years of his death had been, apparently, destroyed and its members dispersed. The enormous subsequent influence of this community issued from the quality of life maintained there for a relatively short period, a life of which nothing can be known with certainty as the earliest extant manuscripts of the *Regula Benedicti* date from two hundred years later.[1]

It seems that the Benedictine house was a self-contained family of men living a simple, ordered life based on the sacred measure of seven and three.[2] The day was divided between liturgical chanting (*opus dei*, work for God, seven times to be produced "in such a way that our minds may be in harmony with our voices"[3]), private prayer and study (*lectio divina*[4]) and manual craft work (intended to rest and anchor the mind after prayer[5]). Provision was thus made for the conscious exercise of the mind, the heart and the body. There is ample evidence that, within this outer order, balance was being sought through the practice of inner discipline. Gregory the Great, who transmitted Benedict's work, wrote: "The discipline of silence is a kind of nourishment of the word. . . . by keeping silence we must learn to speak. . . . I hear what it is that I speak to you."[6]

In the midst of the heightened instability, disorganisation and violence of sixth-century Europe, then, the Western monastery came into being, existing separately from 'the world,' yet within its bosom; a special place, enclosed and stable, dedicated to a definite kind of work, both inner and outer, which must be named as the purification of emotion through obedience.[7] The monastery was a "workshop" (*officina*[8]) in which the brethren themselves were the raw material, a workshop for which they qualified through the force of their self-denial, their ability to renounce their own will and submit to the Rule and the Father Abbot, held to be the representative of Christ Himself amongst them. They aspired to become "workmen" (*operarii*[9]) of God, by "unceasingly" using "the tools of the spiritual craft" (*instrumenta artis spiritualis*[10]): they were working on themselves, upon egoistic habits of thought, emotion and movement. What must a man pass through and find in himself in order to be able "to keep death daily before one's eyes" or "to utter truth from heart and mouth,"[11] and why? From the oral tradition of the early monks of the Egyptian desert, amongst whom the Christian monastic experiment is considered to have begun and whose ascetic teachings underlie and complete the *Regula Benedicti,* stories have been preserved of the moment when the master's call to obey comes so decisively that the scribe is able to stop the movement of his hand in the middle of the action of forming an individual letter. It was said there that to be a monk meant to be intentionally at war, to eschew an easy life inwardly as well as outwardly, not to expect "peace," to carry in all circumstances the question "Who am I?" to work in such a way that "he can lay a new foundation at every moment."[12]

Entering a Benedictine monastery, a man was asked to work "altogether shunning forgetfulness," "while there is still time, while we are in this body and can fulfil all these things by the light of this life."[13] A remarkable saying has survived from the desert concerning this:

[I]n itself forgetfulness has no power; it is sustained by our negligence and corresponds to it. Do not say, What can I do? I do not want it (forgetfulness) and yet it comes. This is so because you have neglected what was necessary when you remembered. . . . If, according to the Scriptures, the cause of all that is involuntary lies in what is voluntary, no one is a man's greater enemy than himself.[14]

Benedict also called the monastery "a school of service of the Lord" (*dominici schola servitii*[15]): "our life in this world" was a ladder between heaven and earth whose sides are the body and the soul (*anima*), upon which the brethren ascend through humility and descend through self-exaltation.[16] Humility is just the consciousness of one's real place on this great scale. "The work of obedience," which is "the first degree of humility," is connected specifically with being able to listen with "the ear of the heart";[17] the "sloth of disobedience" is the state in which all live who blindly and choicelessly obey only their own desires. Real obedience is possible, says Benedict, only upon awakening from that sleep of which the New Testament speaks so consistently.[18]

Benedict stated that "the full observance of justice is not established in this rule," but, although only "a little rule for beginners," it could nevertheless lead eventually along "the narrow way" to Christ's religion of Love, that is, to "our Creator."[19] This was his hope. In this sense, the monastery he conceived was not yet a house in which men could be said to be Christian, but a place of preparation for this, a forecourt, a possible bridge to another life: an experiment of mutual relationship in pursuit of a common aim, in which like minded men joined together to help and remind each other in the struggle with their weaknesses, supported by an ordered and harmonious daily rhythm. The Way of the Monk, it is implied, began only *after* this bridge had been crossed.[20] But, historically, the monasteries of the Black Monks, as they were called, became a channel through which Christian teachings were given recognisable and tangible form, and, as such, were able to enter as a certain kind of influence into the life of Europe, with incalculable results for good and evil.

The paradigmatic monastery of the early Middle Ages which developed from this experiment was a nucleus of structures centred upon a church, girded with subsidiary buildings for guests and services, a kind of sacred village derived from the vernacular architecture of the secular village or manorial complex. The monastery represented, not an isolated place estranged from 'normal life,' but a heightened and perfected state of normality, partaking of both worlds in which man lives, visibly present while available to another order of influences.[21]

While the deep meaning of the tradition may be sensed, we must beware of assuming. How can there be a normality free from the influences of 'the world,' especially for the Christian? Is not 'the world' all that he must struggle with? What does practicality mean here? 'The world' is also, necessarily, in the monk, who, facing himself anew in this special place, must be brought again and again into question, unto 'fear of the Lord'—the beginning of real understanding. Was it Benedict's thought that the exterior, habitual, involuntary aspects of the novice's being, his 'fallen' and 'sinful' nature, could be experienced more directly and fruitfully under the guided influence of an ordered life and the continual reminders of a teaching directed to another, 'normally' dormant, part of him? The evidence indicates that the monastery was a place where the crucial struggle between 'the world' and 'the spirit'—corresponding to the fundamental duality of human nature—might proceed more intensively for those who sincerely sought it: our two natures are not on the same level. 'The world' is indeed necessary to the monk, and is, anyway, evoked by its denial. If there can be no normality without its presence, there can be none if he is entirely absorbed in it, for this is not a question of 'two,' of comparison, but of 'three.' Being himself the battlefield, the more the conflict rages, if it is under his eye, the more profound may be his experience of himself, of what he is and is not. Does living more consciously with this duality, *between* these two contrary forces, bring the balance and normality of relationship with another level, because it effectively calls down the reconciling Spirit?[22] These questions run like a thread through all that follows, for they are obviously not exclusive to a formal monastic context.

The monasticism of medieval Europe was a descendant of this remarkable school, its persistence as a Christian norm a measure of the influence generated by the informed struggle for this balanced normality. Monastic legislators made intentional adaptations of emphasis to suit changing conditions, but each new formulation of the Rule acknowledged the spirit, aims and authority of the *Regula Benedicti*.

Yet, by the thirteenth century, the qualitative influence of the monastic life upon society had, imperceptibly, altered. Challenging new forms of the religious life had arisen, the numbers of the monks had grown prodigiously, their lives had become physically and psychologically easier and safer through innumerable evasions, the calibre of men attracted to them had changed, they had acquired property contrary to their vows and begun attending universities in large numbers to waste their heritage by theorising about God and their own experiences: they had become identified with the values of ordinary life to such an extent that their assimilation to the socioeconomic fabric of 'the world' proceeded without their effective resistance.[23] Unlike earlier intentional and farsighted adaptations, these changes were at first overlooked, and then sanctioned in retrospect. The meaning of service was being renewed outside the monasteries, in the midst of life by the Mendicants, and through the increasingly individualistic abnegations of anchorites and visionaries;[24] the intellectuality of theology from the twelfth century on, was matched by the emotionality of affective devotion, a growing imbalance in a nominally Christian culture which surely reflected men's psychological divisions. Not only had the monks lost their unique balance, but perhaps even the reason and the means of its seeking; not moving, they had become an obstacle, a resistance to be overcome. Their multiplying critics[25] pointed both to their worldliness and to their escape from the natural challenges and common duties of men: what had begun as a way of facing more impartially the whole scale of human reality, had become a means of evading even those ordinary responsibilities which bring normal self-respect, in other words, had fallen beneath the level of life as it was being lived by those who had never aspired to anything else.[26] From containing the most powerful question, the monastic life had come to represent a dogmatic literal answer.

By 1500, the life of the *Regula Benedicti* was all but extinct in England, save possibly among the small handful of Carthusians and Bridgettines. When the abbeys were dissolved it was found that many inmates had never even seen their rules, which were written in a language—in every sense—that few now understood.[27] The observer can only marvel, somewhat uncomfortably, at this ability to continue when all meaning has fled.

This is the general picture of monastic decay, widely accepted by historians. And yet, at the heart of this tradition lay an essential and unconditional authenticity, capable of renewal. The Christian morality of a thousand years was derived from and informed by the enabling asceticism of the *Regula Benedicti*. If the real aim of this asceticism was the purification of emotion, it was founded—as will become plain[28]—upon the inward freeing and gathering of the energy of attention from its automatic and habitual dispersion in the repetitive associative thought, shallow emotional reactiveness and isolated sensations of the 'self': these entrance and dominate the human organism and the common life of people, impoverishing and deforming man's nature, created in the image of God, reducing it to the level of lower animal forms and depriving man of his intended place in the greater World. All our evidence implies that asceticism, in this sense, constituted the real 'withdrawal from the world' and 'denial of the body,' the necessary preparation for the reception of higher influences 'of the Spirit' and for right being in this life. The impossibility of understanding this organic process without living it, without experiencing over a long period the supremely difficult work of reorientation, surely explains the numerous historical distortions and falsifications of asceticism and the profound and rightful suspicion and incomprehension its substitutes evoked in the Protestant reformers. Taken from its context within a balanced discipline touching all sides of a man's life, divorced from the necessary preparatory inner work, reduced to an idea or moral precept, self-denial must tend to become forced, with poisonous consequences.

The root of the word 'asceticism' is from the Greek for 'exercises' and signifies the tuning and balancing of all human functions which was the aim of the training of the athlete and gymnast in ancient times. Early ascetics were sometimes called 'athletes of Christ.'

It is necessary to lay aside the modern associations of the word 'world,' in order to find its earlier significance. The medieval mind inherited from antiquity the idea of scale, of many worlds hierarchically organised from the Foot of God's Throne to Outer Darkness, one contained, as it were, within the other. Analogically, man was said to contain the corresponding order.[29] What does it mean, then, 'to withdraw from the world'? It cannot rightly mean to deny Nature and natural Life, for nature is Creation, all worlds, the vast range of universal reality, *in saecula saeculorum*. 'Nature,' in the sense of the world of appearances, is misleading only if men assume the part to be the whole, for the world as ordinarily experienced is incomplete. 'Withdrawal from the world' is consistently referred to in the sources as if it were an inner movement whose ultimate end was the love of God, a way of being which could become a consciously dutiful service of universal purposes in the midst of this great Wholeness. The Christian tradition affirms that Nature has been deformed (disordered) through 'sin' and can only be reformed through 'grace.' The 'world' with which man has become identified is all that is lower, within himself and without: 'lower,' not according to some arbitrary or fixed moral judgement, but literally and materially. He is called by authentic religion to turn in another direction, to remember himself and God.[30] 'Withdrawal from the world' is perhaps the *only* initial movement possible for us.

This inner direction, like a hidden spring, was to feed a medieval culture which, despite all its excesses, was permeated with ideals of order, balance, obedience, service and faith deriving from the experimental normality of the monastery. This turning-within sustained Francis and Dominic in their attempt to bring the spiritual life into the world in the thirteenth century, reappears among those hermits and mystics of the later Middle Ages who sought the Way regardless of form or reproach, underlies the philosophical religion of the Renaissance Platonists[31] and informs the 'mixed life' of the contemporary New Devotion.

The Brethren of the Common Life sought a living relationship between action and contemplation which would serve as a bridge between the life of the world and the Way of the monk. They gave 'the mixed life' a method through their spiritual exercises, which they believed to have originated with the Desert Fathers, and through their educational work they gave it a place in society. Their influence entered the congregations of reformed 'Observant' canons, permeated the Carthusian and Bridgettine orders, was present at the formation of the Jesuits, and, although the Brethren did not survive the Reformation as an historical movement, the 'new devotion' continued to inform the direction of lay Christianity. The ground for the 'mixed life' had been prepared by vernacular writings addressed to the neglected laymen of the church by late medieval mystics and Christian humanists. In England, devotional literature connected especially with the Bridgettines and Carthusians, was naturalising the 'mixed life' by adapting its practices to secular existence and by affirming the essential monastic ideal.

Although the gradual supplanting of the monk and hermit by the "true Christian man in this world," was an external result of many causes which culminated in 'the Reformation,' a search for reorientation within existing traditional forms, preceded by centuries the efforts of the Protestant reformers. It could be said that this search provoked the crisis of the sixteenth century, because a church that had become unable to mediate effectively between the conflicting claims of the world and the spirit, could not harness its restless force.

The sources I have concentrated on emphasise, above all, the need for a certain quality of sincerity towards oneself, if the world man inhabits is to be touched by the action of the higher laws of which traditional religion speaks:

> What does it profit you to have written and understood these things unless you read and understand yourself? Therefore give diligence to inward reading, and read and understand your own self: that you may read and love God: that you may fight and overcome the world, and all your enemies: that your labour may be turned into rest, and sorrow into joy: and after the darkness of this life you may see the springing of the bright morning.[32]

Consider also these words of a present-day scholar:

> All interpretation is to conquer a remoteness, a distance between the past cultural epoch to which the text belongs and the interpreter himself, . . . [I]t is thus the growth of his own understanding of himself that the interpreter pursues through the understanding of the other.[33]

All conclusions are provisional. The material I am presenting has been part of my own search. What we describe, describes us. We are captured by what we see; but active vision reveals a witness, the presence of a question, the intimation of another world. Conscious observation of ourselves is commensurate with the essence of these texts—and thus a tool for understanding them—because spiritual exercises "originated . . . from the Fathers observing what happened to them when they were in a state of prayer."[34] Drawing on this experience, normally excluded from academic research, we cross a threshold; inwardly we have already crossed. Another scholar, after attending a celebration of matins according to eleventh-century practice, has stated:

> I will only say that from that day on everything was different. It was the actual experience of the liturgy that provided us with our greatest single advance in understanding. . . . Research is more than solving puzzles; its ultimate goal is understanding, and thus it is essential, now and then, for something to happen that brings us back to reality, to what it is that gives the material its significance.[35]

The note which has sounded contains an inner octave.

ONE

The Three Lives

[S]loth, idleness and vain rest that come of your flesh under colour of contemplation.

Walter Hylton

[A]nd if we work manually, what prevents us from raising our heart to heavenly things and retaining unceasingly the thought of eternal love?

Richard Rolle

[B]ut because all may not be men or women of religion, therefore of every degree in the world God has chosen servants.

Richard Rolle

The harmony of Christian society, the great body of man, was traditionally held to depend on the balance of three functions, government, labour and prayer,[1] in conformity with the structure of human nature and the science of types. The scholastic thinkers of the thirteenth century, synthesising a tradition reaching back at least to Cassian and Dionysius the Areopagite, divided the spiritual life into three 'ways,' purgative, illuminative and unitive.[2] Religious literature dwelt on the correspondence between the three aspects of God and the three powers in the soul of man, His Image.[3]

The idea of the three lives, active, passive and reconciling, can be traced back to the amalgam of Greek thought and Christian teaching which emerged from the disintegration of the Roman Empire. It is probably much older. Through the work of Clement of Alexandria, Philo and Origen the Greek divisions of 'philosophy' became part of the traditional material of medieval thought. Augustine regarded Socrates as the exemplar of the active way of seeking truth through living, and Pythagoras of the contemplative, through the elucidation of natural causality.[4]

Although the opposites of 'action' and 'contemplation' dominated men's literal thinking, the rumour persisted of a third life, the way Christ Himself had lived with the Apostles, reconciling all opposites. Worthy representatives of the reformed monasticism of the twelfth century, imbued with the ascetic writings of the Desert Fathers, claimed to embrace all three lives. The *vita apostolica* was the aspiration of the Military Orders and permeated the symbolic literature of the Grail quest; it inspired the lay guilds, informed the rise of the Mendicant Orders and was expressed in the lives of remarkable contemplatives like Bernard of Clairvaux, Hugh of Avalon and, later, Jean Gerson, who played an active part in the events of their time. In the later Middle Ages, the New Devotion and the *imitatio Christi* became its chief vehicle.[5]

Traditional ideas had been manipulated in the university schools at a cost. During the internal struggle, through which European culture passed in the fifteenth and sixteenth centuries, the yearning to return to a purer, older valuation at first disturbed and then—as supposed ancient canons in art, scholarship, literature and religion were rediscovered—began everywhere to upset the weight of prevailing custom. With the attention of the newly forming intelligentsia focused on their broader cultural heritage, medieval accretions were stripped away. Augustine's vision of 'a life' as a search for truth had been imperceptibly supplanted by 'a life' as a particular state of existence without specific meaning. The moral ascendancy of the monks during the 'Benedictine centuries' had sown a passive belief in the supremacy of 'the contemplative life,' with which the activities of existing monasteries were then identified. As the numbers of professional religious increased and the spiritual initiative passed elsewhere, this identification hardened and invited refutation.

'Holy poverty,' long associated with the contemplative life as an expression of its complete opposition to the values of 'the world,' was compared by Tudor propagandists to the poverty of social outcasts, and pronounced as such to be an offence to the commonweal. Robert Parkyn adds a fourth life to the traditional scheme, the "miserable living" of vagabonds who "shall have no mead or reward of God for their poverty."[6] As a codicil to a venerable legacy this is absurd, because 'selling all one has' and 'poverty of spirit' have nothing in common with vagrancy, but also fitting, because once the religious life had become indistinguishable from the life of society at large, it naturally became susceptible to the judgement of that society as to its usefulness.

The study of religious history must be generally this: the following of a descending movement, of the loss of truth through its inability to be lived. We are trying, however partially, to comprehend the reality of another history, which concerns the contrary movement of return and renewal. To gauge the scale of the question: what a distance separates the monk-as-tramp from the world of those Fathers of the Monastic Way who said, "if you have not first of all lived rightly with men, you will not be able to live rightly in solitude," and again, "if you want to go to the monastery, you must be careful about every encounter and everything you do, or you will not be able to do the work of the monastery; for you will not have the right even to drink a single cup there," and again, "you cannot be a monk unless you become like a consuming fire."[7]

Although a shift in popular attitudes certainly took place during the fifteenth and sixteenth centuries, and bulks large in the accessible records, the reorientation of religion began on a different level: practices belonging to what we can only call a teaching were being introduced into life, in accordance with changing needs and conditions. Most of our study must deal with the former shift, but in places the quality of our material bears on the latter movement.

Practices supporting 'the mixed life,' intentional spiritual exercises grounded in a coherent traditional psychology and verified in the experience of countless Christian contemplatives reaching back into the Egyptian desert and beyond, were passing into a stream of popular devotion which was to be of great significance for the next century and a half and which remained in many ways untouched by the upheavals of the Reformation:[8] a devotion 'new' but deeply traditional, eluding formal definition, colouring the surviving records but not identified with them.

Mons Perfectionis (1496), by the educational and social reformer, Bishop Alcock of Ely,[9] based on the enigmatic text from the story of the destruction of Sodom—"in the mountain make thyself safe"—was a late encomium of the monastic ideal addressed to the Carthusian order, widely regarded as still undeformed.[10]

He asserts, with a mixture of hope and wishful thinking, that the monasticism which had been under increasing attack since the twelfth century[11] was the way of life most concordant with Christ's precepts and the monk the highest type of man. Christ taught his disciples the secrets of love "on the mountain": this "signifies religion . . . a mountain in which God is well pleased."[12] On this "fertile mountain reigneth all perfection that should feed man's soul," the "roses" of charity, the "lilies" of chastity, the "violets" of obedient humility and the melancholy-curing herbs flowering in the "desert" of their life.[13] It was the dream of medieval culture, the relic of analogical thought during monastic *lectio divina*,[14] in origin anything but naive. The exhortation to "go up to the mountain of the Lord" refers to the development of the soul possible "in this world," for as Augustine said, "if heaven may be on earth, it is in the cloister or study."[15] The repetition of twelfth-century sentiments on fourth-century authority at the end of the fifteenth century was to be challenged within a generation by reformers who, claiming a genuine relationship with history, proceeded to destroy what was left.

If the virtues enjoined by Christ are perfected in the monastic life, it becomes the mark for all Christians.[16] This claim haunted the last days of the medieval monk like an old memory. The fifteenth-century Bridgettine manual, *The Myroure of Oure Ladye*, pictured the saints of the Bible using the monastic *horarium* in their devotions,[17] and it was said of Abbot Feckenham when defending the Marian houses in 1559, that he "to exalt the authority of his own profession . . . placed Nazirites, prophets, nay even Christ Himself and His Apostles in the monastic orders."[18] Thus Alcock glosses the strange words of Jesus from St. John, "I said, Ye are gods," with "this is to say: Ye true and faithful religious men, living according to your religion, I say unto you, ye are gods."[19] Protestants were wont to call the monks "perverters of Scripture."[20]

Alcock's thought was coloured by contemporary trends He quotes Jerome and Chrysostom, Fathers whose limpid style, broad classical learning, ethical bias and penetration of religious pretence had made them humanist oracles.[21] Nor was he untouched by the contemporary movement for 'Observant' monastic reform. The second half of his tract exhorts observance of the Biblical bases of the Rule: "therefore every man principally should take heed what precious thing is committed unto him; and what vow he hath made before God and all His Angels, that he would truly perform it."[22] Like the Bridgettines Whytford and Bonde, he believed renewal could come from reexamining an existing commitment and nowhere calls the universal validity of the Monastic Way into doubt: he represents one pole of the situation we wish to examine.

More penetrating minds were trying to confront the situation. Replying to a zealous Dominican, who had asserted at the Council of Constance that lay attempts to pursue the evangelical counsels of perfection were unmeritorious and even sinful unless they joined a religious order,[23] John Gerson arrived at the following revaluation of the monastic ideal by reasoning:

[T]he religious orders, created by men, are improperly enough and by an abuse of language and somewhat pretentiously called 'states of perfection' . . . there are . . . as everyone knows, people far from perfect among the professed. . . . the said expression is very badly chosen . . . it does not mean that the religious possess or have acquired perfection . . . but only that they ought to acquire it. It is clear that perfection to be acquired is a very different thing from perfection that has already been acquired. Furthermore, religious profession would be better named if it were called the way and the means of perfection or the habit tending thereto rather than the state of perfection. And, verily, if the religious state helps and leads a certain number of people in a more perfect manner, it turns aside and ruins many others who would have gained their salvation much better in the world. For 'an unfaithful and foolish promise displeaseth God,' a promise rashly made and not kept.[24]

Gerson's six sisters had intended to enter religion, but he advised them to live differently without leaving the family home.[25] At this Council he had also defended the Brotherhood of the Common Life against charges of heresy, whose founder Gerard Groote had written:

If devout women separate themselves from the world, and try to serve God in the privacy of their own homes, without taking monastic vows, they are just as religious as nuns in their convents. To love God and worship Him is religion, not the taking of special vows.[26]

It was this religion—in the world but not of it—sought by the Brotherhood, which came to be known as 'the New Devotion,' a prepared bridge between medieval forms and those of the sixteenth century, both Catholic and Protestant. The Brothers of Zwolle declared in 1415: "We have decided to live in cities, in order that we may be able to give advice and instruction to clerks and other persons who wish to serve the Lord."[27] The growth of a specifically urban culture heightened the relevance of 'the mixed life':[28] hence Erasmus, trained at a house of canons influenced by the New Devotion, was to say at the beginning of the sixteenth century, "I pray you, what thing else is a city but a great monastery."[29] Luther was an admirer of *De Imitatione Christi* and of Gerson, particularly for his views on monasticism.[30] Gerson, like Gerard,[31] had allowed that the Orders could help in some cases, even if "created by men," an unbearable conjunction for the Protestant reformers.

The crescendo of antimonastic criticism and resentment during the fourteenth and fifteenth centuries was obviously significant in the formation of Reformation thought and sentiment. English historians have tended to focus on the academic Wycliffite heresy, popular Lollardy and the ground swell of social discontent and satire—'the Piers Plowman tradition'[32] —as harbingers of the theological controversies, fierce anticlericalism and declamatory Erastianism of the sixteenth century. The public capital of the monks had been subject to a steady process of attrition by these movements, which explain negatively the fate of the monastic ideal, but the possibility that the fundamentally orthodox tradition of late medieval vernacular devotion, informed by the experience of the mystics, and much more influential, widespread and rooted than Wycliffite views, could have had a positive bearing in turning men towards a different understanding rather than merely away from monasticism, has been less widely canvassed. Its writings are neither theologically reformist nor intellectually sensational and have tended to be monopolised by students of English literature and spirituality. Their researches have demonstrated the important influence of writers like Rolle (*c.* 1300–49) and Hylton (*c.* 1330–96), magnified by the new printing presses, on the piety of literate, non-Latinate laymen in the early fifteen hundreds. The expanding genre of devotional guides continued to bear new directions after the Reformation, as we shall see later;[33] but it is with the balanced, clear sighted outlooks of Rolle and Hylton, a tangible result of their respective searches, that the remainder of this chapter will be concerned, for in their thought the foundations of "the mixed life" can be discerned. Rolle's writings tangentially and Hylton's directly, show some of the ways in which the monastic ideal was being positively transformed during the century before the Dissolution: they were antennae for the coming age.

Rolle's books were among the very first practical religious guides available in print in England. A modern editor of the extensive literature by, or attributable to, him has said that, "at the time of the Reformation 'Richard Hermit's' influence was as great, or greater than, that of any other medieval writer of devotional works."[34] His views on monasticism, largely elicited in response to criticism by local Yorkshire orders, came to have a very wide currency. Rolle, whose individual search made him a figurehead for the contemporary movement towards personal asceticism and solitude,[35] affirmed the layman's religious responsibility to be just in the place where he was (a fact deeply understood by a hermit), not by fleeing outwardly from the world, but by serving God inwardly while continuing to fulfil all his social duties. When the religious value of asceticism came to be seriously challenged,[36] Rolle's views, taken from their context and reinforced by more radical denials of the monastic ideal and by the positive trends of lay piety, contributed to the final collapse of the established subjective division between 'religion' and 'the world' in the early sixteenth century.

> I do not say that you should flee physically from the world or from worldly goods, for they are principal occasions, but I counsel you in heart and in will that you flee all such vanities. For though you be lord or lady, husbandman or wife, you may have as stable a heart or will as some of the religious that sit in the cloisters. True it is that the most certain way is to flee as the religious do, but because all may not be men or women of religion, therefore of every degree in the world God has chosen servants.[37]

This was first published in 1506 and reveals the breadth and potential cutting power of Rolle's thought. The nature of his Tudor audience is suggested by the company his books kept. The influential Carthusian mystical compendium, *Speculum Spiritualium,* addressed both to pious layman and professional contemplative, reprinting in Paris in 1510 was bound with an enlarged version of Rolle's *De Emendatione Vitae* at the expense of a certain William Bretton, citizen of London. Another fifteenth-century work, the *Abbaye of the Holy Ghoste,* treated of man's inner life on the analogy of a monastery and its inhabitants:

> Of the abbey of the Holy Spirit that is in a place that is called conscience. . . .
> I see that many would be in religion but they may not, either for poverty, or for dread of their kin, or for the bond of marriage, and for them I make here a book of the religion of the heart . . . that all those that may not be bodily in religion, may be spiritually . . . where may this abbey best be founded and this religion? Now certainly, nowhere so well as in a place that is called conscience; and who so will be busy to found this holy religion[?] That may every good Christian man and woman do, that will be busy thereabout.[38]

Scholars have rejected its attribution to Rolle, but its theme of the real possibility of leading a religious life in the world shows the position with which he was associated.

The old question of how God may be pleased raised for Rolle all that was most hidden in a man, his 'inner life.' What a man loved was more important than what he did: what he loved, he was.[39] If he beat his breast in church, but thought all the time of his business, what use were his devotions, his heart being far away? "The devil owns many whom we reckon good."[40] Rolle taught from experience that, through prayer, meditation and invocation of the Holy Name,[41] the heart might be freed from the world and stabilised on another level. To be able to love God was the essence of Christianity:

> Different men on earth have different gifts and graces of God . . . the diversity of love makes the diversity of holiness and of reward. In heaven the angels which are most burning in love are nearest God: also men and women who have most love of God, whether they do penance or not, they shall be in the highest degree in heaven.[42]

The question of the quality of their emotional life could arise, whatever people did.

Although considered by many to have been an enemy of the monks, Rolle sometimes used the accents of the monastic reformer. He wrote to a nun:

> If you have delight in the name of religion, look that you have more delight in the deed that falls to religion. Your habit says that you have forsaken the world, that you are given to God's service, that you delight yourself not in earthly things: look then that it be in your heart. For nothing may make you religious but virtues and cleanness of soul in charity. If your body be clad without as your order wills, look that your soul be not naked within—that your order forbids.[43]

Respect for the ideal is implicit, and to our knowledge Rolle nowhere contradicted its aims, but he did quarrel with the excesses and pretensions it fostered. In falling to the level of life in the world the monastic life became far worse, for, in so doing, it betrayed its place in God's scheme, the great world.[44] To relinquish everything and then to live only as if one was a monk, as if making an inward turning (conversion), was "the height of madness." And only too comprehensible: the little extra thing necessary was to be able "to direct the whole heart and all the affections of the mind and thoughts of the spirit to God," but Rolle was an independently motivated seeker and it is probable that the enabling knowledge of this inner movement was rare among the religious of his time. If, in his words, it has to be "better to remain torpid in the world, than to enter religion and not to have the fervour of love,"[45] it is not that he wished to empty the cloister, but that sincerely putting a question about the limits of choice, that is, the freedom of attention, he has to subvert the usual order for a moment. If profession in religion was neither an indispensable qualification for being able to love God, nor even necessarily a help, to be between stools was to have the worst of both worlds.

Rolle, by virtue of his own search and character, was disturbing, not least because he took a greater view. Because of our common helplessness, the monastic was " the most surest way," but human beings had different qualities and possibilities, and nature requires many kinds of work. The paths on which God may be served were many, but Rolle's words echo the unity of his vision:

> [N]evertheless they come all to one end, that is to say to the life that ever shall last. And thither they are brought and led by diverse ways and by one charity, the which is more in one than in another.[46]

Although he himself finally became a hermit, declaring that "the special gift of those that lead solitary life, is for to love Jesu Christ,"[47] he viewed solitude as a condition of the heart which could be found also in the midst of worldly occupation. His question is at the heart of our subject:

> And if we work manually, what prevents us from raising our heart to heavenly things and retaining unceasingly the thought of eternal love? And thus we shall be at all times of our life fervent and not stupefied, for otherwise our heart will not at all be withdrawn from sleep.[48]

Speaking of an inner awakening and activeness of the heart, he wrote, "this solitude is of greater merit than if one fled to a hermitage and was able to live there on roots and water.[49]

The traditional injunction to turn from 'the world' towards God is restored to meaning as an inner turning, incomprehensible to the ordinary mind for 'the world' is also in the heart. Hence Rolle did not consider it particularly significant whether a man 'did penance' or not. In the struggle for ones life the outer world could be a battlefield just as the cloister or cell: "get who get may, this world is wide enough and good enough to win heaven in; and it is rich enough and pleasant enough to win hell with, flee who flee may."[50] A religious life was founded on an inner dedication to and relationship with God, in the absence of which either inside or outside the cloister was a hell.[51] The real hope of layman and monk depended on the same thing. Whether Rolle anticipated Protestantism[52] or not, he insisted always on the primacy of the love of God, his own essential and secret experience: without this inner sense of great scale, these questions are comprehensible, but relatively meaningless.

He is saying that men must find their own way, as he himself had done.[53] The Carthusian who said Rolle "made men judges of themselves,"[54] pre-echoed Luther's critics. The quality of guidance to be gained from an institutional church, split by schism and weakened by national politics and internal corruption in Rolle's day, may well have deteriorated further in the hundred and fifty years after his death, but this begs the question. Rolle's 'traditional' certainty could never have been cheap: "The highest path goes to him that loves God most . . .

which love makes God to dwell in him and he in God . . . " Man can do nothing
of himself, only search for an active submission, 'choose' to be chosen:

> [N]o man may by his own might set himself in any of these paths that go to
> heaven, but it behoves him to take that path meekly that God has chosen for
> him . . . for that is hid in a man's true love that he has in his heart, that no
> man may know but God alone, for there is nothing that man may do out-
> wardly to bring him to so high a path as true love of God.[55]

A native tradition strongly imbued with Rolle's views was the stock on which the
Reformation was grafted, a fact which has led some scholars to trace 'the Puritan
temper' to medieval Yorkshire rather than Geneva[56] and which helps to explain
the conservative nature of later sixteenth-century devotion.[57] Rolle's practice of
the internal prayer of the Holy Name fostered a cult and current expositions like
Suso's *Horologium Sapientiae* were translated by his followers and even attributed
to him. This cult was characterised by a warmth of feeling for the person of Christ
that had previously been reserved for the Virgin and the Saints, and persisted in
various forms throughout the fifteenth and sixteenth centuries, as the popularity
of the *Jesus Psalter*, attributed to the Bridgettine Whytford, attests. The simplifica-
tion of devotion occurring during the Reformation was eased by a tradition cen-
tring on Christ. Rolle wrote only one (adolescent) work in praise of the Virgin,
and there is some evidence that her cult lapsed in Yorkshire during his lifetime.[58]

Rolle's affirmation of the place of religion in the world may effectively have
prepared for the Protestant doctrine of 'godly vocation,'[59] his influence combining with the New Devotion to assist at the birth of "the true Christian man in this
world" in the sixteenth century. The 'personal' aspiration to be consciously
related to God, central to the vocation of hermit and mystic, passed into the
Protestant and reformed Catholic mentality, although the loving familiarity with
which Rolle addressed his Lord was replaced with a characteristic sense of awe
and incomprehension—the experience of distance—as the pendulum swung
away from medieval affective devotion. Rolle's attacks on the emptiness of externally acquired scholastic learning in comparison with the wisdom taught by "the
doctor within,"[60] also found echoes among the later reformers, as did his far-
ranging use of the Bible against sinners.[61] The view of the English mystics that
grace was given rather than deserved,[62] as popular belief held—and holds, is further evidence here: the last words of Hylton's *Medylde lyfe*—"No man suddenly is
made sovereign in grace, but from little he begins and by process waxes until he
be perfect"[63]—have been underlined in the 1516 edition,

The works of the Augustinian canon Walter Hylton were, like Rolle's, collected
and studied not only among Carthusians and Bridgettines but by generations of
laymen,[64] their influence extended by the early Tudor presses. His *Scala Perfectionis*, a classic formulation of medieval English spirituality, was written for an
ancress and does not deal with the monastic life as such; bound with *Medylde lyfe*,

it was printed in 1494, and again in 1507, 1519, 1525 and 1533. *Medylde lyfe*, conveying "to a devout man in temporal estate how he should rule himself," appeared also in 1516 in the company of works by Bridget and Bernard, and in 1530(?).[65] This little treatise sketches a spiritual attitude to life founded squarely within the tradition, yet of particular relevance to the needs of the early sixteenth century. Hylton's monastic works languished in abbey libraries until they were dispersed, unpublished because the literate public were more interested in ordering their daily lives on Christian principles than reading of the utility of monastic rules and the prerogatives of the religious orders.[66]

Hylton summarises the medieval teaching on the active and contemplative lives in this way:

> Active life . . . belongs to worldly men and women the which are lewd in knowing of spiritual occupation, for they feel neither savour nor devotion by fervour of love as other men do, nor do they have any skill of it, and yet nevertheless they have dread of God and of the pain of hell, and therefore they flee sin and they have desire for to please God and for to come to heaven and a good will have to their fellow Christian: for these men it is needfull and advantageous to use the works of active life as busily as they may in the help of themselves and of their fellow Christians, for they cannot else do. Contemplative life belongs alone to such men and women that for the love of God forsake all open sins of the world and their flesh, and all business, charges and government of worldly goods, and make themselves poor and naked to the bare need of the bodily kind, and flee from sovereignty of all other men to the service of God: unto these men it belongs for to travail and occupy themselves inwardly for to get, through the grace of our Lord, cleanness in heart and peace in conscience by destroying of sin and receiving of virtues, and so for to come to contemplation, which cleanness may not be had without great exercise of body and continual travail of the spirit in devout prayers, fervent desires and spiritual meditations.[67]

Thus the tradition is on one level clear, even dogmatic, yet with an inner dimension, pregnant with the imperative to know one's place in order to be: it can only be understood 'in translation,' by being lived.

Christianity was the religion of love. For those who had not been touched by the love of God and did not "have any skill of it," the two commandments of the New Law[68] were their guide: that is all! If responsibility depends on the quality of experiencing, the level from which the tradition comes and at which it begins to be operative is clearly revealed. Those who had been so touched were called to contemplate, to a life of a certain kind of work, a continual quest:

> [T]his work is not of one hour, nor of one day, but of many days and years, with much sweat and stinking of body and travail of the soul . . . cease not but seek busily.[69]

Their aim was the striving to clean their hearts and come to "peace in conscience by destroying of sin" through the practice of prayer and meditation, in which they were supported by the accumulated wisdom and transmitted techniques of the Christian spiritual tradition. In the teaching of the Desert, central to all that follows, 'action' and 'contemplation' refer to the dual nature of man, reciprocal aspects of a process of transformation which can take place, at this stage of the religious way, within the individual: contemplation denotes the reception of that force from Above with which vice could be 'actively' overcome.[70]

Hylton is restating what were to him objective truths, rather than passing judgement on his fellows: different degrees of religion being proper to different kinds of men,[71] it has no meaning to consider one 'life' better than another. Each has its place within a wholeness greater than we know. He neither extols contemplation unconditionally above other works,[72] nor makes it synonymous with the monastic life: it is a special and rare kind of activity for which a man can only prepare himself—if he is called. If the 'desire for God' is indeed more whole in contemplative prayer than in outward actions for one's neighbour, only an unbalanced literal mind would find in this a reason to denigrate these actions rather than an important question. Hylton distinguishes between 'bodily' and 'spiritual' action, not between life in the world and the monastery. 'Action' and 'contemplation' are not only abstract concepts. Habitual outer devotion, which so enfuriated the Protestant reformer, is merely characterised by Hylton as "uncunning." If ignorant men believe they are not desiring God unless they continually speak His Name, they do not know themselves and beg the question. Pious formulae are good, formed in the heart or enunciated, for they can stir the dormant feelings, but a "clean thought" of God without words, is the only sign of "soothfast desire."[73] Protestant thought was to cut across this view of temporal-active and spiritual-contemplative in the belief that just those who had not forsaken "all open sins of the world" could indeed be saved without having to make themselves "poor and naked." In this they were in accord with the thought of the Italian Renaissance.

During the twelfth century the *vita apostolica*, hitherto seen in terms of their own experience by monastic commentators, began to be reinterpreted by increasingly influential orders of quasi-monastic canons with pastoral duties, the religious forebears of both Hylton and Luther. The appearance of the Mendicants in the thirteenth century parallels a shift in spirituality from monastic asceticism to devotion to the humanity of Christ, and eventually the *imitatio Christi*. The *vita apostolica* of 'ambidextrous' prelates like Bernard and Gerson seemed to unite action and contemplation (even East and West in the person of Francis, one of the few Western medieval saints to be honoured in the East), and "thus develops into a new vision of life which is in but not of this world and which is open to laymen as well as to clerics and monks."[74] Whether such adjustments were providential or accidental, it is against this background that Hylton goes on to speak of the life of ancient bishops, potent exemplars in the reform atmosphere of early Tudor England hungry for proofs of the *vita apostolica*, idealistic about primitive Christianity and ripe for more searching pastoral care:

> [T]hese holy men left not utterly the administration, the looking after and the dispensation of worldly goods to give themselves wholly to contemplation with as much grace of contemplation as they had, but they left full often their own rest in contemplation when they had well rather have been still, for love of their fellow Christian, and engaged themselves with worldly business in helping of their subjects, and truly that was charity, for wisely and discreetly they parted their living in two: one time they fulfilled the lower part of charity by works of active life, for they were bound thereto by taking of their prelacy, and another time they fulfilled the higher part of charity in contemplation of God and of spiritual things by prayers and meditations, and so they had charity to God and to their fellow Christian, both in affection of soul within and also in showing of bodily deeds without."[75]

This ideal for the secular clergy was interestingly restated by Chancellor Melton of York in his *Sermo exhortationis* (1509–10):

> Every craftsman who uses his hands has, besides the stall for his wares outside, a workshop for his craft within, and if he does not work diligently in it for many days he will not easily earn for himself through his craft the necessities of life; similarly, besides the temples and shrines of God in which by daily prayer and psalms we, as it were, display our wares to passers by, we must make use of our inner workshop or study with sacred reading and teaching, that we may become rich in learning and have no lack of the necessities of life eternal. . . . Nor may we have any other source to expound to the people the holy consolation of God's word."[76]

Melton was a close friend of John Colet, the owner of a humanist library and one-time tutor of John Fisher. His younger contemporary Richard Whytford, a member of the same circle, was also to write of a religion blending action and contemplation in terms of the discipline of learning a craft:[77] this attitude was completely traditional.

The idea that being Christian 'in the world' needs to be based on the kind of special discipline, hitherto the exclusive property of the committed contemplative, underlies Hylton's account of 'the mixed life.' The ability to respond to both outer demand and inner call, in conformity with "the order of charity," must be learned, because for the most part it has been lost and will not be formed by itself. The 'mixed life' is not an ideal by default. One of the Desert Fathers said of the religious life, "what is the good of giving oneself to a trade without seeking to learn it."[78] Hylton declares:

[M]ixed life . . . belongs to some temporal men which have sovereignty with much favour of worldly goods, and have also as it were lordship over other men for to govern and sustain them, as a father has over his children, and a master over his servants and a lord over his tenants, the which men have also received of our Lord's gift grace of devotion, and in part savour of spiritual occupation. . . . if these men standing the charge and the bond they have taken will leave utterly the business of the world, the which ought skilfully to be used in fulfilling of their charge and wholly give themselves to contemplative life, they do not well, for they keep not the order of charity, for charity . . . lies both in love of god and of your fellow Christian, and therefore it is that he has that charity to use in working now to that one, and now to that other. . . . on the contrary wise whoso has so great regard to work of active life and to business of the world that for the love of his fellow Christian he leaves spiritual occupation utterly after that God has disposed him thereto, he fulfills not charity.[79]

This speaks of a 'new' possibility,[80] the acceptance of inevitable conditions of life just because there is no choice, and their skilful use for the fulfilment of our duties to man and God, rather than allowing them to become an excuse for our inevitable limitations: the possibility to stand up between the outer and inner worlds, to touch a depth of responsibility born of an awareness of the demands of the two opposing directions we bear by virtue of our humanity.

In a general way, the technique of the mixed life showed how the father, the squire, the magistrate and the merchant, among the most commanding types in sixteenth-century society and imagination, might become Christian realities. Hylton's challenge to the influential layman—"for what are all your works worth whether they be bodily or spiritual, but if they be done rightfully and reasonably to the worship of God and after His bidding: soothly right nought"[81]—prefigures the attempts of religious leaders in the fifteenth century to impose moral restraint on developing commercial interests,[82] which continued under the Tudors and became very marked in the 'godly guides' of the Elizabethan and Stuart Puritans. The mixed life, concerned not with imposing restraint at all costs but with the practical reconciliation of 'the world' and 'the spirit' in the sphere of the individual, with discharging the responsibilities of life without neglecting "spiritual occupation," was the enabling force of this movement. Nor can it be unconnected that, although the temper of the sixteenth century has been called "activist," its spirituality became increasingly centred upon the "intense cultivation of private prayer."[83] Within the new religious orders of the Counter-Reformation there was a corresponding development away from the exclusive performance of the liturgical *opus dei* and towards a more active involvement in 'the world' sustained by intensive and systematic spiritual exercises. These are questions of balance. Hylton's warning to the man of affairs not to allow piety to interfere with his obligations seems a little fantastic until we recall the contemplative excesses, eremitical fervour and apocalyptic expectations of the late fourteenth century.

Hylton can be said to anticipate the characteristic sixteenth-century sense of social conscience, but he is summoning a much older vision. . . . The responsibilities of the magistrate are viewed in relationship to 'the mystical body of Christ,' the traditional symbol of "holy church." Medieval thought was heir to powerful ancient teachings of unity concerning the correspondance between all the hierarchies of being, between microcosm and macrocosm 'as above-so below': men's action and inaction has consequences at all levels because the World is One.[84] For the sake of the deep human need to be conscious of the Whole, Hylton is asking whether the powerful thrust of earlier medieval religion towards the inner world, in the form in which it had entered popular culture, was a dangerously partial understanding: a living tradition is able to adjust itself through the integrity and sensitivity of its members. We may be beguiled by outer responsibilities, but when they are neglected for what is called worship, the head of this mystical body is beautified at the expense of its other parts:

> [Y]ou leave His body with the feet ragged and rent and take no keep thereof and there you worship him not, for it is villainy and no worship for a man to be curiously arrayed upon his head with pearls and precious stones, and all his body naked and bare as it were a beggar: right so spiritually it is no worship to God to crown His head and leave His body bare. You shall understand that our Lord Jesu Christ as man is head of His spiritual body which is holy church, the members of His body are all christened men: some are arms, some are feet and some are other members after the sundry workings that they use in their living. . . . His feet are your children, your servants, your tenants and all your fellow Christians . . . you make yourself to kiss His mouth by devotion and spiritual prayer, but you tread upon His feet and defile them.[85]

Our sense of the different levels on which an authentic symbol calls to us, demanding to be understood, appears and is as soon lost, as we ponder this extraordinary passage. Of the source of this image—the Immaculate Being of Christ and the sacred mystery of the Last Supper—who can speak? But, having deferred, we must grasp tightly what we can. What, on our level, is this 'body'?

It is clearly, in some way, 'our' body, what we belong to, and yet, equally clearly, it is not ours for we do not know it: becoming aware of itself, and thus of its lawful allegiance, it belongs to a higher consciousness, but, as things have become and are, right order has been subverted. Fragmented, dispersed and our 'truth,' it is being called to an inconceivable re-membering, to re-ligion: to receive, obey and serve the scale of energy which could act within it, take its place in the greater world, it must become conscious of itself, become one. Therefore, Hylton says, we need to wash Christ's feet (His head is fair enough), to pay attention to the lower—as even God must do—for the sake of the Whole. The conditions for this are provided, yet we turn away.

Hylton's vision needs to be related firstly and intensely to a level which we can, but at present do not, comprehend: if the World is One, this is possible, and if it is not, it is necessary! It is only through an opening of consciousness experienced fully in the body, that the transforming power of new understanding could begin to inform our outer behaviour. Becoming truly and unmistakably aware of ourselves, others appear: unity, however relatively experienced, leaves an imprint and a lawful question. Effective worship is the action of a man who is able, however momentarily, to live on two levels, to be open to the two differently directed currents of energy within himself, who, through this, begins to sense a greater whole, and, with that presence, suffers correspondingly for his sins, actively, that is, consciously.

Erasmus' early sixteenth-century vision of the mystical body as three circles of humanity centred on Christ, the fountain of everlasting fire, shared Hylton's sources. In the introduction to the *Enchiridion* he says that the common people, laymen, constitute the outer circle as the grossest part of the great world, although still belonging to the body of Christ: feet, legs and other parts have their proper work in relation to the Divine Presence at the centre, and, performing it, their honour and hope, for the foot may in time evolve into a higher part.[86]

These great images, cosmic in scale, were diminished into the Tudor "Commonwealth," an idea whose influence has reached the present day.

Protestant political thought supported the obligation of the magistrate by enhancing his dignity as the guardian of religious purity, but Hylton, for all his future relevance, never had such an intention. He was recalling them to responsibility, which, at the level of their own awareness, must be experienced as dual. 'Charity' calls us to face in two directions, knowingly: because their contact in us directly and urgently evokes the need for their proper relationship. For the sake of this, "You should do both works in diverse times and with as good will the one as the other, if you might." The outer demand might become a check on the inner state, "so shall you put away by grace of Our Lord, sloth, idleness and vain rest that come of your flesh under colour of contemplation."[87] Abstracted from its place in the inner drama—a living sense of which is always the first casualty—a more apt description of 'monasticism' in Protestant eyes would be hard to find.

There are further echoes. The association of pious layman and secular cleric in his exposition of the mixed life evokes the grand Lutheran ideal of 'the priesthood of all believers,' while the tradition that Christ Himself was its exemplar[88] could not fail but deeply impress a generation that had devoured Thomas a Kempis and were currently coming to terms with the *philosophia Christi* of Erasmus. But Hylton is again more subtle. He refers to Christ as an inner presence revealed through certain experiences, our unconsciousness and neglect of which constitutes the sum of all that is lacking in our lives: it is not exactly this presence which is absent:

"I mean not this word Jesu painted upon a wall, or written by letters on a book, or formed by lips in sound of the mouth, or feigned in your heart by travail of your mind, for in this manner wise may a man out of charity find Him."[89] It may be that Hylton anticipated the fierce Protestant antipathy to religious externals, but that is not what this text is about.

All our sources recommend an intentional beginning to the day. Here is Hylton's description of the morning exercise, referring perhaps to sunrise or earlier still, after monastic practice:

> In nights after your sleep, if you will rise for to pray and serve your lord, you shall feel yourself first fleshly heavy, and sometimes lusty; then shall you dispose yourself for to pray or to think some good thought for to quicken your heart to God, and set all your business for to drawe up your thought from worldly vanities and from vain imagination that falls into your mind, that you may feel some devotion in your saying; or else if you will think on spiritual things . . . there are many manner of meditations.[90]

An invitation to question is always touching, however indirectly expressed, in material concerning faith. Conventional meditations and prayers are at hand, but how does a man find himself before them, are his emotions sluggish or preoccupied, his mind a hostage already to imaginings arising he knows not where or how, is he being governed from below, by the state of his body? Can he approach God like this? Can he even approach his day? Such questioning is not mental in the ordinary sense. Behind Hylton's simple words lay worlds of possible experiencing.

'Monastic knowledge,' based on a tested spiritual psychology, concerned the 'how,' rather than the 'why,' of religion. The experience hitherto of committed contemplatives it was being shared during the century before the Dissolution, and intensively on the eve of the Reformation, passing more and more into general currency, for better or worse, through the agency of the presses. Even where the monastic life was not suppressed the same process can be observed. Fray Francisco de Osuna said of his *Third Spiritual Alphabet*, published in Spain in 1527, "the chief reason for which I wrote this book was to draw everyone's attention to this exercise of recollection." The monastic authorities had objected to his making such things available, but he believed that all who were able, including those with families, should have the possibility of trying in this way: the Devil might well lurk in these matters, but he also lived, it was said, behind the church door and this had never been made a reason for staying away![91] The exercise of recollection was central to 'the new devotion.'[92]

Hylton gives another example of special knowledge:

> I tell you forsooth you may make of other men's sins a precious ointment for to heal your own soul when you have mind on them with compassion and

sorrow for them; this ointment is precious though the spicery of it be not clean, for it is an antidote made of venom for to destroy venom; that is for to say, your own sins and other men's sins, if you beat them with sorrow of heart, pity and compassion, they turn into medicine which makes your soul whole from pride and envy and brings in love and charity to your fellow Christian. This thought is good sometime for to have.[93]

This is knowledge not in the sense of information for the mind but guidance and support for a certain kind of inner experiencing, perhaps more balanced, for new alchemical combinations of thought, sensation and particularly feeling. It is implied that to practice religion in 'the world' requires cunning, even a quality of slyness, not least towards oneself: learn to discriminate in the inner world, take nothing for granted, for 'good' and 'evil' are divided only by the fine line along which a man must find his own balancing and travel, listening to his own deepest promptings for guidance. Later we shall meet the idea that life, in the fullest sense, is the guide. The religious man in the world has much in common, paradoxically, with the hermit.

The 'mixed life' is clearly not for all, requiring both simplicity and slyness, even the qualities of the dove and the serpent:

[S]trive not too much with yourself for you might so lightly fall into more darkness unless you were more sly in your working, and therefore I hold it then most certain unto you for to say your Pater noster and your Ave, or else your Matins, or else for to read upon your Psalter, for that is evermore a certain standard that will not fail . . . and if you may by your prayer get devotion, look then if this devotion be only in affection, that is to say in great desire to God with spiritual delight; hold forth then your saying and break not lightly off, for often it falls that praying with the mouth gets and keeps devotion, and if a man cease of saying, devotion vanishes away. Nevertheless if devotion of prayers bring into your heart a devout thought of the manhood of our Lord . . . and this thought should be letted by your saying then may you cease of your saying, and occupy yourself with meditation till it pass away.[94]

Attending to what is taking place as if it mattered, willing to watch the darkness, thought is felt and feeling thought and, however fleetingly, a finer sensitivity appears, indicating both a more genuine submission and the capacity for independent responsibility: the reestablishment, momentarily, of this connection with the inner life bears impressions of a forgotten language, whose wordlessness is its strength, a language replete with contradictions, their reversals and resolutions. A language forgotten twice over, because Hylton refers to the staple of a traditional Way, long since abandoned by our culture, and because we have neglected to nurture its essence. 'Devotion' signifies, here and throughout, not what it has come to mean in our tired and involved vocabulary, but just that differently centred and precious quality of feeling resulting from the joining together in us of that which is usually sundered: it is the forecourt for the reception of that talismanic love to which these texts always hungrily return, the intelligence that is the consciousness of the heart as a cognitive organ, a consciousness lawfully able to illuminate its actual place in the physical body. Suddenly in possession of the reins, able to be, as it were, his own guide, he listens to what is happening in himself—as it is happening, not retrospectively—and receives the corresponding impression in order to become less irresponsible. "A truly devout man," said John Ruysbroeck, "relies on himself," and this, together with the practice of attentive self-observation while in a state of prayer, is absolutely in accordance with the inner tradition of Desert asceticism. Hylton's words also recall the old proverb, often cited in late medieval spiritual writings, "better is art than evil strength."[95] From where should the 'art' come, if not a kind of study, supported by the tradition? What are its tools?

Hylton's significance for us lies not only in his exposition of the interrelationship of 'the three lives' and his later publication at a critical time, but in his lifting the veil on the inner life of the medieval ascetic and in the importance he gives to a certain "desire," common to all men. If this desire did not exist, neither would this book, for there would have been no need at any time for men to have sought anything in themselves. This, the holy desire, is not the love of God, but the wish—however buried—to taste it: in the language of the time, "a great yearning for to be present to Him in His bliss, and fully for to be oned to Him in love."[96] One of the fundamental 'ideas' of the New Devotion was that knowing—in the sense of living in the presence of—this desire, would in itself bring about a reorientation. It is always there, says Hylton, but men do not remember it, for they are seldom engaged in what he calls "thinking with intent."[97] From the context it is clear that he refers to a special kind of working together of thought and feeling—our 'intention,' 'wish' and 'attention' being rightfully indissoluble, although rarely experienced as such.

> [H]e that has this desire of the gift of God, if he sleeps or else thinks not on God, but on worldly things, yet he has this desire in heart . . . but anon as he thinks on God, or on cleanness of living or of joys of heaven, then works his desire to God as long as he keeps his thought and his intent to please God either in prayers, or in meditation, or in any other good deed of active life.[98]

Transliterated from a haphazard early sixteenth-century modernisation of Hylton's rhythmically alliterative fourteenth-century English, these apparently ordinary words, 'the soup of the soup,' still indicate an extraordinary sort of experience, unconditioned by time, the erosion of language and everything else: being active, this "desire" can act in him, and he becomes able to receive. Therefore, "all our business be for to stir this desire and use it by discretion now in one deed, now in another after he is disposed, and has grace thereto."[99]

This is an excellent description of the 'mixed life' and must be borne in mind in all that follows, for what we are wishing to follow is just this process.

TWO

Revaluations

Honour thyself.

Marsilio Ficino, quoting Pythagoras

[N]or, when we judge all that we understand to be little,
should we invent for ourselves dreams and inextricable fic-
tions.

Pico della Mirandola

Let him who is in the world flee to the cloister, but let him take
care that he does not sleep there.

Gabriel Biel

[T]he flame of religion is extinguished.

Jacques Lefevre d'Etaples

[R]epute yourself to be in a monastery, wheresoever you be
conversant among them that love truth.

Desiderius Erasmus

[C]ertain conditions are necessary . . . in order to remind us
that we must seek even the breath of life.

Wessel Gansfort

The Italian city-state of the fifteenth century was for the cultural forms of the
next three hundred years the kind of experimental laboratory which the
medieval monastery had been for the preceding. An intense yearning for freedom
meeting with rediscovered ancient wisdom produced a radical revaluation of
existing forms of thought, feeling and sensibility, with the result that in the consciousness of a small group of active and influential intelligentsia, "an old way of
seeing reality disappeared and a new way emerged."[1] In the characteristic mood
of the early Renaissance, Petrarch the precursor wrote in 1338: "there is perhaps a
better age in store; this slumber of forgetfulness will not last forever. After the
darkness has been dispelled, our grandsons will be able to walk back into the pure
radiance of the past."[2]

Historical accounts convey the impression of two mutually independent lives coursing north and south through the body of Europe at this time: was the integrity of a common life revealed at their confluence? Were 'revaluations' formal adjustments, the result of the collision of two forces alone? The sense of spiritual awakening among these men deserves our respect, however difficult to relate to our theme. Existing forms, identified with long established social, political, religious and artistic attitudes whose spirit had departed, contradicted the fundamental movement of life by excluding the needs of the increasingly lay dominated urban society developing in fifteenth-century Italy.[3] The dream of *historiae novae* ('the Middle Ages') had been the realisation of a Christian society on earth, but the wish now was to awaken. Perhaps the city was a 'monastery.'

The emerging 'Renaissance' culture was based on an altered relationship with the past. Italian history, in which the identity of her people resided, was not what it had seemed. What Salutati and Bruni did for the historical horizons of the Florentines,[4] other humanists later accomplished for the French, Germans and English, while more visionary thinkers demonstrated the same truth for all Europe on a philosophical and spiritual level, namely that the cultural roots of Western civilisation extended further and more widely than had been allowed and men were richer than they had known. The surviving remains of the ancient world— schools of thought, literary genres, works of art, canons of architecture, religious doctrines, magical traditions and scientific, metaphysical and cosmological knowledge—all were searched out and scrutinised for authority and relevance. This material of *sacra vetustas*[5] became a touchstone for the thought and feeling of the Renaissance. The "explorator," Pico della Mirandola, brought forward, for example, "those things that I have dug up from the ancient mysteries of the Hebrews . . . in order to confirm the holy and Catholic faith."[6] In all spheres the wisdom of the distant past, hitherto inaccessible, came into contact with the hunger of the present. This movement exactly parallels the making available of practical spiritual help discussed in the previous chapter, and was to have equally far reaching consequences.

The reformulation of an ancient vision of man's role in all worlds presided over this renewal.[7] Man must make himself: upon the nature of his work in this life depended his real significance and use. This is much closer to the essential attitude of the Christian devotionalists in the North than might seem, for man's dependence and independence are inextricably linked, and, whether emphasis is placed upon God's remoteness or upon His presence, man's part is still to be sought. Pico's deeply traditional words, as disturbing to our aimlessness as the teachings of the medieval mystics, expressed the characteristic energy of the cultural renewal and distinctively coloured it.

He therefore took man as a creature of indeterminate nature and, assigning him a place in the middle of the world, addressed him thus: "We have made you neither of heaven nor of earth, neither mortal nor immortal, so that with freedom of choice and with honour, as though the maker and moulder of yourself, you may fashion yourself in whatever shape you shall prefer. You shall have the power to degenerate into the lower forms of life, which are brutish. You shall have the power, out of your soul's judgement, to be reborn into the higher forms, which are divine." . . . On man when he came into life the Father conferred the seeds of all kinds and the germs of every way of life. Whatever seeds each man cultivates will grow to maturity and bear in him their own fruit. If they be vegetative, he will be like a plant. If sensitive, he will become brutish. If rational, he will grow into a heavenly being. If intellectual, he will be an angel and the son of God. And if, happy in the lot of no created thing, he withdraws into the centre of his own unity, his spirit, made one with God, in the solitary darkness of God, who is set above all things, shall surpass them all. Who does not wonder at this chameleon which we are? . . . [M]an is not any inborn image of himself, but many images coming in from the outside. . . . Let a certain holy ambition invade the mind, so that we may not be content with mean things but may aspire to the highest things and strive with all our forces to attain them: for if we will to, we can . . . the patriarch Jacob . . . sleeping in the lower world but keeping watch in the upper . . . will advise us through a figure . . . that there is a ladder extending from the lowest earth to the highest heaven, divided in a series of many steps, with the Lord seated at the top, and angels in contemplation ascending and descending over them alternately by turns . . . two natures are planted in our souls; by the one nature we are lifted upward to the heavens, and by the other, shoved downward to the lower world.[8]

If we can receive these words innocently, free from all accumulated associations about 'Renaissance individuality,' 'romantic willpower' and even late-twentieth-century 'new age philosophy,' we begin to appreciate their force—even in translation—like a discovery. The aspiration they express, although by no means the corresponding ability, was evoked by contact with real ideas, with what Pico called "philosophy," a totality of knowledge conceived by him as the revelation, for those able to receive it, of one sacred tradition embracing and uniting the wisdom of the ancient Egyptian priesthood, the mystery religions and philosophical schools of the Greeks, the psychological lore of the Persian Magi, the Hebrew Prophets and Cabbalists and, finally, the Fathers and Saints of Christianity, who were its crown.[9] Clearly such "philosophy" is, and remains, inaccessible to a partial intellectual attunement, unlike its worldly namesake: it is a teaching, or part of a teaching, a traditional Way, leading through purification and unification to liberation,[10] the call of whose ideas reentered life during the Renaissance. Although we know of it only indirectly through the literature and art it generated, it can be recognised as something distinct from the philosophy, classical or otherwise, with which we are familiar, the subjective exercise of speculation focusing on one world at the expense of others. It was maintained that "lawful Philosophy is no different from true religion, and lawful religion exactly the same as true Philosophy."[11] "Philosophy" had, inconceivably, to be lived: "Indeed, fathers, there is multiple discord in us . . . moral philosophy alone will still those wars in us."[12]

This Renaissance synthesis completes the cycle of medieval thought[13] and, by establishing its unity with pre-Christian traditions, begins a new cycle: in general, by transmitting to the coming age a body of ideas, however fragmentary, capable of serving the renewal of an intellectual life imbued with moral and spiritual aspirations,[14] and, in particular, by providing the motivation for a renewed search for man's place in the cosmos, from which arose what we call science[15] and the concomitant need for a universal religion.[16] The sustaining vision of man's unique position in all worlds, his possibility of evolving or involving, thus unites past and future. Dante had spoken of man as the horizon between heaven and earth. The experience of the medieval mystics could thus find a place in the 'post-monastic age' because, when its inessential medieval associations and forms had faded, it retained meaning as an expression of the basic search for truth;[17] without this Renaissance revaluation, the significance of their example would have evaporated with the passage of time. It is not only the swing of the pendulum: there is an economy in these matters.

Renaissance intellectuals did not prize originality of thought in the modern sense. Eclectic and syncretistic,[18] they sought to reconcile the apparently contradictory truths of their rediscovered sources with the Christian tradition in order to find practical guidance for their own lives, in the process of which they acted as more or less effective mediums through which a large quantity of ancient thought from many different sources passed into the life of the time. Their philology, for example, like that of their classical mentors, was made to serve the daily needs of urban life and was not limited, as it has now become, to a theoretical study of antiquity.[19] They sought always the application of knowledge, the passage from poised thought to balanced action. Incurably didactic, their writings were addressed to educated laymen, noblemen, businessmen and students; the works of their North European heirs were devoured by the widening circles of the middle classes.[20] This secular moral literature was directed mainly to individuals[21] and in this mirrored the religious imperatives of the late medieval mystics and the early Reformation.

How can we rightly order our lives? The question lay at the heart of these revaluations, as it had lain at the wellsprings of medieval culture: what else was the *Regula Benedicti* but a response to this? Truths not renewed by being lived become static, their own opposite: the medieval 'answer,' ceasing to touch men's innermost need—serving here inertia, there self-interest, was thus no longer able to inform all aspects of existence, the life of the body, the aspirations of the mind and the emotions of social life. A 'new knowledge' of thought entered the body of Europe during the Renaissance, resulting in a gradual reorientation in all spheres, which became, in turn, subject to the influence of the renewed spirituality, based on a 'new knowledge' of feeling,[22] represented by the New Devotion and the rediscovered Platonism. In the following account, material has been chosen to illustrate this changing emphasis rather than to project a particular theory of humanism.

Underlying all was a tension experienced as the wish to be free. At the turn of the fourteenth century, groups of Italian intellectuals were beginning to be intensely dissatisfied with the values and orientation of contemporary learning. However splendidly conceived and subtly elaborated, theological and philosophical systems that failed to teach men how to live more fittingly were, in Petrarch's words, no more than chains about us:[23] "it is one thing to speak wisely, quite another to live wisely." Challenging a scholar in 1390, Salutati wrote, "the truth cannot be in all these distinctions, questions and suppositions. Take away the sophistic dressing, give us back a knowledge of reality."[24] Expressing the same dissatisfaction, the young Bruni had written to his mentor in 1407, that he wished to learn (ancient) philosophy, "that I might understand on what basis our life must be established and how conducted."[25] Intellectuals were in search of practical thinking.

The open addressing of these questions, the staple of ancient thought, was a distinctive feature of the early Renaissance. Despite the classical dilettantism their words have an earnestness common to the search of every age. It was irrelevant for a starving man to learn how to define food, wrote Poggio Bracciolini, and proceeded to outline the priorities of the emerging culture: Cicero was greater than the intellectual Aristotle, for he "brings the virtues themselves down into the battlefield and puts them in the front line, making them speak and instruct; he offers a way of life and precepts, tells us what virtue allows and forbids, what should be the office of a good man, and thus he finally directs our actions to a certain rule of life."[26] Pass this inquiry into real, liveable values through the intensification of religious feeling occurring at the turn of the fifteenth century, and the ensuing popularity of manuals offering "a certain rule of life" for "the battlefield" becomes comprehensible, even inevitable.[27] This literature, a reflection of the search for new integrity, encompassed depths of feeling ranging from *The Spiritual Combat*, attributed to Lorenzo Scupoli, through Erasmus" *Enchiridion* and Elyot's *Governour* to the most jejune handbooks for the unlearned: its keynote being always an insistence on what was most useful for this life, upon action now.[28] "Thou must needs perish if thou know not what is to thy life profitable, that thou mayest seek for it, and what is dangerous, that thou mayest eschew it."[29] The merciless insistence of Socrates that philosophy should descend into men's homes and answer their deepest needs in the midst of life, his uncompromising practicality—albeit filtered through the stylish decencies of Ciceronian ethics—became the widely admired ideal.[30]

Other thinkers, while retaining the emphasis on practicality, were suspicious of crude attempts to synthesise Classical and Christian values. Alberti's dialogue

Della Tranquillità dell' Animo shows a humanist trying to approach profound questions of meaning by cobbling together fragments from ancient sages. Everything is in this conscienceless pillaging except the kernel of truth. The vital question includes oneself: how can we live the indifference to ill fortune, of which the philosophers speak, when in fact the goods of this world are what we all live for? It is necessary to learn, not how to "put a good face on things, but inwardly to avoid the perturbations and to purge the soul with a certain reason and method." Stealing from ancient ruins does not bring us this possibility![31] The prevalent 'humanist' mentality made a "muddle of so many opinions" that "what one finds is everything returning confused into a sort of false ancient chaos."[32] Alberti continued his probing in the Lucianesque *Momus*, in which he ridiculed the pretensions of all philosophers: virtue is never found among them, although they talk unceasingly about it.[33] The penetrating writings of Lorenzo Valla also systematically destroyed current beliefs and assumptions without providing any obvious solutions.[34] His thought was taken up in Northern Europe, particularly by Erasmus and the Christian humanists, for he finally came to find something of what he sought in the Pauline and Patristic corpus.[35]

The received tradition of 'the three lives' was of great interest to the humanists and its dispositions were examined in the light of ancient thought by Salutati, Bruni, Landino, Alberti, Ficino and many others. How often did the zeal for a literary-oratorical topic mask a question of burning personal relevance? In looking at how the the legacy of 'the lives' was being reshaped, we must grapple with personal reactions to the conventions of humanist prose: a formal transparency which obscures force of meaning, an elegant balance which frustrates attempts to weigh the thought and feeling contained, a love of oratorical devices and rhetorical effects and an emulation of classical sentiments which rarefy personal conviction and the authentic voice. Their words ensnare through poise and reasonableness, yet the impression evaporates soon afterwards: in a word, they lack body. In expression, Luther and Erasmus, for example, are opposites.

"The philosophers," according to the popular *Mythologiae* of Fulgentius, "have decided that the life of humanity consists of three parts, of which the first is called theoretical, the second practical, the third pleasurable: named 'contemplativa,' 'activa' and 'voluptuaria.'"[36] One of the most important discussions of action and contemplation is to be found in Landino's *Disputationes Camaldulenses*. The active life of engagement in community affairs is extolled as practical obedience to the Gospel commandment to love one's neighbour; the professional sage, isolated from his fellows, engaged in no business, forgetful of the world and his own body, is only half a man, a lazy drone feeding on the honey of others. The really wise men of antiquity were not wise for themselves alone, but benefited all by putting themselves at the service of the state. If there are two kinds of action proper to man, rational living and the care of the community, and the contemplation of truth and ascent through self-knowledge to the higher degrees of being which feed the soul, let the wise man be active insofar as human nature, family and country demand, yet let him remember that he was born to this dilemma of being between two worlds: let him seek his highest good in knowing the truth.[37] Although such formal debates can be tedious in their mannered abstraction, they recognise in their own way the fundamental duality of human nature, the outward and the inward directed, which is so important for a better understanding of the later material of this book. Ficino wrote to Lorenzo de Medici that to pursue any one 'life' at the expense of the others was not only misguided but blasphemous.[38]

It has become an historical commonplace that renewed emphasis on the 'active life' during the Renaissance decisively influenced the religious orientation of the whole of Europe. It is true that the 'Stoic' view of the inherent goodness of sociopolitical organisation, of the world as a theatre of human effort in which men rightly strove to express themselves in "magnificent and large things" in order to satisfy their legitimate ambition[39]—in contrast to the *otium* (leisure) advocated by some classical philosophies and personified by contemporary monks—made a strong appeal to the emerging, self-interested 'capitalist' society of fifteenth-century Italy.[40] By the 1530s these attitudes had passed into the intellectual life of Northern Europe, helping to explain the righteous horror of Tudor Englishmen at Italianate sophistication: toned down, they permeate Elyot's *Governour* and Starkey's *Dialogue*, and were surely contributory to the spread of the doctrine of the 'godly vocation' invented by the German Protestants.[41] But the view that Renaissance culture was fundamentally irreligious begs many questions. The dogmatic 'medieval' judgement that 'activity' precluded a religion that had become synonymous with 'contemplation,' as well as the conventional Renaissance equation of 'action' and 'virtue,' must be discarded if we wish to penetrate further: what do these words signify? In many cases pragmatic thinkers imbued the 'active life' with a religious sense comprehensible to the urban bourgeoisie, making its closest medieval parallel not the 'active' but the 'mixed life.'

Although the medieval division between temporal and spiritual was replaced with the Ciceronian between things human and divine, and a stand was taken squarely within the former,[42] modern scholars have developed whole interpretations of humanism based on its latent religiousness.[43] Petrarch said that learning, however profound, could never bring happiness if divorced from the Presence of Christ: "if wisdom is God through whom all things are made . . . the true philosopher is a lover of God."[44] Salutati affirmed the interdependence of things human and divine, the understanding of which was "the sum and perfection of wisdom," the result of "a certain mean" which was easier to imagine than discover.[45] Bruni spoke of the active life as a mean between the medieval opposites of action and contemplation, rather than a classicizing of the former, and cited the lives of Dante and Cicero as examples of the participation in economic, political and social life perfecting intellectual work, for the "flowering of the whole man" must be the result of both action and contemplation. Filelfo's commentary on the

Aeneid also emphasised the relationship between the two: wisdom without the ability to act rightly is nothing, and virtue without contemplation of the truth is impossible.[46] Behind these cultivated antitheses they perceived the divisions inherent in man and wondered about their reconciliation, their 're-ligion.' Weighing their words, it becomes clear that understanding at all levels is the result not of knowledge alone but of becoming-able; in the religious sources of the 'mixed life' we shall meet the idea of 'spiritual doing,' the possibility dormant at the intersection of action and contemplation.[47]

The humanist critique of the unconditional supremacy of contemplation was, effectively, directed against the contemporary monastic ideal, because the literary defenders of contemplation were not only underwriting existing religious institutions but justifying their own positions within them: but if they attacked 'religion' it was on practical grounds, for they were trying, in different measures and according to their lights, to define the place of a religion without quotation marks, a possibility for all men. Salutati advocated the 'active life', not because it denied religious obligations but because it provided a more certain and honest ground for their realisation:

> Do not believe that to flee the crowd, to avoid the sight of beautiful things, to shut oneself up in a cloister, is the way to perfection. In fleeing from the world you may topple down from heaven to earth, whereas I, remaining among earthly things, shall be able to lift my heart securely up to heaven. In caring for your family, your friends, your city which comprises all, you cannot but follow the right way to please God.[48]

Salutati considered, like Petrarch, that the will with which a man loves his good was more important for his orientation than the intellect, with which he knows his truth, and so concluded, unlike Petrarch, that 'active' life, in which virtue was sought, was more valuable than contemplative, in which knowledge of truth was the goal.[49] The "true and moral wisdom," which Salutati believed could arise from action, was essentially received from God in the midst of daily engagement: all other wisdom was relative ignorance, for without grace man could neither do nor know anything.[50] Nowhere did these early Humanists bring the quality and origins of action or contemplation directly into question; perhaps they didn't need to, although the later Neoplatonists endlessly debated their abstract meanings.

The religiousness underlying the civic humanism of the early Renaissance makes the redefinition and reestablishment of the primacy of contemplation by the Christian Neoplatonists and occultists of the school of Ficino a natural development, the answer to a cognised need rather than an antithesis, because their discipline required no external withdrawal from life: with them the humanist aspiration approached realisation. Humanist theories on the preeminence of the Good presumed the existence of an independent, innately intelligent will, but the

Platonists emphasised forcefully the chaotic and almost hopeless inner situation of man, the disorientation and unreality of his will, a diagnosis they shared—together with the terrible insight that man was literally asleep—with the contemporary New Devotion of the North.[51] "The chief reason" why man's life is so troubled on earth, said Ficino, is that he is upside down in himself. He cited "a certain play" to illustrate this extraordinary situation,

> [I]n which people have their legs extended upward and walk on their hands and heads—trying to look with one eye at all earthly things, with the other at things celestial; attempting to grasp with the nose, lips and fingers whatever is going on below, but to touch with their feet whatever hangs above them. . . . Oh friends, of such a kind are we almost all of us. . . . We stupidly make reason, which is the head of the soul, subservient to the senses, which are the feet of the soul. Moreover, with a mind so immersed in the depths, we have faith that we shall know both celestial and earthly things. With the lowest soles of the soul we try in vain to touch the highest parts of nature. . . . Just as everyone is in himself, so are the things he receives. We can complain not so much of our destiny as of our choice. We think continually of evils and evils trouble us everywhere. . . . Know yourself! O divine race clothed with a mortal vestment; make yourself naked, separate as much as you can O minds too ignorant of yourselves, O blind hearts! Please arise from this deep sleep since you cannot grasp foreign things through anything but yourselves, how will you ever grasp outward things when you have lost the inner ones? Why do you seek goods far away, as foreigners, when they are near, or rather within yourselves?[52]

Deepening the humanist intuition, Ficino argued that, because the Good was above the True, the will must be reoriented, an aspiration central to the New Devotion.[53] The Renaissance Platonists stood for the renewal of contemplation and its revitalisation from the sources of Western culture: the thought, and it is said the practice, of Pico and Ficino reunited the medieval tradition of spirituality with its ancient roots in order to point a way forward,[54] just as the New Devotion was renewing an ancient Christian discipline as a bridge to future forms of the religious life.

For all its elusive diversity, humanism shared fundamental religious attitudes with the New Devotion.[55] The Renaissance search for a more balanced religious orientation amidst daily demands was essentially for a 'mixed life' of action and contemplation. Humanists, Platonists and New Devotionalists urged 'being good' rather than pursuing knowledge about virtue in endless distinctions, each attempting in their different ways to cut the Gordian knot of scholasticism with renewed ancient knowledge and common sense. Consider these extracts from *De Imitatione Christi*:

What doth it profit thee to dispute deeply about the Trinity, if thou be wanting in humility, and so be displeasing to the Trinity? . . . I would rather feel compunction than know how to define it . . . all is vanity, but to love God and serve Him alone. . . . Cease from overweening desire of knowledge, because many distractions are found there, and much delusion. . . . Happy is he whom truth teacheth by itself, not by figures and passing sounds but as it is in itself. Our own way of thinking and our sense often deceive us, and see but a little way. What signifies making a great dispute about hidden and obscure things which we shall not be reproved in the judgement for having been ignorant of? Wonderful folly! that, neglecting the things that are useful and necessary, we give our attention unbidden to such as are curious and mischievous! Having eyes, we see not. And what matter is it to us of 'genera' and 'species'? He to whom the Eternal Word speaketh is delivered from a multitude of opinions.[56]

The atmosphere of the expression is distinctive, but how different is Petrarch's message?

It is safer to strive for a good and pious will than for a capable and clear intellect. The object of the will . . . is to be good; that of the intellect is truth. It is better to will the good than to know the truth. The first is never without merit; the latter can often be polluted with crime and then admits no excuse. Therefore those are far wrong who consume their time in learning to know virtue instead of acquiring it, and, in a still higher degree, those whose time is spent in learning to know God instead of loving Him. In this life it is impossible to know God in His fullness; piously and ardently to love Him is possible.[57]

The practicality of the classical moralists endeared them to Gerard Groote as well as the humanists:

[T]he wiser among them such as Socrates and Plato, turned all philosophy into the consideration of moral questions and if they spoke of deep matters they dealt therewith as in a figure and lightly, dwelling upon their moral aspect . . . so that some rule of conduct might always be found side by side with knowledge. Seneca too, following this principle, as often mingles moral dissertations with his discussion of natural philosophy, for whatsoever doth not make us better or induce us to avoid evil is harmful.[58]

Such studies as most pursue are "an unprofitable expense of time and are of no help for good living," he said, dismissing the whole late medieval knowledge of arithmetic, geometry, dialectic, grammar, poetry, rhetoric and law.

In fact humanists of all shades produced a large body of devotional writing and lay sermons on the themes of medieval religious thought, especially the relationship between man and God, in which they paid most attention to the quality of the inner life and the need for its utter reorientation; they considered the status of the monk, the lives of the saints, the Four Last Things and the Sacraments, particularly penance and the Eucharist, their views approaching those of Luther and Erasmus and reflecting the sacramental revivalism of late medieval devotion.[59] Fontius, for example, emphasised the inner disposition of the communicant rather than the mediating role of the priest:

> [I]f either the priest or the one to whom the injury must be recompensed is lacking, it still can be rightly done. For God does not require the work of lips or hands, if we are not able to perform them, but only the will. For it is in the judgement of the heart and the intention of the will and mind that true penance consists.[60]

This work, *Donatus seu de poenitentia* (1489), was translated into the vernacular. The Florentine Platonists were also directly involved in the lay devotional life of their time. Ficino's Academy included statesmen, merchants, poets, orators, physicians, jurists, musicians and theologians, but very few philosophers as such. He intended it to be a spiritual community and school and it was constituted on the pattern of the old lay religious guilds, with which he had a strong, albeit unclear, association. Research is gradually revealing the pervasive influence of these guilds, not only on Ficino's circle but on the drama (*sacra rappresentazione*), music and religious literature of the Renaissance as well as the oratories of the Counter-Reformation. Many of the most important works of Ficino, an active priest and vernacular preacher as well as physician and musician, were translated into the Tuscan vernacular by himself and his pupils, and the number of manuscripts extant suggests that they were widely read by laymen; his influential letters of spiritual advice were closely modelled on the traditional *lettera spirituale* of the guilds. The foundation of the Florentine Academy in the early 1460s was followed quickly by other foundations all over Italy.[61] In this sense, the Platonists were not remote from ordinary life, although they tried to point beyond it. Their influence gradually spread through Europe with consequences which began to wane only during the nineteenth century.[62]

At every opportunity Ficino affirmed the fundamental unity of religion and philosophy. Because man was divided, the two disciplines—philosophy fortifying the intellect and religion the will—had become separated and antagonistic, the former profaned by impiety, the latter by ignorance. It had not been so among ancient peoples whose philosophers had also been priests and physicians: "and that," he declared, "was right." The soul's return to God, its heritage, depended on the harmonious development of both reason and feeling, sustained by bodily health.[63] He pointed to a succession of legendary and historical sages—initiates—who had passed on the ancient teaching of unity. In his call for a purified religious philosophy and philosophical religion converging towards the same meaning on a higher level, Ficino saw himself as a worker in this tradition, not for the sake of the past but the future.[64] He was baiting a trap for the coming age to lead men back to simple religious faith by awakening their reason. It was too late to move the clever, impious minds of his contemporaries by conventional preaching:

> Stronger measures are needed: either divine miracles manifested on all sides or at least a philosophical religion . . . in these times it pleases divine providence to confirm religion in general by philosophical authority and reason until, on a day already predestined, it will confirm the true religion, as in other times, by miracles wrought among all peoples.[65]

The children of his foresight, or that of his teachers, were not only the *philosophia Christi* of Erasmus, which blended the piety of the New Devotion with the classicizing thought of humanism, but also the researches of scientific seers like Paracelsus, Campanella, Patrizi and Bruno, whose empiricism was interwoven with the magical and miraculous. Counter-Reformation Catholicism emphasised anew the authenticating miracles of the sacraments, particularly the Eucharist.

Ficino's thought was grounded in his own experiments in self-knowledge, and in his search he touches, however different his mode of expression, the essence of the New Devotion:

> We are all thirsty for true goodness and we all drink mere dreams. . . . What may we do, therefore, so that we may watch and be healthy in the right way? Our life must be converted into its contrary. We must unlearn those things which we have learned; by learning them we have hitherto not known ourselves. We must learn those things we have neglected; without knowing them we cannot know ourselves. We must like what we neglect, neglect what we like, tolerate what we flee, flee what we follow.[66]

Was this attempt to intentionally break habits, to 'like what it doesn't like' in order to "watch," the beginning of that "certain rule of life" which Poggio had been seeking? 'Self-denial,' in order to see, and be seen for, what one is and is not—that another influence might be received—was the instrument of traditional monastic asceticism.

Such "philosophy" is far indeed from speculation about truth: it is the reflection of a complete traditional teaching,[67] revealing man's intended place in the universal scale, together with a practical method[68] for bringing his disparate powers[69] into an order of relationship receptive to universal laws of creation and return. This is what we seem to glimpse, however indistinctly, in Ficino: he and his pupils were engaged, like Plotinus, in something more than vague and lofty thoughts, idealism and good deeds. They had a discipline and perhaps a way. We shall find commensurate material in the New Devotionalist, Zerbolt.[70]

It is just at this point that the opposites represented by 'philosophical' Platonism and 'religious' New Devotion may be related.[71] Despite their different frameworks, emphases and language, their common aim was the experiencing ('knowledge') of oneself, through separation from the 'unreal' world, leading to the possibility of practical study guided by the newly available experience of the past: whether the *prisca theologia* of the sages or the methods of the Desert Fathers. New 'knowledge' supported the search for wholeness, the awakening to another level of meaning—"the Divine Essence" and 'the love of God.'[72] Ficino, in his certainty that he had a solution, and in his technical terminology, may be compared with Bernard of Clairvaux. We shall attempt to examine the elusive practices of a psychospiritual discipline when discussing the exercises of the New Devotion. To say that such practices were the inner core of the Platonist's doctrine of the convergence of philosophy and religion, even if true, raises indeed more questions than it answers, questions which threaten to lead us off the known historical map into quite another place.

Ficino described his search with timeless and deceptive simplicity:

> I have often looked for myself. . . . First I have touched my chest with my hands, then I have often gazed at this face in the mirror, but I could never say that I have touched myself with the one or seen myself in the other. For, when I seek myself, I am certainly not looking for another but for him who seeks. Indeed, it is exactly the same Marsilio that is both seeker and sought. Who does the seeking? He who wishes to discover. Who wants to discover? He who knows that there is something worth looking for. Who knows this? . . . [W]henever I have drawn the sharp sight of the mind back to itself, hoping that I might see myself in this way, I have by no means thus attained what I desired. For in this inward search I find neither much delight nor rest. . . . I do not find myself in myself.[73]

These remarkable words tell of his efforts to live in the present moment. He exhorted his pupils to free themselves from the passage of time. Time was "an unwholesome physician," beguiling the patient each day with expectations of the morrow, leading men "to death in a fallacious hope for life," while evils accumulated all around. In God, he said, yesterday and tomorrow are nothing else but today.[74]

> [I]n the name of the eternal God, spend the precious money of this short time sparingly and prudently, that you may not someday repent in vain your prodigality and irreparable loss. . . . Free yourself, I pray, from this miserable prison while you can; and you can only today. Belong to yourself today for the first time. Believe me, it is not fitting for a wise man to say: I shall live. The life of tomorrow is too late, live today . . . do not promise me tomorrow anymore; you promise what you do not possess. . . . Nothing is more fallacious than that tomorrow; it has deceived all the men the earth has produced. . . . We all suffer heavily from this sickness. . . . We hardly possess the present time, for we have it so lightly that we cannot hold it even for a short

while. But the future is nothing . . . mad and miserable people, we throw our hopes into nothing and always misuse the treasure we possess, but we desire to use well that which we do not possess. So we are all sick unto ruin.[75]

Laetus in praesens (rejoicing in the present) occurred more than once among the aphorisms inscribed on the walls of Ficino's Academy.[76] The followers of Gerard Groote also worked for a living presence, a conquering of time through remembering their own death. "You are a man," wrote a correspondent to Ficino, "for whom no moment is free from the dread of death."[77]

Humanists and Platonists were trying to harness the 'active life' to spiritual values, the New Devotion to discover how to be in the world but not of it. Traditionally, contemplation which did not issue in right action was judged dangerous and imperfect: Martha and Mary, the types of the two directions, live under "one roof" in the symbolic language of the Bible, both having their rightful place, for "repose is not given unless thou hast first laboured."[78] In effect, this is 'the mixed life.'

We are not saying that the Platonists and New Devotionalists followed an identical discipline—their formal orientation was quite different—but that psychologically and spiritually their practice was deeply related, even cognate. They had both received a direction and were addressing themselves to the same buried need. The Platonist's aim to purify the mind and the Devotionalist's to purify the heart,[79] must necessarily touch each other in practice within one body. The characteristic and exclusive formal languages in which they expressed themselves reflect the different languages of thought and emotion as enshrined in the historical traditions of philosophy and religion. If an incongruity remains for us between piety and understanding, is it not because, encumbered with modern associations, we are unable to envisage that transformation of meaning which is both the child and the purpose of an experiential discipline? It was this practical possibility which Ficino, Gerard and others received from their teachers and brought into the body of Europe for their time: that intellect and will, knowledge and love, thought and feeling, might not always be so divided, that, with right preparation, a relative unity—a higher level of being—might actually be experienced. Although further work is undoubtedly necessary to clarify historical, psychological and spiritual relationships of this order, these two movements bore the hope of a period of transition.

This renewed seeking within the conditions of ordinary life inevitably reflected back upon the status of the monastic ideal and its corollary, the position of laymen. Before we can examine in detail the nature of the New Devotion, we must review the tensions within late medieval monasticism.

All our evidence indicates that by 1400, if not long before, the monasteries had ceased to effectively transmit the authentic mystery of Christ's teaching in all its immensity and power, that they were no longer able to command their position within life as the gateway to another world. Not every community, but enough, had fallen short, for the sum total of their qualitative influence in this direction to have become negligible. At the same time, the appeal of monasticism as a way of life had inevitably widened and the numbers of the professional religious increased: broadening at the cost of shrinking.[80]

During the twelfth-century renewal, their purpose had been formulated thus: "to occupy oneself with God is not idleness, but the work of all works."[81] Summoning men to his side in the remote Jura, Bernard had written:

> Would that God might in his goodness let fall upon His poor servant a drop of that rain of His free choice which He keeps for His own inheritance, that I might pour it over thee and hear from thee in return how its touch had moved thee! Believe one who has experienced it. Thou wilt find among the woods something that thou didst never find in books. Stones and trees will teach thee a lesson thou didst never hear from masters in the school. Thinkest thou that honey cannot be drawn from the rock and oil from the hardest stone? Do not the mountains drop with sweetness and the hills flow with milk and honey, and the valleys abound with corn?[82]

The monasticism condemned by the fifteenth- and sixteenth-century reformers for failing to be occupied with God was not the movement of Bruno and Bernard, although they were still revered, their foundations still existed and men still lived, as it were, according to their directions: names survived, but what they signified had altered by a kind of legerdemain. But we should not assume that the search for this "work of all works" disappeared with the erosion of its medieval monastic form: on the contrary, it intensified. During the years that had elapsed since the foundation of Clairvaux, individuals had continued to seek these lessons, but more and more rarely within the monastic orders. The monasticism with which the current of new enquiry came into contact was an entrenched feature of social life, an obstacle. In the clash of this contact the 'mixed life' is revealed as the expression of Christian teaching most in tune with the conditions and needs of the age. Moving between North and South among humanists, pietists, monks and radicals, we will try to explore in the rest of this chapter some of the results of this contact between new and old, letting the scale of our subject emerge gradually, as it will.

To follow Christ's teaching must mean in some sense to become a warrior. What echoes did this call awaken? For centuries it had meant entering a religious order.[83] Common sense, the practical search of the mystics and the 'new' values of Italian civic humanism concurred that the battlefield was in the midst of daily life. This life was already full to bursting with conflict, but to what end? In 1513, John Colet preached before the English court "on the victory of Christ, exhorting all Christians to war and to conquer under the banner of Him, their proper king."[84] Erasmus' *Enchiridion* (1505), subtitled in its English translation "the Handsome

Weapon of a Christian Knight," consisted of advice on combat for all Christians, for whom "life here below is best described as being a type of continual warfare . . . the world, like some deceitful magician, captivates their minds."[85] Men could no longer excuse themselves by disclaiming membership of 'religion,' for had not all sworn in baptism to 'die to sin,' namely to become monks in spirit? The proper path for all Christians was effectually that once trodden by the monks alone.[86] This was the hope of the age. Thomas More appended twelve rules of Pico della Mirandola to the translation of his *Life*, "partly exciting, partly directing a man in spiritual battle," and also "twelve weapons of spiritual battle which every man should have at hand."[87] In his *Werke for Householders*, addressed to laymen on the ordering of their lives, the Bridgettine Whytford pictured the objections, as his friend Erasmus had done, to the monastically derived exercises he was advocating: "Some of you will say, 'Sir, this work is good for religious persons and for such persons as are solitary.'" But if they would be prepared to suffer all manner of hardship for a friend, a master or the king, if bidden, why not for their own sake?

> Venture upon it, go forth withall. Every beginning is hard and of great difficulty, but importunate labour does vanquish and overcome all things.[88]

The idea of the battle imbued the Ignatian *Exercises* and the profound expositions of Lorenzo Scupoli's *Spiritual Combat* (1589), as well as the mass of Elizabethan and Stuart guides for the godly, and was not limited by religious persuasion.[89] An anonymous manuscript, *A Discourse of Life and Death* (1623), describes how he who wishes to follow his "reason" must inevitably "swim against the stream," "resolve to fight in every part of the field" against "the world itself" and "a thousand treacherous and dangerous intelligences among his own forces."[90]

Although the Christian struggle, the ancient *psychomachia*,[91] clearly became (and on the individual level was always tending to become) a 'manner of speaking,' practical knowledge of its method had survived from earlier times. Inner war intentionally initiated and continually renewed implanted 'monastic' striving in the world. This 'new devotional' attitude, bearing the perception that different levels had become confused and wrongly opposed, was naturalised by the researches of Christian humanists and granted entry by the moral seriousness of Northern pietism.

The Observant reformers of the fifteenth century, touched by these new imperatives as children of the New Devotion, emphasised the need for preparation for the religious life, itself only a preparation according to Benedict.[92] The Windesheimer, John Busch, wrote of certain incorrigible monks:

> [L]et them, when they beg for leave of absence, promise that they will live in the world according to priestly rule . . . for in the world, being solitary, they will comport themselves better through the fear of man than they do now in the monastery, when they fear no man.[93]

The implication that a former spiritual elite had become insensitive to everything except the 'worldly' morality of fear, approaches the characteristic Reformation insight that the monk who had fallen inwardly to the level of the layman (who had never promised anything) was in a worse case.

In the intellectual erosion of the monastic ideal a crucial role was played by the humanist Lorenzo Valla with his dictum that the man who overcomes greater danger should have the greater reward, while he who is sheltered and even then fails to do his duty should be the more punished.[94] In *De Professione Religiosorum* (c. 1441) he systematically denied the supremacy of the monastic ideal and redefined the status of the lay Christian as potentially the peer of the professional religious, even his better. Although little known outside Italy in his lifetime (*De Professione* remained in manuscript for many years), his thought was seminal, his common sense prophetic, his views antennae for the future.[95]

The special position inherited by the religious orders, he said, did not correspond to their reality as Christian sects whose life differed from the rest of society only in its pretension.[96] To a pioneer of Renaissance philology, a subject with philosophical, psychological and moral dimensions since lost, it was a matter of the integrity of words. Humanist-influenced reformers hated religious hypocrisy and were preoccupied with the promptings of 'the spirit' because they believed language to be a true expression of the inward state: hypocrites falsified their actual condition and hence prostituted the Word. The "unchaste" latinity of the Papacy reflected moral and doctrinal impurity.[97] To speak of 'religious orders' was a devaluation of language, which, since God was the Word and language a divine gift, was a devaluation of very much more. When 'religion' was the description of the activity of the monk, it was not only language in question but reality.[98] We distort language because we do not see things as they are, and, if our view of others is the result of our view of ourselves, it is not only discrimination but self-respect which is lacking. "For what else is it to be religious than to be a Christian?"[99] To take words as facts was superstition. Monastic vows were being taken as oaths, which could not, in themselves, make a man more virtuous. 'Vow' comes from the same root as 'devotio,' a sincere wish, and only if the vow corresponds to this reality can it signify, because it is the inner attitude of the man, like the kernel of meaning in the word, which is important. Poverty, chastity and obedience are meritorious whether they have been professed or not, and, Valla added, "truly, these things are not necessary for everybody."[100]

In what sense was the relationship entered into by the obedient monk useful to him? Was there not a healthier position, more difficult to sustain, which avoided self-abasement or elevation? Monastic (and all traditional spiritual) literature refers to practices of submission, founded on an inner logic: the means of developing qualities of faith and feeling,[101] contradicting reason and self-respect as usually understood. If Valla knew this, he ignored something so opposed to humanist self-cultivation; with his own valuation, he looked for expressions of freedom and self-respect in the monastic life, and found a void.

> Is there no middle ground so that we only either have servants or serve? . . .
> Not all are lords and not all are servants, and not all are teachers and not all
> are disciples; they do not obtain a lesser degree of merit who are in the mid-
> dle. And as desirable as it is to belong to the status of prelates and preceptors,
> just as miserable is it to be in the number of subjects and disciples. Certainly
> this is of far less dignity than to be . . . in the middle and for one to be able to
> be without a lord and to live and know without a master. I do not venture to
> say that it is a sign of an abject and ignorant soul to commit oneself to the
> charge of a tutor in the manner of a boy . . . but if he is able to admonish,
> teach and rule others, why does he subject himself, especially to others who,
> as frequently happens, are ignorant and unworthy? . . . [Y]our pledge of
> obedience is a kind of servitude . . . while I would prefer to be the master
> rather than a servant of others, I certainly prefer to be the master of
> myself.[102]

Can we detect here the aspirations and grievances of an urban bourgeoisie whose growing vitality, at first in the Italian city-states and later throughout Northern Europe, was demanding new religious forms?[103] The influence of humanists, whose emphasis on moral virtue made them the natural counsellors of this class, tended to polarise the old distinctions between clergy, religious and laity. Valla seems to echo their healthy independence, their mingled resentment and exasper-ation at a religious ideal foreign to their experience, whose principles were obscure and whose values appeared inappropriate, even opposed, to their own lives. Or was he rather speaking of a psychological position of insecurity and exposure which looks forward to Luther and beyond? He makes the point,[104] to be repeated by Protestant and Christian humanist reformers, that the original lay baptismal vow of obedience renders the monastic vow superfluous,[105] that in later life it was necessary to remember and live according to this lay vow and that, in the absence of this effort, entering religion would not help. His words, "to be able to be without a lord and to live and know without a master . . . to be master of myself," haunted the European mind for centuries.

An honest, balanced, practical way of life becomes the aim. Poverty has no objective value unless 'of the spirit,' yet the monks are not even poor in material possessions. If the Rules are man-made they are unworthy of attention beside God's rule (felt by humanists to be perfectly accessible in the Gospels), and if they are its equivalent they are unnecessary.

> To obey the rule is to obey God, not man, which we laymen also do. Nor can
> another rule be held better than the one handed down by Christ and the
> Apostles.[106]

The ideal of poverty ran counter to the social mores championed by the humanists. Did the obligations inherent in Valla's position as scholar and family man
really place him beyond the religious pale? Innocence and wealth were not mutually exclusive:

> [I]t is sufficient if I do not revel in riches and renounce them not in fact but
> in spirit . . . money is necessary to me to buy codices. You, if you do other-
> wise and hand it to paupers are stupid and do not love yourself as your
> neighbour.[107]

Extremes were suspicious and dangerous—"it is much better to be safe in the
middle than on high with danger of ruin"[108]—as the multitude of sixteenth-century encomiums of family life and the duties of the married householder were to
agree.[109]

Valla concludes by defending an ideal which may have had bourgeois overtones
that others were soon to develop, but which is unjustly described as such at this
stage: we must accept our duty in the world fearlessly and strive to understand
what is demanded of us in the fullest sense, for the respective value of the lay and
monastic lives depends on how they are lived.

> You obey: I assume the care of others. You live poor and continent: I live a
> life equal to yours. You have bound yourself for keeping this, I have not
> thought that servitude necessary. You do rightly by necessity, I by choice;
> you out of fear of God, I out of love; perfect charity drives away fear. If you
> had not feared that otherwise you could not please God, certainly you never
> would have bound yourself . . . all the way of the vow, all imposition of a
> fast, all oath and finally all law (your profession is a certain law), was
> invented on account of fear, that is . . . on account of bad people. . . . I don't
> know what else you can ask of God except the fruit of obedience, poverty
> and continence. But you are not content with this and demand that you be
> placed above others on account of danger. But if you consider the danger of
> punishment among you, consider in my case the danger of sinning more
> easily, who am bound by no anchor of fear This makes the same act of virtue
> greater in me than in you. . . . Therefore let us make both you and us equal
> in the manner of Paul, who of those eating and not eating said, "each
> observes in his own sense."[110]

Valla's sanity begs the question of level.[111] In the humanist's division of outer and
inner life, their opposition of the positive life in the 'world' to the negative life of
the monk and recourse to 'the spirit,' the dubious legacy of medieval dualism
lived on.

In this vein Petrarch had admired the Carthusian life with its clear objectives,
because it seemed an escape from the responsibilities and distractions which so

taxed him.[112] Despite this attraction he retained his independence: *De Otio Religioso* was a sermon to himself encouraging him to be religious without joining an order. When his tentative classicism became a full-blown cultural programme in the Italian city states of the fifteenth century, the sole value of monasticism came to be seen as the opportunity it afforded for *otium liberale*—peaceful retirement for writing and study,[113] an astonishing analysis but perhaps a true verdict on the path the monks had taken since the days of Bernard. Petrarch left unquestioned the tacit assumption of language that to be religious meant to be 'a religious,' but his successors (with the important exception of Valla) bypassed philological conundrums in their single-minded concentration on classical values, reading into the life their own subjective preoccupations. Erasmus wrote his early work *De Contemptu Mundi* while he was an Augustinian canon at Steyn, having entered religion in the belief that seclusion would enable him to concentrate on classical letters.[114] The peace, liberty and *voluptas* of his life there was the "safest way" for a young man threatened by the dangers of 'the world.'[115] It seemed to him then that the monk was freer than the layman because he wishes for nothing that is not permitted, and thus (!) may do as he likes: having discovered bread he does not desire acorns.[116] For the scholar there is the *voluptas* of "sacred studies," leisure to browse in the library and "muse" in the gardens.[117] An exercise in citing classical myth, ethics and history, it makes no mention of the daily round of the office, mass and chapter, ignores the traditional monastic virtues and passes over in silence the love of God, once considered the heart of monastic purpose. Of the fruits of meditation, however, he does speak respectfully, for he had heard about them from his fellows: "I am unworthy as yet to be admitted to come to these delights, although I have a little slenderly tasted thereof."[118] Naive and enthusiastic as it is, this peculiar little treatise expresses fundamental attitudes of his later life, including the preoccupation with personal freedom which was to drive him back into the world within six years. Written circa 1490, it was published in 1521, and the 1523 edition carried an additional chapter bitterly attacking monasticism and offering an alternative.[119]

Its original form was deeply coloured by the advance of North European humanism. Goswin of Halen, the humanist rector of the Groningen Brotherhouse, declared in 1529 that the monastic morning should be devoted to the study of philosophy and the afternoon to the enjoyment of the company of friends, the cultivation of one's health and the reading of poets and orators. In his list of recommended authors, the classics and early Church Fathers predominate,[120] but among the moderns he approved Pico, and, indeed, in his translation of Pico's *Life*, More quotes a eulogy of the contemplative life by Pico which reads like a summary of Goswin's programme of *otium liberale*.[121] Although More and Pico seriously considered it, neither became professional monks. Ambrogio Traversari, the director of the Camaldulensian Order, was the type of the humanist monk, similitudes of which began to appear in England at the turn of the century.[122] While Pico was describing a personal contemplative regime unconnected with organised religion, Traversari stood for the infusion of degenerate monasticism with the new hope of philosophical and religious synthesis, but both embraced the ideal of *otium liberale*. More, who sincerely admired Pico and dedicated his translation to a nun, finally found his personal meaning in active commitment to public affairs sustained by an intense inner religious life. Erasmus, in the seventh rule of the *Enchiridion*, exhorted the lay Christian to the essential monastic work of loving Christ, but in 'the world' and with the tenacity of a scholar of the New Learning seeking natural knowledge. Pico, More and Erasmus were deeply but differently influenced by the idea of 'the mixed life.' During the restructuring of monasticism in the sixteenth century, Renaissance *otium liberale* escaped from the cloister to inspire generations of literary scholars, philosophers, poets and scientists, but the personal independence and private agonies of More typified the life theme of the century's innumerable and many-coloured religious martyrs.

According to the chronic polarity in human attitudes, the monastic life's potential for reflective scholarship had only to be grasped by one party, for another to begin ridiculing abbeys as dens of malingerers unwilling to face the difficulties of life. Thomas Starkey's account in the *Dialoge between Pole and Lupset* (1533) begins by discussing the difficulty of leading a balanced life in 'the world':

> For the which purpose, as I think, many men of great wisdom and virtue fly from it, setting themself in religious houses, there quietly to serve God and keep their minds upright with less jeopardy, which thing is surely not amiss done of them which perceive their own imbecility and weakness, prone and ready to be oppressed and overthrown with these common and quiet pleasures of the world, by whom they see the most part of mankind drowned and overcome. Howbeit, meseemeth they do like to fearful shipmen which for dread of storms and troublous seas keep themselves in the haven and dare not commit themselves to the dangerous tempests of the same.

Following closely the line of Valla's *De Professione*, he makes the issue turn on the question of proper strength and weakness, courage and fear.

> [L]ike as he that in great tempest and troublous time governs well the ship and conveys it at last to the haven . . . is called a good and expert mariner and much more praiseworthy than he which for fear and dread keeps himself in the haven still, so he which in dangerous prosperity . . . governs his mind well and keepeth it upright is justly to be most perfect and wise man; yea, and much more deserves . . . than he which for fear of the same dangers runs into a religious house, there as in a haven quietly to rest, without so much trouble and disquietness . . . you shall not think that such as live in

prosperous state of this life present are thereby excluded from the felicity of
the life to come, but rather, when prosperity is well used, it is a mean to set
man's mind in that state whereby he shall attain higher felicity.[123]

Starkey goes on to express, in the style of the pamphleteer Simon Fish, the typical
Reformation insight that the religious are "nothing but burdens to the earth . . .
the third part of our people living in idleness, as persons to the commonweal
unprofitable drone bees in a hive which do nothing else but consume and devour
all things as the busy and good bee with diligence gathers together."[124] Ideas formulated in the debates of the Italian intelligentsia a century earlier were now common property. Landino had said the same,[125] while Poggio's *De Avaritia* refers to

> [T]hose hypocrites hanging about the market place who get their living
> without sweat or labour under the guise of religion, preaching to others the
> poverty and contempt for property which is their own rich fortune. Our
> cities will not be maintained by those idle and bewitched men who live in
> repose, but by men who are devoted to the upkeep of the human race.[126]

This was the way humanists liked to think of themselves.

Their attempts to 'understand' the relevance of monasticism did not end with
the transposition of *otium liberale*. In *De Seculo et Religione* Salutati associated the
moral probity of Republican Rome with monastic virtue. Present-day customs
were criminal compared with the purity of ancient society,[127] but men had
become so corrupt in the dotage of the world[128] that they were no longer able to
understand the heroic struggles of the early monks, let alone the life Christ Himself lead, and so Salutati was loath to propose them as models. The Golden Age
might be regained only if the whole of society would take the vow of poverty, like
a great monastery.[129] The Roman Republic and the Church may be compared
because both were founded by paupers and ruined by wealth: the coming of
Empire and the conversion of Constantine were equivalent tragedies.[130] As elsewhere, Salutati is hinting at a kind of lay spiritual monasticism, without which life
in the terrestrial city, the humanist's main concern, will never be tolerable, let
alone truly civilised. The monastic ideal, once the ark of Western culture, has
become historical myth in the dream of intellectuals, and the seeds of post-Reformation nostalgia for 'the age of faith' were already germinating: sixteenth-century
yearnings for the peace and solitude portrayed as 'monastic' by humanists easily
became tirades against "the filthy worlde" and rhapsodies on the simple life,[131] for
sentimentality and violence are closely akin. The longing felt by Elizabethans for
the Golden Age mingled with their idealisation of a monastic past they had never
known, and which, in truth, had never been.[132] The humanist's dream of
medieval monasticism sounded its death knell.

The nature of monasticism was fundamentally a question of the meaning of
religion and of man's need, but it was also, subjectively, a matter of whose religion, whose need.[133] The sources at our disposal are becoming increasingly sub-

jective. Erasmus' concern was with his own idea of liberty and its hidden agenda: "if anyone examines more attentively the life and rules of Benedict, Francis or Augustine, he will observe that what they wished was only to live with willing friends in liberty of spirit close to the gospel teaching."[134] He reverses the traditional, and latterly trite, medieval view of Christ as the first monk, by using the worthy origins of monasticism as a flail in the battle for his favourite notions of the purity of the past and the virtue of unconstrained observance. Views of primitive Christianity were shifting, for each age 'creates' in its own image. The Protestant preacher, Hugh Latimer, looked with his own social gospel in mind: "Abbeys were ordained for the comfort of the poor."[135] Had he heard that they once had other purposes, his forgetting must be weighed with that of the majority of the monks, who had been wont to cite their founders as authority for present behaviour as if conditions and understanding had not changed: the new thought grasped the sense in which history did not travel in straight lines, how what begins purely curves always towards impurity. The Observant Friar John Ryckes wrote that "if Saint Austin or Saint Benet were again alive (whom they take as fathers and authors of their rules and orders of their living) I think they should not know them but say there was never thing that they more disapproved than such living as is now in many places."[136] The impression of dynamic historical decline and renewal, drawn from ancient historians and implicit in the Renaissance experience, was challenging the (apparently) static medieval view of time.

Renaissance thought, which tried to grasp the universality of the Christian heritage but whose force was often vitiated by literary sentimentality, was to combine with the radical toughness of a vigorous popular tradition of dissent in early sixteenth-century England to produce such typical works as the anonymous *Sum of Scripture*, proscribed in the 1530s. The *Sum* said, "In times passed all that lived after the gospel were monks and gave them to that life," but the first monks had lived centuries before Christ: since the sixth century, the very time from which conventional wisdom dates (and still dates) the historical appearance of monasticism, it had actually been in decline. "The monks after our Saviour's ascension unto Saint Benedict and Gregory's days, made no vows nor profession; they might eat, drink, fast, pray when they list, they had no certain masses, nor hours to sing daily." By comparison, contemporary religious life was "a superstitious subjection unto certain vain ceremonies."[137]

The desire for freedom from externals became a keynote of Reformation thought. At the critical juncture when a certain truth had cut through, where could men turn for support? Was their own subjectivity any more reliable than the outworn truths of the established order? At the moment of awakening from one dream, were they not threatened sevenfold by another?

As the monk became more and more indistinguishable from the layman, the vision of layman-as-monk grew. "Now," wrote Ryckes in the 1530s, "there is little difference between lay persons, priests and religious in crimes and worldly living."[138] The original truth of monastic separation from 'the world' had been the search for an actual connection with the higher level which contains it, with God as it was said; historically this separation had meant the actualisation of special conditions intentionally organised ('the Rule') to support intensive work for such a connection. Without this meaning the religious Way became imaginary, supporting—however sincerely followed—only repetition, that is, 'worldly' habit, although such a life might be unusually altruistic and worthy. The monk's fundamental purpose as the exemplary medieval human being was to find and love God, to experience both higher and lower influences and turn in the heart consciously in a direction diametrically opposed to 'the world'. Involution, the contrary movement away from God, leads lawfully through repetition back into 'the world.' The disappearance of the medieval form of monasticism during the sixteenth century was thus surely a necessary result of causes both mechanical and providential. Eventually only the impulse to be free from superstitious impedimenta was left, the last generation turning against their austerities as meaningless and self-defeating, their negative criticism sometimes combining with an aspiration to embrace a more honest life in 'the world,' their attitude both reflecting and encouraging the spread of Protestant and Erasmian ideas on the pointlessness of monastic observances as well as representing the culmination of a long process of decline. Of the Observants, who were exceptions to this, we shall speak later.

If the perceptible influence generated in a monastic community by the sincere confrontation with the mystery of man's calling had once evoked the instinctive respect of outsiders, regardless of personal understanding and commitment, by the fifteenth century this response had generally given way to scorn and envy. The ancient name of the monk, formerly honourable before God, had become a reproach and a laughing-stock before men. The stricter orders, Carthusians and Bridgettines, tended to retain admiration, yet they too were to fall from their pedestal. During the last days of the London Charterhouse, the precincts were overrun by hostile and curious members of the public who proceeded to annoy, deride and strike the bewildered brethren,[139] for what is incomprehensible, if it cannot be respected, becomes an object of fear. But in what sense had the monastic life originally meant to be comprehended by those outside? If the monks themselves had ceased to understand, public nemesis, judgement from below, must needs follow. Numerous contemporary statements suggest that many monks did not know what their rules were: hence the eleventh-hour surge of vernacular translations at the turn of the sixteenth century.[140]

Tudor monks, enthused by the new ideas, chafing at the remnants of their ancient discipline and anticipating a new climate, their resentment encouraged by the 'divide and rule' tactics of Cromwell, provided him with evidence of the state of English religion which continues to divide historians by its extreme partiality.[141] A letter from the Benedictine Chapter, probably early in 1520, had complained to Wolsey that, if his proposals for enforcing regular observance were to be implemented, there would be a wholesale rebellion together with a drastic reduction in recruitment: "since in these times, when the world is already declining to its end, very few and very rare are those who desire austerity of life and observance of the rule." If all houses had to submit to the discipline of the Bridgettines, Observant Franciscans and Carthusians, the authors added, they would be emptied overnight.[142] Continental evidence concurs. In 1549 a section of the Chapter of the once 'Observant' Bursfelde congregation petitioned for a dispensation to eat meat (that is, for legalisation of the now customary meat eating), arguing that suitable candidates had long been deterred by the ban, "a thing which men, as they are affected in these days of ours, regard as too strict and almost unbearable" and that, unless it was lifted, their order would wither away.[143] In this emotional atmosphere, common sense, surely suspended for the wrong reasons, was resuscitated with a vengeance. Since he had been professed, wrote Nicholas Rawlyns of the London Charterhouse,

> I have had never my health a fortnight together . . . and if I do continue long in this Religion it will shorten my life sooner than I should die, if that I were abroad again in the world, which Religion is against the Law of God, whereby it should shorten any man's life . . . the Religion is so hard . . . that there is not vi whole monks within this cloister, but that they have one infirmity or other, the which will be their death sooner than God would that it should be.[144]

Similarly, the Carthusian doctor Andrew Boorde wrote to the Prior of Hinton, "I am not able to bide the rigour of your religion," to Cromwell of the "great thraldom, both bodily and spiritually" of their regime, and finally, on the verge of leaving the order, to the English Province from the Grande Chartreuse in 1535, "I cannot, nor never could, live solitary, and I amongst you confined in a closed air might never have my health."[145] At the last, the instincts rebel: if heaven proves unattainable, at least a man can look after his health. In the *Lamentable annotations taken forth of our Rule* (1534), Carthusian rigour is measured logically against the simple force of Gospel precepts and found wanting:

> [T]he Lord commandeth his disciples when he sent them forth to preach his word, that they should take for their refection such meats and such drinks as were set before them . . . our statutes commendeth that we should never eat flesh but evermore fish, yea, if we chance to be sick and like to die and the physician say that flesh will save our lives yet we shall not have it; thus I cannot see but we have professed to be men killers.[146]

The characteristic Protestant truth, that the law of man had diverged utterly from the law of God, is here filtered through the straightforward Tudor mind. The twelfth-century Carthusian *Consuetudines* had laid down that, "mindful of the purpose taken up by them, they should bethink themselves that, as they when well ought to differ from healthy secular men, so when sick they ought from secular sick, nor ask for those things in deserts which are hardly to be found in towns."[147] The anonymous annotator was bitterly attacking, not so much the rule, as he thought, but its mindless application, the stupidity of repeating practices as if their purpose had not been forgotten. Monasticism was indeed a way against nature, but which nature? These passages imply that faith and hope arising from partial emotion are weakness and slavery. Traditionally it was said that faith must seek understanding.

The meaning of asceticism, the place of the physical body in religious experience, is at the heart of our subject.[148] Medieval monasticism had become identified with the blind imposition of physical hardship, with narrow adherence to the traditional answer without continuing to experience the question,[149] an atmosphere in which serious engagement was naturally evaded and personal compromise flourished. The body denies the spirit: where then is the work of the religious man?[150] Bodily austerity that had become an end in itself was stupid, probably harmful and, anyway, not the whole suffering of which the Gospels spoke. 'Superstition' means literally that which is left over. Taverner wrote in 1531 of "the blind superstition of men and women which cease not day by day to profess and vow perpetual chastity before they sufficiently know themselves and the infirmity of their nature."[151] And, indeed, what is the meaning of bodily chastity in the service of religion? William of St. Thierry had written of the body, "it is not so to be kept as though for the sake of it we lived, but as that without which we cannot live."[152]

The revaluation of austerity was part of the broad movement to spiritualise religion, originating doubtlessly in the source of contemplation but carried within the establishment by the stricter fifteenth-century orders like the Bridgettines and Franciscan Observants and aided and abetted by the current of Renaissance inquiry. By 1500 the emphasis had shifted decisively from bodily fasting to fasting from sin, from sacramental to inner penance. Valla had written in scorn of blind asceticism, "it is not the exterior man, but the interior, who pleases God."[153] Its unconditional value was deeply questioned by such dissimilar figures as Luther and More, Savonarola and Egidio da Viterbo, Denck and Contarini, Zwingli and Ignatius, as well as by the lesser-known English writers we shall discuss later. At the same time complacency had been ruptured, enabling the dark side of human nature to be seen, if not borne:

> Who sees not that he, Satan, uses to put on a visor of holiness of the punishment of the body and austerity of life as often as he minds thoroughly to deceive? Which thing he has most perfectly brought to pass in all the orders of Antichrist, of Popes, cardinals, Bishops, priests, monks, canons, friars etc., to the perfect establishment of buggery, of whoredom and of all ungodliness

and to the universal ruin of the true faith of Christ's true religion and of all virtue and godly life.[154]

Among the 'new' opinions the authorities were trying to ban in 1530 was this:

> He that is compelled outwardly to abstain from women, inwardly full of lust, is a dissembler, and it is double lechery. Mark what foul slayers they be, that provoke foolish youth to a vow of chastity compelling them to nourish inwardly hidden malice.[155]

A living spiritual tradition supports the whole man in the process of discovery as he approaches God and is therefore able to be reconciling for the inevitable shocks: if its representatives lose touch with their source, nothing real reaches those outside. The revelation of imbalance cannot be properly received without extraordinary support: only the truth wounds, and only the truth heals, but who sees?

The writers touched by the New Devotion considered the usefulness of ascetic practices while emphasising the importance of the individual's balance. Wessel Gansfort wrote to a particular nun: "What is the use of all this needless hardship in trying to attain the impossible?"[156] Traditional wisdom held that contact, however momentary, with the force of a higher level—nearer God—must be at the expense of upsetting the habitual relationship between the human functions, in itself already a kind of balance, and that it was dangerous to change anything without corresponding guidance. Unconscious and uninformed attempts to dominate the human organism by the deluded self (our 'ego'), from motives arising from its manifold unseen weaknesses, of course did not, and could not, disappear from post-Reformation religion, despite all warnings. Evidence of a more precise and broader understanding of the place of the body in the religious life lies half hidden in earlier Christian ascetic writings and can still be found in some quarters during this period.[157] Gerard, the founder of the Brotherhood of the Common Life, thought asceticism often a "tool of the devil," associated with "mental diseases, anger or pride." Not understanding their inability to do good by themselves, men imagined their efforts could bring Christian results, did not see outward religiousness masking inward viciousness. "Every ascetic practice," he said, "such as fasting, flagellation, watching, chanting of psalms or wearing a hair shirt, all this has no value except so far as it produces righteousness and peace and joy in the Holy Ghost." The "possession" of these things "within ourselves" constitutes the Kingdom of God, "which is above us." "We ought to aspire with all our energy" towards this Kingdom, "which means that we should attain nearness to God and that God should dwell in us." No external exercises must take precedence over this. Gerard brought exercises of another kind.[158]

Gansfort's *De Sacramento Eucharistiae* insists that it is possible—indeed necessary—to look at the world and oneself in a new way, so that guidance can be received from the difficulties of life itself. "If we had open eyes . . . we would be fed" by the world about us, for everything that exists has its existence "through the Word," which is the "light of men." Everything that was made, was "not only worthy to be made, but was so sublime in the Word that it makes alive anyone who apprehends things in the Word and illuminates him with wisdom." Hardships and austerities, naturally arising or sought, may remind us, thus helping to produce what is necessary, but they cannot replace it. Gansfort was speaking of living with a "clearness of vision [which] goes far beyond the natural limits of the mind." In words recalling Bernard,[159] he affirmed:

> In all things therefore it is possible to suck honey from the rock and oil from the stone and find manna upon the face of the earth and wine—provided, however, one has open eyes and ardent desire. . . . Nay, what is there that has not been given for the accumulation of riches unto him that hath open eyes, since the necessities of poverty and weakness, nakedness of the body and all the causes of hunger, thirst and weariness are to him the means of wisdom and righteousness? For certain conditions are necessary to us in order to remind us that we must seek even the breath of life. Nakedness is always unseemly. Raggedness is always productive of shame. Hunger, thirst, weariness, wakefulness, sickness are always irksome, in order that we may be urged to seek bread and wine, the bread of salutary wisdom . . . the wine of spiritual delight . . . in the embrace of our beloved. These hardships, therefore, have not been inflicted to torment us, but have been appointed to serve as warnings to us, if we are wise; so that as often as we suffer them, we may be reminded to seek true blessings. O wisdom! How like a father thou art, in that even while angry with us thou dost give us the help which is our heritage.[160]

There is no implication that the professional religious are privileged in this search, about which there is indeed nothing specifically 'religious.' In his letter to a nun, affixed as a preface for publication, Gansfort enjoins her to find "that which is necessary for us all." Before so great a mystery all are equally beggars, but this poverty has special meaning. Hardships and joys have equal value, "provided . . . one has open eyes." This fascinating allusive passage implies the balance of the 'mixed life' and the practice of the kind of systematic inner meditation that he elsewhere described, which is continually mentioned in the writings of the New Devotion and was later elaborated by Ignatius. Gansfort's education began under the auspices of the Devotion and he maintained this contact throughout his life.[161] His theme in *De Sacramento*, the necessary predisposition to receive help from the greater world, from what is already being showered upon us from above, brings to mind Ignatius' definition of spiritual exercises as means to dispose us to be free of attachments. On what does this 'disposition' chiefly depend?

The linking of asceticism with new balance appears in many places, high and low. Ignatius tells in the *Confessions* that he had first tried to adopt the ascetic ideals of others:

> [I]t seemed to him then that holiness was entirely measured by exterior asperity of life and that he who did the most severe penances would be held in the divine regard for the most holy, which idea made him determined to lead a very harsh life.

In the light of later experiences he realised this to be misguided, so when "he began to be consoled by God . . . he gave up those extremes which he had practised before and cut his nails and hair."[162] The members of his subsequent society were advised to eschew fasting, going bare footed and begging, as these interfered with their activity and the effectiveness of their meditations. The asceticism of the *Spiritual Exercises* is intended to produce nonattachment, the equivalent of the *apatheia* of the Desert Fathers, a state of essential balance, openness to oneself and God's Will.

Robert Parkyn, an obscure Yorkshire representative of the *devotio moderna anglicana*[163] and a student of Rolle and Hylton, has also left us his thoughts on asceticism. Writing in the late 1550s he warns the "true lover of the spiritual life" that, although he might "with wisdom" deny himself his favourite foods, "yet let him not destroy nature and his body with intolerable abstinence and with too much rigour and sharpness that he taketh upon him at the judgement of his own head and pleasure," in other words, "let him keep a mean."[164] Rolle, simply "the hermit" to his admirers, had counselled the man who would love God above all, firstly to pay attention to his own balance,

> [F]or it would be better for him in ignorance to exceed the mean in a small matter, while he doeth it with a good will to support nature, than to begin to flag with too much fasting and through bodily weakness have not the strength enough to sing . . . the true lover of Christ and him taught by Christ doth with as great zeal beware of having too much as of having too little.[165]

The *Epistle of Prayer*, an anonymous fourteenth-century work printed in a spiritual miscellany in 1521, emphasises "reverent affection" for God rather than "any other manner of doing (as is fasting, waking, sharp wearing and all these other)": austerities "are needful inasmuch as they are helply to get this, so that without this they are nought."[166] This was the view of Gerard and Gansfort. The considerable interest in the native mystical tradition on the eve of the Reformation gave these views currency so that the *Epistle* and other writings of its quality became instruments of a delayed transmission:

> I would by this knowing that thou charged and commended each thing after that it is: the more 'the more' and the less 'the less'; for oft times . . . unknowing maketh men to charge more and commend more bodily exercise

. . . than they do spiritual exercises in virtues or in this reverent affection touched before.[167]

Hylton has the same advice: even if great austerity does not become an end, it can be an ineffective means.[168] The minimising of bodily mortification in Counter-Reformation writings issued from these earlier views, although the lives led by Catholic missionaries to Elizabethan England were probably hard enough:[169] 'the world' having replaced the cloister as the field of spiritual endeavour, the ascetic monk was ousted by the Jesuit priest as the hero of the new martyrologies.

The traditional view of a 'world' without aim and a 'desert' charged with meaning may be compared with the Protestant interpretation of a famous legend of Desert monasticism, telling of Anthony's realisation at prayer in a remote cave that he was less perfect than a certain cobbler of Alexandria: "in this story you see how God loveth those that follow their vocation and live uprightly without any false-hood in their dealing," wrote Latimer in 1552, for "this Anthony was a great holy man, yet this cobbler was as much esteemed before God as he."[170] Revered through the Middle Ages as 'the first monk,' even Anthony is made to acknowl-edge the advent of a new order.

The distance between Bernard's wish to convert Europe into a great monastery and the Protestant assertion of the godliness of the secular vocation was spanned by the decline of monasticism as a spiritual force and the emergence of a 'new' lay religious ideal, based actually upon the same elusive and conditional human pos-sibility as the monastic way and drawing on the same essential techniques and experience, but which was, nevertheless, enshrined as a contrary orthodoxy dur-ing the upheaval of the Reformation. What causes a possibility to become a mere ideal? In an upside-down world, ancient doctrines connected with the unity of the Bodies of Christ were adduced to justify the instability of a revolutionary situ-ation, but such powerful ideas, partially remembered, could cut both ways: thus Whytford, the friend of Erasmus and later staunch Bridgettine, gathered together the fragments of the vision of Rolle and Hylton to refute Luther's attack on the monastic ideal,

[S]ome one person or persons out of religion monastical may keep the reli-gion of Christ as perfectly and precisely as any person within the same . . . soldiers, courtiers, merchants, men of law, artificers, husbandmen, labour-ers, with such other married persons . . . parsons, vicars, priests . . . all be of one religion, all brothers and sisters, all disciples of the rule and religion of Christ, all members of the mystical body of Christ.[171]

Recapitulating the material of this chapter from Valla to the Carthusian anno-tator, Erasmus translated the ideal of the layman as true monk in this way:

In times passed . . . a religious life was nothing but a solitary life. And now these be called religious which be altogether drowned in worldly business. . . . And yet these . . . do challenge such holiness to themselves, that they account all other by comparison no Christian men at all. Why do we make so strait and narrow Christ's religion, which He would have so large. . . . I pray you, what thing else is a City but a great monastery. Monks be obedient to their abbot and governors, the citizens obey the bishops and curates, whom Christ Himself made rulers, and not the authority of man. The monks live in idleness, and be fed of other men's liberality, possessing that among themself in common, which they never laboured or sweat for. . . . The citizens bestow that which they have gotten with their great labour and travail, to them that have need. . . . Now as concerning the vow of chastity, I dare not be bold to express what difference is between the religious man unmarried and the chaste matrimony of the other. And to be short, he shall not very greatly lack those three vows of man's invention, that does keep and observe purely and sincerely that first only vow which we all, solemnly, make unto Christ, and not unto man, when we receive our baptism. And if we compare those that be evil of one kind with those that be evil of the other, without doubt the temporal men be much better. But if we compare those which be good of the one sort, with those that be good of the other, there is little difference, if there be any at all: saving that those appear to be more religious which keep their religion and duty with less compulsion.[172]

The commentators of the ancient world had seen the Egyptian desert colonised by Christian ascetics blossoming into a "city,"[173] but now the city was to become a monastic colony, for laymen were the only religious. The curious episode of Savonarola's "renovation of the church" through the institution of monastic austerity in Florence, the 'holy cities' of Calvin's Geneva and John of Leiden's Munster, the philosophical visions of J. V. Andreae's Christianopolis and Campanella's City of the Sun,[174] were expressions of a deep, if strangely and variously felt, aspiration.

Erasmus wrote more, and less, than he knew. Why does the famous *Enchiridion*, a proclamation of values for the "Christian knight" and the distillation of his spirituality, make so little impression? For all its clarity and patent sincerity, it lacks weight and credibility,[175] being somehow even a little cheap. Only an impenitent idealist could have written about the life of a city in that way. Erasmus dreamed the contemporary dream to perfection. He had been touched by, and attempted to synthesise, all the influences of his day: fired by patristic and early Christian ideals, imbued with the spirit of the New Devotion, inspired by the Classical worldview and explicitly concerned for the poor and weak, he was an intellectual universalist and social satirist, ill at ease in the climate of the Reformation he had unconsciously abetted. Luther represented a reality he could not bring himself to accept, yet behind his own Christian ideal lay another reality of which, to judge from his writings, he was not fully aware. His definition of the religious place of the layman is meaningless unless related to the teachings of the 'mixed life,' the specific search for balance between action and contemplation through the intentional practice of spiritual exercises to harmonise the three powers of man within life, as represented for his time in the (originally lay) Brotherhood of the Common Life. What is the source and actual meaning of his words in the *Paraclesis*:

> [W]hat other thing is this doctrine of Christ which He calls the new regeneration, but a restoring or repairing of our nature which in its first creation was good.[176]

The Brethren, whose records deal with very little else but this restoration, claimed only to be renewing an ancient path,[177] among whose followers may well have been counted that nameless cobbler of fourth-century Alexandria.

Where, behind the shifting patterns of this chapter, can the rigour and simplicity of a true search be discerned?

THREE

The Search for the True Image

He did not consider what is popularly deemed religion to be really such.

Erasmus, of Colet

For all things are received in each case according to the measure of the receiver.

Colet

If we look well upon holy scripture and upon the old living of good Christian men, if books be true, we may see and know that we be now out of the way and full unlike to the priests and religious in old time.

John Ryckes

In attempting to fathom the unrest from which European life emerged so altered by 1600, we have been drawn magnetically to the evidence for a search in daily life, acting as a leaven, which the Brethren most clearly embodied for their time. Unrest produces formal adjustments, but from where could real change come, and be sustained, on the scale of the individual as well as the common life? Here are worlds within worlds. For the individual the New Devotion brought the inner action of renewal, the work for a change in the heart; on the larger-cultural scale a new valuation was also being sought. In what follows we may begin to see how the 'smaller' world contained the larger.

The element of personal search in the lives of Colet, More and Erasmus can hardly be doubted. They mutually supported each other's enquiry[1] and were in touch with like minds throughout Europe.[2] In their respective ways, they united the spiritual values of the Platonic revival, the *ad fontes* scholarship of Christian humanism and the pietistic and mystical traditions of late medieval devotion.

Only one of Colet's works appeared during his lifetime (1466–1519), and only one more during the course of the Reformation.[3] Yet, one humanist wrote in 1533 of his many "friends, his familiars and his scholars, or rather godsons (for full many he did regender and get to God)."[4] His influence was felt through the school he founded, through his English preaching,[5] and, particularly, through personal contact.[6] To More he was father confessor, "the director of my life."[7] Erasmus based some of his *Colloquies* on their discussions, which he frequently related in his correspondence.[8] Colet kept his own counsel: "from numbers of the tenets most generally received," he "widely dissented, and would at times discuss them among his private friends," but "with others, he would keep his opinions to himself."[9]

Although deeply read in the New Testament, the Fathers and the ancient and modern schools of Platonism, and although an heir in many respects of the Rhineland mystics and the New Devotion,[10] he sought throughout his life for his own attitude and truth: being neither a follower, nor wishing to have any, his position is difficult to define. His researches in heretical literature, which he is said to have preferred to the scholastic, led him neither to public condemnation of any doctrine, nor identification with any sect.[11] Protestants claimed him as a forerunner and Catholics as an inspiration.[12] Believing in the unity of truth, he rarely quoted the numberless authorities of the church in his biblical exegesis, seeking for the one personally meaningful sense rather than the manifold senses of convention, and often taking words literally where allegory had been the rule.[13] He refused dogmatism even when framing the statutes of his school, preferring to leave his successors to confront altered times with their judgement unfettered: he "did not show any anxiety to perpetuate his own particular views by means of the power which, as the founder of the endowment, he had a perfect right to exercise."[14] Yet all the evidence speaks of his personal force and decisiveness.

His distrust of monasticism was well known, although he ended his days among the Shene Carthusians.[15] According to Erasmus:

> Though no one approved of Christian devotion more warmly than he, he had yet but very little liking for monasteries, undeserving of the name as many of them now are. The gifts he bestowed upon them were either none or the smallest possible, and he left them no share of his property even at his death. The reason was not that he disliked religious orders, but that those who took them did not come up to their profession. It was in fact his own wish to disconnect himself entirely from the world, if he could only have found a fraternity anywhere really bound together for a gospel life. And he had even commissioned me to seek for such a one when I was about to visit Italy, telling me that among the Italians he had discovered some monks of true wisdom and piety. Moreover, he did not consider what is popularly deemed religion to be really such, being as it often is mere poverty of intellect. He was accustomed also to praise certain Germans, among whom there yet lingered, as he said, some traces of primitive religion.[16]

These are surely veiled references to the New Devotion.[17] Colet entrusted the management of St. Paul's to a board of married citizens of the Mercer's Company rather than to a monastic chapter or clergy, for:

> [W]hile there was nothing certain in human affairs, he yet found the least corruption in these . . . he was in the habit of declaring that he nowhere found more unblemished characters than among married people, on whom such restraints were laid by natural affection and family and household cares that they were withheld, as by so many barriers, from rushing into all kinds of wickedness.[18]

The inexorable demands of life could become a discipline, not a series of impositions to be, by turns, passively borne, desired or evaded, but opportunities to be welcomed for the sake of the coincidence of the outer and inner world. They could, at least, be a corrective. Such a view, if correctly attributed to Colet, was founded on the deep human need to be 'in the world but not of it,' and aligns him with the New Devotion and their sources,[19] with the idea of 'the mixed life':

> [I]t was a great thing for Colet, in worldly circumstances such as his, to have steadily followed the call not of natural inclination but of Christ.[20]

Other members of his circle found the same orientation. Richard Whytford, after entering Syon, wrote instructing laymen in religious and devotional exercises using the traditional analogies of athletics, archery and craft.[21] His attempt to establish a mark or target in his readers' lives was a translation of the Brethren's *intentio*, for, as he said, the sense of one's effort lies in the "inforce" of the will, not in the outer achievement.[22] Before mastering a craft the apprentice must learn how to work: religion, being no less practical, does not begin beneath the level of life. Becoming able to "do that which is in him," a man needs instruction in order to be the disciple of his own experience, for "by many experiments or experiences . . . art or craft is gotten."[23] At the moment when the monasteries were passing, this advice had a particular significance.

His "familiar friend" More had also been drawn to the monastic life and had lived experimentally with Lily among the London Carthusians for four years while studying the law, participating in their devotions and exercises without taking the vow,[24] in the manner of the Brethren of the Common Life. His decision to leave and marry was influenced by Colet, and perhaps by the example of the layman Pico della Mirandola, whose *Life* he had been translating. Colet had written of the married state that "no one lives outside of society unless he is above humanity or below it."[25] More's version of Pico's letters reveals an ideal of simple piety and study without monastic withdrawal, based on the alternation of outer and inner work, the intention "not so to embrace Martha as to forsake Mary" which was at the root of the New Devotion. The patriarchal household he estab-

lished in Bucklersbury and Chelsea with its monastic devotions, private austerities, philosophical discussions and resident fool was both a Platonic Academy on
Christian lines and a living expression of the 'mixed life' as More conceived it.[26]

Colet's belief that "God's desire is that the entire world might be nothing but a
priesthood" complemented Erasmus' view of the city as nothing else but a great
monastery.[27] Colet felt that if a layman did the "work of a priest," freeing himself
internally from "all weights which . . . dragged him down" and uniting himself to
God as a "fellow worker," he was indeed a priest; likewise a priest who lived heed-
lessly was no more than a layman. "He is not a priest which is one outwardly, but
he which is one inwardly, in the Spirit."[28] Colet's account of man's possible liberation from "multiplicity," "disorder" and "unreal evil," by way of the "stripping
bare" and "collection" of the soul ("purification"), the reception through grace of
"spiritual being" and then "spiritual doing," the practice of watchfulness and the
imitation of Christ, indicates the practical teachings of the New Devotion and the
powerful reality of an ascetic tradition.[29]

Colet's conviction of the spuriousness of ordinary religion,[30] including the
sacraments ("but the emptiest shadows, if the reality be not existing in the
soul"),[31] was expressed in unpublished papers and in discussions with friends but
never publicly broadcast. Nevertheless, his preaching finally brought down
charges of heresy: it was said that he had incited men not to worship images.[32]
Although finally dropped through the intervention of the Archbishop of Canterbury, these accusations raise the question of his orthodoxy and, beyond this, the
perennial question of the reception in life of the tradition which he represented.
The American scholar Leland Miles, positing a split between his views and the
later orthodoxy of More, assumes that More invented a treatise called *The Image
of Love* in his polemic against Tyndale in order to repudiate the "spiritual Christian" views of the Dean which resembled heresy. More did not imagine this work,
which will be discussed at length later in this chapter. The fact that the extracts he
quotes are closely paralleled by statements of Colet[33] becomes, therefore, more
interesting. The *Ymage of love*, written by an Observant Friar, describes the search
for the true image of Christian love, first in outward life and then within the
seeker himself. Its intimate relationship with Syon underlines Colet's affinity with
that handful of reformed monastic centres transmitting devotional meditations
and spiritual exercises proper to the 'mixed life' on the eve of the Reformation.

The third main figure of this group, Erasmus, made his life's work the restoration of theology along the guidelines given by Colet.[34] His avowed ambition was
to refind the source of the spring whose entrance had been gradually earthed in
by the priestly caste,[35] and then to provide the documentary basis, through translation and commentary, for the layman's personal discovery of sacred literature,
and thereby, of a religion which could be a practical and effective way of life. In
his conception of a living Christian devotion he shared with Colet a debt to the
New Devotion and the Renaissance Platonists.[36] Like Colet, he had long since

rejected existing monasticism as a viable way[37] and spoke directly to the devout, educated laity, bypassing the daunting accumulations of scholastic theology that buttressed the exclusivity of the religious establishment and ensured lay isolation. His message was not an incitement to storm barriers but a reasoned exhortation to remain in the 'world' and, with open eyes, at all costs find a higher allegiance: the enlightened spirit of original monasticism operating within daily life could lead a man to Christ:

> When thou hast got the knowledge and understanding what thing the true religion is, after thou hast assayed thy wit, thy body and thy mind and when thou hast spied out a kind of living, meet for thy purpose and when thou hast found out a fellowship, which altogether with one assent, have fully determined their minds to live after Christ: then get thee hither. . . . Now peradventure thou wilt say to me, that all monasteries displease thee: nor there can be found none where a flock that hath pure minds consented to live after Christ. But yet look that thou so leave and forsake the world that thou mayst accompany thyself with whosoever be most innocent: and repute thyself to be in a monastery, wheresoever thou be conversant among them that love truth, pure chastity, soberness and temperance, and do both in word and deed express the same.[38]

Whytford wrote of the same search in his *Werke for Householders*: "every honest place of good and lawful occupation" could become a place of religion, "for God is there present where he is duly and devoutly served."[39] The *Ymage of love*, directed to Whytford's nuns, develops the theme:

> [T]he temple of God is a holy thing that is none other but your self. The temple of stone is not holy but by reason of the living temple, therefore that is more holy & needs more to be maintained and adorned. Should we then go lay up or spend our riches in the stony temple & suffer the quick temple to perish, either bodily or spiritually?[40]

The argument of this forgotten work might well have appeared divisive at the time of More's polemic. In the heretical Lollard sources breaking cover during the instability, we find: "in each place where a man is he owes for to pray to God in spirit and truth, that is, with will and devotion and cleanness of living . . . the place hallows not the man but a man hallows the place."[41] The *Ymage* was deeply indebted to the medieval mystical tradition, whose contemporary custodians were the orthodox Bridgettines, Carthusians and Observant Friars.[42] 'Orthodoxy' and 'unorthodoxy' were in such flux that it is difficult, and unprofitable, to assign the *Ymage* to either camp. The passages quoted refer to a 'mixed life': the centre of gravity shifts from the outer to the inner temple, because "in each place where a man is" he is called to pay attention to himself, seeking a prayer at the heart of his life.[43]

The details of the *Ymage*'s printing history indicate the confused intellectual climate of early sixteenth-century England. In December 1525, Wynkyn de Worde, in a written deposition to the authorities, admitted printing the work, sending sixty copies to Syon and selling as many more. Another printer, John Gough, claimed to have received the manuscript from a certain Edward Lockwood of St. Brides parish in London, to have translated it and sent copies to Oxford and Cambridge.[44] There is no further record of the case. De Worde was associated with Syon as Whytford's printer[45] and the magnificent library of the order possessed many heterodox works, including a fine collection of mystical literature.[46] Internal evidence suggests that the exhortation contained in the latter part of the *Ymage* was addressed to the Bridgettine nuns.[47] It was reprinted by De Worde in the altered atmosphere of the early thirties and the author identified as John Ryckes, an Observant Friar.[48] The volume included *The Myrour or Lokynge glasse of lyfe . . . for comforting of the soul whiche desyreth the lyfe eternall. The worde of God shall ever endure*; an epistle of Erasmus, *concernyng the forbedynge of eatynge of flesshe and lyke constitutyons of men* and the *Dialogue betwene a knyght and a clerke concerninge the power spiritual and temporall*. The appearance of the latter suggests the hand of Cromwell and his advisers, who were turning to anticlerical Erastian literature of the fourteenth century, exemplified by Marsilio of Padua's *Defensor Pacis*, to fuel the propaganda campaign against Rome.[49] The *Ymage*'s radical potential was highlighted by the company it kept: opinion was rapidly polarising and More's polemic was widened to include a qualification of the *Ymage*'s teaching. Its nature as a forerunner was confirmed by a further printing in 1587 under the title *The True Image of Christian Love*.[50]

The *Dialogue concerning Tyndale* emphasises the *Ymage*'s controversial aspects. The author "layeth sore" against elaborately carved and painted images: books for the ignorant perhaps, but the discerning should "labour only for the lively quick image of love." The saints of old had nothing superfluous in their churches—their images were wood, their priests gold—but we have reversed this. If we do not escape from the shadows of the Old Law and penetrate to the spiritual worship of the New, we are Pharisees. More says that he has read the book and regards the author as surely "a right good man," but one who had

> run up so high in his contemplation spiritual, that while he thought he sat in God Almighty's bosom upon high in heaven, he condemned and set at nought all earthly things, and all temporal service done to God here . . . among poor silly men in earth.

However, if his fervour has led him into indiscretion, "verily of his intent and purpose I will not much meddle."[51] His real quarrel was with the attempts of the *Ymage*'s unconscionable sponsors to exploit the imbalance of the time for their own ends.

The *Ymage* concerns the search for the real love of Christian teaching, a search which begins in the market place of the world and ends—to begin anew—within the seeker himself. He travels from a realisation of need, through disillusionment with existing religious forms, towards an acknowledgement of inner poverty and a sense of new hope. At the end he becomes able to invoke the Trinity for the establishment of right order in himself. After a certain stage his path is lighted by a guide who is a channel for the wisdom of the Old Testament and the teaching of the New. The view of contemporary religion presented owes much to Erasmus, but when the seeker begins to realise his situation he turns unequivocally to the medieval mystical tradition.

The search begins in the very midst of life. It is New Year and he wishes to find a gift. What does he most deeply desire? An image of love enters his mind, but what is love? Natural love draws him, but he already knows that this child of Mother Nature fades daily, however brightly coloured its image at the beginning. This is the common portion of wise men and foolish, and of the animals. (It is, somehow, his own love, the capacity proper to him alone, which he seeks.) Experience shows that the image of family love blinds men, unless the Holy Ghost assists in its fashioning: Jesus could not be found when sought amongst his kin. The love of the senses for their objects, the soul for the body and man for woman are only "well painted" if the Holy Ghost orders the relationship: (the love of 'two' must include a 'third,' the influence of another level.)[52]

He next encounters a strange allegorical figure, as if from the Renaissance *ars memorativa*, which represents the classical art of friendship. Like many of his contemporaries he is at first impressed, but he notices its downturned face and cruel expression towards enemies, and remembers Paul's verdict upon a culture that knew God, yet, secure in its own wisdom, failed to honour Him. This thought, together with the aphorism of Christ that to love those who love you is of no value, "caused me to seek further."[53] Colourful symbolic figures representing different kinds of love cross his path, but in each case he discerns their essential hollowness[54] and wastes no time on them.

Meditating on the Bible, it dawns on him that his ordinary experience of love is the obstacle separating him from the charity that is spoken of: who loves? His search for the true image is bound up with the question of his true nature as a man, created in the Image of God: three in one.[55] At this critical juncture when he is beginning to grasp the scale of his difficulty, he is tempted by the wares of contemporary religion, despite his strong inner sense that "the very image of love was not there." Just when he is about to capitulate, he meets a guide:

[T]here were many goodly images which I thought should steer a man to devotion & to the love of God. And because it was hard to find the very true image I set my mind to buy one of these, & as I was choosing out one of the goodliest there came to me a holy devout doctor rebuking me.[56]

The guide (identified with St. Jerome in a marginal interpolation) calls him to open to the situation of which his question forms a part: "see you not the goodly living image of God most pitiful, fade and decay every day in the great multitude?"[57] A higher level is invoked, as in Hylton: the 'mystical body of Christ' which suffers inconceivably because of the way we are.

This movement—from Above, outwards—into 'the world,' became the emphasis of early Protestantism, the social legislation of sixteenth-century governments, the development of Counter-Reformation orders out of missions to the poor and the material of countless homilies, sermons and tracts.[58] Its proper counterpart is the movement inwards, as the seeker will find: to love the neighbour as I am able to love myself. From this point of view monasticism had focused a rightful egoism, for behind the love of God for one's own sake lay the love of oneself for God's sake. Such altruism, 'love of kind,' as had been accumulated during the Middle Ages, became the foundation of the Christianity of the succeeding age. But the movement out and the movement in, begin from the same place.

Not only the need of others but our own superfluity binds us, says the guide, "and he alleged for him the gospel of Christ."[59] Nothing that a man possesses is his own, least of all his goods: he owes everything, and above all his life, to God. In this sense all men are brothers.

> It is the bread and sustenance for the hungry that you retain with you; it is the clothing of naked men that you lock away in your presses; it is the redemption & relief of them that be in thraldom and prison, the money you hide in the ground."[60]

Apart from their value in sustaining our lives and maintaining our degree (within reason and honesty), riches have no use except as alms for the poor and as means to provide "necessities" for "Christ's church." Luxurious images are not among these. The sense of balance has been lost: the significance of images as books for the unlearned has nothing to do with expensive elaboration, which evokes the "spice of propriety" in the owner's breast more effectively than piety in the beholder. A good man is the true image and the best influence.[61] The seeker is "almost confounded," but the guide relentlessly holds up a vision of primitive Christianity as a mirror to the contemporary church:

> "Aha," said he, "I see it is but vain to preach & teach men to learn & take example of Saint Ambrose, Augustine, Gregory, Exupery, Nicholas, Martin, holy bishops . . . in whose time were but little of such things: they would have all things that belonged to the church and specially to the sacraments, honest, pure and clean, but not costly nor curious. Then were treen chalices & golden priests, now be golden chalices & treen priests, or rather earthen priests; then were religious clad with hair & sackcloth & now they disdain or

grudge to wear woollen cloth; then were monasteries hostelries for poor men, and now they be palaces for lords & estates; then they were apparelled with meekness, poverty chastity & charity, now with silks, cloth of gold, pomp and vanity."[62]

This is reforming thought in its pre-revolutionary phase, exemplified in the works of Erasmus. Ryckes' membership of an Observant order of recent Italian origin suggests the scope of his intellectual and emotional reference: elsewhere he shows familiarity with Renaissance attitudes[63] and here he quotes Savonarola,[64] whose career had already aroused interest in England[65] and whose 'Protestant' sounding Psalm meditations won a place in several reformed primers.[66]

Having absorbed this shock, the seeker is able to pass, strengthened, beyond mere condemnation. His reason, assisted by the guide, leads him to confront his original question from a different angle: "As the people be, so are the priests."[67] The church is composed of men like himself, but because he has no power over others, he must look first to himself: "the temple of God is a holy thing that is none other but yourself."[68] If the living temple has been given over to strange gods, then before the true image can be found room must be made, inner idols deposed.

Men have forgotten God's commandments and follow only each other, but Christianity teaches renewal of the Law, the passage from shadow to light, the pursuit of truth.[69] The Gospels can be heard telling him that he has been looking in the wrong place, that he has not been worthy to find the truth: before he can live, he must first, inconceivably, die:

As I stood conjecturing what I might do, scripture spake to me and said, 'O foolish man, why do you seek a living thing among dead things, light in darkness, a spiritual thing among earthly things, incorruptible among corruptible: it is not there . . . the image that you seek cannot be seen of the bodily eyes, but only with angel's eyes and pure, with them that be dead from this world living with Christ,' & he said also all that ever I had was nothing to the price thereof. Nevertheless I would fain have had it.[70]

It appears hopeless, and yet, at this very moment, there is help from within: buried in his experience is an intimation of what he seeks and its worth. In his remembering is the seed of hope.

[F]or though I saw it never, I remember that a shadow I saw thereof in a glass, which passed by me suddenly without any tarrying & delighted me so that ever since I have such a desire to it, that I would be glad to give all that I have for a little sight of it."[71]

Like many before and since, does he have any choice but to continue, in the face of all difficulties?

At this point of intensity there is a shift of emphasis, a deflection; Ryckes turns to address his audience directly, and, from now on, progressive revelations of the nature of the true image alternate with exhortations to an unnamed group of nuns. He quotes *Psalm* 45:9–15:

Kings' daughters were among thy honourable women: upon thy right hand did stand the queen in gold of Ophir. Hearken, O daughter, and consider, and incline thine ear; forget also thine own people, and thy father's house; so shall the king greatly desire thy beauty: for he is thy lord; and worship thou him. And the daughter of Tyre shall be there with a gift; even the rich among the people shall intreat thy favour. The king's daughter is all glorious within: her clothing is of wrought gold. She shall be brought unto the king in raiment of needlework: the virgins her companions that follow her shall be brought unto thee. With gladness and rejoicing shall they be brought: they shall enter into the king's palace.[72]

Our conclusion that the *Ymage* was addressed to the Bridgettines of Syon is based on this text, which is woven throughout subsequent explanations. The lack of direct reference is not surprising in a controversial work at such a time and is in keeping with the allusive, punning habits of contemporary thought. The house was royal in origin, in composition and, according to many witnesses, in quality. St. Bridget herself was a member of the Swedish royal family and Syon took a high proportion of noble entrants, who became, indeed, daughters of a royal house, founded by Henry V. Medieval thought pictured the nun as 'bride of Christ,' and at Syon, widely regarded as one of the highest spiritual families in the land,[73] their liturgical manual was wont to dwell on the Psalmist's frequent reference to "Syon."[74] There was, moreover, a strong kinship between the Bridgettines and Ryckes' Observant Franciscans, based on their recent introduction to England, their royal patronage, their origin in the last wave of medieval monastic reform, their familiarity with the newest currents of European thought and their study of mystical teachings.[75] He will later quote extensively from the Victorine school as the culmination of his message, as did Whytford in his translation and commentary on the nun's rule.[76]

Ryckes then interprets this psalm after the highest ideals of monasticism, perceiving in it a symbolic account of the journey of the religious from inception to consummation: "for all the glory and pleasure of a king's daughter is inward spiritual in the soul: you be the daughters of the heavenly king, espoused to his son Jesu." The second verse, "hearken . . . and incline thine ear," is very like the opening of the *Regula Benedicti*,[77] while the forgetting of "thine own people and thy father's house" becomes the ancient monastic intention to forsake all worldly attachments and make oneself "naked of all earthly things by poverty and chastity." Only then can "the king, my son, . . . covet thy beauty" and reclothe them in goodness.[78]

Thus I doubt not he that hath called you from darkness to so great light of grace & hath now taken you unto his spouses, he hath now shewed you this image & given it to you much more goodly than I can describe it as it is, for it is infinite and incomprehensible, yet it pleaseth him to shew it to all meek souls, after their capacity, calling them his daughters, saying . . . 'Hear, my daughters, in true faith & meek obedience . . . and see what I have done and do daily for you, see what you do again or have done for me; see also what I do prepare for you.' The beholding of these three things I think should leave some print of this image in our souls, but much more in you that be his special spouses.[79]

He is referring to Syon's discipline, for the "three things" are a summary of the subjects for systematic meditation given in the first part of Whytford's *Dialoge*,[80] the words "print" and "behold" underlining the association with the special receptivity of the state of meditation. The passage implies the traditional view that all are called by Christ, but the religious more directly, their position placing them above the layman in the rewards it commands and the obligations and difficulties it entails.[81] The Bible can be understood as proclaiming the monastic Way leading to the spiritual marriage, but Ryckes is not writing a conventional encomium of the monastic ideal, being concerned rather with the passage from outward religion to inward observance, from the unreality of 'the world' to life more abundant. He implies that this concern was comprehensible at Syon, but nowhere rules out the possibility of its being found elsewhere, for "daughterhood," as he describes it, could never be exclusive to the religious.

Monasticism had entered the stream of history as exemplary Christianity: by the form of their lives the monks were to teach religious truths. Mindful of their corporate deviation, late medieval reformers who respected the monastic ideal looked to individual houses to reinhabit the traditional role. This was Ryckes' interest in Syon. He counsels the nuns to "attend to" and "delight in" the real image of love, which is none other than the reflection of God in man, the true life within them. As "king's daughters" their "glory" should be their inner life;[82] they are "living temples of God," upon whose "altars" the image of love should be raised and honoured. Ryckes' urgency stems from his sense of the human condition, on their behalf and his own, but also his sense of the times. He felt, with many, that

now is the time that Christ spoke of to the woman of Samaria, saying: 'The hour is come when the very true worshippers of God shall worship him inwardly for spiritual things, in truth unfeignedly & not . . . only after the outward observances as the Jews did, that kept the outward observances of their law in sacrifices and prayers with their mouth but their heart & love was far from God.[83]

The spiritual renewal for which Europe waited appeared outside the old orders. Ryckes quotes extensively and almost verbatim from Erasmus on religious hypocrisy,[84] ending with the favourite monastic precept, "the body is kept in within a little cell, let not then the mind be wandering all about the world"; within twenty years this passage from the *Enchiridion* was being rendered, "in thy body thou art closed within a strait cell, and in thy cogitation thou wanderest throughout the world."[85] Through a slight rearrangement, the monastic connotation has been expunged and the individual interiorised, even isolated, within themselves.

In looking for a (selective) monastic leadership of a purified Christianity, Ryckes follows the New Devotion, whose intention was to build a viable bridge between ordinary life and the monastic discipline; his own Observant friars were closely related to the Observant congregations that had grown from the Brethren of the Common Life.[86] He shares with these groups an attitude to worship informed by the use of spiritual exercises to awaken deeper participation through strengthening the power of attention.[87] The fullness of this does not appear in Ryckes but is often implied and would have been inferred by the Bridgettines, the strength of whose inner life is vouchsafed in many sources. It could be glossed: upon the quality of relationship between inner and outer depends the degree of profit. The individual's despair at the hollowness of helplessly habitual outward observance (not only others', but his own) could lead to a dividing of the ways: to a desperate wish for freedom through dispensing with all ceremony—the words of Christ to the woman of Samaria were used to justify many violent Reformation excesses[88]—or to a committed search under guidance for the bridge between outer and inner life. With presence, the outer form can have its place together with the inner subjective state, provided neither is rested in. These considerations underlie and substantiate Ryckes' words and relate him to the New Devotion, whose lack of violence on this question combined with a sharper insight and a deeper feeling and whose records touch more fully on the indispensable practical means. Ryckes' exposition, which frequently assumes in his audience an experience of practical means unknown to us, must remain somewhat equivocal.

> [I]t is very well done oftentimes to accuse our self before a priest of our sins; it is truth if it be also before God . . . when we utterly hate our sins & forsake them with inward contrition for the true love & fear of God, for an inward wound must have an inward medicine; if you hear the word of God which is most necessary for the soul, hear it inwardly . . . hear so God's word outward that you may say with the prophet: "I shall hear what my lord speaketh in me[89] with fervent desire to accomplish in deed what is shewed in word, that it may be said to you, blessed be they that hear the word of God." . . . [W]e should not lean nor trust too much unto outward observances and ceremonies more otherwise than the truth does assign they be little acceptable

but if spiritual and inward working goes withal. We may not leave off the honourable and devout customs & holy ordinances of the church . . . these it behoves not to omit nor leave off, but to observe them. The other, that is the spiritual & inward observances, are necessary & must needs be done, if we will have any profit of them.[90]

The danger lies in the habitual confusion of outer and inner life and the consequent atrophy of discrimination; the meaning lies in the clarity given at the moment of their separation and realignment, in the redistribution of 'our' energies, however slightly. We have been formed to receive, and obey, a higher influence. For outer and inner are one life at the corresponding level, only their right relationship has been subverted. Religious tradition insists that this inherited condition be lived consciously and faithfully, so that the question of our two natures be incarnated. Thus Ryckes is advising the voluntary freeing of the force of attention from its customary sleepy confusion and its direction to the inner exercise, so that the outer observance be really inhabited, that it not be utterly mechanical. His injunction to listen outwardly in such a way that one is also able to listen inwardly means not to listen passively impacted in 'oneself,' blindly absorbed in dreams and associations, but more consciously, as if to something new: to listen in such a way that the channel is reopened with that place where the desire to act and the wish to be are one ("fervent desire to accomplish in deed what is shewed in word"), where the ability to do may be rightfully born: that "spiritual doing" often referred to in our texts. Is this the sense of the story of the centurion, "I also am a man set under authority," to whom Christ came (*Luke* 7:9)? Ryckes conveys the traditional focus on the fulcrum of human potential, the point at which change, with grace, can begin. A present-day Cistercian, Thomas Keating, describes the inner work of the medieval monk, the discipline said to lead to the contemplative knowledge of God, which was now passing into 'the world' through books like the *Ymage:*

> The method of prayer for these monks . . . consisted in a practice known as *lectio divina* reading scripture, or more exactly, listening to it. They would repeat the words of the sacred text with their lips so that the body itself entered into the process. . . . It was primarily an exercise of listening. Listening can be at different levels. It can be with the bodily ear, with the imagination, with the heart, or with the whole being. The monks sought to cultivate through *lectio divina* the capacity to listen at ever deepening levels.[91]

Ryckes' advice on listening inwardly to the 'word' relates him also to the contemporary spiritual reformers of the 'Radical Reformation' and clarifies the suspicion of heresy attaching to the *Ymage*. Compare his words with the more intense, personal tone of Hans Denck writing of his own search:

By the side of these [my] inborn foibles, I feel and perceive in me a 'something' which . . . awakens in me a longing towards a better life. . . . [W]herever I find 'something' on this earth which harmonises with this inner feeling, I will always listen to it, whether it comes from a high or a low source and wherever it hunts me, there will I flee. If I do not respect this voice of conscience I shall not be able to understand the holy scriptures; but as much as the 'something' impels me, so much do I understand them. . . . [I]t [the Bible] is an echo of what is being uttered deep in my own bosom. . . . [H]e who seeks Him in truth already has Him and without this inner spirit to guide and direct him, one cannot find God, even in the Bible. . . . [T]he darkness of my soul . . . makes it impossible for me always to understand the holy scriptures rightly. . . . [W]hoever does not pay attention to the manifestation of God in his breast . . . but dares to expound the scriptures to himself, as only the godly can, makes out of God's secret laid down in the scriptures a wild abomination.[92]

Behind his special pleading and the hypnotic language of the Psalmist, Ryckes' 'intent' is to reveal the religious love set forth in the Scriptures, in order to help the nuns receive it in their meditations ("this printed image . . . that you know better than I"). He is like a blind man wishing to share the tremendous significance of sight. Through studying St. Paul he has been given a mirror and exhorts them to look into it, for what he and his readers seek cannot be seen directly, only "by a glass in a dark similitude." In his own looking he has seen "nothing but mine own face foully deformed":[93] despite his attempts to "get me to the light," the glass has not yet reflected the true image, but he has begun to see.

He visits a monastic spiritual guide "for to clarify my sight that I might at the least once see this image." He explains to this father that the splendid solemnities of the Abbey "moved me for a time unto religion" but this beauty was not evidence of the love he sought, which has nothing in common with "the inordinate love to our self," for "it is not all gold that shines as gold."[94] In his criticism of "all the gay singing & playing, or multiplying of orisons," Ryckes is addressing nuns whose liturgical ideals, like the canons of the New Devotion, were simple and austerely traditional.[95] The Rule of Syon, newly translated by Whytford, was concerned essentially with love in the Pauline sense: Ryckes uses Paul to describe the love which culminates in the *imitatio Christi*, of which his audience could now read in another translation of Whytford, *The folowyng of Christe.*[96]

The guide, "a good religious man," speaks of the slavery enjoined on the monk who inwardly yearns for freedom and joy in worship,[97] of the wish to return 'to the source' and of the inescapable truth that the way of the ancient fathers had become its opposite. Although this way is the 'historic' foundation of religion, it is in no sense its equivalent, much less its justification, for the line connecting past and present is by no means straight. He says that, if they understood their tradition, if they could love, if . . .

[T]he life of the religious should be much more joyous, pleasant & easy than it is, where now we see it contrary, heavy, painful, laborious, full of superstitious observances & vain customs, leaving from them the true way of life, the following of Christ, the old manner of living that was used, taught and shewed by our holy forefathers, Saint Austin, Saint Benet, Saint Jerome, with many other, so that now there is little difference between lay persons, priests & religious in crimes & worldly living, to whom it is said. . . . Be not conformable to the world . . . if Saint Austin or Saint Benet were again alive (whom they take as fathers & authors of their rules & orders of their living) I think they should not know them . . . they will say that they ordained that manner of living after the rule of Christ & his apostles & not after the superstitious manners of the Jews that made gay & fair all things withoutforth & were withinforth full of ravine, venom, sin and malice.[98]

The Brethren of the Common Life spoke of discovering "a certain delight" which kept them "unharmed" in all their exercises, as in the Psalm "I remembered God and was delighted."[99] If spiritual exercise does not separate a man, however fleetingly, from 'the world' within himself, his religion must remain on the level of ordinary experiencing, with whatever is undertaken strengthening only the 'upside-down' psyche:[100] outwardly his behaviour becomes more conformable to his ideals, but inner malice grows unbeknown. He travels not towards unity, but multiplicity. Desiring spurious riches, he becomes an idolater. Receiving an "image of love" from the first Christians, the monastic founders set it up in their communities to be studied, to be forgotten under pain of cursing,[101] but their methods have been lost, the image dethroned and a counterfeit of the good, an image of new formation,[102] substituted. The old, right and, in a sense, initiatic way to which we are called to return leads simply to acquiring the ability to act from love "in Christ."[103]

The seeker passes beyond the monastery with a deeper vision. The true image has a quality both concrete and miraculous, not of this world yet at its heart; informed with magical force

it has this marvellous effect, that whatsoever is wrought or done where that is present, it is sufficient & good, though sometime it appears evil to some persons."

Action undertaken in its absence, however seemly, is empty in reality. Its power transcends the influences of ordinary life in 'the world,' for

it unites and makes many men all one, and confederates them so fast together, that nothing can sunder them; it covers the sin of penitents & redeems their forfeits and transgressions."

It is a talisman, drawing down beneficent influences to earth:

it makes peace & concord, it sets all things in order . . . yes, and sometimes it raises the dead to life; it is so attractive that it draws all good things to itself & then makes all common.

Truly the lodestone of myth, it has the power to orientate its possessor aright in every situation:

it mourns with mourners, it joys with them that be glad, it weeps with weepers, it takes away all suspicions and misjudging from the heart of man, it abhors all strife, envy, murmuring & contention, it hates all evil & loves all that is good.

The true image belongs to the real world, where it is the subject of the eternal struggle between the forces of good and evil, light and darkness:

there is nothing that pleases God more than this image & without it nothing can please him; there is nothing more desirous of the devil than the destruction of it, & to that intent he applies all his labour.[104]

That this invisible world of the higher levels should enter life here and now, is the significance of the search for the true image, of spiritual exercises and meditations to deepen participation inwardly and outwardly, of the call to the whole man with which our material re-echoes. Unless this image, "that is none other than charity"[105] appears in our midst, the reality behind what is known, felt and sensed cannot penetrate us.

Charity is a living image & the spirit of life that alone gives life to the body.[106]

Searching blindly for a life more abundant among dead things, he has been brought to the threshold of the practical spirituality of the Middle Ages.

A simple and immense perspective opens up, and perhaps the beginning of a path. Ryckes affirms, in language rich with allusions to the medieval mystics, Paul and the Neoplatonists, that the "patron" of the image is the "invisible God." We are similitudes of God. The divine power, wisdom and love are reflected in us as in a mirror, but, living as we do, we experience nothing of it: we do not even feel the question. Why is this? Traditional teachings say that man's soul is actually dead, or so unawakened as to be only embryonic, and that he is very far from the real world. His possibility to know God begins, in a sense, with his possibility to know himself, to "keep the glass towards the light." Love is a sacred capacity of being, the "life of our souls," "without which we are but dead." Through becoming able to love, the divine image in us may be "renewed" and "quickened," but unless the divine image is renewed we are unable to love. As we are, we are unable to love as Christians: "in man can be no charity but if God be present unto his soul." In God's apparent absence, it would seem that the Devil presents himself to the mirror and it gradually ceases to work. Unless it can be restored "betimes," it may be ruined: "many times it is broken before it can be made clean." God is "always present": who then is absent, and what does this mean? A man "sins" when God's image in him "ceases & has no being." Conversion, literally, is to turn altogether in a different direction. If the "glass" receives no light, a man cannot see any direction, and so goes "he knows not where":

> not in default of the light of grace, nor for the charity of God is not present, [but] because the glass is turned from the light & then it is so infected & defiled in darkness that it is unapt to receive the light of grace & the image of charity again.

A man's proper wish, Ryckes concludes, can only be to turn again that he may receive life.[107] It is not a matter of 'doing good' or of acquiring anything new, but a question of inner order and relationship, of not hindering the action of what is already there.

Traditional thought held that all phenomena manifest, and were manifestations of, a hierarchical order. As the physical body had five senses which love their objects, so there are, analogically, five kinds of love proper to the spirit.[108] The loves of this higher body were said to depend on the right functioning of the lower loves. If the love of a man for his kin, his neighbours and "every reasonable person" is not "grounded in a better respect than of nature," not the automatic result of conditioning and heredity, how then can he love his enemies, let alone God? "It can not be." It is not the powers of the spirit which have decayed, for a man is still sometimes moved by their reflection, but the ordinary, 'lower' functions of the physical body which have become disordered, fragmenting the whole.[109] Among these functions, Christianity focuses on the state of our primitive, disorganised emotions:[110] because the love of kin "may readily & unawarely be disordered (as we see by experience), it is hard to order discreetly the tasting of meat & drink & appetites of the flesh." Hence traditional ascetic practice to 'keep the heart,' to 'watch and pray' lest the ordinary affections become inordinately infected with egoism, "lest they diminish or destroy the other senses of love."[111] If the soul of the body departs, the bodily senses degenerate; if charity departs from the spiritual soul, the senses of love decay.[112] Ryckes concludes that a finer, more discriminating intelligence participates in an ordered love, the ego having made way:

> it is necessary to love discreetly, so that I love every creature in God and for God, after the goodness of it, not for profit & pleasure, for so the cat loves the mouse; & not to love more that thing that is less to be loved, & less that is more to be loved; for charity is not exception of persons, but loves in word and deed every person after their virtue & goodness.[113]

Discretion, the separation of what is usually conjoined: for the sake of the questions which arise in this most elusive and subjective area of our experience, it is asked that we realise its innate capacity to reflect a more objective world.

The confrontation of ignorance and self-delusion was inevitable for all who searched in this way, and our texts return again and again to the importance of discrimination. The Bridgettine William Bonde's advice to the nuns of Denney Abbey (1535)[114] on how to discriminate between "holy" and "servile" fear of God in themselves, was an early example, although rooted in medieval experience, of a persistent sixteenth-century concern to validate the individual's religious sense. Later came Calvinist guides to 'signs of election' and Jesuit manuals of self-analysis. Under the heading "to know when it is a true image" Ryckes restates the old aphorism that genuine love seeks no reward but the good of the beloved, meaning, at the highest level, that conscious love helps God:

> Some men declare that we should love our neighbour as our self 'in god, unto God and for God'; in God, that is, for that he is a special creature of God; unto God, that is, for he is made to his image, wherefore our intent in loving should have respect unto God; for God, that is, for that he should come to bliss & help us to the same.[115]

Clearly this is not love as ordinarily experienced, but neither is it impossible according to the tradition for which Ryckes speaks: such love is the expression of order in the whole man, in the 'three parts of the soul,' memory, reason and will.[116] Only if their ordinary counterparts develop, if memory can forget its usual preoccupations ("as be injuries done to us, which, when they be called to remembrance, be as iron left in a wound"), if the force of reason can appear where there has been only the laxity of associative thought (reason able to direct "without any error . . . subduing the wit and understanding unto meek service of Christ . . . enforcing with whole desire to the knowledge & sight of him") and if the will can be fearless, only then can he begin to love as a Christian.[117] All his parts must learn to work together harmoniously for a man to receive the help ('grace') to enable him to love consciously, that is, "in God, unto God, for God."

Such a possibility represents the 'unknown' in us, but at moments its hem sweeps close. The tradition we are investigating claims that we live far from it because we have become "subject to things" (Zerbolt), because we do not "belong to ourselves" (Ficino):[118] hence a new intent, "keep diligently thyself."[119] The questions of every age become its answers. We are on the verge of the 'spiritual exercises' of the sixteenth century, which renewed earlier attempts to confront the human condition and live closer to this possibility. Christ was able to love His enemies. Ryckes wonders, presciently, what it would mean to "use" persecution "well." Why did the martyrs' enemies help them more than their friends?[120] It was believed that exercises embodied the early Christian tradition.[121]

The spiritual exercises developed among the Jesuits were founded on the threefold division of man according to traditional spiritual psychology and were intended to support the reintegration of these functions so that God might be more truly served. Jesuit meditations therefore comprise exercises for mind,

senses and feelings, separately and in combination.[122] For the sake of discrimination, Ryckes describes love's opposite, the image of envy and malice, inviting his
audience to recognise it with their minds, know it through the senses and hate it
with the will. His method derives properly from the allegorical tradition of
medieval literature: he cites Ovid and Chrysostom and draws attention to "pic-
tures of the devil & of tyrants under the feet of saints."[123] Yet, by drawing on a
practical, as distinct from an academic, psychology, by insisting on self-examination and by implying the use of exercises, he prepares for the Jesuit experience.
Meditation on artistic iconography was fast giving way in early sixteenth-century
England to an obsessive concentration on the printed word:[124] Ryckes stands for
an older, more symbolic way of thought connected with the heart and analogy, a
way still natural for the New Devotion, which was to guide the young Ignatius.

It was the form in which the mysticism of the twelfth-century Victorines was
expressed, and the *Ymage* concludes with the words of Hugh of St. Victor, whose
works were well represented in Syon's library and whose commentary on their
mutual Augustinian Rule had recently been translated by Brother Whytford.[125]
Syon was a centre for the study of the Rolle corpus, upon which the Victorines
had been a major influence[126] Hugh's Parisian Abbey had been reformed by John
Mombaer, who had known both Kempis and Gansfort and whose outlook was
indebted to the New Devotional canons of St. Agnietenberg.[127] Mombaer's cryp-
tic writings on meditation, considered by many historians to systematise the spiritual exercises of the New Devotion, had been presented to the Syon library by
Whytford.[128] Hugh is called by Ryckes as a witness to the primacy of love in the
Christian life, and, by virtue of these correspondences, stands guarantor of Syon's
receptivity to the teachings of the *Ymage*.

Through Hugh, Ryckes recapitulates his theme of the search and its cost:

> O charity, what shall I say of thee, how shall I praise thee? If I felt thee or per-
> ceived thee I should somewhat cast in my mind what thou art worth: if I
> knew thy value I could esteem some price for thee. But perchance you exceed
> my poor scarceness . . . & yet will I give all that I have.[129]

He renews his commitment to the unknown. Like many, before and since, he has
heard about love but does not really know what it is; in the sincerity of his wish,
he knows his poverty, but acknowledges that he must pay for what he lacks; payment and sacrifice are interdependent. The real search, for which this has been a
prelude, begins when, realising his all to be nothing,[130] he still persists.

Ryckes' hope for the Bridgettines, whom he casts in the traditional role of the
religious as exemplary Christians, underlies all his expositions. It is at the
monastery within, the inner altar of the heart, that they must meditate, there
behold and contemplate "the two images": of God as incomprehensible and
uncreated love, and of "our little love" caused by His Image, "as a little image in a
glass, but yet . . . very precious and good, by means whereof the soul has life &

spiritual senses." Upon this 'altar' they must strive to "set up lights" and gradually learn, "both by doctrine & grace, whereby you may work, teach and shew examples of light."[131] If the religious, dedicated to Christianity, do not feel the quality of this love, they cannot ever communicate the teaching. Traditionally, the real health of the community depended on the presence of those able to "set up lights" in this way. If others are to be shown why and how they can love, the truth of it must be embodied in the teacher, for it is not people's minds alone that need to be instructed. Hugh said:

> [T]hey that have charity in exhorting of other to charity, they enflame themselves with love & they shew, not only inward but also in deed to every man, how sweet the love of God is & how sour & bitter is the impure & deceitful love of the world. . . . Charity thinks that thing to be sweet to all men, that savours well to herself, that thing to please them that she loves, . . . that thing that she knows to be manifest to all . . . it discovers itself where it is, for it will not abide only withinforth in the will, but it must go withoutforth by shewing of good works in outward conversation.[132]

It discovers itself where it is.

By grace, action may feed contemplation and contemplation action: a description of the 'mixed life.' As the quality of action changes, another balance may appear momentarily, psychological divisions weaken and the outer and inner become one:[133] the search opens the door to another life, a different order, and the end becomes the beginning. These ideas have come down to us from the journeys men have taken into the unknown.

This whole area is further illuminated in the *Revelations of St. Birget*, anonymously translated into English in 1530. (In this translation, it is nowhere suggested the contemplative need be a professional religious,[134] although in one place essentially monastic precepts are enjoined.)[135] "The house of the contemplative man is his heart," and it is necessary to practice a detached attitude towards what takes place there. He must learn to properly entertain his "guests," that is, those thoughts, feelings and impulses that visit him there. With his vices and weaknesses there is this particularity, that "all those vices when they come they shall in manner be as guests that be asleep," but, by not consenting to or delighting in them,[136] it may be possible "little and little through the help of grace to remove them clearly out of the heart." If he cannot do this, he must suffer them patiently, like a good host, for God's sake, and in this way they may eventually profit him. And he must care for his guests, "clothe" them with compassion, "feed" them by alerting himself on their arrival and not dissembling "as though he were asleep"; he must try to reason with them and remember his intention—to disregard his own egoistical pleasure and care only for the honour of God and the health of his soul—"such a will is meat and drink for the guests that come." He must try to pay especial attention to those guests who come when he is in a bad, inhospitable state, "that is to say when the heart is drawn from beholding of itself," when his ears are desiring only praise and his senses gratification, when the spirit "lays excuse of its frailness," when it seems insignificant not to care "and when there comes a painfulness and a hardness to do good deeds and a forgetfulness of things to come."[137]

The meaning emerging from this recalls Bernard's maxim "Keep diligently thyself." The religious man is asked to be as fully conscious as he can of all that takes place in him He serves God in the way he serves his "guests" and he serves them in the way he serves God; above all, he must know it, he must be in between:[138] this is the real asceticism.

The text states that change is a practical possibility under certain conditions: if the guests can be cared for in the right way, their nature may be transformed. Self-knowledge, a certain kind of struggle and "fire" are the means of change. The contemplative must thoroughly familiarise himself with his guests, weigh their fundamental character and tendency; he must lay in "dry sticks," by taking heed of the motions of the flesh ("that it rebel not against the spirit") and by diligently increasing "works of pity" and by prayer; and he must find how to light a "fire" with these "sticks," that the guests may be warmed and illuminated.

> Such thoughts and such guests . . . be in manner as they were asleep, but they be illuminated with the fire of the Holy Ghost: the which fire comes into the heart when he thinks how reasonable it is to serve God and when he thinks he had rather suffer all pain than wittingly to provoke God to wrath . . . then also the heart has heat of this heavenly fire . . . when the soul thinks and discerns to what intent every guest, that is to say, every thought, comes and whether it move the mind to covet joy perpetual or transitory and that he leave no thought undiscussed nor uncorrected with the dread of God.[139]

Despite conventional picturings, then and now, the traditional Way of the monk and of faith was based originally on an exact psychological knowledge which still echoes in this 'late' period. "Fire" is produced, literally, by friction between man's two natures, called here "flesh" and "spirit": it is a certain kind of suffering inevitably resulting from the way he is called, perhaps guided, to search.[140] These references to intentional meditations and self-study find their proper source in the struggles of the Desert Fathers, and bear comparison with Whytford's proposals in the Dialoge and with those later made in the Spiritual Exercises of Ignatius: like all the material cited in this book, they give the lie to the assumption of apologists that laymen were being poorly fed on the eve of the Reformation.

The experience of a new truth, potentially able to touch all sides of life, threatens a new imbalance, but, also—because everything is connected—invites a new sense of responsibility. The material of these texts, however conventionally expressed, concerns the relationship of human energies.

[H]e must specially know and consider that where a fire is made in a close vessel that hath no avoidance, anon the fire goeth out and the vessel waxeth cold. So it is with the contemplative man: if he would not live to nothing else but that he might do honour to God, it is expedient that his mouth be opened and that the flame of charity go forth.[141]

In his own rightful self-interest he must risk manifesting his state, must "labour all that he can, that convenient avoidance may be had for his flame": to surmount all the difficulties this will entail, he will need to be as cunning as a fox.[142]

This whole analogy from the *Revelations*—an example of symbolic thought— puts flesh on the bones of Hugh of St. Victor's advice and leads to the same con- clusion as the *Ymage*, that the end of the religious life is its beginning.

The image of love has been revealed as the heart of the Christian life. Upon the relationship with it depends the orientation of both outer and inner life, the pos- sibility of the soul; its action determines the conformity of man's inner order to the image of God, for, by opening him to the higher influences, it governs his place within a greater order. In the wish to be between higher and the lower, in order to receive what has been prepared for man, Ryckes finally invokes this beneficent image in a prayer:

[B]eseeching you to come into my soul for to kindle it in love, to light it with grace, to dilate my heart, to stretch out my desire, to open the bosom of my mind, to enlarge and establish thy dwelling place in my soul, that it may receive the Good Lord, Father, Son and Holy Ghost, most high charity into my reason, will and memory, for a continual dweller in me: and likewise in you good ladies perpetually. Amen.[143]

What can we discover about the background of this remarkable, today forgotten text? The *Ymage's* teaching derives from a medieval tradition of practical religion which sought to experience the ancient idea that man was created in the image of God. A web of correspondences link the work and its author to the religious life of the continent, revealing elements of a common late medieval nonscholastic spirituality which entered significantly into the movements of Christian human- ism, Counter-Reformation Catholicism and even Protestantism. Here, all roads lead through the experimental asceticism of the New Devotion to the truths of an earlier age. The New Devotion was a bridge.[144]

The *Ymage* draws on the medieval mystics, the broad Augustinian tradition in which the Victorines worked and the native school of Rolle and Hylton;[145] its imagery connects it with the Christianised Neoplatonism of the Renaissance. It was addressed to the Bridgettines of Syon, prominent in the transmission of mys- tical traditions,[146] and, according to their library catalogue, fertile soil for the revived Platonism.[147] Ryckes' order, the Observant Franciscans, were newly established, decidedly international in outlook (as their resistance to Henry VIII was to show) and natural allies of the Bridgettines;[148] they constituted a link between England and Renaissance Italy,[149] where they had originated, and with Flanders, the home not only of very influential schools of mysticism and ascetic theology and a galaxy of lay heresies in the fourteenth and fifteenth centuries, but of the New Devotion itself and some of the most radical sixteenth-century sectarian thought.

Specific enquiry into early Tudor devotion substantiates these relationships. The prayer *O bone Jesu*, associated with the Observant Friar, Bernardino of Siena,[150] which appears in most late medieval English Books of Hours and most of the early printed Hours,[151] was introduced from Flanders,[152] probably through the travels of Flemish Observants transmitting the prayer of a newly canonised saint (1450), the most famous representative of their order. England at this time was replete with foreign friars, particularly from north Germany and the Low Countries. The first Observant Franciscan community in England was closely associated with the Low Countries, most of the recruits hailing from Northern Europe: probably all the original Greenwich settlement were foreign.[153] The Cult of the Holy Name fostered by this prayer was practised not only by the reformed Observant houses of Canons Regular and by the Black Monks in Flanders, France and Germany, but was central to the New Devotion, as attested by Kempis in his life of John Brinckerinck, one of the original Brethren of the Common Life. Because of its association with the suspiciously heretical Beguines,[154] the practice was controversial: Brinckerinck defended his brethren's use of it thus:

> [T]o them, their great honour and their chief joy is this Holy Name of Jesus, which they call upon continually and reverence deeply; and before all and above all the names of the saints they love and adore Jesus, the son of God, whom you mock and despise, because these Brethren and Beguines rejoice to call upon His name, devoutly praise it, saluting one another therein.[155]

The Brethren's founder, Gerard Groote, translated one of the most famous late medieval devotions on the Holy Name, Suso's *Cursus de aeterna sapientia*; manuscript translations of Suso were widespread in England (along with other writings of the Rhineland and Flemish masters, Tauler and Ruysbroeck, who had been Gerard's teacher)[156] where this work was often attributed to Rolle, the best-known English "lover of the Name."[157] Syon became a centre for Rolle texts[158] and the popular sixteenth-century manual of the Cult of the Name, the *Jesus Psalter*, was attributed in its turn to the Syon monk, Whytford.[159] The cult survived into Counter-Reformation lay devotion, as a part of the schemes of intensely ordered 'monastic' daily life which embodied the principles of the New Devotion.[160]

The Observant Friars, Bridgettines and New Devotionalists were further linked in a common aim to 'observe' the religious life, to obey the tradition as it had reached them. The fifteenth-century Observance movement, in which the New Devotional canons of the Windesheim congregation played a leading part, was closely paralleled among the Italian Friars and Benedictines. The words "observance" and "reformation" first became current in Franciscan circles. In 1380, Gerard had advised the school rector, John Cele, against joining the Franciscans because none of the local houses had been reformed. Ruysbroeck, at whose feet Gerard often sat, spoke stingingly of monastic "inobservance," and surely guided, if not initiated, his protégé's attempts to inaugurate reform, for Gerard went on to become an early advocate of observantism.[161]

Information is scanty regarding the principles on which Windesheim was founded after Gerard's death, by his pupil, Florence Radewijns (1386–87); but the union of four monasteries to form the Windesheim congregation (1394–95), clearly associates the New Devotion with Observance. Their petition to the Pope states that union was sought because monasteries from all parts of the Church were failing noticeably to progress in the religious life and to properly apply the Rule. The Windesheimers hoped that their organisation with its fraternal visitation and annual chapter would be able to maintain the desired observance, and the form of such chapters became characteristic of all fifteenth-century congregations. Henry Pomerius, author of a life of Ruysbroeck, wrote in his chronicle of Groenendaal that his order of Augustinian canons had been reformed "in newness of spirit," and were thus able to preserve the severity of order under the observance of one chapter: they had begun to expand from a desire to lead others to this observance. John Vos of Heusden, head of the Windesheim congregation, described their life as the maintaining of the Rule, the perpetual striving after observance.[162] Through the influence of Windesheim, this observance spread to other orders in the Low Countries and beyond, for they had touched a need. The meaning of the association between the New Devotion and Observance lay in the nature of spiritual exercises as a preparation for being able to accept more wholly the discipline of the Rule. The Brotherhood was a bridge between 'the world' and the cloister.

It can be said, with proper caution, that Observantism began around 1400 in the Order of Canons Regular as an element in the movement later called the New Devotion: "to the extent that Windesheim was implicated in this movement, this reformation can be considered to form part of the Modern Devotion."[163] Parallel with this, convents and monasteries emerged in the Low Countries which took at first the Third Rule of St Francis, particularly adapted to a religious life in the world. They probably originated among lay groups living communally with no particular rule, such as were usually suspected of association with the quasi-heretical Beguines and Beghards: apparently desiring a stricter life, they often introduced enclosure and adopted the Rule of Augustine, perhaps under the influence of Windesheim.[164] These movements were contemporary with the monastic foundations of Bridget in Sweden and, subsequently, of Syon in England (1415, enclosed 1420). Syon followed the Augustinian Rule and was distin-

guished throughout its life for the fidelity of its observance. The Windesheimers"
only pastoral duty was the care of nuns of the convents belonging to their congregation, a relationship equivalent to the Syon brethren, who cared for their own
nuns, heard their confession and administered the Eucharist.[165] The Bridgettines
Whytford and Bonde were prominent among the advocates of observance in early
sixteenth-century England, as was Bishop Fox of Winchester, who commissioned
a translation of the Benedictine Rule to facilitate observance,[166] and who had
been one of the prelates entrusted by Alexander VI with the introduction of the
Observant Friars into England.[167] The *Orcharde of Syon*, published at the expense
of the nun's lay steward in 1519, included in its prologue a letter to an Observant
Friar extolling observance as the only solution to religious decadence and referring indirectly to the excellence of the Cult of the Holy Name.[168]

The Windesheim congregation, the Bridgettines and the Observant Friars represented both the last wave of 'medieval' reform, in that they accepted and
worked within the monastic ideal, and the first 'modern' reform, in that their 'dis-
coveries' within the tradition entered as important ingredients into the new religious syntheses of the sixteenth century. Among the ideas which these reforming
orders regenerated, were the virtue of the vernacular for religious instruction,[169]
the authority of the Bible as the only sure external guide,[170] the need to instruct
laymen,[171] the helplessness of man without grace[172] and the importance of systematic meditation.[173] These trends in New Devotional and Bridgettine writing
(although by no means exclusive to them) were present in the *Ymage* and were
crystallised in the next generation of developing Protestantism and stirring
Counter-Reformation.[174] Whytford, Bonde and Ryckes wrote of Observance in
terms which were akin to Erasmian freedom,[175] while the language and some of
the values of observance found their way into the Protestant vocabulary.[176] There
is some indication that Ryckes himself became a Lutheran.[177] Whytford interpreted the Christian humanist ideal of religiously educating the laity in terms of
transmitting the devotional attitudes and practices of Syon.[178] It was a time of
new and unexpected blendings, and of inevitable confusion.

The intense contemporary experience of search in these transitional conditions
is mirrored in the *Ymage*. The ancient idea that man is a similitude of the Whole,
'the image of God,' pervades Ryckes' search and, indeed, all the material of this
book. It derives from the bedrock of Christian tradition to which the most vital
fifteenth-century thought, feeling and practice strove to return. To be understood,
an idea must be lived: like an instrument which has an action. The question of
man's true nature and service, the search for right relationship in all worlds,
secretly united Platonists, pietists and laymen. It was essentially a call, not for
introspective self-analysis, nor the intensification of ordinary thought or emotion, however profound or ecstatic, but for the development of a different quality
of attention, an awakening from sleep, in order that ancient religious and philosophical teachings might again have meaning. This is the *Ymage*'s deeper context.

Confronted with the dazzling image of "the love of this world," the seeker spies "a very living thing called the worm of conscience" amongst the flowers, beasts, birds and insects upon the hem of her garment and he ponders the gospel teaching that the world entrances men by making them forget God. If these lower forms of life are bewitched humanity, as the Prophet David said, this image is a terrifying picture of the real world.[179] Here is the key to the *Ymage* and one of the seminal ideas of our period: the lack of right order within man and without. He has become assimilated to the level of lesser beings as a result of the corruption of his will ('love') and the ignorance of his true nature and rightful place in every world. Because he embodies the Divine purpose, his animality places him beneath the animal. This is the ground of his search.

> Man, lord of all creatures, having in himself the image of God (whereof he ought to draw out the very image of love) to his high honour, knew not his degree and high estate that God hath made him to, but set his mind more upon these vain outward images through the which he is compared & transformed to beasts most unreasonable and is made like unto them.[180]

What is the meaning of the extraordinary capacity—and absence—implied in Pico's statement, "man is not any inborn image of himself, but many images coming in from the outside"?[181]

As a vehicle, the *Ymage* is related to a corpus of contemporary writings which, for all their heterogeneity in other respects, converge on the idea of the 'mixed life.' The spiritual psychologists of the New Devotion spoke of "original justice," the right inner and outer order from which man has departed.[182] Italian writers emphasised man's original dignity in order to portray more vividly his present condition: Pico told of man's forgetfulness of the Father and service of "the beasts" within, the result of the upside-down supremacy of his 'body' over his 'reason,' contrary to his true nature as God's image. In this syncretic "poetic theology" the myth of Circe was often cited in illustration.[183] Northern writers concentrated more on man's fallen state in the tradition of vernacular piety. More, commenting on Circe and citing Pico, stated that if men would observe themselves closely they would see the beasts within, whose dominance deformed their true nature as men, images of God.[184] This understanding is often shown in art by a human head placed in the lower part of the body.[185] More's friend, Whytford, used the analogy of the rider asleep on his horse ("sensuality")—which, consequently, cannot help following its accustomed ways. The evidence of the New Devotion emphasises again and again that true prayer begins with watching: the 'rider' must awaken to his sleep. The possibility of learning from one's thoughts, of which Whytford then speaks, depends on this.[186]

The diagnosis of man common to these accounts unequivocally makes self-knowledge the first aim of the search. "In consequence of giving little heed to understanding ourselves," said Pico, we have been disinherited, condemned to "follow after the steps of the flocks," our lower, passively 'sensual' nature. Thus disinherited—for God intended us to lead our flocks—and in ignorance of our state, we are "violently separated" from ourselves, unhappy indeed.[187] Perhaps it is better that we do not know it. If we would advance in reality, follow the steps of the Prophets and Saints rather than "the beasts that are in us," then "let us enter into our very selves . . . so that we may successfully recognise in ourselves not only all the worlds but also our Father and our home."[188] Dean Colet's *A ryght frutefull monycion concernyng the ordre of a good chrysten mannes lyfe*, addressed to laymen, contained a more homely, but no less significant invitation to self-discovery. It is not only "high wisdom," he wrote, but "great perfection" to know and "despise" oneself. The Christian had inherited a vision and must, somehow, bear it: man's psychological, physical and spiritual organisation reflected the Trinity, therefore, by virtue of being born into a lawfully ordered Creation, his real justification and search lay in striving to conform voluntarily to that order, to obey God, as it was said. Colet saw this in terms of faith and practical discipline, leading from externals to the inner life. Man's relationship to his outer life, his needs and responsibilities, depended on his relationship to himself, his self-knowledge supported by the Christian teaching: temporal goods were meant to serve the requirements of the temporal body, the temporal body to serve the soul, the soul to be ordered by reason and grace, with the help of which his duty to God and neighbour became clear. It is the impartial vision of order embodied in orthodox historical Christianity: serve that which is higher if you would be served by that which is lower, but if you do not obey, evil will be done: become a master!

Like all traditional teaching stemming from a quality of comprehension almost irrecoverable today, it is simple, but not easy to understand. In this court, however compromised its authority had become, the fundamental questions continued to sound, evidence of law-conformable levels of consciousness in ourselves, 'our' world and—if human beings are the Image of God—in All Worlds, everything above and below the place of our precarious foothold on this ladder of reality. There may be little to choose between the kind of fool who thinks ladders lead only upwards and the one who believes them to be historical relics, if not figments of the imagination; but the question remains. Without the wish, and by moments the capacity, to see what is, the social cement solidifies in our absence.

[B]y all common reason, if thou keep this convenient order to God and his creatures, they shall keep their order to thee. But if thou break thine order to them, of likelihood they shall break their order to thee. For how should thy wife, children, servants and other creatures, with which you have doings, do their duty & keep their order to thee, if thou dost not so to God and to them. And also think thou of a surety that if thy sensual appetite be not ordered by reason and grace, thou art worse ordered than a beast: for then thou livest out of order & so doth not a beast, which is a great shame and rebuke to thee a reasonable creature & without the great mercy of God, it shall be to thine eternal damnation.[189]

What sort of morality was at stake?

Colet's manual outlines daily exercises of meditation, mindfulness and discrimination, which derive from the experiments in daily living of the New Devotion,[190] supported by the Renaissance vision of man's place and duty. If relationship is all, right and wrong behaviour has cosmological significance:

> Earthly things are subject to man and the heavenly bodies befriend him, since he is the bond and link between heaven and earth; but they cannot both have peace with him unless he, who in himself sanctifies their peace and alliance, is at peace with himself. But let us beware, I pray, that we do not misunderstand the greatness of the honour we have been given. Let us always hold it in our mind's eye as a sure, proven and indubitable truth that just as all things favour us when we keep the law which has been given to us, so if through sin or evasion of the law we forsake the beaten path, they will all be unfriendly, hostile and dangerous. It is reasonable that to the same extent that we do injury not only to ourselves but also to the universe, which we encompass within us, and to almighty God, the creator of the world itself, we should also experience all things in the world as the most severe punishers and powerful avengers of injuries, with god among the foremost.[191]

Man's dignity depends on his consciousness of responsibility: on this ground philosophy and piety can meet.

Pico and Colet were speaking, like Ryckes, of the search for the true image: for the Observant Friar, man's discovery of his true nature as the image of God was the revelation of deep feeling and faith; for the secular priest and confessor of souls, Colet, it was submission to daily discipline and the (high) level of common sense; for the philosopher-poet, Pico, it was a more conscious participation in all worlds, within and without, of returning home. Renaissance thought was founded on a vision of the essential truths uniting all creeds, the burning relevance of ancient values to the contemporary situation; Colet's circle stood for intellectual and emotional integrity, a blending of the sincere simplicity of vernacular devotion with the radical idealism of a revived Neoplatonism and the hope and vitality of the 'new' learning. Originating within a reformed monasticism, the *Ymage* called the committed religious to conform to their ideal and a clarified Pauline tradition, that they might become torchbearers of a spiritualised Christianity for the coming age. All these writings speak eloquently of the need for renewal and its possible bases, but it is to the New Devotion that we must now turn for the clearest evidence of how it might be begun.

FOUR

The New Devotion

A truly devout man relies on himself.

John Ruysbroeck

The knowledge of all knowledge is for a man to know that he does not know anything.

Gerard Groote

He is indeed a brother and a friend of another who hates his defects and helps him to surpass them.

Florence Radewijns

The New Devotion lies at the heart of this enquiry because it represents the closest approach to a living teaching of Christianity that we have been able to discover within the period of research. What this movement stood for gives meaning to all the material being presented and the key to further work.

'The New Devotion' described the values and exercises communicated by Gerard, called 'the Great' (Groote, latinised as Gerardus Magnus), 1340–84, and Florence Radewijns, 1350–1400. These men and their companions became the nucleus of the Brotherhood of the Common Life, and, after Gerard's death, of a house of Augustinian canons at Windesheim based on the same newly understood principles. Founded in 1386, Windesheim had become by 1496 the mother of about a hundred related houses, including twenty nunneries, to which the name New Devotion referred by extension, although they were subject to other influences by this time. Their 'new' methods were being distinguished from the 'old' devotion of the majority of monasteries, as well as from the wishful sentimentality of popular cults and the scholastic impenetrability of official theology. The 'new devotion' denoted a 'modern' renewal of religion. The Brotherhouses established by Florence and his pupils helped men to find the necessary intermediate stage between 'the world' and active religious commitment.

The Brothers were pious men, who exercised themselves in devotion. 'Devotio' expresses the idea of personal consecration and 'pietas,' duty. Gerard said, "it is

81

our duty to make ourselves worthy habitations where Christ will be pleased to dwell."[1] "Devotion," wrote Florence, "is nothing other than the desire of the soul for God."[2] The early companions of Gerard were known simply as "the Devout" or "the Servants of God," the latter echoing the name of Augustine's companions and of certain groups of Desert monks mentioned by John Climachus in the seventh century.[3] The Brothers believed themselves to be essentially related to these men in their understanding. Gerlach Peters wrote of their life:

> The servants of God have greatly longed for the glory of heaven and panted after it with their whole heart. Therefore their chief study has been to gain the joy that is given to the saints here below in the knowledge of truth and wisdom and to refashion their inner man after the likeness of God and to conform their outer life to the life of Jesus.[4]

In their view it was an ancient and forgotten craft they studied. Information concerning it, deduced and pieced together from the records of their experience, reveals something of greatest interest today, for our civilisation is even more highly 'evolved' and distant from its sources than theirs. Their claim to be, in effect, links in a chain of transmission, makes nonsense of accepted views of linear historical evolution and is one of the ways in which they challenge us.

The pervasive influence of such an unassertive and, as it were, invisible body, constitutes the Brotherhood's challenge to historical thought. Noting that many outstanding figures acknowledged the New Devotion with respect and gratitude,[5] historians have equated it with almost every intellectual and religious trend of the fifteenth and sixteenth centuries. Taking their ethical approach out of context, some commentators have seen them as humanists manqués;[6] others, enthusiastically simplifying, have claimed them as initiators of a 'Christian Renaissance,' encompassing not only religious humanism but also the Reformation and Catholic revival.[7] A recent monograph cautiously upholds the Brethren's significance but, due to lack of evidence, systematically denies them any more than local influence: "too many things are too easily attributed to the Brethren, because not enough is known about them."[8] In our view, the difficulty is not so much in the quantity of our knowledge, although the evidence has its limits, but in understanding what we have.

Perhaps scholars assume their influence to have been necessarily vague and subjective—corresponding to modern conceptions of piety—capable of being all things to all men. The evidence, however, speaks rather of the strong and definite shock of their example upon all who came into contact with them.[9] To further deduce their characteristics from the varied and contradictory results of an indeterminate 'pious' influence produces a naive and unconvincing picture of their work, a reflection of our own confusion concerning everything spiritual. It is more helpful to regard the Brotherhood as a consequence rather than a cause: a visible consequence of a hidden Christian life, connected, as far as we can see, with certain Carthusian houses and the circles around the Augustinian canon John Ruysbroeck,[10] a life as hidden to contemporaries as to modern observers.

The study of spiritual movements is fraught with particular difficulties. We are facing not only the intractability of the evidence but—speaking personally—a deficiency of understanding. Their work was founded on an essential faithfulness in people which has become rare today. Information, couched in a religious language no longer living for us, is scarce for the vital early days, becoming more detailed only as the movement was beginning, in the judgment of its leaders, to degenerate.[11] We are forced to rely for evidence of the Brotherhood's origins on these later writers, whose reverential anonymity and studied naiveté, deriving stylistically from established literary-devotional models, effectively blocks a modern curiosity accustomed to feed off sensations of self-expression. The very blindness of these Brother authors to the kind of reality we habitually seek in the past, tells us something important.

A superficial examination reveals many contradictions. They appear highly orthodox, especially in their reverence for the Eucharist,[12] yet *De Imitatione Christi* says that anyone who knows devotion could experience 'communion' without going near a church and the early Brethren were consistently called Lollards and Beguines, generic terms for heretic.[13] Their influence may have undermined the sacraments.[14] Their teaching placed great value on the love of the neighbour[15] and their pastoral work and care for one another was remarkable, yet the Windesheim canon Gerard Zerbolt, a profound theologian and psychologist trained by Florence, questioned about the crowds when he went abroad, said, "it is to me as though a herd of swine were passing: what is it to me that they wear the form of men?"[16] They regarded the monastic state highly[17] and many Brethren became monks in the houses founded from Windesheim, yet Florence's successor at the Deventer Brotherhouse stated that all men had the possibility of self-perfection, contrary to the Church's view that this was proper only to the monastic elite.[18] They took no sides in the theological debate between the *via antiqua* and the *via moderna*. Founded by Gerard Groote, reputedly a master of magic[19] and one of the famous doctors of his day, in whom all the branches of knowledge were said to have been united, they are best known today for their uncompromising rejection of academic learning: yet brilliant scholars like Gansfort and Biel kept their company.

Are these contradictions irreconcilable—or even real—and where is their seat? They come from a kind of manipulation, an inability to accept the material on its own terms. Trying to define these people by establishing their position in relation to issues, as if they were a modern pressure group, they will continue to elude—or will be rendered a lifeless conformity, which comes to the same thing. This undoubted elusiveness to analysis constitutes another significant fact about them. We do not know what they were. Much depends on the way we question. Our interest is centred on the meaning of the Brotherhood's coming together: in what did 'the common life' consist? We are seeking an inner-world influence which leaves the least perceptible trace in the records and is the most inaccessible to the modern historian. For this reason, in all that follows the Brethren have been allowed as much as possible to speak for themselves.

The story of Egbert ter Beek's entry among "the servants of God" illustrates the kind of influence felt fifty years after Gerard's death. From the start they had sought relationship with the young.[20] Egbert first met them as a schoolboy and was so impressed that he imitated their dress and manner. Growing up and beginning, as the chronicler says, to "pant after the things of God,"[21] he became disillusioned with university and remained unmoved by the monasteries he visited. In 1438 he entered the Brotherhouse founded by Florence and then began a struggle with his family, echoes of which have reached us. His wealthy father wanted him to become a dignitary of the church and offered to establish a vicariate for him in their hometown. He visited his son among his new friends and tried to influence him. Egbert addressed "his father according to the flesh" as follows (the chronicler has transposed the subtleties of authentic dialogue and the Edwardian translator has transposed further):

> Because you are a circumspect man, listen, beloved father—your secular priests carry on from day to day, as is apparent to all, alas, in drunkenness and intoxication of their hearts and bodies contrary to the evangelical precepts and, what is even worse and usually follows from this, they proceed to luxurious indulgence of the flesh. There is no doubt, taking into consideration my natural weaknesses, that it would be impossible for me to live with such men and not become as they are.[22]

His father suggested he live at home and pursue a life of prayer, reading and spiritual exercises on his own.[23] Perhaps he might become a good influence on these evil priests. Egbert rejected this picture:

> It will be easier for me, dearest father, to be perverted by them than for them to be converted through me. Why? I am not ignorant of my own weaknesses nor of the devil's wrestling, and so it will be more useful for me to persist among the many in this holy and praiseworthy society, where each companion [socius] is a supporter, where the adroitness of the enemy is known through the daily exercising in spiritual warfare, and where it is terrible for the world, the flesh and the devil on account of their resolution and courage. The forces of a camp that has been wisely ordered cry out, "woe to the man on his own, because when he has fallen there are none to raise him up!"[24]

His father gave his blessing and became a friend of the Brethren. Egbert, with the particular help of Otger, Deventer's procurator, whom he came to regard as "the father of his soul,"[25] persisted through all difficulties and rose to a position of responsibility. His words give a glimpse of the Brethren's influence on a young man's aspiration at a turning point and indicate the straightforward yet deep meaning with which the internal life of the Brotherhouse invested conventional Christian ideals. His references to inner order, the touchstone of all our material, are particularly interesting.

The historical appearance of the Brotherhood can be dated to around 1380 in the Low Countries, contemporary with revolts in England, Italy and Bohemia, the Great Schism, the spread of heretical movements and natural disasters of all kinds,[26] during one of the periodic crescendos of confusion and disillusionment in the life of Europe. Practical accounts of religious meaning, based on the experiential formulations of mystical theology rather than the divagations of the Scholastics, providentially began to appear: they focused on the obstacles ('vices') in the individual's inner life which hindered the awakening of those higher faculties which bring the possibility of real obedience to the precepts of religion. One of these writers, John Ruysbroeck, played a crucial, if enigmatic, role in the career of Gerard. Whether these writings verged on heresy, as some then judged, is a matter for theologians; they were taken up selectively by Protestants, 'spiritual reformers' and religious revolutionaries of all stripes during the reintensification of discontent preceding the Reformation, but they deal essentially with an inner revolution, as do the treatises of the Brotherhood.

The sources agree that Gerard was the focal point around whom the groups later called the Brethren and Sisters of the Common Life formed and that he had been specifically prepared for this role at certain monasteries, although he never became a professed religious. John Vos of Heusden, prior of Windesheim, declared on his deathbed in 1424 that

> Groote was the first father of this our reformation, the source and origin of the new devotion; he was an apostle in this country who kindled the fires of religious fervour in the cold hearts of men and drew them to God.

A little later Kempis described him as a "living voice," able to prick the heart and address the individual need.[27] Of his mission, Kempis said:

> The eternal wisdom of the Father and his celestial mercy provided that there should be sent such a great and good master as an ambassador from heaven to a world which was now ageing and always turning to even worse practices: one who had put on the breastplate of faith, and was sustained by sanctity of life, so that through him sacred religion might be made to flourish again and the devotion of Christian people, being instructed by his discourses, might be rekindled to practice the worship of God, the observance of the commandments and merciful works to the poor. It was not the work of an ignorant man to resist the malice of so many enemies and call souls that were perishing out of the depths of sin into the light of truth, but this man was very skilled and one who had moreover made trial of many things and upon whom had been

bestowed by divine grace the power of speaking. He excelled other men by the worth of his life and by the heavenly doctrine, in which he had been instructed: he was thus able to convince his hearers to despise the world not in words of human wisdom but through the example of his holy way of living.[28]

For details of Gerard's life we are dependent on tales circulating among the second and third generation of his followers. He came from a prosperous background and was scholastically successful, studying law in Paris, acquiring a thorough knowledge of patristic thought and developing an interest in astronomy, astrology and magic. His life ran smoothly enough, no doubt, until one day in Cologne when a stranger confronted him as he wandered the busy streets and challenged him with a question:

Why are you standing here like this, intent on empty things? You must become another man.

The stranger, according to one tradition a member of the hidden "Friends of God," then disappeared into the crowds.[29] Gerard sought out various people, whose significance and even names have been lost to history,[30] and fell seriously ill. Subsequently he experienced a 'conversion.' It was at this crucial time that he made contact with Ruysbroeck: accompanied by his close friend, the schoolmaster John Cele, and guided by a certain shoemaker, he visited the old hermitage of Groenendaal in the forest of Soignies. Ruysbroeck came upon them in the grounds and said, "before I saw you, I knew you were coming."[31] He advised Gerard to withdraw to the Charterhouse of Monnickhuizen.[32]

It was the beginning of a fruitful relationship. The influence of Ruysbroeck and his friends was decisive for Gerard's orientation: he said later that he wished only to be a footstool for these men, that he was "renewed" (*renovare*) by his visits to them and that he was more attached in love and reverence to them than to any other mortals.[33] On at least two occasions he was to send them people wishing to profit from their kind of experience. (He recommended one be set to brewing beer as a test.)[34] The bones of an exchange tell of their relationship. Gerard was earnestly questioning John about passages in his writings which had aroused the suspicion of the authorities. He answered that he had "never written anything except by the guidance of the Holy Ghost." Later, "Master Gerard endeavoured to imbue the devout prior with the fear of hell, but did not succeed." Ruysbroeck considered that Gerard "was wounded more by the dart of fear than by the spark of love," and, on being told that he did not have enough fear, replied that, "hitherto he had certainly not been disquieted by any fear, but that he was ready to accept whatever God had adjudged for him, whether it was life or death."[35]

Kempis records the belief current at Windesheim that Gerard had conceived the foundation of their house as a result of his experiences at Groenendaal:

He was chiefly led to institute this order of a rule on account of singular reverence and love for the reverent lord John Ruysbroeck, the first prior of Groenendaal and the other brothers of the same, who were of the order of [canons] regulars and who conscientiously lived a most excellent life. He had visited these men personally in Brabant; in them he had observed and from them he had taken a way of great constructiveness, on account of the extent of their humility and their wearing of simple clothes.[36]

Gerard translated into Latin some of Ruysbroeck's works, versions which had a very wide circulation in their day and ensured his thought an influence beyond Northern Europe; he concerned himself with the publication of Ruysbroeck after his death and actively defended him against his critics. In his dealings with Groenendaal he called him "the father."[37] His translations of John of Leeuwen, Ruysbroeck's cook, anticipated the work of John Ketel in Florence's kitchen and a tradition of practical spirituality that was to reach at least into the seventeenth century and the Carmelite cook Brother Lawrence.

Ruysbroeck's influence on the New Devotion has been minimised by commentators unable to connect the philosophical and theological content of his writings with the known outlook and activities of the Brethren. It is a question about the relationship between thought, feeling and action. What quality of thought could guide what the masters of Christian asceticism called "spiritual doing." The religious exercises of the Devotion were not invented from nothing and, by their nature, were not broadcast to all: a serious study of the inner life of the Brethren, were it possible, would make a good beginning by trying to penetrate—and not merely academically—the kernel of Ruysbroeck's teaching. If Gerard did not imitate him outwardly, nor repeat his thought, substantial matter was exchanged: indicating Gerard, he had once said, "he understands my words."[38]

Gerard and his friends were at Groenendaal between 1374 and 1376, whence they were sent to study with the Monnickhuizen Carthusians for three years, between 1377 and 1379. Gerard returned to Ruysbroeck just before he died in 1381,[39] three years before his own death. His sojourn with the Carthusians was in no way accidental: he went, as his legend says, because "by this means he would first learn in person that of which he must afterward become a teacher." It was "these wise and religious brethren" who determined him to preach and gather like-minded men on his return to the world, "when, by the ordinance of God, the time of his fruit bearing was at hand."[40] Upon rejoining his countrymen, Gerard gave up his prebends, wound up his affairs and began to speak of what he had learned. He was slandered and hated for this, because "he struck his finger on the place."[41] Others were drawn magnetically, their receptivity granting them legendary status in the later account of Kempis.[42] The records, although retrospective, were closer to the influence in question than we: they show Gerard crossing the threshold, having been intentionally prepared for a particular task, and the wisdom and foresight of his teachers being vindicated by the response he evoked. Was his anonymity in the records the result of a lack of 'individualism,' his conformity as a vehicle?

His surviving letters are mainly concerned with practical advice to young monks, nuns and novices[43] and with attempts to persuade religious authorities to behave differently. His writing is intense, his expression obscure and contorted, studded with biblical phrases like fragments of some ancient and forgotten code, in the manner of Bernard; yet it still arrests, despite the silence of that "living voice" for which he was noted.

> I constantly try to write that which can and must strike straight to their hearts (not laved by milk nor shaped by earth and flesh, but open to the brightness of the eternal sun and renewed after the image of God in the knowledge in [sic] Him and reformed according to the inner man) and be heard by them with love.[44]

The contents of the letters cannot be added together to produce a single set of views, but, behind the contradictions of their advice in different circumstances, an intense simplicity and constancy of purpose can be felt. They tell us little, however, about his *socii* (companions), the *spirituales* as he also called them,[45] those men and women in his more intimate care, who became the nucleus of the Brothers and Sisters of the Common Life: with them his contact was personal, his advice oral.

Beginnings are difficult to locate in time. As early as 1374, according to some sources, Gerard opened parts of his house to women who wished to benefit from his guidance; they studied and worked manually and he defrayed the cost. Similar groups arose in neighbouring towns. Gradually groups of laymen began to gather around him and his friend Florence in Deventer. They lived together, exploring questions of the religious way, copying and broadcasting texts of the early Fathers. The life of these associations was based on certain principles: we know what they did, if not why or how. They wished to conform to the essential ideals of poverty, chastity and obedience, but took no vows and were free to leave at any time; they lived frugally and wore simple clothes, but not a monastic style habit; they took food together in silence; they read, meditated, prayed and regularly exchanged together on questions of the inner life; they supported themselves by copying texts and manual work, eschewing the begging adopted by lay groups suspected of heresy; they fed and clothed the poor.[46] They had combined to help each other towards the common goal: to live in a better way, according to Christ's instructions. These "disciples and brothers whom he had first faithfully built up and set on fire by the grace of that new light wherewith he himself was filled"[47] were not formally organised until after his death in 1384: under Florence's guidance, and presumably in line with Gerard's instructions, the Brotherhood took on the form perceived by historians. Members increased, funds were amalga mated and individuals ceased to pay their expenses directly.[48] The Brethren took experienced and impressionable young students under their wing in hostels which became a regular feature of later Brotherhouses (the schools of the Low Countries were famous and drew pupils from a wide area).[49] Gerard's great friend, John Cele, had been a schoolmaster.

The Brethren continued to lead a "common life" with no constraining vows, but the gradual assimilation of the movement to the existing religious orders was leading to the introduction of vows by the end of the fifteenth century.[50] In the early years, when the Brethren were unusual enough to be feared by the establishment, the absence of vows invited accusations of heresy. They had begun as a lay association[51] and lay involvement was associated, in the mind of authority, with heresy. For his own reasons, Florence "chose rather to be called an abandoned Lollard with his brethren, or to be reputed insane by laymen, than to be named a great lord and master."[52] How far are we, with our hindsight, from ill-informed contemporaries unable to distinguish between this group and the Beghards and Beguines who had flourished in the Low Countries for at least two hundred years?[53] It must be admitted that we know little of the inner life of either.

Two fundamental features of the New Devotion should be noted: deep respect for the example of the early Christians, particularly the Desert Fathers, and a singular attitude towards knowledge.

The Devotionalist's writings, developed often from *rapiaria*, collections of texts for meditation,[54] frequently quote the aphorisms of early monastic ascetic literature and uphold the model of the primitive church. Where we speak of their 'respect' for the early monks, they would have felt it as a relationship: not the abolition of distance but making it come alive. Surely there is such a channel between movements of spiritual renewal, acting always in the 'now,' and the sources of their tradition: ordinarily, the past chokes the future, or vice versa. Recalling the atmosphere of the "ancient house" of Florence and the impressions of his youth, Kempis wrote:

> [H]ere the memory of the ancient fathers and the pattern of the holy conversation of the monks of Egypt—which had lain, as it were, half dead upon the earth—were restored to life; and the manner of life of the clergy rose to that standard of the highest perfection which was set by the practice of the primitive church.[55]

The later written constitution of Florence's house bears this out in more formal language:

> Our house was founded and endowed with its small rents and goods by a certain devout matron in order that, after the manner of the primitive church, devout priests and clerks with a few poor laymen might live there in common by the labour of the hands, namely the work of writing and from

the returns from certain estates; attend church with devotion, obey the prelates, wear simple clothing, preserve the canons and decrees of the saints, practice religious exercises and lead not only irreproachable but exemplary lives, in order that they may serve God and perchance induce others to seek such salvation.[56]

Gerard believed, with others, that the present time was so poor because of the distance separating men from the influence of the founder of their religion. He did not reject current eucharistic practice, for example, but characteristically tried to find a reconciling understanding in the light of his vision:

> In the primitive church all the faithful were used to communicate, in the place of which communication the pax is [now] given, as if it were something of a communication of Christ's body. The reason, in my opinion, why the body is not given communally is that in the primitive church men were better from the heat of the blood of Christ and religion was vigorous and at its acme, which is now grown old, wherefore He has withdrawn Himself.[57]

How, then, should Christians organise themselves? He thought that the decrees of the church should be perused thoroughly, "that thou mayest see the material fruit of the primitive church," and in order "to know what was determined of our forefathers."[58]

We do not begin to understand these Brethren until we realise their hunger for instruction. Lists of writers given by Gerard and others show a commitment to early Christianity, the practices of the first monks and the medieval mystics: most favoured were Augustine and Bernard, with very frequent reference to Cassian, Climachus, Dionysius, Gregory, Jerome, Ambrose, Chrysostom, Isidore and the Victorines.[59] It is clear from context that all were valued for their practical guidance. A letter from the rector of the Zwolle Brotherhouse to the Brethren at Culm, speaks of the vital need to understand works which "define the progress of the spiritual life," which outline a "way" leading to the love of god and neighbour, a way "revealed by a previous complete and utter conversion and by subsequent sound instruction, by the suppression of faults, the fostering of virtue." Such a way, he considered, was revealed by Bernard, Cassian, and Climachus, and in *De Vitis Sanctorum Patrum*, and if it is not followed, "you will help neither yourselves nor others."[60]

Exposure to ancient texts could be, then as now, highly disturbing. Gerard Zerbolt compared the original Christian attitude to Bible reading, as he understood it, with the present authorities' insistence on restricting it to the latinate clergy: had not the Fathers told their people to search the Scriptures for guidance? He believed that, in the course of our heedless daily living, the "natural law" written in the heart became overlaid: laymen returning from their occupations should have the possibility to read the sacred writings which expressed that law, to know themselves as the first Christians had done. Zerbolt was the probable author of *De libris teutonicalibus et de precibus vernaculis.*[61]

As well as providing material for comparison, early writings gave details of monastic ascetic methods, and there can be no doubt that the founders of the Brotherhood made practical study of them. The profoundly simple tales of the Desert Fathers in the *Vitae Patrum* and the deceptively intelligible accounts of their ascetic teachings given by Climachus in the *Scala Spiritualis,* run like a thread through all the material of this book.[62] According to one scholar, the essential orientation of the New Devotion came from "the traditional line of thought received from the fathers and other holy men of the Latin church with the addition of the results of the spiritual intuition of men such as Tauler and Ruysbroeck."[63] We would emphasise the practical application of this received wisdom, for the Brethren were neither dreamers nor enthusiasts. Gerard, for example, strove often during the day "to offer himself to the Lord," and is said to have reproved himself once for only having made this offering ten times.[64] This truly important inner movement is frequently mentioned, directly and indirectly, in the writings of the Brotherhood. Gerard believed the early monks to have engaged in the same struggle for the same reasons:

> It seems to me that the Fathers in the Desert offered short and numerous prayers so that the heart might be always uninterruptedly raised to the Lord and might not be scattered in things, but be dragged away from things, and thus must one act.[65]

His conception of the religious life was based on his opening to the force of the tradition embodied in Cassian, Climachus and Bernard, as mediated in the practice of the Carthusians of Monnickhuizen[66] and Ruysbroeck. His task was to bring what these men and their teachers had gathered into life, into 'the world,' in every way possible. Referring to one of these ways, Kempis wrote:

> [H]e was not only assiduous in thoroughly reading the sacred books but also wrote and carefully published at the earnest desire of others certain short works based upon the genuine sayings of the saints for the use of them who sought his guidance that he might teach those whom he could not reach in person and instruct by word of mouth.[67]

Florence Radewijns based his tracts *Omnes inquit artes* and *Multum valet* on Cassian, dealing, for example, with eight capital sins, a number uncommon in medieval thought but found in early monastic literature.[68] They pose the fundamental questions: What is our duty and our task? What is the fulfilment of God's will and what prevents our co-operation? The discussions or "collations" on practical spiritual problems, recorded by Cassian and others as an important means (and the immediate source of much early ascetic literature), were reflected in the vernacular collations held at the Brotherhouses.[69]

The exemplary teachings of the Desert touched all who were influenced by the New Devotion. Among the English Bridgettines, the study of Cassian and Climachus, being practical, supported their spiritual exercises: Whytford and Fewterer made a translation (now lost) of the *Scala Spiritualis*; Whytford translated two works of Kempis, and frequently quoted Desert sources in his books of simplified religious exercises for laymen; Fewterer translated a book of meditations on the passion which drew deeply on the work of Abbot Cisneros of Montserrat, an important link in the spread of 'the Brethren's' exercises and the development of Ignatian practice.[70]

The orientation of the New Devotion invites comparison with the humanist avant garde in Italy.[71] Both sought to communicate with early sources and broadcast their findings, the Brethren focusing on early monastic and medieval mystical texts, the humanists upon classical and patristic texts; both began the century by copying texts and ended it with the new presses. It is said that one-quarter of all manuscripts and printed books extant from the fifteenth century passed through the hands of the Brethren, who were called "brethren of the pen" in Liege.[72] The first Windesheim canons searched out old scriptural codices and collated them to produce an authoritative Bible for their own use: they discovered "three or four great volumes of the Bible written long ago in very old characters," including one from a house of the Brothers of St. John in Jerusalem, compiled, it was said, from the library of Jerome; the Brotherhouses" constitutions insisted on pure texts of the Bible, "lest one's conscience be hurt by some improper version."[73] Italian scholars scoured the libraries of Europe and Asia Minor for traces of ancient culture, their researches perhaps differently angled, yet their contemporaneity surely more than coincidence. Busch's comment that the Windesheimers esteemed the old witnesses more than the new, catches well the spirit of this broad cultural revaluation throughout Europe.

There was similar companionship over the question of useful knowledge. Petrarch had written passionately that our knowledge never related us to what was really important. He felt, somehow, that he must change himself, rather than continue to accumulate such uselessness: strive to develop the will, not the mind, so that he might be able to love the good and do it, rather than just know about it, while remaining helplessly as he was.[74] He drew much on Augustine, but his followers found a similar message in the classical moralists. Gerard praised these too and frequently quoted Seneca on useless learning.[75] Like Petrarch, Ficino and even Erasmus, he regarded religion as properly the same as philosophy and understood Socrates" aphorism, that virtue was learning, in this sense.[76] Contemporary philosophy, on the other hand, was for him a shadow, a hotch-potch of insubstantial information: "God, God, what a mixture comes forth from the rind and pith of the holy scriptures and the song of the sirens!" Such philosophers erring from the good, lose the truth.[77] The Deventer Brother John Hatten said, "the scripture has a nose of wax and is pinched by different people in various directions."[78] Petrarch had called the true philosopher the lover of God (*amator Dei*), the truly wise man a "philosopher of Christ," phrases later made familiar by the erstwhile student of the New Devotion, Erasmus, but patristic in origin.[79] In view of these correspondences, it is interesting that a fifteenth-century rector of the Zwolle Brotherhouse based his *Advice on various difficulties* on Petrarch's *De Remediis utriusque Fortunae* and that the Brethren printed Petrarch's *De Vera Sapientia* in 1473.[80]

However, in order to follow the Brethren further, we need to look more closely at their attitude to learning, for it shows the quality of experience they sought, and is not so accessible as it might seem. Best known from *De Imitatione Christi*, it is expressed throughout their writings; often labelled 'anti-intellectual,' and reacted to emotionally, it has been little understood. It was knowledge gained in the service of—not ethics, exactly, nor piety in the sense it is usually understood, but a relationship with a higher level, "order," "a portion of the Spirit," "the Fear of the Lord," the opening of another part of the mind to its proper nourishment. It involves a stripping away of the inessential.

> Much study is of little profit unless it be directed to the amending of one's life and to ordering oneself diligently in right conduct . . . a portion of the Spirit is better than much knowledge without devotion, for to acquire the trick of beautiful language is easy but to find the way to good works is harder[81] Since there is no limit to the number of books and treatises and each writes according to his conviction, let us listen to . . . all the readings necessary for sanctity, that is: fear God with childlike fear and keep His commandments with love.[82]

Useful learning must include knowledge of oneself. The Brethren felt called to study differently from the way people were then (and are today) conditioned to study: they sought a knowledge which could, eventually, serve the wholeness of man: 'usefulness' implies an aim, so here is another question.

Scholars have, naturally, seen a contradiction between the scholastically trained Gerard and the views of the Brethren. He was indeed "sated with knowledge": a list of books copied by him and that he liked to possess, comprises almost all known Christian literature, while he could cite without pedantry in one letter, Vegetius, Cassian, Dionysius, Hippocrates, Gregory, Anselm, Climachus and Aquinas, as well as the Bible.[83] (His letters were, however, always couched according to his correspondent, in this case an over scrupulous and intellectual Carthusian.) In the studies he pursued before his conversion, he admitted he had "followed after the shadow of a great name,"[84] and some of his letters do give the impression of mild bibliomania. It is interesting to note, in passing, that his love of books was taken into the Brotherhouses and turned into work: their workshops pioneered the revival of traditional blind-stamped bookbinding.[85]

The equally educated Gerard Zerbolt also took a high view of those "sacred codices" which gave him access to the experience of the Saints: it was remembered that he used to say: "These books declare and teach what we are not able to speak about; for the holy books are the light and comfort of our souls and a true medicine of life, which we are not able to be without in this sojourn here any more than the church's sacraments." He loved the books of sacred theology above all the riches of the world ... for he knew ... that those men who have dedicated themselves to sacred study shall be filled with wisdom and merit to be admitted to the secrets of heaven. . . . Therefore he held books in great reverence, reading in them with great longing.[86]

These words, "light," "comfort," "medicine," should be weighed: traditional metaphor and analogy seek to make comprehensible the experience of a higher level in terms of the one with which we are familiar. These men were simply seeking to be informed, to discover what is not already "known," to hear "what we are not able to speak about." If the ability to inquire from this simplicity must be earned, what must be sacrificed? The study to which they aspired began only at that moment to which Gerard referred, when he said: "the knowledge of all knowledge is for a man to know that he does not know anything."[87]

Gerard suffered from, and for, the way he had studied. He wrote to Ruysbroeck in 1381:

there is nothing new to report about myself. I am always useless, always talking, always greedy and more than greedy for books: to which habit I am forced to set an end, partly for lack of cash, partly because I get tired of dealing with writers and all connected with that.[88]

Kempis tells, in a story recalling St. Francis, that he tried to remind himself of this, intentionally using books that were poorly bound and unadorned:

when he saw one who had a book sumptuously ornamented and noted how carefully the owner looked at it and turned the leaves, he said to him, "I had rather that a book were my servant, than be servant to a book."[89]

He wrote to another scholar:

I can tell you from my own experience that those who set out to study without a firm supernatural foundation will remain jackasses and blockheads forever, even if they study a hundred years.[90]

After his conversion, Gerard's preoccupation with his own learning gave way to the intense question of how to learn, how not to 'remain a jackass forever.' The movement initiated by him set great store on learning which was actively directed, rather than selfishly idle, on study as a practical approach to the sacred rather than an aimless accumulation of information in the outer man. The relevance of his words on conventional learning are not limited to the scholasticism of his time:

Alas how misguided are the young people today, that they, depending solely upon the personal word of Aristotle or of another philosopher whom they personally esteem very highly, persuade and convince themselves of many opinions which they scarcely understand, or indeed even before they have penetrated to the heart of them—solely on account of the person who expresses them. . . . [I]t arises from the fact that when reflecting on the intelligible, people take account of such an incidental thing as another's pronouncement on the subject. . . . [A]nother greater and more widespread hindrance . . . lies in philosophy itself, namely that . . . all students of philosophy, when concerning themselves with the essentials of things, their natures, quiddities, their matter and form and their genera and species, do not direct their minds to reality but for the greater part only to the verbal expressions themselves. I must confess that I philosophised in this manner for a very long time.[91]

In other words, "all learning is pernicious that is attended with loss of honesty."[92] An authentic sound can suddenly be heard, despite its translation, demanding an active search for one's own understanding, subverting our picture of 'devotion.'

The ordinary learning 'of the world' had a crucial part to play in the drama of this search. Gerard wrote of one of his pupils, "he is suitably initiated into the various branches of the *artes,* which help not a little on the way to God."[93] But later, other questions arise. Consider the young Gerard Zerbolt's burning zeal for knowledge, his self-questioning and discipline, and his progression from the university schools to the 'school' of the Brethren:

[He] thought upon the purpose for which he had come [to university] and the reason for which schools were founded, wherefore he applied himself zealously to study; and so wisely did he profit thereby as afterward to deserve to become a learner of that wisdom that is eternal in place of the wisdom of the schools; for by the ordinance of God he came at last to study at Deventer and having found the devout brothers there he attached himself closely to Florentius and being by this time sufficiently instructed he quitted the unstable worldly life for the sake of the love of Christ and his own salvation.[94]

It is a description of the process whereby an individual subject to one set of influences gradually falls, by virtue of his search, under another. The questions of these obscure medieval figures—what is the value of my present knowledge, what must I learn in order to be saved, how can I study in order to be free?—are faced by us also, if we wish to put ourselves in their place and recognise something of what they came together to seek: they are not only 'historical' questions.

Traditional sources state that what a man can understand is a matter of what he is. "There is a knowledge that may be useless and vain . . . that follows truth out of curiosity."[95] Learning included self-knowledge, or perhaps the other way round: it was expensive. In its absence, learning was based on, and fostered, self-delusion, resulting in a further disorientation of man's capacities. In his *Conclusa*, Gerard spoke about what was at stake:

> Through honours and favours and through avarice, which all men study for, a man is polluted and by such a greedy wisdom he is darkened, impassioned, his natural straightness made crooked and his desires poisoned so that they cannot properly discern those things which are of God, nor what is right, nor what is good for his body. Hence it is most rare that the man who clings to knowledge for greed . . . is correct or balanced in his reasoning, just, right or at peace in his living.[96]

What good is knowledge which does not lead to an enlargement of understanding, which limits and weakens what a man is, rendering him less able to live than his uneducated fellow?

Knowledge and understanding ('wisdom') are not the same. On the scale of this tradition, the reception of wisdom meant the awakening of the powers of the soul, upon which the harmonising and reconciling of the whole man depends: it is a question of the quality of man's being, and, therefore, his doing. 'Knowledge,' leaving out the man himself, is—relatively—harmful and external, 'of the world,' necessarily giving birth to unbalanced and partial action: it implies, and depends on, a man's ignorance in other spheres (Gerard mentions the needs of the body), and, particularly, on his ignorance of himself. Our knowledge is rooted in complacency and issues in hypocrisy:

> Most people know many things, but they do not live the better for it. Oh, how they are to be punished, who recite "do this and this," and do not do it themselves.[97]

It was not knowledge that the Brethren sought, but wisdom:

> The Masters of Arts teach the arts of this world but the divine wisdom is taught by the inspiration of God, without any intervening means. Divine wisdom is placed in and impressed into the hearts of men by divine illumination, but the other words by pen and ink written on parchment. As things are, many ecclesiastics rely entirely upon their letters and leave the truth alone . . . take the leaves and abandon the fruit . . . use up their silver, that is their understanding and knowledge, but not for bread, that is, not for such things as strengthen and nourish the soul. That is why there are so many that are sick and weak, that they cannot grasp or comprehend the things that belong to the soul . . . why so many sleep and close the eyes of their souls wherewith they should see God. For they have placed their perfection only in external works and remain there, and do not hear what our Lord teaches:

namely that one thing is needful and that we must pass through our good works and exercises and come to the love of God and union with Him.[98]

Both in relation to the state of affairs that has developed 'in the heart,' and in relation to the possibility 'of the soul,' our learning is a charade. Gerard worked for this to be confronted in his Brethren, that the voice of conscience might be heard and the consciousness of a more whole truth stir a sense of religious duty: a renewal, a new devotion indeed.

In order to communicate concerning these questions, New Devotionalists borrowed the technical, analogical vocabulary of traditional spirituality, but used it distinctively, emphasising certain words which related to their particular way of working.[99] References to 'feeding,' 'mastication' and 'digestion' should not be dismissed as literary conceit or vapid metaphor: in the scale of our material, they reflect a vision that the processes of growth and nourishment are based on the same principles at all levels, that is, whether 'the body' or 'the soul' is in question, a traditional understanding which was always in danger of being dissipated and becoming mere metaphor, through not being lived. Lubert Berner, an early Brother, speaks of an observed process:

> Approach study so as to take food for the soul, in order that, having been reinvigorated in reading, the soul may learn to be occupied with that which it reads and to forget ephemeral things and refrain from offences. At the same time there is not much, indeed not enough, use in studying without mastication and prayer: to masticate it with prayer and longing and send it to the stomach of the soul to be transformed into behaviour and virtue, so that the soul may be sustained by this, like food.[100]

Florence said that the study of a Christian must not be blind or haphazard, and cited Bernard on the need to strive during reading to awaken love, and through love, prayer, so that in studying one may also become able to pray. We shall return to this seminal question of the transformation of energies in "the stomach of the soul," when considering the importance of attention in the Brethren's work.[101]

The Brethren's study was not the functioning of the isolated mind, but an activation in which other faculties might awaken and participate: only then could understanding appear and learning begin. Useful study was work, and work prayer: something being fed. Florence said that a Brother must be prepared to stop studying at a sign and go to other work, wherever he was needed, and in this exercise the New Devotion truly continued the asceticism of the early monks.[102]

Our discussion begins to turn on questions of personal meaning and practical training, the 'why' and 'how' of religion, generally skirted in historical accounts of religion for good reason, but which are central to our subject of reorientation: they will come increasingly to the fore in what follows. The Brothers sought personal and collective reorientation: it was the purpose and significance of the New

Devotion. The fruits of their experiment slowly entered and worked in the consciousness of their time, with far reaching results for the religious life of the sixteenth and seventeenth centuries: but, unless we can grasp something of its inner dimension, the quality of this influence will remain mysterious, for the extant historical material is strangely unresponsive to comparative analysis or enthusiastic intuition.

For a limited period, circa 1400–1500, and in given conditions, men and women from all walks of life joined together for the sake of a common aim; they worked together to find a new way of living, a way in the midst of life rather than apart from it (even the 'monastic' Windesheimers were canons), a way based on ancient Christian principles, yet transmitted to their founders from contemporary monastic groups; they sought a way combining and reconciling the opposites of contemplation and action, in order to have the possibility of being in, but not of, 'the world,' and believed this to have been the sense of Christ's teaching. Borrowing the terminology of Walter Hylton, we have called this way 'the mixed life.' Now we must look more closely at what it could mean.

FIVE

The Mixed Life

We are not members of a religious order but strive and desire
to live in a religious manner in the world.
                                             Peter of Dieburg

While they were working they had recourse to ejaculatory
prayer.
                                             Thomas à Kempis

[B]e inwardly free and master of yourself . . . with the left eye
gaze at the transitory and with the right the heavenly.
                                             Thomas à Kempis

"**B**eing in, but not of, the world," describes a medieval form of the religious life, the essential call of Christian teaching and an elusive human possibility, unconditioned by time, place and tradition.

The meaning of man's place in the world, the purpose of religion and the nature of freedom shifted as monastic religion emerged into ordinary life with the regular canons, the Mendicant orders and the lay heresies of the later Middle Ages, a process continuing through the New Devotion and the Society of Jesus. These 'new' forms were both a working out of material inherent in original Christian doctrines and the result of the search of individuals on the border between orthodoxy and heterodoxy.

Although historically these attitudes were not new, for the individual they were a discovery: this was their significance. The secret of the great influence of the New Devotion lay in small groups having found a new attitude for themselves which corresponded also to the unconscious need of their contemporaries. On the scale of the individual, we see how the appearance of a new attitude to one thing naturally effects everything in a way perceptible to others, whether or not they understand or welcome it: in such a way, it is likely, a certain force was conducted through these groups into the life of their time, with the power of action proper to it, no more and no less. In the fact that new vision, if granted, is intermittent and a better balance precarious, that, without renewal, the old reasserts itself with greater strength (as the gospel story of the seven spirits[1] may be understood), we have one approach to the New Devotion's rapid assimilation to existing monastic forms.

The examination of the relation of 'the mixed life' to current monastic practice and the aspiration for freedom, lead naturally to the fundamental questions of the next two chapters: the Brethren's view of man, his religious duty and practical work, the foundation of their 'new' attitude.

The monastic houses with which they shared their valuation were very few.[2] Gerard rarely discussed monasticism as such, except to imply that the majority of establishments had little to do with religion. His letters show him at one moment directing someone towards a house he respected, at another strengthening an aspirant in his resolve and at another advising an intimate friend flatly against taking vows. Although we lack real knowledge of the context of his words, his high view of the possibilities of the religious life under right guidance is apparent:

> Hasten thou to the places where the Blood of Christ is glowing, in which the presbyters are following the canonical ordinances and living the life of the saints, until Christ be formed in thee and, being spiritually taught, thou art able to walk worthy of God and to recognise and drive back the fire tipped darts of the Devil, the flesh and the world.[3]

Elsewhere he addresses the Monnickhuizen Carthusians as "true imitators of Christ," practicioners of "the discipline of the saints." Here he writes to these same "fitting physicians" on behalf of a certain Ricoldus, with whom he had been discussing religion:

> So far as I can judge, Ricoldus devoutly desires a place in your monastery. He has given the matter a great deal of thought and he thinks with me, surely and certainly, that the monastic life is to be desired and striven for above all things in the world. Therefore we ask you, he and I, to consider his application favourably. I dare to add . . . that, in my opinion, he will . . . in time bear fruit.[4]

He outlines the character and likely difficulties of the candidate: he regarded this monastery as a stable for training horses.[5] In another letter he tells a young novice that the monk's way was, as it were, safe, but by no means easy, demanding profound commitment: the sacrifice of his personal history and the sense of identity it maintained. Payment in advance, a kind of responsibility, was necessary:

> [T]he way of simplicity which you choose now is the best and most agreeable to God. Being received into a monastery is like a second baptism, a putting off of the old man, forgetting what is past: your people, the house of your parents, because the king has desired it. Apply yourself to the internal

affairs which belong to your order and only think of the world to pray and do penance for it. For God is your heritage.[6]

Because of his understanding, Gerard's letters emphasise that monastic discipline was a means. Like his near contemporary Richard Rolle, he recognised the validity, the necessity even, of other ways, with the independence of mind and intuition born of a questioning faith. He wrote to his friend, John Cele, the companion of his expedition to Ruysbroeck, advising him strongly against becoming a Friar: his wish to take vows was an inspiration of the Devil.[7] Once he wrote to John asking him to help a certain man, "because he is yours, poor and humble. . . . Blessed be God, who gives you the opportunity to care for yours, entirely without *votum*."[8] In another letter to a close friend, "old tenant of my heart," who was thinking of becoming a monk, he wrote:

> As I see it, I would not dare to advise you to enter religion, although I have no confidence nor ought you to trust me, because of my ignorance of the way of God. The desire I have in my heart—and yet it may be silly—is that you might remain in the world and not be of the world, because the world will hate you and many so called religious will hate you, since they are of the world and seek their good. But the true religious considers neither this nor that, neither the place, the time, nor the man; they seek not that which is dependent upon the world but the whole world itself or rather what is above the world and all men, both eternal and all embracing, just as you, your father and brother may be united and embraced in an unparalleled way.[9]

This letter, advising someone he regarded as a "true religious" to go to Groenendaal, unequivocally associates Ruysbroeck's teaching with 'the mixed life.'

Traditional religion concerns liberation ('salvation'), but our understanding has been conditioned by the influences of a civilisation in which this plays almost no part: how can we begin to evaluate, as the material bids us, the consciousness of our tradition, now buried in us? Christianity states, in its own language, that man is unfree and that the meaning of his life ('justification') is liberation, whereby he becomes able to serve God. The 'three lives,' corresponding to the three forces of the soul, were essential paths based on traditional knowledge and experience, leading, from their respective starting points, towards one goal: paths always there, whose approaches have to be cleared and refound in each generation. The understanding of freedom informing the medieval versions of the religious way is central to our theme. What slavery prevents men from corresponding to their nature as images of God?

From early times men had sought their freedom outside themselves, according to their lights, in opposition to the heart of traditional culture. Since the Renaissance this external searching has intensified, with the official sanction of a civilisation rapidly developing aims and values running counter to all earlier culture. Despite

the Protestant aspiration to confront at all costs man's inner poverty and the degeneration of religious forms, this shift of focus was facilitated by the Reformation: the
reformers may have wrestled in themselves with their alienation from grace, but the
freedom they won for their new churches was an external freedom from traditional
authority. If the workings of the individual and the lot of multitudes are incommensurate, how is the gap bridged? Did the force of the reformers' turning-within
require compensation? What was the relationship between the violence of their
denial and the external results of the Reformation, its divisions and contradictions?
When speaking of the New Devotion and medieval religious ways we are trying to
penetrate things foreign to modern experience and values, but which had a definite
meaning in the scale of tradition. The Brethren of the Common Life compared their
outer freedom with the restrictions of the religious orders, but the purpose of their
'mixing' action and contemplation was to work for an inner freedom in their life
together, an essential aim of the original asceticism of the monks.[10]

To understand something of the freedom of 'the mixed life' is to pass beyond
the conventional late medieval accounts, for, as the Brethren themselves found,
such descriptions of freedom lacked the sense of urgency proper to such an
important inquiry, being either theoretical and over-generalised or merely
restatements of earlier thought out of context. The question of freedom had been
tied to the monastic vow and needed to be separated: in order to uphold, rather
than diminish, the significance of what a human being is able to vow. In considering whether an action performed as the result of a vow was more praiseworthy
than the same action performed without, Aquinas had resolved in favour of the
vow, on the grounds that to act thus strengthens the will.[11] As fourteenth- and fifteenth-century scholastic thought became increasingly unrelated to life and
actual monastic practice, his pronouncement, together with the saying of Augustine, "repent not of your vow, rather rejoice that you can no longer do what you
might lawfully have done to your own detriment," were 'understood' unconditionally and frequently repeated. Such was the view of the ardent young Erasmus,
that the monk was freer than the layman because he wished exclusively for what
was permitted,[12] and Salutati, in his bland defence of the monk, who merited
greater "benefits of God" than those "who without the vow offer only works."
Salutati mentioned, almost certainly for rhetorical effect and without personal
knowledge, the holocaust traditionally held to be consequent upon the vow, "a
total consumption and burning up in which all that we are and can be we commit
to God."[13] Gerard, whose experience in this matter is less suspect, identified this
as the true state of being a monk: he knew, however, that monastic conditions
were not indispensable for such a purifying process to take place.

Richard Whytford, the early friend of Erasmus ("sincerest Richard")[14] and later
Bridgettine, considered the fathers of the Desert to have striven freely, "without
any bond, profession or promise," to follow "the rule and example of the old
church of Christ . . . in himself and by himself alone." They legislated decisively

in their monastic rules only when a voluntary way of life had begun to decay, in order to restore and support the necessary Christian virtues of poverty, chastity and obedience:

> and so ... those three said virtues, which before were counsels of liberty to everyone, are now commandments and bonds of necessity to those who deliberately profess them.[15]

Does freedom lie in accepting bondage, in being able to submit, or in refusing all external authority? Was the intentional sacrifice of illusory freedom the first real step, as tradition affirmed? Such questions cannot sound truly if they remain theoretical: all depends on the quality of the sacrifice, on whose acceptance and whose refusal, which bondage and intention, freedom from what and for whom. 'Like' it or not, we are already under authority. In some religious organisations the sacrifice of intiative might well be the end of hope. Could a real path demand the assumption of obligations in complete ignorance of one's strength? The monk was asked for his faith, but this is not an explanation. The adducing of authorities and vanquishing of imaginary opponents, with which so much of our second and third hand material is preoccupied, is a poor echo of the magisterial conformity of a living tradition: a turning towards multiplicity—the 'yes' and 'no' of ordinary discussion—in the face of a real question.

Of what is the vow an expression? Gerson pictured a devil travelling about the world confusing everyone, particularly monastic aspirants. If it is men's nature to live in society, why do they wish to flee the world, where their salvation may be found under the one abbot, Christ? The law of freedom given by God and purchased by His Son, should be enjoyed by all: to assume the extra obligations of the Rule, when we cannot even obey the basic commandments, is to court unnecessary sin.[16] The distinguished preacher of Mainz, Gabriel Biel, seems to have taken lessons from this devil. He joined the Brethren in 1465 and wrote of their work in *De Communi Vita*, three-quarters of a century after Gerson: they lived in the freedom of Christian law under the said abbot, without obligatory observances and beyond the precepts of the monks, humbly fulfilling the apostolic admonition to remain in the station to which they had been called. In Biel's view they were freer, because they did not vow in excess of their strength. As for the Way of the Monk: "He who is in the world, let him flee to the cloister; but let him beware of sleeping there."[17]

In search of awakening men had turned, from time immemorial, to the intellectual, emotional and physical disciplines of the traditional spiritual Ways. The degeneration of the medieval monastic way of faith and the systematic intellectualisation of theology, philosophy and metaphysics, constituted the real crisis of our period and made the renewal of a practical Christian discipline a necessity. Every necessity has a history. The Hildebrandine Papacy's affirmation in the eleventh century of the distinction between sacred and secular had become, slowly but surely, identified with the unconditional upholding of ecclesiastical authority, thus losing its real force and meaning. Medieval monasticism reflected the consciousness of this distinction in all its phases, but, with the coalescing of a more urban civilisation, a search in the conditions in which people found themselves—a life governed by dualities—had to find its focus: much was at stake. The Christian 'way in life' was a reaffirmation of traditional teaching, although its interpretation during the sixteenth and seventeenth centuries became mixed with an outlook beginning to diverge fundamentally from the traditional.

The 'mixed life' had been explored amongst the Military and Mendicant orders and tertiaries, in the *vita apostolica* of the twelfth-century canons,[18] in numerous charitable and craft fraternities and, not least, in various heretical groups. The vernacular discourses of the Dominican Meister Eckhart (*c.* 1260–1327) contain the essence of all the Brotherhood worked for. The 'lay monasticism' of Erasmus the populariser was not formulated in a vacuum.

There were parallels to the Brotherhood in fifteenth-century Italy. We have already heard Valla arguing that to be religious was to be a Christian, irrespecive of clerical status, that a life pleasing to God could be lived in 'the world.' By the beginning of the sixteenth century, groups of laymen and women wishing to follow Christian teaching without altering their outer circumstances were disturbing the authorities. These Italian "evangelicals" were trying to "emancipate the ideal of Christian perfection from the monastery and carry it into everyday civic life, to seek self-sanctification not in the convent but in the home and office."[19] In one of his popular *Dialogues*, Bernardino Ochino, the Capuchin General and later Protestant, discusses this question with a certain noblewoman. "I have a good wish to become perfect," she says, "but I would not wish it to be too difficult." She does not wish to enter a nunnery or take vows, because "that obligation to mortal sin seems to me to send one into great danger." Ochino replies that she should enter a new order, so to speak, the perfect Christian state in the world, for monastic religion was superfluous in her case:

> This is a religion so perfect that there, where it is, everything is divine. Here it is not necessary to change places, just manners; to change one's way of living, not one's way of dressing; to cut away all sad thoughts and desires, not one's hair; to pray to God with the heart, not with a mouth glued together, to obey God, not men; to be modest with the heart and the mind, without feeling for earthly things, having all the virtues for company.[20]

In moving outside the monastery, religion had to move inside men. This was the drama of the age.

In France, during the 1490s, John Standonck had established a community of scholars in the old College de Montaigu. They lived under an ascetic regime but took no vows. The young Standonck had fallen under the influence of the Brethren at Gouda and is said to have stocked the college library with the works of Gerard Groote, Mombaer, Zerbolt and Kempis. The scholars made *rapiaria*, collections of extracts from their reading as material for meditation, practised a daily 'examination of conscience' and confessed their faults to each other, all usages of the Brethren.[21]

In England on the eve of the Reformation, literature issuing from the Bridgettines and Carthusians introducing spiritual exercises into daily life expressed the same movement and will be extensively dealt with later.[22] The Dominican William Peryn's *Spirituall Exercyses and goostly meditacions,* was dedicated to an exiled Bridgettine nun in 1557, but intended "generally for all others that desire to come to the perfect love of God and to the contempt of the world": it prescribes intensive meditation on Christ's life leading to a virtual *imitatio*, a radically new experience in which activity and contemplation are organically related. In his sixth exercise, to obtain a "conformity" with Christ, he speaks of the way in which the body is included: the meditation is a "printing deeply in your soul and flesh His passion and death, that they shine out of you like a lantern," a striving to conform all thought and manifestation to those known to have been Christ's, so that

> wheresoever you be seen, heard or touched, there be nothing found in you, but that which was in Jesu Christ and then shall be seen in you, that you are a very Christian, a servant and lover of Christ.[23]

According to Peryn, if this conformity is desired sufficiently intensely in heart and mind, and if self and self-will can be, "in a manner," forgotten, a new state may appear, in which

> for the vehement, burning love of Him, your mind may run so much upon Him that you do take no heed . . . what is bitter, what is sweet, neither hour, time, nor space, nor place, nor mark not one person from another, but in all things you must seek, consider and remember your Lord God, and His blessed will, pleasure and honour, seeing verily your saviour Christ in his members. And thus doing you do live a contemplative life in an active life. For in your outward doings you have contemplation spiritual of God and find Him everywhere, and in every thing specially you do recollect yourself wholly and do enter into your heart and searching the bottom thereof, resolving and resigning yourself, do put yourself wholly in the hands of God.[24]

Without direct experience of the darkness which has taken the place of the 'recollection of oneself,' the drift of this remarkable passage communicates a dubious, possibly pathological state; without practical knowledge of these exercises, how can they be impartially judged? It is partly a question of the subjective historical language of *imitatio* description, but also, more urgently, whether something far more fundamental is being expressed between the lines. Is it not the whole meaning, that the Master is absent? The fruit of this exercising, by which we are known, is a deep need arising from the realisation that the recollection of ourselves—the real 'I am' of which the saints and prophets spoke—is, in fact, in abeyance, its place having been usurped: just that elusive sense upon which the hope of all genuine religious teaching is based, but which, by a strange delusion, is regarded by almost all of us as already a permanent and secure possession. The essential material of this book points again and again to this unknown diagnosis.

There are similar passages in the Brethren's writings. Peryn's account marked a stage in the broadcasting of exercises which had, hitherto, been practiced under guidance in special conditions. He was describing an experience which, if his humility is to be believed, he had not himself undergone.[25] The *Exercyses* were based on the work of the Fleming, Nicholas Van Ess, in which scholars have discerned a marked Jesuit influence: the presence of the New Devotion in the life of the monastery of Montserrat at the time Ignatius came seeking his path must again be noted. Peryn's book is also closely related to the native tradition of devotional mysticism discussed in our first chapter.

If this way, harmonising action and contemplation, actually corresponded to the life lived by Christ Himself, as was believed, and as such lay outside time, its influence as an ideal became associated with a great variety of impulses and aims: the common desire of all fifteenth- and sixteenth-century reformers to return to the Christianity of the Gospels; the iconoclastic urge to root out the accumulations of the past and rediscover a radical Christian path; the pious striving to imitate Christ through prayer, exercises and meditations on the Passion, in submission to the authority of tradition; the individual's wish to find a place within himself—rather than in a monastic location separated from life—to which he could return through his own discipline, in search of the freedom to be religious. The New Devotion was an important focus for these diverse impulses in the century before the Reformation, a central influence on the shift of values from the monastic to the lay religious ideals of the sixteenth century. In the words, not of Luther or Latimer, but Gerard Groote:

> Christ would rather see a wife obedient to her husband and quietly performing her daily tasks, than any ascetic doing penance and not obedient or kind hearted.[26]

The wish to experience ritual, especially the sacraments, more deeply, was fundamental to the work of these fifteenth-century schools of 'imitation' and meditation. At the basis of all ritual, had there once been an empirical method by which might be obtained the experience needed to use external forms more intelligently, and thus verify their content?[27] The raw urgency of this wish, at the level of the individual's need, was to break the surface of early-sixteenth-century society, conflating levels, confounding his separation, demanding a response: the tradition must be verified, its meaning renewed, or it must be abandoned. But the work of the New Devotion translates as the renewal of participation. Wessel

Gansfort's *De Sacramento Eucharistiae* (*c.* 1500) gives an insight into these techniques of remembrance and recollection which lay at the heart of 'the mixed life.'

He exhorts "ordinary men," that is, laymen, to be "constantly remembering the Lord Jesus," because "there is no nearer, shorter, straighter way to the blessed lot and better portion of Mary, the sister of Martha."[28] Although Martha and Mary were the conventional types of action and contemplation, they are not seen here as the antithesis of lay and religious, for the layman's conformity to Mary lay not in joining a religious order, but in practising the inner discipline of "remembrance."

Christian life is a path upon which there are beginners and those who are advancing, objectively differentiated by the degree to which the Kingdom of Heaven is awakened and active within them:

> Here on earth it is small and still sleeping, and though so potent, is like a dead grain of corn; yet with advancing cultivation it is to be aroused from that sleep of death and inactivity.

The Christian "is still, in a certain sense, lying dead and buried."[29] The beginners on the path are babies: "in regard to the deeds of the higher life they are asleep and therefore are like unto the dead." They may have faith, but they cannot do works.[30] He is not equating these "little ones" with the laity, nor the professional religious with those who advance, nor even meaning the majority of people, lay or religious, when speaking of "little ones," for he states clearly that these already have faith.[31] There is another agenda. The work of the "little ones" is to "remember," while those who advance must "consider."[32] "Remembrance" is "the stomach of the soul," the technique of the mixed life, that which unites the two sisters. Through the "wisdom" of remembering, "we may sit at Jesus' feet with Mary and at the same time minister with Martha."[33] To "remember" means to contact the life within us,[34] which can deepen the experience of the sacrament and our whole existence, becoming a bridge between our ordinary life and our religion, enabling us "to be fed" by the world around us in a new way.[35]

> Remembrance . . . is the proof that he truly eats. For Christ says, "whenever two are gathered together in my name, there am I in the midst of them."[36]

The indispensable preparation for this spiritual-sacrament lies in the participation of the whole man—"heart, spirit, soul and brain" and "the mental acts of the three faculties of the soul"—in the taking of 'food.'[37] We are what we eat, says Gansfort, and so we must work for better food, "food that perishes not":[38] what the Desert Fathers called "bread of angels."[39] If a man can practise these things, "his heart will be strengthened unto a higher step of life,"[40] and he may become fit, in time, for "the service of love," "genuine love" that is not egoistic, through which "he saves himself": "to love is to live."[41] This is the true worship, alone worthy of God: coming to it, a man may enter "the holy of holies" in the "Temple of the Lord," already a "priest," indeed, "whatever his order, degree, sex, age or condition."[42]

Although these few extracts hardly convey the depth of Gansfort's thought and feeling, they do illustrate his particular intensity and allusiveness,[43] common to all New Devotional writers who worked in the same practical tradition. He is saying that God is approached more effectively with the help of an inward discipline of meditation and remembrance, discernment and love, which open the heritage of ritual and sacrament, than through ordinary submission to the external framework of conventual discipline in such schools of Christianity as most monasteries had become. This effective approach is made through unknown psychological territory, where nothing is as it seems. In his wish to revitalise Christian forms from within, he focuses on the degree of human wakefulness ("remembrance") as the missing ingredient of a real spirituality.

Gansfort's teaching informs two directions, towards religion in life and life in religion, thus embodying the New Devotion as a bridge between daily experience and monastic commitment: a bridge admits movement in two directions. Windesheim had been founded to protect the Brethren,[44] to give those able to benefit from submission to monastic vows in their further journey along the path begun in the Brotherhouse, the possibility to do so in conditions infused with the same understanding and principles. Later, when congregations of canons regular affiliated to Windesheim had spread through northwestern Europe, the Brotherhouse, under pressure to conform, became more often than not a stepping stone to the monastic life, but this had not been so at the outset: then there had been a choice, the transition had not been automatic. A letter of Florence to the prior of Windesheim discusses the case of a certain cleric who wanted to enter a monastery:

> I would not, however, have you commend him much or draw him in to take the vow if he show unwillingness. For there will be danger to our community, dearest Father, unless we are cautious in looking to the persons we accept, or whom we send forth from us. If any of those whom you purpose to invest, wishes to belong to us rather than to join your society, I should doubt whether I ought to advise him to take the monastic vows without the adequate desire to do so on his part."[45]

Choice and responsibility: experience with the Brethren was helpful, perhaps crucial, to the future monk and the passage to conventual life was encouraged if deemed helpful to the individual in question, but it was not automatic. In this can be felt the care of elders and the significance of 'free-will.' The Brotherhouse existed to prepare men for a more becoming ('mixed') life, wherever it might be.

Neither Gerard nor his disciples were monastic reformers, although later Devotionalist-canons like Busch turned to this. Florence's successor at the Deventer Brotherhouse reputedly said on his deathbed: "although according to the church the monastic state is more perfect, yet if anyone has lived perfectly in a humble state he will receive the reward of a perfect man."[46] Gerard Zerbolt, in his defence of the Brotherhood against the Inquisitors, used the word 'religious' to refer to the devout, rather than as a synonym for the regulars, and, bearing in mind the Papal prohibition of new orders, went on to differentiate between the Brothers and the monks.[47] Gerard had reasoned about the matter as follows: the monastic life is a complete dedication to the service of God, and the way to this is through a veritable holocaust, yet for this experience the monastic life is not indispensable; the same conditions of study and service, mitigating the subjection of man's higher parts to the desires "of the body," are necessary whether a man is a monk or not. The New Testament teaching, which the monk tries to obey, must guide also those striving for perfection in 'the world.' He considered, like Colet and many since, that the religious did not necessarily merit their name, and that there were people who, never belonging to the official "state of perfection," attained very much.[48]

The Brotherhood founded by Gerard represented this possibility in life. His spirituality, according to one scholar, had a strong lay character intended to direct the "man in this world" towards the love of God in all things.[49] The head of each Sisterhouse was called "Martha"[50] and we find frequent emphasis upon action and activity in the writings of the New Devotion. "Learn," said Kempis,

> how much greater is the virtue that is tested by action and thus rendered clearer and truer, than that which depends only on thought and imagina-tion.[51]

It is said that Gerard intended to form a 'city of God,' comprising clergy and laity of all social ranks, united by one aim: the "common life" could be lived in any cir-cumstances, in a secular community of copyists, such as existed under Florence's guidance, or in lodgings in private quarters, or, for that matter, under a monastic rule.[52] On this path each Brother was sustained by his fellows, by the renewal of his own *intentio,* by his religious exercises and by obedience to his superior in experience. Godfrey Toorn, rector of the Deventer Brotherhouse (1410–50), said that if the Brethren behaved like people in ordinary life, they were even worse, because they had an aim: other people, he implied, had none.[53] Their focused atmosphere made a vivid impression on the young Kempis:

> Never before could I remember having seen such men so pious and burning in the love of God and their neighbour. Although they lived in the world they had no part in ordinary life and were not effected at all by its affairs. Remain-ing at home quietly, they worked carefully at copying books and were insis-tent in studying continually sacred literature and devout meditation. While they were working they had recourse to ejaculatory prayer for their relief.[54]

In the early days, when the relationship with the original Brothers was intact and the inner demand great, Windesheim was not easy to enter. We are told how "certain devout and competently learned men" and others "of less education, very strong and constant men," were turned away, while "laymen of good will" and men who were "of no learning in the world yet of good experience" were accepted into the company.[55] The grounds of this discrimination are significant. The Brothers themselves continued to attract laymen: a certain Rodolph, for example, who "took high views of our system and its exercises,"[56] and Matthias, who managed external affairs at Deventer, "placing himself in the midst of cares and outward errands, so that the Rector and Procurator and the others might remain in peace . . . and he managed these cares as if without care." Matthias read studiously and practiced meditation during his work, so that, in the words of the mid-fifteenth-century Brother chronicler,

> he became so illuminated that, as regards the remedies against vices and the practice of virtues he knew how to give such clear counsels and to bring forward such apt proofs from the Scriptures, as to seem rather to be a cleric than a layman. . . . Moreover he was united to his clerical brothers in hearty affection and good will; nor did he, as is the case with laics, readily differ from them or turn from them with grudging ill will.[57]

By the end of the fifteenth century the individuality of the Brethren had been undermined. There are reports of them canvassing on behalf of the monasteries among the students in their hostels, and even, according to Erasmus, forcing them into religion in collusion with the Friars,[58] the very orders with which Gerard had refused to deal. By 1485, nearly all the German Brotherhouses, and perhaps some of the Dutch, had become, in effect, houses of canons, their chapels, collegiate churches and their rectors, provosts; the time given to choir prayers had expanded and even their terminology had drawn closer to the monastic with the use of words like "order" and "habit."[59] Peter of Dieburg, Rector of the Hildesheim Brotherhouse, responding to a suggestion in 1491 that the Pope be petitioned to rule those priests apostate who left the Brotherhood without entering a monastic order, took the opportunity to restate their principles:

> We are not members of a religious order, but strive and desire to live in a religious manner in the world. It would seem to me to be to our disadvantage to try to obtain an order from the Apostolic See that such persons should be compelled either to enter an order or to return. It would do us no honour to sell our liberty, the great glory of the Christian religion and with great difficulty obtain chains and prisons in order to please and copy the religious orders. We should then become slaves, just as if we had taken a solemn vow. The only thing to do then would be to accept a monastic rule.[60]

Did their assimilation to the monks signify the dissolution of the mixed life into its constituent parts, the loss of that balance between the active and contemplative lives within which they had taken their stand? Situating themselves in life but separating themselves from the influence of contemporary monasticism, they had worked for a true inner freedom within that life: if their gradual assimilation to religious bodies that had become passively subject to the influences of the world, actually meant that they lost the possibility of working for this freedom, then it was indeed a degeneration.

While staying at Monnickhuizen, Gerard had formulated his "conclusions and propositions, without the vow, in the Name of God."[61] The Brethren's view, that the vow was not a tool for beginners, was based on their understanding of human nature, on their conviction that the Christian's dedication needed to be perpetually renewed. The vow could not do for a man what he could not do for himself. Their daily religious exercises, which will be discussed in detail in a later chapter, were concerned precisely with this renewal. Whether the ability to be continually renewing intention is a necessary precondition for the effective once-and-for-all renunciation and rededication of the vow, and whether, without this, there is no possibility of advancing on the monastic path, cannot rightly be answered, even perhaps understood, by the academic who deals in generalisations while standing apart.

The Brethren were, undoubtedly, practical men who distrusted theorising in these matters. They had seen through a certain hypocrisy and it made them intent:

> Some consider it of much worth that they fast much, keep vigils, sing and study much and do other outward works, and such people think that it [religion] consists in just that . . . they sparkle and gleam outwardly because they have the appearance of being devout, but inwardly they lack the true virtues and do not possess the true freedom but only the appearance of such . . . they have a false taste of the sweetness and they arrive at the wrong things: they lack the taste.[62]

This text goes on to emphasise the significance of the inner *intentio*, rather than the form of behaviour, and refers the reader to Cassian, the recorder of the Desert Fathers. Kempis writes in the same vein:

> This must be realised, that many stand in the place of the saints, who, in their manner of living, nevertheless are very different from the saints. Many actually bear the name of religion, who are, however, stupefied by the life of the world. Many outwardly rest from official occupations who are not at all wholly at rest from desirings for outward things, many seem to be placed in quiet who do not strive to use it for themselves, as is fitting.[63]

The outer ('active') and the inner ('contemplative') life are represented in Christian teaching by 'Martha' and 'Mary.' According to the New Devotion, the right relationship between these two sisters is when each does the work proper to her. We have called this right relationship 'the mixed life,' and Kempis describes it as follows:

[T]hese two sisters should not, however, be separated from each other, nor should they contend concerning their function, but rather let them apply themselves equally to receive Christ with hospitality, so that in all things they may be able to stand perfectly.[64]

Both monk and layman courted an imbalance in themselves. How could Christ be "received hospitably," so that a man might be able to "stand perfectly," how could he use "quiet" for himself "as is fitting," how should he not separate quiet from activity, how might the "true freedom" of a right relationship be "tasted": by what means had these simple men found a way in to the practical meaning of Christian teaching that they were able to experience these questions? It was said of John Hatten, the cook's servant at Deventer, that

although with Martha he was attending in outward things, yet with Mary he was continually directing his attention towards those things which were needed and longed for ardently within, as much as he was able.[65]

The study of these texts brings us to the deceptively simple conclusion that it was just this division of attention which lay at the heart of the New Devotion. Without this practical work, the mixed life became only another ideal, of as little significance as the monastic in its decadence.

If the Brethren's particular struggle for the freedom of genuine religious feeling prepared the ground for the fundamental Jesuit experience of undergoing the *Spiritual Exercises*, it also entered into the specific Protestant experience of moral dilemma and separation from God, when an ideal somewhat like the 'mixed life' supplanted the monastic as the framework for a reformed Christianity 'in the world': the current generated by both these experiences in the next century was very significant. The Brethren's influence became mixed as it entered life.

The desire for freedom, "the great glory of the Christian religion" was the issue of the Reformation The annalist of the New Devotional house of Doesburg perceived the early followers of Luther to be united by their attitude to personal freedom, rather than by any belief in the theological tenet of solifidianism, which has been promoted as their intellectual credential in modern historiography. The monastic converts to Luther were now valuing the freedom from the 'weakness' of accepting the restraints of the Rule. The annalist added, thoughtfully, that Luther's views on monasticism and the importance of freedom in Christian life were probably sound, but that many of his followers understood wrongly the general idea of freedom, and Luther's use of it in particular.[66]

The New Devotionalists often spoke of freedom, not as a revolutionary slogan, nor even as an aim, properly speaking, but as the lawful result of an inward state of service, that is, right order:

that freedom of the spirit which is the principal good of the spiritual life. For the affections are fettered by many things and, having been fettered, they are controlled. Such affections, infecting the soul [*anima*] resist the peace of the heart and the quiet of the mind, which is very often defiled and disturbed by the cares connected with them.[67]

Gerard's words convey something of that freedom of impartial self-knowing which pervades the ascetic writings of the Desert. The freedom he valued was to be found as much within the tasks of everyday life as at prayer, not surely without great discipline, search and, in a sense, violence,[68] but without doing violence to one's true nature; while, in our view, the freedom which tended to become the goal of the Reformation was a freedom from various external 'injustices,' from Papal control of the church, the monastic rules or ecclesiastical convention, a freedom it was hoped would inevitably result if these 'causes' were abolished. When it was drawn into the turbulent stream of life, this is what the desire for freedom became. Yet freedom must be found in life, for where else should it be?

What difference can be divined between Valla's words to the monk, "is there no middle ground so that we only either have servants or serve . . . [how] to be able to be without a lord and to live and know without a master . . . to be the master of myself," and this summons to mastery from *De Imitatione Christi*?

> [Y]ou ought diligently to aim at this, that in all places and in every action or external occupation, you be inwardly free and master of yourself and that all things are under you and not you under them; that you may be the lord and ruler of your actions and not a slave or mercenary, but rather a freeman and true Hebrew having passed to the lot and to the liberty of the sons of God, who stand above present things and see the eternal, who with the left eye gaze at the transitory and with the right the heavenly, whom temporal things do not draw into adherence, but who rather draw these things to serve well, just as they were ordained to do by God and appointed by that supreme craftsman, who has left nothing disordered in His work.[69]

The question of the relationship between inner freedom and order leads us directly to the material of the next chapter.

SIX

The City of the Moon

See, man! You have now reached the land of estrangement.
> Gerard Zerbolt

My lord God, deliver me from my enemies . . . in truth, I who
have lived against myself until this hour will begin now, with
your grace, to live to myself.
> *The Meditations of Saint Bernard*

Traditionally, religion had been concerned with man's liberation from the
power of illusion, and so it is here. The objectivity of Augustine's, "God is
truly worshipped only by faith, hope and love,"[1] becomes, in Gerard Groote, a
question of experience and an experienced question, truly subjective, like an
inner avowal: "Man will consider himself master of his lower self as long as he has
not sensed the lack of faith, hope and love in his mind."[2] The illusion of mastery is
the mark of the citizen of "Jericho," the city of the moon, and his plight, everyman's, is the subject of this chapter.

But, let us pause. In an attempt to discern a coherent complex of traditional
ideas and practical instruction—a living teaching—in the opaque historical fragments left by the Brotherhood, we have come, with the material on which this
and the following chapter is based, to the heart of our search. Having arrived at
an intensification of meaning, we arrive also at an intensification of difficulty.

How is it possible to present with clarity powerful ideas, whose function it is to
awaken men to their deep self-ignorance and heedlessness, to their personal nullity, without taking them seriously on their own terms? And what would it mean,
to take them seriously? Is discussion of these questions as if they were understood, inherently dishonest? If we take the traditional vision renewed by the
Brethren as merely furnishing evidence for a particular historical trend, we are in
danger of forgetting that they were being called to face their own truth, that
receptivity to ideas could be a matter of life or death. To accept or reject their
stark diagnosis, even tacitly, is to miss the point, for it concerns the actuality of

115

the human condition, as it had been established in the Christian psychology reaching them and as it was being verified in their own observation. And the reason why the knowledge and understanding of Christian teaching are not the same, is implied time and again in the material.

Its central theme of man's almost hopeless inner disorder and the need to seek a remedy, is related directly to the essential meaning of 'religion,' the act of binding together again. Is a teaching not the bearer, through its own force, of certain specific experiences? This material points to a fundamental experience, at once new and deeply remembered, in which a natural acceptance of the necessity of working for salvation ('spiritually exercising') is confronted by an equally sincere acknowledgement of the virtual impossibility of doing anything. The question of *how* men might stir themselves is not passed over, indicating the kind of source from which this renewal of the teaching came. The ideas of this new devotion discover a Christianity which is part of the forgotten inheritance of the modern world.

Entering this world of sacred myth and tradition, we hear that man is analogous to God, made in His image, although on a different scale and level, but that this verisimilitude of the whole has been grievously defaced, due to a calamity which befell our forefathers in very ancient times. Since then, our manner of living has, inevitably, been the result of a disordered functioning, our passive acceptance of which 'normality' constitutes the terror of our situation. Christianity taught there were 'three powers' in man which form a lawful trinity, but which have been disharmonised, preventing the higher trinities, for whose reception we were created, from working in us. These powerful ideas are restated in the writings of the New Devotion and in the sources they studied. To grasp their meaning anew, laying aside what has reached us through the conventional channels concerning 'the fall of man,' would be the beginning of understanding the Brotherhood and their exercises.

It was said, with that strange mixture of literal truth and allegory characterising spiritual tradition, that we, being made in God's Image, have yet gone down from "Jerusalem," our fatherland, the holy city of peace, into "Jericho," the city of the moon,[3] where we now exist in states of constant mutability, "subject to things."[4] We live under the influence of the moon. This is a result of what befell "a certain man," our ancestor, but also of the way we live now, which causes in us that "uncleanness of heart," through which we have become used to this unworthy dependence and love it.

Gerard Zerbolt, one of the first Windesheimers, describes the psychological consequences of this situation with great acuity in *De Spiritualibus Ascensionibus*. By the "law of descent" (inheritance), we are no longer what we were intended to be, have lost our way, forsaken and forgotten "the mountain," our home, and live in "the valley" of another and distant land. Therefore, a "great labour" is necessary in order to return.

In truth, the distance between the valley of tears where you are now established and the place in which the Lord once placed you, namely the state of your uprightness, is great and beyond measuring. And that is why a great ascending is necessary, or rather, in fact, many ascendings. There is a need for a great labour, if you wish to return to that place. . . . Indeed, as the holy gospel says, you have gone away into a very distant region.[5]

This refers, above all, to our psyche, our so-called inner life, and means that, in actuality, we have been

brought into conflict and made narrower and, in all the energies and powers of an excellently ordered soul [anima], deeply damaged.[6]

Our distant ancestors had in themselves "original justice," harmony as the saints have known it, "an excellently ordered soul," the obedience of the lower in them to the higher, freedom, being in God's Image, 'paradise.'[7]

But we are in chaos. At the beginning of his exposition, Zerbolt makes a crucial observation: our situation, although desperate, is not irredeemable, because it *is* possible to know ourselves, objectively. Knowing that we sleep, we awaken, or— we are "totally insensible."

These very energies and states of thinking and feeling, having fallen from their condition, have been correspondingly fragmented and disordered. They are not, however, utterly destroyed, but have in themselves a rhythm contrary to their former; their movements are themselves alternating and their impulses quite different and inconsistent with each other. In fact, you are experiencing this every day, not to say continually, unless you are totally insensible.[8]

In this last sentence, Zerbolt surely addresses his fellows; he may refer, indirectly, to the collations, or exchanges of personal experience of their struggle.[9] He is saying that the first step for anyone wishing to escape from this alien valley is to study the terrain directly, not merely through the accounts of previous travellers, however wise or holy.[10] The situation, although universal and impersonal, is also particular and individual: the saints may have struggled, but it is I who am unfree.

The states Zerbolt proceeds to describe were not intended to be our lot: they are not 'the will of God.' Their main characteristic is that nothing in us does the work for which it is best suited and which it was meant to do. We are, in this sense, unjust. Florence writes on this:

[R]eason blinded by sin often accepts falsehood for truth; the warped will takes evil for good; the unstable memory busies itself with those things which cause it to grow restless and vacillating, as it no longer concentrates itself on the highest good, where it might have everything.[11]

In such disorder, we do not—and cannot—remember God, or ourselves, and this is unjust. Zerbolt, who almost certainly knew Florence personally, describes the significance of these states in greater detail:

> [N]ow these same energies and operations are set in motion in quite a different way than that which God had implanted, disposed to evil and falling always into unlawful desiring. Since that, the reason itself, having been rendered aimless, wandering and blurred, often accepts what is false as if it were true and frequently entangles itself in useless and inquisitive enquiry. The will has been rendered crooked and perverse: it often chooses the lower, loves what belongs to the carnal body, while not valuing at all what is spiritual and heavenly. Moreover, the power of desiring is destitute of its proper object and, in a way, slides into eager desiring which arises from the body and its pleasures, and from the eyes, namely, gluttony, luxury and avarice. The irascible force is truly disordered and has slid into the pride of life and glory of the world. Hope does not hope in God but in its own deserts, or in money, either hoping more or less than is justified. For example, we are unhappy if we lose money or at the disapproval of the world, we are happy in gluttony and luxury. We are angry at our brother.[12]

Action, so-called, issuing from this inner disorder is 'of the world' and cannot be other than 'sinful.' The early monks censured a living which was only 'active' in this sense, because, from the standpoint of the activation born of contemplative order, it is blindly lower. At the same time, guilt about such 'sin' is inappropriate and ineffective, the result of wishful thinking and misguided self-condemnation at the very same level. More wholesome was the possibility of directly knowing this inner situation, elsewhere described as 'sleep,' for what it is—with help, and from an awakened conscience, turning in another direction: as it was said, towards God. The tradition of which the New Devotion was an expression affirms everywhere that this was the point; for us it is the question.

Zerbolt could not have written as he did if the work of the New Devotion had not been based, like the Desert Fathers', on the ancient dictum 'Know thyself,' and on the search for an inner, self-cognising attention, the indispensable practical means.[13] The subject of the Brethren's study was themselves in relation to a higher level, God, and its object was the possibility of changing this relationship. Study was never an end in itself. The conventional formulae of Christian doctrine must be challenged by this new attitude. In what sense has Christ's inconceivable sacrifice saved 'the Christian'? What is his responsibility before this awesome deed? What does it mean, actually, that Christ has destroyed death and released the world from sin, as the liturgy has it? Although Christ died for men,

> [H]e has by no means restored us to the state of original uprightness, nor transformed the powers of the soul [anima], but he has left their transformation to us, to be striven for and earned through holy exercises.[14]

Disorder, 'sinfulness,' is *our main help*, if it can be faced.[15]

The crucial question for the would-be Christian is the content and quality of his emotional life. What does he actually love? Zerbolt says of "the state of wretchedness into which we fall,"

> we must put order in the heart by ascents of raising ourselves, so that we are able afterwards to arise again from this place.[16]

Sow now, reap later. Without better order in ourselves nothing new can take place, yet men have grown to love all that perpetuates their disorder, all that binds them in "the city of the moon." This kind of 'love' is "impurity of heart" and it is maintained, almost continually and unconsciously, by the way we live: our "gold" has become increasingly intermingled with "baser matter," our higher part more and more "subject to things" and, through love of them, kept in subjection. Above all, it was a question of habitual thought and emotion:[17] thus Augustine, pointing to the text in *The Song of Songs*, "order love in me," had written of Lazarus lying in his tomb beneath the "mass of habit."[18] All this is spoken of in the Bible, but, in the absence of self-observation, is it understood practically?

He continues his diagnosis of man's low level of being:

> [W]e have incurred a disposition to eagerly desire the lowest things and, unless we continually withstand these eager desires, we are compelled by their impulse to stoop even lower. But, in truth, you have not only not with-stood, but, bending to them, you have gone down with them and adhered to desires, states of mind and emotion coming from the body and things of the world, and, consequently, you have let go the inclination to good that remained in you, whether it came from your natural or spiritual gifts. Over and above this clinging always to valueless things by desire and emotion in this manner, you are rendered conformable and of like nature with them in a way, and thus you gather a kind of filth, as it were, or stickiness in your desires and energies and, being connected with an even lower place by this as by a glutinous slime, you are held in check there in a certain manner. . . . See! You discern what uncleanness of heart is, about which you read in the Scriptures and perhaps you do not understand it. It is, without doubt, those states of thinking and feeling by which you, in disorder, bend down and hang on to the lowest part, and whether through these states you are drawn to gluttony, luxury, vainglory, pride or the praise of men, it is called unclean-ness of heart. This uncleanness has been brought about by the fall of the first man, but you have added much more to it by your habituation, your mental and emotional states and your adhesion to them.[19]

Although the impression must remain that words of this kind, like those of the Desert Fathers, originally derive from an exact and merciless self-observation of inner processes as they are taking place, supported by a precise and subtle spiritual psychology, it is easy to sense how, through repetition and blind faith, they could degenerate, in the absence of this conscious direction, into the suppositions and assumptions of mere moralising. How quickly does perceiving the darkness become dreaming of the light! With the historical records of the New Devotion we are still, just, with unfreedom as a materially experiencable fact in man, rather than an idea or belief with which to beat others.

In the symbolism of the Bible, all men are prodigal sons who have squandered their substance on prostitutes, who exist in an estranged place (*regio dissimili-tudunis*),[20] feed swine under compulsion, and have nothing for themselves—and who have yet to realise that something is wrong. Exactly this is the condition of mankind, our common plight, according to our own tradition. Their personal intuition of this truth gathered Gerard Groote's original friends and their individual attempts together to "put order in the heart by ascents of raising ourselves" related them subsequently within the common life as Brothers. To those who came after, they were examples. The Bridgettine, William Bonde, wrote one hundred and fifty years later, in a work aiming to make available the "secret doctrine of perfection" according to "the sentences of illumined doctors . . . and the spiritual exercise and experience of holy fathers," that "in the cleanness of heart stands the end of our journey."[21] Whether we regard the Brethren's diagnosis of man to be the fruit of unbalanced superstition or of an enlightened and terrible insight, they felt themselves to be in question: the truth of their situation, beyond opinion, lay in testing it against their fidelity, through their exercises.

Their experience released a force into the life of the time, touching directly those in personal contact and gradually diffusing more widely. Although the subsequent multiplication of manuals of systematic meditation and exercises for introducing order into everyday living was strongly coloured by the formulations of Ignatius, behind the Jesuits stood the New Devotion, drawing on a broad and deep medieval tradition of practical spirituality reaching back at least to the Desert and fed by many diverse streams.[22] Ignatius invented nothing. The Abbot of Montserrat, Garcia Cisneros, at whose house Ignatius studied in 1522 during a critical time in his own search, wrote of man's condition and its possible transformation in exactly the manner of Zerbolt and his teachers:

> Most beloved brothers, in the book of Psalms it is written that that great man, the prophet David, said 'I have meditated in the night with my heart and been exercised frequently and searched my spirit.' Consequently for the dedicated religious, who greatly wishes to transform his spirit [*spiritum*], which had been made "in the Image and likeness of God" but has slid from Jerusalem to Jericho, that is, from a condition of stillness and peace to so great changeableness of state, and to restore it to its original condition, it is indispensable that, taking the example of the most honourable prophet mentioned above, he should correct, cleanse and purify his spirit from

imperfections and errors as well as from spoiled mental and emotional states, that he may be healthy in order to be able to have the capacity for gifts of grace and of the spirit. For it is written that "into the ill disposed soul [*anima*] wisdom will not enter, nor will it live in a body subjected to sin." And because, as Augustine says, order is that through which peace and still-ness in the soul takes place, and that which is not ordered is not able to be permanent and still while that which is ordered is permanent and still and manifests great strength in the soul, becoming to its enemies terrible like the ordered forces of a fortress, therefore it is valuable and necessary to give some way and assign some exercises that have been determined upon, so that knowing what we must do, we may always be still and, frequently exer-cising ourselves in these things, we may transform our spirit to the original dignity that it has lost.[23]

Cisneros wrote for his monks, Ignatius for a religious order in the world and his sixteenth-century adapters for ordinary laymen, steps in a process of transmis-sion that had passed already through the Brotherhouses and convents of the Devotion.

Our subject becomes densely interwoven at the turn of the century. During the 1490s Cisneros returned from Paris with copies of works by Zerbolt, Radewijns, Kempis and Mombaer. The latter's *Rosetum exercitiorum spiritualium* (1494) refers in the prologue to the search for "the man," oneself:

I was troubled, and I searched out the man who had fallen away, from Jerusalem into Jericho, stripped of his original justice, dignity and purity. It will be worthwhile to reshape and reform him, and to restore him to his for-mer level, first by cleansing exercises, after the example of the most radiant prophet David: to search that spirit, and purify and correct it from vices and corrupt effects.[24]

Cisneros may well have met Mombaer,[25] who was in Paris in 1496 with John Stan-donck, introducing Windesheim's discipline to certain Augustinian houses. Cis-neros' *Directorium horarium canonicorum* and *Ejercitatorio de la Vida Espirituel* outlines a system of meditations and exercises intended to strengthen the atten-tion during the performance of the canonical hours (*horarium*) and celebration of the Mass, and speaks of reestablishing internal order and balance in the spirit of the New Devotion.[26]

All our material concerns the practical relationship between religious ideas and method. On the one hand, there is the ancient teaching of the microcosm, that the lower was created in the image of the higher, the idea of a universal but hidden order in all worlds, and on the other, there is man himself, in the wrong place: and there is, or has been, religion. Let us remember "the possibility that all gen-uinely religious ideas have an empirical basis, and are embedded in a method by means of which a man may obtain the experience necessary to verify and use them."[27] It is difficult to define 'practicality'—the key to a lived understanding of these ideas—due to the relative coarseness and superficiality of the evidence of religious culture available to us[28] and the shallowness of our experience, but its presence can be immediately sensed: the records of the New Devotion hint at its possibility and the Brethren believed they had a method. The meaning of method must relate to a known way of opening us to the action of genuine religious ideas. Therefore the New Devotion emphasised the growth of the attention of the heart through self-knowledge.

The tradition that the soul comprised three powers, a trinity of memory, will and understanding, had been repeated throughout the Middle Ages, but how often made the subject of genuine enquiry, how often experienced? The humanists used it to support their contention of man's great worth, but man as he was or as he might become? Antonio da Barga, for example, wrote that "the great excellence of man is also shown in that God said 'in Our Image and likeness,'" explaining that this image meant the memory, intellect and love on the authority of Augustine's *De Quantitate Animae* and *De Trinitate.*[29] Augustine had said that the Holy Trinity governed and interpenetrated all phenomena, but that, due to the conditions in this world, the three aspects of the Trinity had become, somehow, separated, and thus acted unequally.[30] We recall, here, the description of "the land of estrangement" (*regio dissimilitudinis*), a place where there are no correspondences. In the world outside us and the world within, there are only vestiges of the Trinity, "God's footprints" as Bonaventure had called them.[31] The idea of a trinity in man which corresponded to higher trinities was used in challenging ways by thinkers like Valla, Ficino and Pico,[32] but was often expressed more simply—reminding us that it is not only an 'idea'—in devotional treatises for laymen.[33] Colet's *A ryght frutefull monycion concernyng the ordre of a good chrysten mannes lyfe* (1534) states:

> [I]t is high wisdom and great perfection to know yourself . . . and most especially it is necessary for you to know that God, from His great grace, has made you His Image regarding your memory, understanding and free will.[34]

In the gulf between ancient teachings of the threefold order of reality and man's actual nothingness, this practical material resounds with the need *and* the possibility of experiencing universal laws, "God's love," in oneself; with the hope that a conscious self-remembering might renew religion.

Before examining the practical work of the Brethren in the following chapter, we must look at one of their most valued guides, *The Meditations of Saint Bernard on acquiring knowledge of the human condition*, an anonymous treatise placed by Gerard Groote directly after the Bible and "the lives and collations of the Fathers" in a list of necessary reading,[35] and widely reprinted in England during the sixteenth and seventeenth centuries.[36] The Cambridge student who made an English translation about 1496, "because I would have so good and so profitable a thing common to many," spoke of the hunger for practical guidance in Christian living in his introduction.[37] Its appearance in print shows a relic of the real quality of an earlier time becoming an influence during a later crisis. This translation was reprinted at least three times before 1525.

Our situation is described in a distillation of the tradition of practical Christian mysticism:

> Many there be that know & understand many other things & yet they know not their own self. They take much heed to others, but they look not well to themselves. They leave their inward & spiritual things and seek God among outward things, the which is within them. Therefore I shall turn from those things that be outward to inward things, & from inward things I shall lift my mind to things above, that I may know whereof I came and whither I go, what I am and whereof I am. And so, by knowledge of myself I may ascend & come to the knowledge of God.[38]

Our knowledge is empty because at its centre there is an absence. We do not know ourselves, do not sense ourselves, *and are not even aware of this*, content to remain unable to pay attention to this essential relationship, little suspecting the scale with which it is connected. To turn towards ourselves, from deep need and with help from 'above,' would be something like 'repentance': but the means for us to look at ourselves in the light of what is greater, while at the same time receiving what is beyond us in the ground of what we are, is not there. A 'bridge' is missing. It means, in relation to the Brethren's exercises, that all of our attention is being caught by, drawn into and involved in whatever is happening, inside and outside us, with which we identify 'ourselves.' We are being robbed, constantly, unconsciously. In the hypnotised belief that we can find purpose as we are, without turning in another direction, our lives will remain empty, our knowledge groundless, however lofty our ideals: and we will not know it, which is perhaps just as well. Disharmonised and unbalanced, upside-down and inside-out—and this refers to 'normal,' not pathological, states—the real questions of a man's life cannot begin to sound in him, as they might: from where can he sincerely ask, which means hear, the question "whereof I came and whither I go, what I am and whereof I am"? The idea of intentionally freeing and directing the force of attention runs through the *Meditations* like a hidden thread.

Why does the author connect the search for knowledge of oneself with the knowledge of God? Augustine was perhaps a source here, where he said, "for you are indeed more secret than my innermost and higher than my utmost." The relationship between 'above' and 'within' evokes the levels of universal order and what Christianity calls grace. Man is a similitude of the Whole: the mind that seeks to know, the understanding that can recognise the truth and the will that can love that truth, resemble in their right relationship the three aspects of the

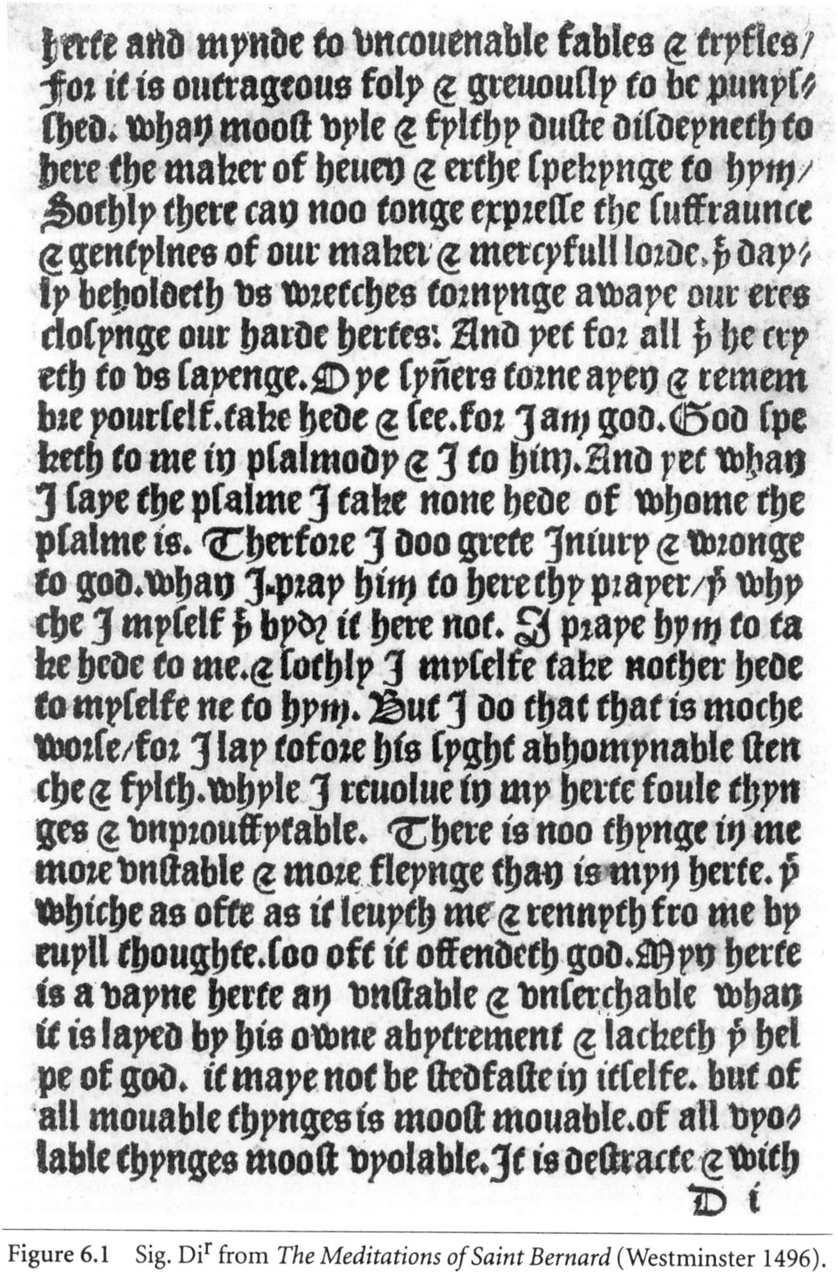

herte and mynde to vncouenable fables ⁊ tryfles/
for it is outrageous foly ⁊ greuously to be punyſ/
ſhed. whan mooſt vyle ⁊ fylthy duſte diſdeyneth to
here the maker of heuen ⁊ erthe ſpekynge to hym/
Sothly there can noo tonge expreſſe the ſuffraunce
⁊ gentylnes of our maker ⁊ mercyfull lorde. ꝑ day/
ly beholdeth vs wretches tornynge awaye our eres
cloſynge our harde hertes: And yet for all ꝑ he cry
eth to vs ſayenge. O ye ſyñers torne ayen ⁊ remem
bre yourſelf. take hede ⁊ ſee. for Jam god. God ſpe
keth to me in pſalmody ⁊ J to him. And yet whan
J ſaye the pſalme J take none hede of whome the
pſalme is. Therfore J doo grete Jniury ⁊ wronge
to god. whan J-pray him to here thy prayer/ꝑ why
che J myſelf ꝑ bydꝛ it here not. J praye hym to ta
ke hede to me. ⁊ ſothly J myſelfe take nother hede
to myſelfe ne to hym. But J do that that is moche
worſe/for J lay tofore his ſyght abhomynable ſten
che ⁊ fylth. whyle J reuolue in my herte foule thyn
ges ⁊ vnprouffytable. There is noo thynge in me
more vnſtable ⁊ more fleynge than is myn herte. ꝑ
whiche as ofte as it leuyth me ⁊ rennyth fro me by
euyll thoughte. ſoo ofte it offendeth god. Myn herte
is a vayne herte an vnſtable ⁊ vnſerchable whan
it is layed by his owne abytrement ⁊ lacketh ꝑ hel
pe of god. it maye not be ſtedfaſte in itſelfe. but of
all mouable thynges is mooſt mouable. of all vyo/
lable thynges mooſt vyolable. Jt is deſtracte ⁊ with
D i

Figure 6.1   Sig. Di^r from *The Meditations of Saint Bernard* (Westminster 1496).

Trinity. But because the *Meditations* is a practical rather than a theological guide, it emphasises that the nature of this resemblance depends on the manner and object of a man's love.[39] We are not saints, perhaps not even men as intended, are only 'images of God' insofar as we are able to receive the influence of this higher order and conform to it: as we are, we bear the name of image unworthily, "emptily" (*in vacuum*).[40] In remembering and submitting to something beyond our little selves, we begin to work as Providence decreed.

> Thus I find in my soul the Image of the high & glorious trinity, to the which. . . . I owe to refer and order all my life, that I may remember Him and put all my pleasure & contemplation in him. . . . It is the Image of Him not only that it remembers itself, understands itself and loves itself, but because it may remember, understand and love Him, which made it. And when it so does, then it is wise.[41]

In the growing certainty that there is another reality within, a quite different sense of responsibility takes root ("I owe"). It is with the quality of remembering, understanding and loving that real happiness, and real suffering, are connected.[42]

There can be no lasting happiness while a man is subject to impossible dreams, contradictory impulses and unstable moods, for it has not been merited. Ignorant of himself and thus irresponsible, he misuses whatever is given to him; believing that his unhappiness is caused by hostile events, that everyone and everything is against him, he is not able to see that, fundamentally, "there is no thing contrary to me but I myself."[43]

If at this point he remembers religion and wishes, as might be, to relax somehow the grip in which he is held, to be still and turn to prayer, this would be the beginning of difficulty and real unhappiness, rather than its end. For what does he find?

> Oft times when I pray in the church, I take not heed what I say. Soothly I pray with my mouth, but while my mind is wavering without, I lose the fruit of my prayer. My body is within but my heart is without. And therefore I lose what I say. . . . My heart is a vain heart, unstable and unsearchable when it is led by its own judgement & lacks the help of God. It may not be steadfast in itself, but of all movable things is most movable, of all violable things most violable. It is distracted & withdrawn by infinite things, and runs hither and thither by innumerable ways, and when it seeks rest among divers things it finds none but bides still like a wretch in labour, void of rest. It concords not with itself but discords from itself. It skips from itself, it alters and changes the will . . . for it will & will not & so it tarries never in one estate.[44]

This condition of instability is verifiably true, not a matter of 'faith': "In fact, you are experiencing this every day, not to say continually, unless you are totally insensible," as Zerbolt said. Thus observed, the heart is like a mill, always agrinding what has been fed into it, including material that may have a damaging effect upon its working parts. The heart and mind never cease from this automatic associating day in and day out, "always dreaming & thinking on whatsoever comes thereto." If there is a lack of material to drive them, they consume themselves.[45]

Is it not naive to expect the God of justice and majesty to hear the prayer of this mad machine? In truth, it is not He who is absent! The prayer of such lack of presence has no quality, neither force nor truth. If a man could listen to God, all might be different, but it is not even a question of this: if he cannot listen to himself, how might God hear him? Nothing is attuned in him, nothing corresponds to a higher level, there is no channel open. Can he know it?

> I pray Him to take heed to me & soothly I myself take neither heed to myself nor to Him. But I do that that is much worse . . . while I revolve in my heart foul things and unprofitable.[46]

Prayer is not evasion. It is just at this moment, when a man senses his own truth without words, that the possibility of turning in a new direction is close and real help may appear—for what is true corresponds to itself. Listening, he may hear. God sees, as it were, that he is closed,

> and yet for all that He cries to us, saying: "O you sinners, turn again & remember yourself. Take heed & see, for I am God."[47]

As this is a practical tradition, a uniquely possible 'action' ('inaction'?) is indicated: perhaps 'activation' is the best description, if we mean by this a connection, however fleeting, with a higher, more conscious level of being. This text in Latin translates literally as: "Return, prevaricators, to the heart, become empty and be aware, because I am God"[48]

What is the value and result of such an experience?: a new attitude and question. 'Love thy neighbour as thyself,' but who is he? Can he be satisfactorily 'known' as before, through emotional reaction for or against? He is our mirror, the image of God in the same sense as we ourselves, to be known insofar as we are able to be inwardly related. Before we can love others, we must learn to love (or at least care for) ourselves—and not the 'self' we consider 'ours,' and not in the way we cannot help loving, that is, egotistically. Impartial seeing of others, from which alone genuine love can arise, depends firstly upon impartial seeing of ourselves: usually, the payment for such seeing is the inability to bear another, genuinely. (This is how I would paraphrase the remarkable text following, but I would like to quote it here untransliterated for once, to share its authentic taste:

> yf thou love me bycause I am ye ymage of god, I am as presente to the[e] as thyne owne persone, for the same thynge that thou arte, I am: sothely every resonable soule is the ymage of god. Therfore he that seketh the ymage of

god in himself, sekyth as well his neyghbour as his owne self. And he that fyndethe it in sekynge in hymself perceyveth and knoweth it in every man. Sothely the syghte and perseveraunce of the soule is the understondynge and knowlege. Therfore yf that thou see thyne owne persone, thenne thou seest me that I am the same thynge that thou arte. And yf thou love god, thou lovest me, that am the ymage of god. And I in lovynge god, love the[e]. And so whyle we seke oo thynge, and goo towarde oo thynge, let us alwaye be present togyder in ourself, that is to saye, in god, in whome we love togyder.)[49]

In the same spirit 'Bernard' says that the common injunction to amend faults is meaningless unless they can be deeply experienced: ordinary, mechanical self-criticism and its attendant guilt is not virtue:

there can no man judge & rebuke himself perfectly, for he is so much occupied & troubled with so many thoughts, that he, in manner, knows not himself, so that he knows not well what he does or suffers.[50]

I am saying that these texts, and almost all of the material associated with the Brotherhood, is practical because of its origin in an oral tradition of experienced spirituality. These "meditations" were carried across (literally 'trans-lated') to the early sixteenth-century literate public, and to us, from the experience of generations of largely nameless contemplatives, powerhouses of the tradition. We tend to associate practicality with comprehensibility, but these instructions are practical because they have been lived. Conformably, but deceptively, simple, indeed they are not easily accessible, being convoluted and (apparently) naive by turns, with traces of the assonance and compelling rhythms of an intense, but reported, speech: the most significant obscurity may well be in us.

Being practical, this teaching is bringing the kind of experience with which a man can cut through. It is saying that, as if asleep, we have become habituated to the inner chaos and lack of right relationship in which we are accustomed to 'live': in division our heritage is wasted.[51] If we could live as Christ indicated, these divisions might be healed, but of what use is it to dream of that while remaining oblivious to the facts of our present life? What kind of religion springs from ignorance? Why is the passage between seeing the darkness and imagining the light so swift? If we were able to follow Christ's teachings . . . an incomplete body of instructions and knowledge, inherited in fragments from ancient times, that have perhaps hardly begun to be understood, even felt, directly. The very sense of 'knowledge' in this connection is unclear. Is it not naive and unwise, then, to talk about 'following' this religion? It may well be that many of these teachings do not apply to men as they are, blind and unmoved by their heedlessness, calling for a level of commitment almost no one is in a position honestly to make, pointing in a direction they are powerless to go and assuming a self-knowledge few possess, or would wish to. 'Bernard' is implying this:

Almighty God bids me give him mine heart and because I am not obedient to him when he commands, I am rebel to myself and therefore I may not subdue me to myself, till I be subject to Him & serve myself against my will, the which will not serve Him with my will. My heart makes more in one moment than all men in the world may make perfect in one year. I am not united & oned with God & therefore I am divided in myself. I may not be united & made one with him but by charity, nor subdued to Him but by humility, nor I can not be truly meek but by truth. Then it is expedient that I discuss & examine myself in truth.[52]

A strange sincerity associated with the glimmering of self-knowing calls us back in shame from the objective, and in a sense impossible, religious injunction, "Love God," to the beginning: a realisation, not negative, of our division and an *intention* arising directly from need, "it is expedient that I examine myself in truth." Ignorant of such knowledge and not demanding it from ourselves, we can come into contact with neither the demands nor the rewards of authentic religion. Therefore "inward reading" of "your own self" is the beginning.[53] The path out of the 'city of the moon' leads through what medieval devotion called "compunction," an altogether-suffering for what we see in ourselves.

'Bernard' concludes by identifying and describing the inner tyrant who rules our lives: a servant who has usurped the position of the real master and holds us in bondage; the "old man" who must be "crucified" on "the cross of Christ," for the three powers to be harmonised as God's justice intended.[54] Of this we cannot speak, nor follow further.

If Christianity is concerned with payment in the deepest sense, it has a high price and must have. The real Christian life of which the tradition tells, begins not from where we are but from a place unknown to us; and from 'nowhere' how can there be a bridge? Our material returns again and again to the importance of knowing where we actually are. It is clear that such a 'difficult' understanding of religion can never be widely accepted, but it is upon this ground that the way of the Brethren and the monk are related. The special conditions and discipline of the monastic life were originally intended as *a bridge* to that unknown place where Christian truth could begin to act (rather than the place itself), and it is just in this sense that we try to understand the work of the New Devotion in the next chapter, namely as a bridge, allowing movement in the two fundamental directions, towards and away from 'the world.' Thus the 'monastic' *Meditations of St. Bernard* could become a seminal work for the Brethren of the Common Life and for later generations of lay Christians. It is very interesting today.

Trying to detect the evidence of a search, we have come upon the union of ancient psychological ideas of man's condition and practical experience of his possible liberation, and have seen some of the ways in which it was being expressed during this period. We are describing, not exactly the transmission of spiritual teaching (this is beyond the range of our evidence), but the making available of specific experiences, hitherto valued in small groups, to a larger, more heterogeneous audience, a process which becomes, in the end, popularisation.[55] "The chief reason for which I wrote this book," said Fray Francisco de Osuna of his *Third Spiritual Alphabet,* published in Spain in 1527, "was to draw everyone's attention to this exercise of recollection."[56] Ignatius used the same threefold division of the psychological functions,[57] directing the exercitant to the "interior knowledge" of himself sinning, the experience, through grace, of the disorder of his manifestations and a true knowledge of what actually happens 'in the world,' that he might be horrified and seek to order himself more rightly.[58] Spiritual writers of the sixteenth century, not only Jesuits, elaborated on the proper relationship of the three powers in prayer and meditation.[59] The Spanish Dominican, Luis of Granada, wrote of the need for the will and intellect to be balanced: the will was a blind power unless the understanding preceded and informed it of its proper object, what is to be loved.[60] It had been proven that "superfluous speculation," which 'normally' displaced the real functions of head and heart, stealing their energy and allowing them no room to work as they might, could make way for a more harmonious relationship.[61] Experiments had been made under the special conditions of monastic discipline, but the results were significant to all who sought. Luis speaks of the practical payment, the possibility of economising the energy available to us.[62] He shared a commitment to the teachings of the Desert with the Brethren, and his writings on prayer and meditation enjoyed remarkable popularity in Elizabethan England.

All the sources touched by this influence agree, that before any real good can come to us, our psychological, physical and spiritual powers must, somehow, be balanced. Luis describes the calling of a "general assembly" within a man for the common weal, and speaks of the soul "recollecting all her forces together."[63] The Jesuit, Luis de Puente, commented on *St. Luke* 10:42, "but one thing is needful."

Thou art troubled and perplexed with many thoughts, affections and cares but the most necessary point is, that thy soul be one, that is to say, united and recollected within itself.[64]

Compare *The Meditations of St. Bernard,* where it says:

[W]atch well & wheresoever you be, be thine own & spend time well and thou shalt be there in surety. . . . [G]ather together thy soul with a whole felicity & joy & abide at liberty in thine inward habitation, walking in the largeness of thine heart. Make ready therein to Christ a resting place and a large chamber. For the mind of a wise man is always to God. We should always have Him before our eyes, by whom we have our being, our life & understanding.[65]

We have discovered a web of historical, textual correspondences with an elusive action at their heart—the recollection of oneself in order to be in the presence of God—the meeting of two histories. The spiritual exercises and meditations of Brotherhood of the Common Life were concerned above all with this movement between outer and inner life. The Devotionalist Rudolph Dier de Muden used to say:

> My years are many and there is scarcely any fruit of them in me; pray therefore for me, that at least in my decrepit age I may be able to recollect myself.[66]

Wessel Gansfort, whose outlook owed much to the long period he spent with the Brethren as a young man, stated in *De Oratione* that, to be able to pray freely a man must disengage himself, in a certain way, from "the outward man," recollecting all of himself, so that the three powers of "the inward man" might work more as they were intended:

> [I]f prayer will be unencumbered and ready at hand it is necessary that a man shall be disengaged from the whole outward man, his faculties recollected from all the parts of images and concepts that have been attached to them, so that he may deliberate, meditate and be able to be effected by what he is praying and not pray from another place according to religious ceremonies in his usual way.

The three parts of the interior man, memory, intelligence and will, each have their proper work, but without "circumspect and attentive" meditation they cannot function rightly: they remain "sterile . . . the coffin of meditation," "blind . . . disabled . . . momentary."

> With these three, if a man is engaged in good, it is good, if in evil, it is evil and dead. Therefore whatsoever shall be a hindrance and barrier to these three turning to the good . . . will impede the reformation of the inner man. And, in consequence, whatever things undermine the first foundation of the inner man, namely meditation, are obstacles to all piety and the reformation of the inner man. In meditation, however, although he may not withstand the multitude and variety of inner speakers, with attention and deliberation he may plainly withstand. Therefore, whoever wishes not to err in choice and counsel, whoever wishes for the fruit of deliberation, let him seek to escape multiplicity and changeableness.[67]

Another exposition of systematic meditation by Gansfort, *Tractatus de cohibendis cogitationibus,* was dedicated to the canons of Thomas à Kempis' house of St. Agnietenberg.

There is an interestingly titled work on the same theme by the canon Gerlach Peters, *The Soliloquy of a certain religious who perseverantly collected himself from the multiplicity of his heart to the one highest good:* it concerns the preparation of oneself for receiving the operation of the higher trinities, "Blessed is he who thus alloweth the divine working in himself."[68] The *Myroure of Oure ladye*, written for the Syon Bridgettines, bearers of the influence of the New Devotion in England, emphasises the prime importance of "keeping the heart," which the author believed to have been the practice of the Desert Fathers. He says that to "stable the mind" and "gather the mind in onehead" must be the "chief labour" and "continual travail" of the brothers and sisters of Syon.[69]

The practicalities of this travail are the subject of the following chapters.

SEVEN

The Daily Work

Let us always watch and pray.

Florence Radewijns

It is not possible to seek the glory of God if a man rushes into a matter so impetuously that all his strength is occupied in it.

Gerard Groote

Without ceasing I will strive to be inwardly renewed before the Face of the Lord. . . . It is not enough to know by estimation merely: but we must know by experience.

Gerlach Peters

If the passage we are about to make from spiritual psychology to daily work seems awkward, what lack of connection in thought and feeling is being glossed over as the transition is made? What, exactly, is incommensurate here?

Conventional Western education since the Renaissance has supported the division between 'ideas' and 'life,' between intellectual aspirations, moral experiencings and physical work, and it remains difficult to bridge, even to experience. Yet we are speaking of men trying to confront themselves and their God within a relatively unified spiritual tradition: faith in search of understanding. The passage between recognising the force of a teaching and its incorporation is 'the daily work.' There is a path to be trodden, a place to be found—intentionally—again and again, between what can receive the imprint of a higher level and what cannot, if the truth of one part is to be distributed to all of a man, that he may become able to live it.

The Brethren's attitude to learning was not ours. Their bridge was sought in their exercises, in the renewal of attention and in the attunement of personal intention to occupy a rightful place before God and between the opposing influences of 'the world' and 'the spirit,' 'heaven' and 'earth,' within and without. Their daily work, supported by a tradition that equated useful learning with unitive understanding, was the exploration of 'Jericho,' the verification in action of spiritual psychology: they worked for self-knowledge. A new, effective devotion could not come from old thought or feeling, of themselves or Christian teaching. The original Brotherhouses were "schools of heavenly exercises," where the ground was prepared for this learning. The exercises were part of a technique, essentially inherited from the early masters of monastic asceticism, for making the passage from belief to faith, ordinary knowing to understanding, relative division to unity, blind slavery to an awakened, self-cognising service. Self-knowledge was not an end in itself.

Thomas à Kempis tells of a young merchant, John Ketel, who, dissatisfied with his life, had conceived "a good inspiration" to serve God, but did not know how. In the 1390s he was interviewed by Florence at Deventer, with "certain other men of good purpose." He was accepted,

> and he entered the school of heavenly exercises in order to learn the will of God in the house of Lord Florence, where many men had gathered together and, established in humility and strengthened in divine love, were serving God.[1]

He stayed for the rest of his life. He was searching for a new beginning and the account he left of his work in Florence's kitchen shows that he persevered.[2] The personal fragments attributed to John and his companions constitute the material of this chapter, but they are not answers in themselves: they are the prime source for any investigation of the New Devotion, because they reveal the inner life as directly as the written word may, yet they are almost incomprehensible to us. This is due not only to the subject matter and language of the texts, but with the limitations of our vision as observers.

Difficulty of understanding is considered to be the result of complexity or sophistication of subject matter; enough knowledge having been gathered, we assume that understanding automatically follows. But that is not the case here, for it is simplicity which confronts us. We cannot take the understanding of the key words of this material for granted: 'attention,' 'work,' 'silence,' 'renewal,' 'meditation,' 'presence,' 'humility' and 'intention.' We think of attention as something we already possess, definite, unvarying and knowable; of work as external doing, an exercise of 'will' imposing our notion of order, and ourselves, on a static situation. These assumptions are misleading. The Brother, mindful of his limitations and ignorance, aimed at service, submission and conformity to a higher will. This was his work, and the material being worked on was, necessarily, himself.[3] This is, indeed, incomprehensible to us. The likelihood that the Brethren's injunctions had a practical, as well as a moral, sense, also calls us to pause. The instruction to refrain from unnecessary talking, for example, refers not only, perhaps not primarily, to 'morality,' to making a man 'good,' but to an exercise by which he might experience something of himself, lighten his ignorance. Is an outwardly silent man any better than a talkative one, particularly if neither can help it? It is implied that inner morality depends on intentional self-knowledge and opening to grace, not the 'choice' we imagine. This material concerns preparation for a traditional religious Way, of which few now have real experience or understanding: the very idea of a 'Way' or 'Ways' is unclear, although in earlier times it had a very precise meaning. The ignorance from which our difficulties stem is not only historical.

The acquisition of self-knowledge and faith in God can be discerned as aims of the Brotherhood, the earlier records focusing on knowledge, the later speaking more of faith. What was this liberating knowledge and saving faith? Knowledge and faith, as we generally experience them, are antagonistic opposites, whereas religious tradition speaks of a knowledge and a faith that are harmonious, as in the saying of Anselm, "I believe in order to understand."[4] The great aims of knowing oneself and having faith in God are at the heart of the Christian teaching, but further from the values and actualities of ordinary life than is often supposed: this interval will be obscured with wishful thinking, or fear, unless aims can be related to practical possibilities, for the far journey must have a beginning here and now, if it is ever to become a reality. These beginnings—renewals—are 'the daily work.' We are told they can bring an inner order, the like of which a man rarely experiences otherwise and without which his religion, and much else, will remain ineffectual. In striving to "turn and remember himself," he acquires a measure, the seed of self-respect.

The focus of all the Brethren's attempts was 'to be in the Presence of God,' whatever one was doing outwardly. This meant a new relationship with oneself, as John Ketel said:

> It is necessary for me to have at all times the presence of God before my eyes . . . and especially to have before my eyes my simplicity and that I am not wise.[5]

It is easier to recognise in this a fundamental spiritual exercise than to know what is to be exercised. These fragments are never directed to inform thought: they are relics of a living experience, the smoke generated by a fire beyond our perception. In remembering the question 'What is to be exercised' as we confront these texts, we may approach the Brother's position in his work between known and unknown, the evil and the good.

With this preamble, let us begin with the candidate for the common life as he enters a community of strangers, foregathered in the name of the most intimate questions. Difficulties of relationship are surely the first obstacle at the threshold of brotherhood. He would have been told, one way or another, that indulgence in idleness and daydreaming was not only useless, but harmful: these comfortable habits had deep roots, as would become apparent if he tried to struggle with them. Gerard had said God could not be sought whilst seeking one's own repose, that his indolence was "useless to myself and others."[6] A certain kind of choice was fundamental to their work.

Our true Brother, according to Florence, is the one who hates our defects and helps us surpass them.[7] These men sought a new relationship with themselves, and therefore with others: a way of working together in which they helped themselves in a certain way, thus becoming useful to others with the same intention. In this work, it may be impractical to begin with altruism. "Love thy neighbour as thyself" cannot refer to the unseen, helplessly egoistical compulsion to help only oneself, which colours most relationships, most of the time. The gist of these texts is that the daydreaming born of idleness results in self-isolation: in losing oneself, one loses others. 'The Common Life' is a deep need, not a fact. The remedy for idleness is anything but senseless busyness.

Later Brethren remembered Gerard as someone who, "fleeing idleness, was always exercising himself in something useful for his own edification."[8] For those moments when one activity changes to another, the Brethren were directed to exercises of meditation, so that while awaiting a sign to come or go, they were not vacant.[9] In the language of the *Meditations*:

> Other things belong to other than us, but time is ours only: therefore watch well & wheresoever you be, be thine own & spend time well and thou shalt be there in surety.[10]

The use of time included the indispensable need to pay for our livelihood:

> Florence wished never to be found idle, but strove to spend his precious time fruitfully, taking utmost care, however much he was a beneficiary, not to eat his bread for nothing and without working for it.[11]

Fantasies had no part in the religion sought here. Florence said:

> [Y]ou must always strive to occupy yourself with some good thing and pay altogether no attention to imaginings (*phantasiae*).[12]

Among the "multiplicity of reasons" given by Zerbolt for the necessity of manual work, was this:

> [B]ecause the enemy gets again more possibility of entrance into us through temptings when we are idle than when we are busy. Indeed . . . he that is occupied is worked on by one demon, but if he is idle he is disquieted by truly innumerable demons.[13]

The equation of "demons" with dispersed energies is interesting. Did these New Devotionalists, who suffered "no time to pass uselessly without special exercise, either inward or outward, mental or manual,"[14] inhabit a different world to those religious satirised by Simon Fish as "these greedy sort of sturdy, idle, holy thieves,"[15] or was it the same world transformed by another attitude?

The Desert tradition of manual work in the service of religion was transmitted to the Brethren by Gerard. Mombaer quoted him as saying, "labour nourishes generous spirits." In his turn, Florence diligently observed what he had learned and received from the venerable master Gerard, whose decision was that no one ought to be taken into the community unless, according to the saying of the blessed Paul, he was willing to work with his hands.[16]

They valued manual work, on the authority of the Desert Masters, because it could help balance a man's energies: if one knew how to work physically, faculties needed in "spiritual work" might be rested and thus, different activities within one body could become mutually supportive, even harmonious. The tradition maintains that the relationship between levels is all and its experienced absence everything. They quoted Cassian, a student in late-fourth-century Egypt, on the folly and vainglory of trying to persevere in prayer without resting oneself in other work.[17] Had not Antony the Great (c. 251–356) learnt from an angel how to balance his labours in this way, "ascending and descending between manual and spiritual work," thus overcoming his weariness of spirit?[18] Manual work could help to curb "the disconnected mind" in all its "worthless babblings," and, at the same time, subdue the "wantonness of the body." Such work was "holy," it purified.[19]

The idea of a work which was holy—the literal meaning of 'sacrifice'—is a great mystery at the heart of our tradition: a pious platitude, an archaic notion of only academic or romantic interest, or a factual description of a real human possibility? Once more, before this question, it must be acknowledged that we do not have the living, direct word of teaching, that our material is incomplete and fragmentary, that something vital is being taken for granted. And we tend to forget, in poring over texts, that verbal descriptions are not the sought-for reality. Our conscious experience is missing. It is said that manual work helps balance, "anchoring" the "unstable heart" and facilitating prayer,[20] but is balance the automatic result of work? Whose work anchors them? Whose work is holy? *What* are we trying to understand? It may well be true that the quality of work is related to the quality of prayer, that the redemption of idleness lies neither in blind hyperactivity nor aimless pottering: our material makes these connections indirectly, yet taken as a whole, it contains a dimension of meaning which remains unexpressed.

For example, Zerbolt says that the most important thing is to work "keeping silence":

> You are bound above all things to keep silence during manual work. For silence is that in which our strength is, according to the prophet, and if it must be watched over and protected always and everywhere, unless necessity restricts us or usefulness recommends other wise, this is particularly true in manual work, according to the well known words of the Apostle: we beseech you in the Lord Jesus that you eat your bread with silence.[21]

We may take this as outward silence, not talking audibly, or as the silence referred to in other passages, undoubtedly a deeper and more complete experience. Nevertheless, the sincere attempt to keep silence, however conceived, could not fail to show the Brother to himself, if he was willing. We have inherited injunctions, but there were practices once associated with them, which concerned primarily the creation of conditions for study and self-knowledge, rather than the alteration of behaviour as an end in itself. Zerbolt contents himself with a passing reference, touching upon neither 'why' or 'how.'

We begin to see how this study, supported by traditional psychology and spirituality, might belong with a practical, anti-intellectual emphasis and ordered daily activity. Self-knowledge, born from direct observation of oneself in movement and relationship, engagement both outer and inner in a given task, the harmony of 'Martha and Mary,' was the prize. Inner states, usually unseen, are results and causes. The experience of work depends on a man's sensitivity to himself and his manifestations, on the degree to which his work includes himself,[22] on his ability not to forget himself in movement. The value of his work and the beginning of learning depended on the quality of his attention. Facing work, he faced a question and perhaps a choice. What was taking place? If this dimension of search exists—and we cannot speak of holy work if it does not—then the mystery is increased rather than dispelled. How can such a way of working be found that leads to God? These texts are speaking of work in no less a sense. That which clarifies the mind, balances the energies of the body:[23]

> thus the work of the hands often subserves the spiritual ascent, inasmuch as it withdraws the obstacles to ascending.[24]

We must feel that the Christianity of these men involved the practical study of human energies in movement—'up' and 'down,' towards and away from God—after the teaching of their exemplars, the Fathers of the Desert. This is well nigh inconceivable for us, used to regarding 'study' as the analysis of static facts by the associative and isolated intellect.

Although there remains a gulf between us and the experiences referred to, the instructions beginning at too high a level, as if the first, practical step has been taken for granted, nevertheless we can recognise the description of a different way of working and the states to which it may give rise: prayer at the same moment as outward activity rather than before or afterwards, a simultaneous inner and outer engagement. They were instructed to stop before they began a task, to pray briefly and then carry meditation into their work, to "digest inwardly" (*ruminare, interius ruminandum*) whilst working. Any man may pray and then work: it can signify much or little, depending on how he prays and works. Alternation of activity in time is comprehensible, but what does simultaneity mean? It must, surely, relate to a movement towards the unity of body, soul and spirit, which the Brethren did not ascribe to themselves as they were. They speak, unmistakably, of their work as a separation in the moment, of "exercising yourself in love and fear," for example, while, (or rather "beneath," *infra*) outwardly acting. This had been "a rule of our holy fathers," said Zerbolt. Attention must be divided.[25] If the kernel of this question lies in the religious aphorism "To work is to pray," what is meant by 'work'?

Traditional spiritual writings, including this material, tell us that man is divided from himself, fragmented and asleep. Perhaps because they were originally directed to men who had recognised, or were on the way to recognising their slavery, these writings say comparatively little about man's 'normal' unawareness of it, except to repeat dogmatic formulations concerning 'sin.' We can conceive of a work proper to a man who is unaware of his divided nature, his poor level of being, his 'sins,' and another, proper to one who is trying to become aware of this. Some of our material refers to this latter work and gives directions about it, and some of it falls between the two. Generally, the religious writings that have come down to us like to describe the work of the saints, but say little directly, for whatever reason, about our own experience and are strangely silent about the crucial first steps toward a higher level. We cannot truly understand them and tend to feel that, however profound, they remain, somehow, irrelevant. The practical advice contained in our material, although uneven and incomplete, is therefore very important. The question, "What is work," depends on whom we refer to. The work of a divided man is not the work of a man who wishes and is able to restore himself. There may, indeed, be a work, beyond our experience, which can become prayer, just as there may be a prayer that is work. We are asking what kind of teaching the New Devotion represented: an outward religion recognisable to us and amenable to analysis and comparison, an inner spiritual way, remote and imperceptible, obeying its own laws, or a possible bridge between them?

In seeking this different way of working, the Brethren were seeking a freedom within themselves. To pray and work at the same time is not the accomplishment of a slave. They sought the freedom of a more whole engagement, freedom firstly from daydreaming and idle fantasies, freedom to find their own intention, to know themselves under the sway of the "city of the moon," a measure of independence which placed them under a different jurisdiction, however momentarily. In this sense, freedom is naturally delight, as in the text, "I remembered God and was delighted" (*Ps.* 77:4 Vulgate):

> Therefore strive to discover a certain delight (*delectatio*) in everything with which you are wont to exercise yourself. For delight keeps the worker unharmed in work. Above everything else dread mental weariness and disgust. And this is bound to be the one aim in all things for you, that you may watch over yourself persevering with delight in all your activities and exercises.[26]

To work more freely is a joy.

Let us look more closely at the form of the Brother's day, or rather at how he tried to find its shape by informing himself inwardly. Whatever was done, he strove to

direct his actions towards God by means of short inner prayers and "ejaculations," which kept alive or revived the "intention" with which he had begun the
day. This much can be faithfully reconstructed from the material evidence, but it
leaves us little the wiser. We need to question the meaning of these things as
deeply as possible.

To speak more precisely, each day began with the previous night. One manuscript describes how a Brother makes the sign of the cross three times, for the
room, for the bed and for himself, while pronouncing the ancient prayer: "Holy
God, Holy Firm, Holy Immortal, Have mercy upon us."[27] Only then does he
retire. If nothing matters but his relation to God, everything matters as evidence:
an awareness of his habitual indifference to the quality of his state, the tone of his
thought, his emotional tendencies, unconscious movements within and without,
can become the reading of his own book. Who, or perhaps what, is he? These
moments in the privacy of his room are like others in the day when no explicit
external demand is being made, but he cannot afford to let them slip by, if he
aspires to live more than externally. For, "with whatever kind of thoughts and
reflections a man goes to sleep, with such does he awaken." Therefore, they said,
"it is useful to pray" at this time.[28] John Ketel made a mental review of the day,
before his final meditation, and upon awakening next morning, tried immediately to apply his faculties to this meditation.[29]

We recognise practicality only in outward affairs, but, to be able to awaken
more totally and immediately in the morning, the Brethren acknowledged the
need to prepare the night before, to pay in advance at their forces' lowest ebb: if
attention was to be engaged at the moment of waking, it had already to have been
gathered. By using their first breath in the service of 'the spiritual work,' by submitting instantly to the discipline of meditation, they sought a counterbalance in
themselves to those "foreign and wandering thoughts," which can so vehemently
seize the fresh morning energy, subverting and dividing us while opening the
heart to a multitude of distractions and extraneous influences.[30] It was a question
of becoming aware of the movement of energies within and without, wordlessly.
Perhaps a blessing could arise in the heart at the moment of a more complete
awakening in the morning:

> awakening to the impulse of the rising bell, say out of the innermost heart,
> "Blessed be the sweet name of our Lord Jesus Christ," or, "Thanks be to God
> that I am alive now."[31]

Could attention to the words, at this moment, evoke their deeper meaning? Having taken physical exercise,[32] surely to answer the same need for a more complete
entry into the day, the Brother would meditate on a text or theme that had been
given. We will discuss the crucial exercise of meditation later in this chapter.

And so throughout the day it was the same. Upon the quality and content of
the early morning hour largely depended the material of the day and his search:

very often a man may be left through the whole day in just those kind of wishes and needs which have been aroused in him in the morning.[33]

Hence the emphasis on "watching" and "remembering": if the whole day needs to be interpenetrated by a new influence, *how* is the current to be initiated, renewed and maintained? This is our real subject.

In a recent monograph, Professor R. R. Post describes succinctly, but without apparent question, the way the Brethren, while observing all outward forms of daily life, including attending church, "attempted, however, to perform them respectfully and attentively, conscious of what they were doing or were about to do, through the renewal of their good intention, through short ejaculations, through ruminating on the matter for meditation."[34] This is exactly so, but *intentio, orationes iaculatoriae* and *ruminatio* are technical terms which require fuller investigation and beg many questions. How can we hope to enter the inner world of the Brethren, in which these terms had an experienced meaning, unless we can enter our own and actively discriminate there, neither introspectively nor retrospectively?

The "intention" most familiar to us is the expression of self-will, arising we know not where, like a demand to be imposed on others, on unruly circumstances or on ourselves. It can have a compulsive flavour, and include assumptions about ourselves of which we are quite ignorant. There is an unknown world here. Sometimes intention stays entirely in the mind, where it may be 'contemplated' pleasantly, while we are actually being a party to something quite different; how rarely do we realise, especially when much time elapses between the beginning and end of an enterprise, that our intention has not been carried out as it was conceived, but has been subtly deflected, even changed into its opposite, without our realising, and that, if we have seen something through, it has been due to a fortunate flow of events, that is, accident; alternatively, how many activities proceed entirely without any intention, cognised or otherwise, on our part. Explanations and justifications aside, what is the relationship between will and self-suggestion, our doing and its result, the inner and the outer world? To allow the touching of our material by such questions, would be one starting point, for the Brethren were men like us. Yet, just because of this common experience, they had united to bend their intention in a more subtle direction, towards a less accessible world, for, unlike us, they wished to commit themselves to a religious way, and were being helped to do so. We must admit, as a working hypothesis, the possibility of there being other kinds of "intention," not only as regards the quantity but in the quality of force they embody.

The Brother's "intention" arose from his morning meditation and prayer and partook of their material substance: remembering his known weaknesses, an inner wish, connected perhaps with a specific exercise which might bridge his far and near aims, was refined and focused in him at this time. It was to be constantly "renewed inwardly" during the day:

Likewise preface all your actions with meditation and a brief prayer on how you should be in this task . . . also in the morning and after the midday meal, establish before your eyes your bad habits, your chief weaknesses, and the virtues for which you are striving, and the way things were during the recent struggle with your enemies.[35]

Gansfort places the "intention" at the summit of his "ladder of meditation," considering it the outcome of the combined results of meditation, understanding and love.[36] Lubert Berner connects it with the struggle to penetrate appearances by staying within oneself and yet avoiding all that is false, the honing of the faculties through prayer, submission and study, the search for real self-denial and much else:

In all temporal activity do not attend too closely to outward appearances and embellishments, but strive only towards the will of God and commit everything to this: turn away heart and eyes from men and stay always within, forgetting the exterior. Reach out to heaven through prayers, sighing, study and compunction, and frequently quicken a mind forewarned by these: flee pretence and presumption, cast away human images from the heart. In this is all virtue, all progress, in following God's will and delighting him. Strive for this, so that your intention may be towards God and according to God, and in the abandoning of the passions of the soul.[37]

Although the "intention" of each Brother might vary, it was, in a sense, the same for every one of them: that which turned them "towards God."

Clearly, once an "intention" had been found, it was vital to remember it, to keep it alive by any means, however 'artificial.'[38] Gerard said, "you should bear in mind that in temptations our aim must be to keep our intention right."[39] In the systematisation of meditation exercises by later New Devotional writers, special means to aid recollection were elaborated. Mombaer gives mnemotechnical verses for reviving the "intention" before singing the office.[40] Such verses were also used during the day to help recall the particular meditation on Christ's life which had been given. In some texts "our intention" is used in the fundamental sense of the common aim in working together.[41]

Details of personal exercises lead us into a subjective, but not entirely unfamiliar, world. Gerard's *Conclusa* and the *Devout Exercises* of Berner and Ketel appear in Kempis' *Lives* as a series of "intentions" and aphorisms, often implying specific exercises. Writings of this kind, notes to oneself, must remain equivocal to the outsider: the knowledge of what they tried does not, in itself, help us to understand why and for what they tried. The obstacle or sin which one man wishes to banish, may be for another a signpost which he must learn to decipher.[42]

There are accounts of inexplicable actions, suspicious, even mad from the ordinary point of view. Lubert Berner would "knowingly falter" when reading aloud during the evening meal, so that he might face correction, and would pretend not to hear, so that his reprimand might be the more severe. He wished to be confounded, to be reputed a stupid fellow. Kempis tells us he had a manly voice, "like a trumpet," and was an excellent reader.[43] What was his intention? If to face his disorder before others, how difficult to remember his intention in the moment, without it degenerating into a pious game! Yet, in this way, indelible impressions might be received and something important seen. Is it clear why humility is a virtue? Whose humility? An organic sense of shame is rarely felt from the direct experience of what we are: something has taken its place. As ordinarily experienced, 'humility' is an unconsciously hypocritical masking of reality, a partial arising by association; relatively meaningless, cheap, properly offensive, it lacks the force of truth. Humility born of self-deception is a double lie. Lubert was challenging himself. What is to be obeyed other than the truth? Therefore, before all things, direct, naked experience of what we are is to be sought intentionally *because* of its cost, for through it conscience may be reached.

It may well be, as religious tradition avers, that a man will be given what he needs if he but ask, but who knows how to ask for this? What is an 'intention' and what is a 'sin' here? Referring to exercises of talking and not talking, another fragment says:

> You must be very aware of the occasion of sin. Often when you are quiet you seem to yourself to be something, but having poured yourself out into exterior things that which was hidden in you becomes apparent. For this you are able to humble yourself greatly. Much talking seizes a man from himself and carries him off, leads him into ignorance, withdraws his forethought and makes known his disorder.[44]

The Brothers did not, therefore, cease to speak, but made it the subject of a particular remembering. They tried, for example, to meditate or to say an *ave maria* in silence before they spoke.[45] Lubert tried to think of the virtue of the other person and to remember his own weaknesses, known only to God, the angels and himself, in order to humble himself inwardly.[46] Gerard had an exercise of speaking only in Latin with his intimate friends: if one of them forgot, he was to fall to his knees and kiss the floor. We are told that once Gerard began to speak in Dutch: his friends were ashamed to tell him, but, seeing their embarrassment, he realised he was speaking and fell to the ground.[47] (We cannot connect this agreement among friends with any abhorrence of the vernacular tongue, for Gerard made translations of liturgical works into Dutch for the Brothers and Sisters.)[48]

What was it they were trying to remember when they were together? In both these examples, Lubert and Gerard are intentionally putting obstacles in the way of habitual, automatic talking.[49] Was their intention to become more aware of the place it held in their lives and to study it? Their writings speak of the knowledge of oneself leading to the knowledge of what is above oneself.[50] If the usual remembering of a man is shallow and haphazard, relatively automatic, the living remembrance of God, the Brethren's' fundamental intention, must be a conscious act.

From this point of view, their exercises can be seen as an intentional interruption of what goes on automatically, in disorder. They were trying to 'take the bull by the horns': "do everything with attention and not habitually."[51] While they worked they offered brief prayers (*orationes iaculatoriae et breves*), abandoning the inessential—in sudden silence as it fell away—to help them remember their intention and face whatever was there, in the midst of the movement of life, within and without. They did not stop working outwardly, but, unless something was stopped momentarily within, what room was there for silence and the sensitivity of prayer? 'Prayer,' in early Christian texts, is an instrument to open us to the teaching, a connection between our scattered parts, the receiving of help, a bridging of levels; the unwitting projection of automatically associative thoughts, emotions and sensations,—moving ceaselessly and independently in us whatever we do outwardly—plus the impulse of piety, is something else. 'Prayer' out of this, does not require our present awareness, has neither force, truth nor honesty, and is almost all we can manage. The religious writings of the New Devotion indicate that prayer is a movement of a different order and quality, in another direction, not such a movement as goes by itself; it needs to be intended and, with grace, initiated, the fruit of an inner and more subtle opening. The Brethren believed these brief prayers to be an ancient practice, a discipline of the Egyptian Fathers according to Gerard, "so that the heart might not be scattered in things,"[52] a letting go and a gathering. His *Conclusa* end with these words:

> Direct your attention so that you may thus perfectly surpass yourself and raise up your heart erectly to God at all times, as the prophet says, "my eyes are always towards the Lord."[53]

The *Conclusa* are believed to date from his stay at Monnickhuizen and to reflect Carthusian teaching and practice. The prior of Monnickhuizen, Henry Egher, wrote in the *Tractatus de cotidiano holocausto*:

> You ought always to come back to the Face of God, by meditating even while you are working, just as the Carthusians are always wishing to resort to brief ejaculatory prayers.[54]

John Ketel spoke of his need to pray "without haste . . . briefly, with attention" while at his kitchen tasks, in order to "have the Presence of God before his eyes."[55] To call attention back from dispersion "in things," to be at work while in prayer, to stand between the outer and the inner and, remembering their unity, be open to the Presence of God, was the essence of the New Devotion.

Yet it was not a 'new' teaching, just a new clothing. Chrysostom, for example, had written:

Everywhere, wherever you may find yourself, you can set up an altar to God in your mind by means of prayer. And so it is fitting to pray at your trade, on a journey, standing at the counter or sitting at your handicraft. Everywhere and in every place it is possible to pray, and, indeed, if a man diligently turns his attention upon himself, then everywhere he will find convenient circumstances for prayer.[56]

Compare *The Meditations of St. Bernard*:

Wheresoever you be, pray within yourself: if you be far from an oratory, trouble yourself not to seek a place, for you yourself are a place convenient: if you be in your business or in any other place, pray and there is a temple. . . . For just as there is no moment of time wherein a man is occupied & needs not the goodness & mercy of our Lord, so there ought to be no moment wherein he has not Him present in his mind.[57]

Reginald Pole is said to have learned to practise the prayer of "elevating the mind to God" during his daily affairs, in Italy, on the eve of the Reformation.[58]

The Devout Exercises of John Ketel indicate the inner struggle informing this teaching and convey the kind of experience valued and sought in the "old house" of Florence Radewijns. In these personal notes, John confronts himself with the question: What can I return to God, from Whom I have received all that I really am? He directs himself to ponder deeply, "with great diligence and all your force," upon his past and present existence. "O dear John," he exclaims, "have pity on yourself!" Although he may feel despondent, he understands that nothing displeases God as much as despair. Knowing himself to be desolate and wounded, a sense that he may die at any time, *in this state*, arises in him. He acknowledges a need for "mercy," for a "physician."[59] His study of the Bible, of Christ's life particularly, has revealed the importance of love, but what is this love? He feels that it is of a very high order, and yet it is commanded: how can he attain it, as he is? Thus he reasons with himself, simply, about his aim and how to approach it. The essence of this self-questioning is of great interest:

If I must attain to that love then it is absolutely necessary for me to look at my weakness and to experience the fact that, in truth, from me myself nothing good is possible and to have without ceasing before my eyes the magnitude of God and His faithfulness and the smallness of me myself and my infidelity to Him, in the which things there is much to be pondered. For if I pay attention rightly to these things they will lead me to subject myself to all men and put small value upon myself in such a way that I may even desire to be scorned. One ought to work at these things truthfully and with unremitting thought, often calling upon God, by Whom, without doubt, it will be necessary to grow. If, therefore, I must come to this humility and to that love, it is necessary for me to have a daily exercises and rule which may guide me to that goal. And, according to the sayings of the saints, it is necessary for me to see my past mistakes and always to have them before my eyes and strive very much to ponder them.[60]

The Way of the Monk, for which the New Devotion was, in one sense, a preparation, concerned the purification of man's emotion;[61] here the preparation is the voluntary finding of a "daily exercise and rule" proper to oneself.

In his "daily rule" John intended to avoid detraction and all curious searching into the business of others, rather to remember their virtues; to meditate from the moment he arises in the morning, thanking God for His mercy and remembering his own misery, and to return to this at certain times of the day; to sit and kneel in an upright posture; not to eat hastily; to be ready to help the servers at the table; to be always occupied with something, never allowing his mind to turn idly; to often break his labour with brief attentive prayer, using, for instance, the moment when the bell rings or when it sounds in church to announce the elevation of the host; to be ready while meditating during his kitchen work to answer the door and give the necessary response to anyone who comes. "To do" and "not to do," might, perhaps, be more exactly rendered in the spirit of his intention as "to be able to do" and "to be able not to do." This deceptively simple, but realistic programme is based on the idea that certain practical means, inviting an inner struggle with his habitual self, are necessary if he is actually to move towards his aim, the imitation of Christ, "that divine mirror,"[62] in which he may see all that he himself is and is not.

It is interesting to note that Florence, under whom John worked, made it intentionally difficult for him, insulting and snubbing him and ridiculing his efforts as a cook, although Kempis says that he was a "master" at preparing food and that Florence loved him dearly as a man. It is recorded that Florence often used such methods for his own ends, even resorting to physical violence upon some of the Brethren closest to him. He once struck John Vos across the face while he was speaking proudly to a new Brother; a rich well-dressed young man was made to wear a ridiculously short patched gown when he entered Florence's care, so that he looked to himself "like a tailless chicken," and later, when he developed consumption, was made to work very hard for long periods without food; these methods were extended to outsiders, as when a group of Brothers rewarded the hospitality of some rich burghers "by pointing out to them the defects of their characters." We are here in a quite different world—adjacent to the Desert of the Egyptian Fathers—from that depicted by popular historians of piety.[63]

Kempis says that John was often found praying before the fire, that he made the kitchen an oratory, "knowing God to be everywhere, he summoned spiritual heat from the material fire." While carrying the pots and pans, he sang the psalms of David.[64] Of John Hatten's work there it was said:

What he had heard sung in the church he sweetly ruminated afterwards during his work. And thus bearing God in his mind he was outwardly active in cooking but inwardly he was actually free (*vero vacabat*) for divine meditating, neither drawing out the time unfruitfully nor neglecting his inner exercises.[65]

The kitchens of the early Brotherhouses were a true centre of their work.

These endeavours correspond to the remarkable Biblical injunctions to "watch" and "pray":

[L]et us not sleep, as do others; but let us watch and be sober. For they that sleep sleep in the night; and they that be drunken are drunken in the night. But let us, who are of the day, be sober. . . . Pray without ceasing. (1 *Thess.* 5:6–8, 17)

Gerard, reflecting on his former academic habits and the harmfulness of unnecessary talking, said:

it is evident that everything must be ordered in praise of God, if it is to have always a good purpose, that is to say, one must pray always.[66]

Florence says the same when speaking of the way we take food, for then the Devil will lie in wait for us, "therefore let us always watch and pray."[67] So important was this "watching," that upon it depended the whole progress of a man in the spiritual life:

Before all things, cognize your vices and passions. Be always vigilant in the presence of temptation and the movements of passion. If you sense them and refuse them at once, they will not harm. Often the whole body is moved according to the passion which reigns in a man, but only when he is not aware of it.[68]

According to the *Tractatus de cotidiano holocausto,* many stay where they are, "because they do not see behind the parts they play nor watch themselves."[69]

'Rumination' or 'mastication,' the last of the technical terms needing special comment, was used by the Brethren to describe the way they tried to absorb food for the soul. There is an idea in this spiritual tradition that rumination, meditation and real study are processes analogous to the reception, digestion and transformation of physical food: the laws governing life, health and growth being the same at every level, for the body and the soul.[70] It is a question of 'level,' because the texts, while maintaining the analogy, imply a qualitative difference between what can feed the soul ("the Word of God") and what serves as food for the body. If a belief in materiality, in this sense, corresponding to the ancient idea of 'the Great Chain of Being,' underlies the Brethren's practice, what are the fine matters needed for inner growth, to what do they relate in our world and experience and how can they be received? We have absolutely no reason to assume that these conceptions were metaphorical or figurative in the modern sense. The same analogy appears in Carthusian writings, and, more diffused but still recognisable, in sixteenth- and seventeenth-century writers on meditation who inherited something of the Brethren's outlook.[71] This understanding makes possible a remarkably practical conception of Christian work. One of the texts quoted below implies that action or virtue cannot be manifested, whatever we may 'intend,' without the presence of the corresponding substance in the soul, and that certain inner organs may decay unless these substances are "separated" and "distributed."[72]

Rumination, said Gansfort, was the function of the "discerning" and "strengthened" heart, connected with the "remembering" of its own life within. "Remembrance" he called "the stomach of the soul."[73] Rumination thus indicates more qualitatively, than the intensification of a man's ordinary thought or feeling. Zerbolt spoke of finding a way to draw from study something which was able to combine—one might say, alchemically—with one's purpose (*propositum*), in order that the act of remembering be strengthened, "that you may be like a clean animal that is used to ruminate." In this way, reading was restored to purity.[74]

We have become habituated to accept, passively, anything within easy reach as food for those sensitive apparatuses, our minds and hearts, and so they are likened in *The Meditations of Saint Bernard* to a mill that has been grinding all kinds of unsuitable substances, gravel, sand and even pitch, in lieu of the grain for which they were intended. We have been desensitised and damaged by this, perhaps even irreparably, so that we may now be unable to discern something as fine as the Word of God, let alone to receive and be worked upon by it, for its transformation in us into corresponding action.[75] This comparison between a man with all his original possibilities and a broken-down, abused and wrongly functioning machine is shocking indeed, yet these texts urge it upon us, for the sake of the innate possibility of self-recognition and love of truth.

The fateful meeting between this need and the intelligence of a spiritual tradition, actualises "the daily work" in an individual, so that an engagement with the whole materiality of life may take place:

> Approach study so as to take food for the soul, in order that, having been reinvigorated in reading, the soul may learn to be occupied with that which it reads and to forget ephemeral things and refrain from offences. At the same time there is not much, indeed not enough, use in studying without mastication and prayer: to masticate it with prayer and longing and send it to the stomach of the soul to be transformed into behaviour and virtue so that the soul may be sustained by this, like food.[76]

The Brethren considered that to study for any other purpose, for example "in order to know and consequently to teach others," was not only useless but harmful, providing no real nourishment, rendering the brain unsound and, generally, having the same effect on the psyche as superfluous humours on the physical body. Such study engendered vainglorious, empty thought, overelevated emotion and disorderly behaviour, mental darkness, instability and forgetfulness of God: it pillaged and crippled the soul, rather than restored it.[77] Wishing for the restoration of wholeness, they had a horror of partiality; intending to submit all their actions to a higher, unchanging authority, all lesser ends were perceived as aimlessness.

> Therefore, to study with moderation and to masticate well reinvigorates the soul more than to study many things without thought and without mastication. It follows therefore that the soul that does not separate the Word of God and distribute it in action and virtues without ceasing is dead, or wastes itself and decays.[78]

Study and rumination, then, were properly part of a life-giving process.

To support this process the Brethren made *rapiaria*, compilations of excerpts from their reading which were personally significant and helpful, notes on their observations and experiences which could remind them of their search.[79] In his account of the day, the Harderwijk Brother records his intention for the evening: "Then, dismissing external things, recollect yourself with regard to what is within, studying a little in *Beatus Vir*, or in an excerpt." He tried to recall whether he had learnt anything of himself during the day. What strong impressions had he received? Had he managed to "imprint" (*signare*) his weaknesses, and what of his intention? Recourse to "this book," said Gerard, "orders your state."[80] In the *Chronicon Windeshemense*, John Busch tells of the "little book" in which he noted "certain remedies . . . which I had found by experience of myself or by study from the Holy Scriptures," in connection with his tendency to criticise or be offended by the behaviour of others.[81] Many of the writings associated with the New Devotion are adaptations of these *rapiaria*.[82]

The Brother's meditation was a means for the fulfilment of his task, called by Florence after Cassian, "the expurgation of weaknesses and desires and the acquisition of virtues." Meditation discovered and intensified the experience of conscience: it was connected with a "higher disposition or arrangement" in a man, rather than with a manipulation of his usual mental or emotional activity, was not merely a holding of an idea or picture in the mind, but a step towards informed action, not only a remembering of God's law with one part, but a preparation for doing:

> It is useless for him who works to meditate upon the law of God to hold in his memory what he does not fulfil in action.

> [B]y meditation a man ought to quicken the prick of conscience in his self-examination.[83]

What do these traditional formulations mean?

Historical studies of spirituality which take for granted an understanding of the basic experiences and difficulties, are vitiated by a lack of honesty: but, given the virtual disappearance in the West of a living tradition centred on the inner life, what is the alternative to theory? It is easy to accept and repeat passively the fine words of Augustine and Bernard, as if we understood them and had a right to do so, and this is a good solution, indeed, if we are content to regard these obscure spiritual practices as entirely 'historical,' their relevance limited by a particular time and place, of academic interest only. There is an outer aspect to the subject, conditioned by the particular historical culture, but its pursuit will lead us only so far: to focus exclusively on these accidental aspects in the name of 'accuracy' does not help if we are to be true to our fundamental question about the essence of the Brethren's work. History is always becoming a dead subject. We have another memory. It is precisely because certain ancient formulations still sound in us, even call, that we are denying the possibility of understanding proper to us when we make do with repeating medieval phrases. Nor can we rely upon the scientific or pseudo-scientific explanations of our time, whose impartiality is suspect, if we wish to reject the traditional view. Clinging to the old words of others, our subject becomes remote, or fascinating, but irrelevant to our lives, yet, do the conventional words and attitudes of our culture quite correspond to the reality in question?

The records of the New Devotion touching meditation are simple and practical, emphasising not the theoretical possibilities of its practice but the importance of strengthening attention, not of where it may lead but of where it may begin. The words used, *ruminatio* and *masticatio*, suggest a material process of inwardly digesting food for corresponding growth. Room occupied by habitually reactive thought and emotion has to be made available for this process, which is not automatic.[84] Is it not just these repetitive thoughts and shifting emotions, absorbing attention in the name of the whole man—whose constant overlapping hinders the reception of that food of impressions of which Gansfort spoke, let alone its proper digestion—which are called 'worldly' and 'of the flesh' in the Christian tradition?[85] (They may, of course, be very 'spiritual' picturings.) These writings point to the facts of man's so-called inner life to show the need for 'prayer' and 'meditation': the Brethren's study of themselves, at first an awkward notion, becomes an obvious imperative.

What, then, is meditation? The tradition affirms there are higher worlds than the one in which we exist, the lowest, most confined and least real, furthest from God. The techniques of the religious way opened men to a consciousness of the Whole, by freeing them from the hypnotic influences governing such an abnormal diminution of being as they were accepting. Religion, where it has not degenerated, does not pretend that this exchange is cheap. The Brethren sought relationship with a level of being higher than 'the world,' to reopen the channel between 'earth' and 'heaven.' Without direct self-knowledge, there is no experi-

ence of levels: why meditate then, and for what? Knowledge of oneself brings realisation of separateness from God, of a deeper unknowing, obstacles, and finally
the acceptance of purgatory, however momentarily. As we are, God cannot be
addressed effectively, nor help from Above truly received.[86] Generally, there is
nothing in us able to be helped. The lawful stages of this process have been named
differently at different times in every tradition, in order to reclaim the unknown
and counteract the baleful influence of the compilers of recipes for success, always
at our elbow. In accordance with their times, the Brethren's meditation was devotional, their work focused on their emotional life: "the expurgation of weaknesses
and desires," the "uncleanness of heart" maintained by 'worldly' living.

In their meditation they sought direct connection with the teaching of the
Bible and traditional writings, for "the divine wisdom is taught . . . without any
intervening means."[87] If the Book can speak, why is our relationship indirect and
what does indirection mean here? Finding oneself somehow unable to take in the
sayings of Christ, and dimly recognising they are not addressed to ordinary
thought and feeling,[88] why are we impenetrable? Our attention is scattered by a
direct call because we do not know where it is coming from. To *whom* is this call
addressed? In the face of words of this quality, our 'knowledge' is, suddenly, ignorance of ourselves. If the Brethren's diagnosis is correct, that understanding is not
the inevitable outcome of knowledge, not the facility to repeat automatically the
words of others,[89] and if, as they also said, our capacity to receive fluctuates constantly, what is missing? Staying always, unconsciously, within what we already
know (and fear to lose), how can anything new be received? It is with the possibility of reaching our own, active understanding,[90] rather than with the elaboration
of known, second-hand thoughts, that real meditation is surely concerned. Meditation which is only a one-way focusing upon the external word must remain bar-
ren. The inner food of meaning, for which the Brethren specifically worked and
which they believed could assist the formation in them of a new understanding,
could not be discovered unless they strove to include themselves in their meditation.[91] Merely to read books, however holy, as they had become accustomed to
read, was not enough: certain books may well contain the necessary raw materi-
als, but, to become digestible, food must be cooked. They were trying to develop
the capacity to receive a virtual impression of their relationship with God. Meditation and spiritual exercises were a spoke in the wheel on which we turn, inserted
for the sake of 'being in the world, but not of it.'

A late-fifteenth-century manuscript, written by a member of the Harderwijk
Brotherhouse, bears practically on this question, although the accuracy with
which it conveys original practices is uncertain.[92] The writer is pondering *Psalms*
46:7–8 (Vulgate), on which he was later to meditate:

Sing praises to our God, sing praises, sing praises to our King, sing praises.
For God is the king of all the earth: sing praises with understanding.

He asks himself what it might mean to praise "with understanding," and reflects that when he acts "with both intellect and feeling . . . both prudently and knowingly" it is wiser; God must be praised totally, in heart, mouth and works, the understanding of which is wisdom. We are being asked, he concludes, to become more whole, to praise God no less than five times in order that we may hold the five senses together wisely under discipline, and, drawing them into one, serve God. This is the material he intends to bring to his meditation on this text before matins.[93] Then referring to another text concerning whole praising and respect for God's temple (*Ps.* 137:1–2, Vulgate), he says:

> Just so, you can ruminate that verse of yours, "I will sing praises to you in the sight of the angels," that is, I will reflect, remembering how much it is necessary for me to be in the presence of Him, and of the angels and saints, and pray with reverence and attention.[94]

Here meditation is not just imaginative mental enquiry, but a pondering and a search, a finding and staying close to a different state in oneself—in reverent attention in the Presence of God. It is a movement and a rest. The Brother knows that it is necessary to bring his separate functions together, mind, senses and feelings, before he can address himself to God. This is in fundamental agreement with the meaning of 'religion,' the act of binding together again.

The records of these practical men emphasise again and again the inner movement of renewing attention. When speaking of the *opus dei* and the way in which the Devil molests all who seek to praise God, the Harderwijk Brother says:

> Therefore attend, little by little and as completely as you are able to and read the hours according to the words of Augustine: what is brought forth in the mouth depends upon the heart. But because your heart easily gives way to empty things, for that reason you are bound to always recall your attention to the purpose.[95]

The manuscript interweaves examples of the thoughts and feelings to be aroused at corresponding parts of the Mass with the imperatives "Attend!" and "Collect yourself!" The writer's intention is to help himself live a "new devotion," to find a practical way to participate more deeply and with more of himself in the ancient sequence of liturgical experience and to support this self-reminding for the future by writing it down. He is transcribing part of a method for his own use; he wished to be an influence on himself by incorporating it. If ritual, prayer, meditation and music had once served as a bridge between men's 'worldly' state and the fullness of Christian teaching, then the means of using what remains of this bridge lie still at hand: in this manuscript, as in the Bridgettine material examined later, it is implied that the key to these means lies in the development of the power of attention. The stated purpose of another contemporary work, Mombaer's *Rosetum*

Spiritualium Exercitiorum, is the fostering of the inner life in the same practical sense. In this vast, encoded summary of tradition, considered by scholars who claim to have penetrated it to be a formulation of the practice and method of the New Devotion, Mombaer describes "three beds" in a "garden of roses," praying the hours, meditation and communion, which could be tended only by not allowing the attention to wander.[96]

In the belief that we know what attention is and that we already possess it as of right, we are likely to find this emphasis on the great need to work for it naive, if not dishonest, confirming entrenched modern prejudices about the childish irrelevancy and superstition of medieval religion. But who amongst us has looked into this question deeply? What is the difference between attention and concentration? Is that attention, which a man thinks he can command, really free, mobile and at his disposal? Is it not continually drawn, that is, taken? If his attention is unfree, where is he then, and how can he know? If there is only one, already known, quality of attention, what is the meaning of the sleep of men and their possibility to awaken, spoken of in the religious traditions? The question of attention relates not only to thought and 'the mind,' but to the virtually autonomous worlds of emotion, sensation and instinct. There is everything to be understood here, practically and experientially, rather than intellectually and theoretically: even a glimmer of this understanding will enable us to be more just towards the Brethren, for we will be putting ourselves in their position.

Consider the words of a contemporary of the Harderwijk Brother, who had pondered the ancient records of spirituality:

> holy men tell us of divers kinds of attention during the Divine Office. But because men in these days are dull of understanding and but little skilled in things divine, few are able to catch the spiritual meaning of what these holy men tell us.[97]

This question permeated the New Devotion.[98] The writer is Abbot Cisneros, a pivotal figure in the formulation of methodical meditation and the conception of the Ignatian exercises; did his clearer understanding of the spiritual inheritance enable him to be a channel in the true Renaissance sense? He implies that the teachings of which this forgotten psychology formed a part, live only through men's ability to embody them.

This perception leads us to the famous but deeply enigmatic formula, 'to imitate Christ,' which became such an important focus in the religious life of the fifteenth and sixteenth century. Unless a man lives as Christ did, he has no right to call himself a Christian. The Brethren found their own rule, voluntarily, according to their understanding. It is well known that their aim was 'to imitate Christ' in order 'to serve God,' if only because of the continuing popularity of one book bearing Kempis' name. Gerard Groote wrote in his *Conclusa:*

> let the root of your study and the mirror of your life be above all things the
> gospel of Christ, because there is the life of Christ.[99]

John Ketel is said to have "studied with love the life of our Lord Jesus Christ,
drawing from it a rule for his whole life."[100] That this was a more widespread aspiration, is less well known, similar statements occurring in sources apparently
independent of the New Devotion by the late fifteenth century. One Italian
humanist, who had adopted the hermit's life, wrote around 1490:

> Christ should be imitated by us in every aspect of life. . . . Do you dare to call
> yourself a Christian if you do not follow the precepts of your author and
> leader Christ, nor imitate His example? if you wish to be called a Christian . . .
> you must not only worship Christ in observing the sacraments but also imi-
> tate Him in your life.[101]

The frequency with which pious humanists refer to this has lead one historian to
speak of an Italian *Devotio Moderna*.[102] Nor was the powerful idea of the *imitatio*
or *conformitas Christi* absent from the reformation upheavals in Germany,
although, to judge from some contemporary accounts, in becoming the property
of many, it was often understood only literally or hysterically.[103] We are by no
means wishing to suggest that the Brethren were saints, or anything like, only that
the teaching they followed was profound and needed many years of directed
study to yield its good. Gerlach Peters described the chief work of the Brethren,
the servants of God, as the gaining of joy in this life through knowing truth and
wisdom, refashioning their inner man after the image of God, while conforming
their outer life to the life of Jesus.[104] In our view, the formula *imitatio Christi*,
made prominent but not invented by the Brethren, summarised the whole of
Christian teaching, as it was received and understood for that time.

It is not known if the original Brethren's meditation was systematic: their
material may have been a personal choice, the result of a direction sensed from
within,[105] or it may have been indicated by those in authority to the individual or
the group. It is among the Windesheim canons that we begin to hear of systematisation, and this became the trend wherever the influence of the New Devotion
reached. At Windesheim, meditations on the life of Christ, the Four Last Things,
sin and the blessings of God were alternated during the week, in such a way that
an evoked experience of gratitude for the love of God might be balanced by dread
of just judgement. Between these polar contradictions, lay the possibility of compunction, the rekindling of intention and fervour, the laying of a foundation.[106]
Various combinations of these were used at the Zwolle and Deventer Brotherhouses, among the Canons Regular associated with Windesheim, and later, in
reformed Observant Benedictine Congregations like Sta. Justina at Padua and at
Montserrat under Cisneros.[107] Concurrently with weekly cycles at Deventer, the
Passion was worked through beginning on Sunday, the Brethren being instructed

to consult the Gospels "for the renewal of memory." Meditations on the significance of the traditional festivals of the church were allowed to interrupt these
sequences at their proper time.

The Deventer records state the understanding on which this alternation was
based: 'justification' is not possible on the religious path without a certain fear, yet
emotional negativity endangers balance.[108] The sacrifice of basic health or the
overthrow of the mind, in this sense, was never their aim.[109] What is the fear that
can lead to hope and how can this take place?[110] Although they used a psychological terminology strange to us, the Brethren were clearly aware of the risks of mental
neuroses and the importance of common sense in submitting to a discipline, an
awareness they inherited from their Carthusian sources and which they communicated to their heirs.[111] In the shadow of the Reformation, William Bonde of Syon
was pointing out the uselessness and harmfulness of "servile fear" in religion.[112]
The Brethren were concerned to find a certain "delight," "for delight keeps the
worker unharmed in work."[113] Our material persistently connects being a Christian with the search for a more complete balance or order in oneself. Without this
search the mixed life makes no sense, even as a concept, and without an awareness
of the lack of order, spiritual exercises and meditations have no significance. The
Brethren believed this balance could not be approached without the relative stability and health of ordinary life; their way could not begin beneath this level.

The question naturally arises: if he possesses this basic normality, why should a
man strive for anything further? The Brethren might have answered with another
question: can a man remain satisfied when he begins to see what he actually is?
Laying aside his ideas about what is good and bad in him (usually equated with
what he likes and dislikes), can he look at himself without preconceptions, at the
nature of his thoughts, for example?

> [T]hough they are by no means base . . . yet, because they are simply ram-
> bling, careless, barren and mutilated thoughts, they prove me to be a man
> maimed, barren, careless and unstable. From the wandering current of my
> thought, I can hope for no good haven. . . . Of what avail are fleeting, ram-
> bling, halting, careless thoughts? They produce nothing that is profound;
> they so weaken the mind that it cannot concentrate upon any point.[114]

This feature of his 'normality' would become apparent in any serious attempt to
gather attention during meditation. Can he really understand anything, let alone
the teaching of Christ, while sunk in the passive stream of such thought? To
become emotionally exalted with talk of God and the soul, all too often means to
lose sight of oneself, yet all the authoritative indications are that the real ability to
speak of such high things flows from, and returns to, the knowledge and experience of oneself:

as the eye of the body, when deprived of the corporeal light of the sun, does not see anything, so our intellect, when deprived of the light of God's countenance, is rendered, so to speak, wholly inactive. Not only are we destitute of this light when sleeping, but also often, when we are awake, we are so stupid, so dull, that we actually find that our minds are inactive. And yet sometimes we are made keen.[115]

Because our 'normal' waking state is not what it seems (it is more accurately named 'waking-sleep'), the call of traditional religion has been, literally, to awaken. This involves not turning to the strangely comforting belief in absolute personal unworthiness ('sinfulness')—untrue, anyway, for "sometimes we are made keen"—but the consciously intentional confrontation with all that is in us, worthless and worthy, materially rather than in imagination. This is likely to be the result of long preparation, for these things must first be known. Therefore, the aim was given "to gather together the soul." Meditation was a means, utilising the existing religious framework, towards this aim.

Thus the Brethren were directed to meditate on Christ's actions, not merely to think about them or picture them imaginatively, but to be present before their evidence, to become a witness to their abiding truth with all of themselves: thoughts, feelings and bodily senses together.[116] Meditation in this sense is not an exercise in imaginative fantasy or self-projection, but, essentially, a call to greater wholeness. Traditional instructions abound in phrases like "be present in spirit," "attend with your whole mind and heart." The late fourteenth-century Carthusian *Of the three workings in man's soul* (from an MS including a list of Ruysbroeck's works) advocates the detailed picturing of the Virgin within "in . . . a fair chamber," in such a way as to evoke strong emotion, while saying the *Ave Maria* fifty times, thus teaching the division and focusing of fine attention: "the three workings" are "thought," "thinking" and "contemplation," and this exercise is "both thinking and prayer."[117] A technique for engaging all the functions of a man to one end was to be elaborated in the Ignatian exercises.[118] By daily practice of meditation and spiritual exercises, Zerbolt said, a man might gradually be freed from the valley of 'Jericho':

He who is able to ascend, let him ascend; let him who can receive, receive; but let the lazy who avoid work depart. Although this state of perfection is not acquired by anybody without the special grace of God, yet this grace is not given to the sleeping, the heedless and those who do not co-operate with it. Therefore love is a form of warfare; away with the lazy; they cannot go on treating it as a side-show and approach the exercises any longer.[119]

By our own power we cannot be delivered, yet something is required, "to do that which is in us."[120]

The gathering together of oneself through meditation was connected, for these religious men, with being more and more deeply "in the presence of Jesus," a proximity which, if real, cannot but influence the way a man acts,[121] according to the old proverb, "Before doing, one must be."[122] In *The Meditations of St. Bernard* we find this distillation of New Testament symbolism, theological psychology and inner experience:

> [G]ather together your soul with a whole felicity & joy & abide at liberty in your inward habitation & walking in the largeness of your heart, make ready therein to Christ a resting place and a large chamber. For the mind of a wise man is always to God. We should always have Him before our eyes, by whom we have our being, our life & understanding. For like as we in our being have Him as author & maker, so, if we shall profit in wisdom, we must have him a doctor & a teacher, and so we shall be blessed, we must have Him the giver of everlasting bliss. And, in that, we know that the image of Him, that is to say that high & glorious trinity, is in us. For like as He is & is both wise & good, so we in our manner have a being, & know that we have a being & are glad that we have that knowledge. Therefore use yourself as the temple of God, for that that is in you like to God.[123]

Any lingering one-dimensional picturing of the Brethren's meditation as the imagination of naive men thinking themselves partakers in long distant events, must give way before such a vivid and resonant statement. A far more profound, subtle and organic process is to be acknowledged here. The search to become as completely present as possible to the truth of one's own experiencing of meditation, points towards 'the imitation of Christ,' because in that work, a place could be prepared within—in which 'I,' as it is said, "abide at liberty"—able to receive an influence infinitely finer and higher, called here Christ's Presence, the aspect of God in our world. Who can say what real suffering, between our nothingness and His Being, and what scope for delusion, lies in the actualisation of these words of *The Meditations*? Gerard wrote that "the cross of Christ is built in meditating on the Passion."[124] When the *Tractatus de cotidiano holocausto* speaks of the thought of God which is denied by the Devil and is a crucifying with Christ,[125] does it refer to any quality of thought with which we are familiar? "Let my thoughts die in me that are carrying to me false delights."[126]

We may discern here the shadow of a Christian teaching of self-transformation, swathed in its medieval garments and inaccessible to us in its fullness, yet with roots in the present experience of every householder. *The Meditations* end with remarkable words *ordering* the crucifying of "the old man," "the inordinate lover of himself," who has usurped authority over almost every aspect of our lives:

> Now are you oppressed with the yoke of wretchedness and thraldom & you are trodden foully under his, the old man's, feet. O you wretched & miser-

able man. Who shall deliver you from the bonds of this rebuke. Rise up God. And fall down this armed man, fall he down & be he all to-broken . . . he is a wicked man, the despiser of God, the inordinate lover of himself. . . . If you understand right you will say with me, he is worthy death, put him on the cross. Defer no longer . . . but hastily & instantly boldly crucify this man. But let it be upon the cross of Christ in whom is health and life, to whom if your man crucified cry he shall hear him benignly, answering & saying: "You shall be with me this day in paradise."[127]

Speaking from the experience of meditation on the life of Christ, clothing his meaning in the language of the Gospel, Gerard links suffering and death with transformation and life:

Was not Christ "to suffer and to enter into His glory"? "And we which live are always delivered unto death for Jesus' sake, that the life also of Jesus might be made manifest in our mortal flesh." For meditation on the Lord's sufferings would profit us little, unless the earnest longing to become like unto him go with it. Therefore in every meditation on any part of the sufferings of Christ we must at the same time hear the voice of Christ above us, "Follow this and thou shallt live," or "This have I suffered for thee and for thy sake, that thou mightest set thy feet in my footsteps." And, oh! how will the soul desire to be tried, despised and persecuted, that it may become fashioned in the likeness of its noble lover and may be pleasing to Him![128]

This approach must remain, perhaps, an invulnerable mystery of a religious way, although, supported by a practical discipline these ideas could take on flesh even now, and surely disturb the familiar world.

Gerard often spoke of the indispensability of this contact between the two worlds. If nothing is contrary to me but I myself, what must be obeyed? To borrow the words of another proverb, in the midst of the adversities inseparable from our lives, strike, or you will be struck: but how strike?

And he said that a man ought not to be thrown into confusion on account of any affair of the world. He who does that which he knows, deserves to know much and he who does not do that which he knows, deserves his great blindness. It is a great thing to obey in those things that are contrary and painful to man—this is true obedience.[129]

And again, in connection with meditation:

I almost always and everywhere teach that the Passion of our Lord Jesus Christ must be unfailingly held in the mind and taken up again often, so that by this there is no adversity which may be able to happen to a man that may not be tolerated with a balanced calm.

In another place, he tells of man's willingness to take up all kinds of crosses, difficulties that are actually unnecessary, and of his abhorrence of that cross which is "really needful for us."[130]

In trying to understand the Brotherhood's life and values for ourselves, rather than merely fashion a description from the words of others, this account has become preoccupied with questions of 'the inner life': to find this thread of meaning, even momentarily, is difficult, but to baulk would be worse.

From the outside, the activities of this Brotherhood appeared incomprehensible and suspicious, particularly at the beginning, when they stood out from the familiar religious orders. What did their commitment threaten? Every stick has two ends: where should we grasp it? They can be distinguished from the Protestant reformers, whose preoccupation with inner questions rent the church, not because they were less radical, but because their search remained inside, not demanding the abolition of given forms but accepting a demand to work within them, for the sake of the difficulty. This wish was the Brother's own concern, in the province of his attention: projected outward in order to 'help others,' it became subject to other laws, another scrutiny. It is not a question of inner versus outer, but of the passage between them and the kind of influence generated. The difficulty of understanding a movement of this nature only from the outside is apparent. Their respect for "the institutions of our ancestors and of the church" was unimpeachably orthodox, yet this respect in its intensity came from their work to prepare themselves to receive the sacraments, in opposition to the unconscionably passive acceptance with which 'orthodoxy' and 'faith' are often associated, then as now. Gerard emphasised the need for a discriminating study of

> the institutions of our ancestors and of the church . . . lest by ignorance of the law you turn your sense of duty into disobedience . . . so that you may perceive the fullness of the fruits of the primitive church.[131]

The Brethren emerged during the Great Schism and Conciliar Movement, "present suffering" which Gerard regarded as symptomatic of an organic deterioration. His letters indicate a circle of loyal clerics and laymen working for the purification of the church "through the discipline of the inner man."[132] It was not a question of adapting the religious inheritance to make it more 'relevant,' but of making use of what had been communicated to travel upstream. Peter of Dieburg wrote that only rumination on the Passion could open us to receive the seven sacraments; Gansfort in his *De Sacramento Eucharistiae et audienda Missa* and Mombaer in the *Scala Communionis* discussed means to this end. Peter remarked that many priests knew nothing about the inner devotion and even scoffed at it.[133] The Brethren had a dialectic and a method. They liked to cite the aphorism *fac quod in se est*, do what is in you,[134] as a key to the religious life, perhaps to true orthodoxy in the steps of the saints. For this simplicity, they urged, one must work.

Consider what Gerard says about attending Mass in his *Conclusa*, dating from his time with Ruysbroeck and the Carthusians. The study of devotion which underlies these notes to himself was a direct learning about oneself. He emphasises the relationship between our physical and psychological postures: outer postures, the manifestation of our habitual inner states, evoke only their subjective equivalents in us. What is a man's place when he begins to realise this slavery? Wishing to worship, and seeing that "bending (*incurvatio*) is wonderfully conformable to the devotion of the mind, on account of the proportional movement of the imagination," the question arises: what inhabits this posture of submission? To be completely attentive in this situation, he says, is to "venerate through the orderly arrangement of the body." This was the renewal of tradition.[135]

It is necessary to begin simply in this way with "the natural body" and to "experiment." Kempis described Gerard as "one who tried many things." He knew "through experiment" how the "natural body" was susceptible to the influence of music, for example, and that outward movements of reverence could be "liars." The 'humble' posture into which the body falls does not correspond to inward humility: this is easy to understand mentally, but their religion concerned wholeness. Such observations, simply arrived at and deeply felt, could bring a man to face his unknown. How has this division between inner and outer life come about, unbeknown to his reason?[136] Religion calls: What is he, not philosophically or theologically, but in direct experience? The body carries on in its own way, his mind is elsewhere, and his feeling . . . ? Whatever he may imagine he loves, to what is he actually attached?[137] The inadequacy of outer worship was a commonplace, but if a man turned away from his poverty with his usual sense of rectitude intensified, he would become only a moralist.

Unless we worship with the mind, the heart, the senses and the body together, Gerard said, we are deceived. He pledged himself, therefore, to observe the set forms, the bowing, the uncovering of the head, but to use them as a means, accepting the challenge to be present:

> I will hear by lowering the hood, I will hear with the ear and I will hear with the mind; otherwise it is just like tinkling cymbals and sounding brass. No voices or words are my own whose sound is not received by me.

At different parts of the Mass, different responses were called for. During the reading, it was most important to listen, to be occupied with nothing else whatever:

> for the powers of perception are less when they are intent upon many things than on one thing. It is enjoined that the words of the Gospel and the writings of the Apostles are attended to during the solemnities. . . . "It is useless

to listen unless we pay attention." . . . [W]e owe attention to the present, or we owe to the gospel, from which we withdraw all that we say and pass through in our meditating.[138]

When the Pax came, he strove to "raise up his ardent longing" and prepare himself watchfully:

> After such a communion from the Pax your ardent longing should stay within and last some time. If, however, you begin to wander, as is used to happen to you when you intend something before you have ordered yourself, turn to the Passion of Christ.[139]

The same attitude and practice was transmitted to the Harderwijk Brother, who wrote a hundred years later concerning his work at the beginning of the canon of the Mass:

> at *Te igitur* collect yourself for the recollecting of the Passion of the Lord or His Advent according to the necessity of the time.[140]

These texts tell of an intention born of watching the interrelation of inner and outer life, meditation in action; behind the religious language, they have something new to say.

Feeling this, historians argue about the meaning of 'spiritual communion,' some wishing to see the Devotionalists as forerunners of the radical reformers of the sixteenth century, others preferring them as prototypes of Counter-Reformation orthodoxy. The last part of *De Imitatione Christi* concerns the preparation necessary to receive the Eucharist:

> anyone who knows devotion can freely have spiritual communion with Christ every day and at every moment to his own great profit; for he shares a mystic communion and is invisibly refreshed whenever he devoutly meditates on the mystery of Christ's Incarnation and His Passion and is filled with a burning love for Him.[141]

Preparation must be everything for absence to bear fruit:

> what profit was the bodily sight of Jesus Christ to Pilate or Herod? It would have been no use to carry, to see, to welcome the Christ, unless one had spiritually conceived and comprehended Him. Moreover, if His corporeal Presence had not been withdrawn from the Apostles, the Holy Spirit would not have descended.[142]

The words, "anyone who knows devotion," refer to the Brethren's special study, a qualification possessed by very few. Even someone "who knows devotion," the text continues, would be wise to attend church, "seeking rather to praise and honour God than find comfort for himself."[143] Whatever "spiritual communion" means, it is not the comfort a man blindly craves. We, who do not "know devotion," who have only heard about it, would be better advised to enquire into the reality of 'ordinary communion' first. The material on which the *Conclusa* and *De Imitatione Christi* were based was intimate, not originally intended for publication: belonging to special conditions of study and experiment, it confuses and energises us as we eavesdrop. From such conditions, support has always issued for the religious forms without which social life would irretrievably degenerate, together with a particular challenge to these forms, for those who could penetrate beyond them.

These writings are the kernel of late medieval sacramental devotion.[144] The idea that specific inward preparation was necessary for participating in the great traditional observances became mixed with elements of popular religious culture. Whytford's *Dialoge* and the Observant Friar Gararde's *Interpretacyon and sygnyfycacyon of the Masse* were late English expressions[145] of the responsibility commonly assumed by the monastic orders for the religious education of the laity. These books were designed for public consumption, but retain, more or less indistinctly filtered, an impress of the New Devotion. During the later sixteenth century, the influence of the Spanish and Ignatian schools of meditation renewed the process, but associated it with the obsessive concern about 'orthodoxy' which bedevilled the age.

The Brethren sought to understand their place, in humility, withing a given traditional framework, espousing an orthodoxy to which a certain kind of search posed no threat. In the space between them and their beliefs their experiment was made and their daily work begun. Finding religion within ordinary activities was a threat to the existing orders and established ecclesiastical hierarchy, insofar as these had hardened around the separation of religious and laity. As their work was intrinsically related to the monastic way of faith, how they believed may have been as important to them as what they believed.[146] If this is so, Gerard and his Brethren stood between the poles of orthodoxy and heresy, evading any classification based on our tendency to think in opposites. The material presented in this chapter shows their experimentation in the midst of duality, a path later formalised into the systematic use of spiritual exercises and meditations. Gansfort's *De Sacramento Eucharistiae* is prefaced by a letter in which he advises a nun to be content with the observance of the Rule, for the sake of the discipline necessary for the body, "but in your reflections and meditations on the Lord Jesus," he adds, "never be content," that you may "often have Him as the sweet guest of your heart and by His counsel, he will faithfully control all your thoughts."[147]

The sources of the New Devotion refer, directly and indirectly, to unity, order, the coincidence of opposites, the relating of 'heaven' and 'earth' in the presence of another level. The 'mixed life' was a meeting between action and contemplation. If growth is connected with the spiritual reconciliation of opposites, the significance they believed the Trinity to have in all processes, as well as the subsequent decline of their movement, becomes clearer. For the records available indicate an increasing imbalance and polarisation in their attitudes and practices.

Hence the appearance of an extreme conservatism among the Observant congregations and, in other quarters, the expression of a 'spiritual radicalism' which held all outward observances and good works as nought:

> religious feeling and the ardent love and desire for God and a loving attachment to Him are sufficient to gain eternal life, even though he had neither hands nor feet nor tongue with which to perform good works.[148]

In this involution, a quality was lost which renders their sayings more comprehensible to us. The theologian and reformer, Gabriel Biel, who came to the Brethren late in life, considered that Gerard's successors had not continued his work in the same direction, noting with dismay the preoccupation with outer forms in the reformed congregations influenced by Windesheim.[149] In the view of Godfrey Toorn, rector of the Deventer Brotherhouse, there were two reasons why the Brethren made little progress:"we observe the hours in a negligent way and . . . we do not prepare ourselves for the Holy Communion in a sufficiently worthy manner.[150]
This suggests that the codification of methods of meditation and prayer went together with a decline in their practice.

The simplicity of their attitude to study and learning came from a willing capacity to discriminate, at the cost of self-importance, between the useful and useless: here is the intelligence of an evaluation, and the intensely personal question of aim. How to apply ourselves in such a way that we are literally fed by the Christian heritage and the world about us, so that we are more deeply awakened, without being diverted into all the paths of cleverness and self-satisfaction; how to know in order to be able to serve God, rather than becoming a mere scholar, another unbalanced intellectual? Gerard had said, "I had rather that a book were my servant, than be servant to a book."[151] This was a positive attitude, but there are many indications that, during the fifteenth century, it tended to become negative, that a kind of fear entered. Imposed restrictions blindly accepted, evoke disobedience in due course. John Vos of Heusden, the first Prior of Windesheim, who directed his canons away from Aquinas and the recent scholastics, that they might persevere in "simplicity," was cited by the fourth Rector of Deventer in his attempts to limit free access to the library.[152] By 1450, the Deventer librarian was horrified at the popularity of "sermons or similar intellectual works," and despaired of the future of the community.[153] The Brethren had a saying, often quoted at this time, "first devout, second scientific and third dissolute," which was glossed:

> the first generation studies devotion together and, then when that first fervour becomes tepid, the ardent desire for devouring books becomes hot, and, then, at last, this also perishes and dissolution comes.[154]

The records of the General Chapter of the Windesheim Congregation after 1485 are full of disciplinary measures and deliberations about building prisons for offenders, reflecting the values and fears of contemporary monks.[155] There are accounts of the inflexibility with which new ways of binding books, changes in kitchen equipment and glazing were being resisted in the name of simplicity.[156] The Deventer Chronicle for the 1480s could only lament that involvement in outer affairs was hindering "the observance of the ancient simplicity, devotion and internal training . . . rare in the present age when evil has gained ground far and wide."[157] Simplicity versus what? Engagement in outer work while remembering the inner was the essence of the New Devotion. Memory, often all we have, is important, although powerless on its own; but there are different kinds of memory.

The outer and inner worlds of man were not seen as irreconcilable by the founders of the New Devotion, but their 'normal' contradiction was fully acknowledged. Gerard thought it only exaggerated by naive religious practices: our 'doing,' when we were most vehemently attached to its result, was likely to be an illusion "of the devil."[158] Scattered through our material are indications, even directions, for another kind of doing, 'the work of God,' the lawful result of a different relationship between outer and inner life. It is like a remembering.

Whatever we make of these fragments of teaching, it is obvious how far the wheel had turned by 1500 for lovers of freedom to be building prisons, exponents of the mixed life to be accused of breaking in boys for the monasteries.[159] The Brethren appear to have been deflected by influences exterior to their work: as they were drawn into the intellectual, religious and social life around them, their independent force waned. Christian ideas, precise instruments within an accepted discipline, took on subjective meanings as they became mixed with material of other qualities; becoming external in their action, they became random, imprecise and negative in influence. Both the radical-libertarian and social-revolutionary wings of the Reformation then drew force from them.

Zerbolt, reiterating traditional exegesis, concludes an account of the value of manual work by quoting the Gospel story that news of Christ's birth had first been heard by the shepherds. In 1552, Latimer repeats the same story, commenting that he who follows his vocation in the world is, ipso facto, more obedient to God, and therefore more favoured, than the idle monk.[160] Idleness had been for Zerbolt a warning and an opportunity, but becomes for Latimer the reason for dismissing a whole class: the viewpoint, sense of 'work' and question faced are poles apart. Latimer is concerned with stable social morality within a harmonious 'commonwealth,' Zerbolt with the mysterious allegorical vision of Scripture and man's place and receptivity before the higher powers. When Florence wrote that work was "holy," we do not take him to mean that any work, undertaken in any fashion, was holy, but think rather of of John Ketel working in his kitchen, striving to render to 'God' and 'Caesar' their respective dues. In a controversial pamphlet of the 1530s we read that, "there is no work better than another to please God: to make water, to wash dishes, to be a fowler and apostle."[161] However true in the special conditions of a small, hand picked community, united by a common search for inner meaning within a given doctrinal framework, wrested from it, such a valuation is bound to be misunderstood, to become crudely revolutionary. The spiritual tradition conveyed in our material shows that a clear conscience belongs to the heart which resists accusing others of falsity, in order to allow the truth of each situation to make itself known. In the crisis of the early 1500s new knowledge was needed, whether levels were confused or not.

When Gerard said that a wife obeying her husband and quietly performing daily tasks was more pleasing to Christ than an absent-hearted ascetic doing penance, he was insisting on the vanity of men's assumption that salvation could be achieved by their own 'doing,' without paying attention to what they were: he was neither denying the value of penance, nor lauding the married state unconditionally above the religious. By the sixteenth century we find many statements to the general effect that:

> matrimony, like as in very deed it is, ought to be called the spiritual estate, other orders worldly and secular: matrimony is of all other the highest religion and most spiritual estate.[162]

The 'mixed life' could blend with the moral values of emerging Protestantism when its original context had been forgotten: ceasing to be a tool, it became naturalised as an ideal.

Where did their force go? Imbalance, complication, inflexibility, polarisation of contradictions and multiplication of aims: it is easy to anatomise the decline of the New Devotion. A leaven becomes a doctrine, changing state. It is easy to talk as if we understood what was being lost, as if the lawful movement into complexity could be evaluated without experiencing the initial simplicity, balance and flexibility. Their meditation, in which a scene of the Passion was intensely visualised, impressed on the senses and recalled at moments during the day, was remarkably similar to the Ignatian, in particular the "composition of place,"[163] both drawing on the techniques of the *ars memorativa*.[164] The Ignatian exercises were widely adopted by the surviving remnants of the New Devotion.[165] What appears as decline, becomes transference, even transmission, if a broader view is taken: what is valuable is not lost, for there is a kind of economy at work in these matters.[166]

We have focused on the elusive 'how' of religion,[167] for it is in persevering to apply a method that force is gathered. The question of method evokes no clear association, except perhaps a suspicion of artifice, for we know only about religious theory, what should be done. On what ground can theory and practice meet, what is the passage between knowledge and work? Our material is important because it gives some insight into this.

The sayings of the Desert Fathers, to say nothing of the New Testament, refer frequently to the practicalities of daily life and work. The practice of religion was compared to the discipline of a trade or craft.[168] Analogy measures the unknown by the known, calling upon a more subtle part of the mind, able to be aware of itself, momentarily, in a place between familiar and new territory. In the face of the simplest operation, theoretical knowledge is useless without the experience of how to do, something incorporated: knowledge needs a body with legs. Could the relationship between the Brethren's wish to serve and their effort, between their theoretical knowledge of the human condition distilled from the spiritual tradition and the challenge of daily life, have been any less practical? At every level, the appropriate movement is elusive. Traces of a psychology and its counterpart, a religious method, may be discerned in their accounts of 'the common life,' a method which, based on an ancient understanding of human nature and its possibilities, informed their work and related their activity and ideas.

To recapitulate: the traditional psychology on which the work of the New Devotion was founded had arisen from a study of the whole man, his actual condition as a citizen of the moon and his potential liberation from its laws; this work was directed towards the experiencing of separation from God and disobedience of His commandments, as a fact; the verification in action of these psychological and religious ideas was by means of exercises aimed at awakening an ordered participation of every part of themselves in a more abundant life; the end of this work was the proper worship and service of God.[169] Taken altogether, the New Devotion, during its short life, was the renewal of a method: their exercises, formulated and elaborated, became the 'methodical meditation' of their successors.

The wisdom of a religion in its fullness affirms the scale of what must be realised, its method shows how, but the crucial question 'why' must sound in a man himself, together with the purpose of his life. Without the intention which can be born of this confrontation, there is neither need nor place for method, and without method there is no Way. The 'mixed life' was a Way, or the approach to one.[170] If the rewards of God are great, as it is said, so must our deeds be: it is surely naive to hope otherwise. We are talking of the means by which religion could become more than the mere subscription to ideals: between fascination with them, and despair at the abnormal conditions of life we have established, lies an unexplored area: until a guide appears, I need a staff. 'Method' is the formulation of that which sincere men have observed in a state of reverent attention before God, and have bequeathed to their successors as a way of measuring the distance between where they are and their goal.[171]

Why is it that the records of religion resound with versions of the wisdom, but are almost silent concerning method, as if it were enough to know about the truth? How does it happen that what should be done is remembered without the need for it to be done being present? Our inability and the question of how a way could be found is passed over. 'Method' belongs to the oral tradition. The dimensions of the historical record rarely comprehend the separation of what we know and what we are and, hence, the fruitlessness of the partial knowledge we try to pass off as our own. Some of the records of the New Devotion convey the missing quality. Spiritual techniques for bridging 'Jericho' and 'Jerusalem' arose from the study of this disunity, and were transmitted by being lived, that is, "orally." Through the proliferation of hearsay about this process, teaching becomes information which can be written about and thence enter the records as the 'typical' Christianity of its day, from which religious ideals derive. The Brethren were further upstream, their intention being more practical than idealistic. When transmission becomes harnessed to enthusiasm for the truth of an ideal, the reflection of wisdom in the absence of real search and enabling method, a kind of violence enters: the 'truth' becomes incomplete and, in a sense, dishonest. For whose sake do men preach what they cannot themselves realise? Can such action ever raise the level of society? The 'others' we accuse of falsity are also within ourselves. The real experience of wisdom and knowledge of method does not die out, but, disappearing from view in the records of one time, is providentially renewed in another: in their conviction that they practised the discipline of the Desert Fathers, the Brethren may serve as one example of this.

This chapter has been concerned throughout with the New Devotional method and will end with a detailed examination of one exercise. Mombaer claimed that his *Chiropsalterium* revealed an entire method, "whereby one can accomplish more in one hour than else in a whole day."[172] He tells, for example, how a man might associate an intention with each part of his hand and then stroke his thumb against them whilst praying the psalms.[173] Traditional formulae, such as "sorrow for one's sins" and "the imploring of divine mercy," divided into three constituent acts, were used. What lies behind this?

We must look beyond any initial reaction against 'artificiality.' It is certainly not 'natural' to remember in this way. It is, indeed, 'natural' to forget, particularly those subtle perceptions and intimations which can gradually give substance to a nonegoistical wish.[174] We remember mostly in thought that something was intended, without reexperiencing a connection with its meaning, effectively forgetting why. If what is to be remembered is real, then any method which combats forgetfulness is justified: if men were right as they are, which all traditions deny, artifice would be unnecessary. What is, and must be, artifice for beginners, may later become that 'art' of which the old aphorism speaks: "better is art than evil strength."[175] The Brethren's art was based on a practical spiritual psychology. Whilst we can only agree with the later Protestant comment (c. 1578) on the superstitious use of such methods in connection with repetition of the Name of Jesus, "it is a matter of understanding, sense and feeling, truly to speak of Jesus, it is not a matter of fiddling with ten fingers,"[176] our reading of the material prompts deeper enquiry. Is there not, just here, a clue to their 'art'? It was a funda-mental principle of the tradition that all of a man, mind, body and heart together ("understanding, sense and feeling") is called on to respect what is above him.[177] This opens the question.

If they sought a more whole participation, in their daily work and their perfor-mance of the Office, we wish to know what this meant, practically. The Lollards were accused of thinking 'the world' and 'heaven' were the same level. It is a ques-tion of unity, and therefore scale. What was the Brother's part when the Christian truths he tried to understand on the small scale of his own life were reviewed before him in the awesome symbolism of the liturgy? If this ritual remembering in the Office was intended to be a bridge between the action of the teaching and the place in which a man finds himself,[178] then the quality of his participation is crucial. What, exactly, is being remembered in the Office?

The particular exercise to which we refer must be understood in connection with a man's state, and his underlying need, when called to prayer. We recall a passage already quoted from the *Meditations of St. Bernard*, describing the shift-ing inner states observed during prayer.[179] Let us draw a picture. Being able to watch and wishing to be sincere, he sees that his relationship with what is hap-pening is relatively shallow, partial and disjointed. He is intermittently and, as it were, distantly aware of his own words and thoughts, of those around him, the place and ceremony. He may become absorbed in one aspect at the expense of everything else, being drawn by it, almost unawares, into an associative internal debate, interwoven with pleasurable and painful memories and anticipations, in which he further loses touch with all he is continuing to do or say and with what is happening around him. In trying to pay attention, he sees how weak he is, how he constantly loses the thread. He may simply begin to daydream or imagine him-self to be experiencing something. He mouths words automatically, but what he is saying is lost to him. He may suddenly have a fleeting sense of these haphazard movements within what he thinks of as himself, of his disorder and lack of inde-pendent will, and may connect this direct experience with what he has heard about man's 'sinful' condition after the Fall.

New questions appear, as his perceptions are refined and a contrary move-ment begins. What does he actually receive of the ancient words of the liturgy, how do the truths of the faith sound in him, if at all? In what sense is he partici-pating? In this situation, what does it mean that there are different degrees of attention?[180] In the concentration he now tries to muster, is he becoming more alive to the meaning of his prayer, or is he closing himself off, becoming fixed? His watching *is* the question. It is damaged immediately he strains to project a meaning or becomes greedy for reward. Of what quality is the attention of his ordinary piety, and is it all that is demanded of him? What is the place of the body in prayer: is he even aware of it? If so, what does his posture tell him of his inner state: of whom does it speak, to what is it conformable?[181] Is there not

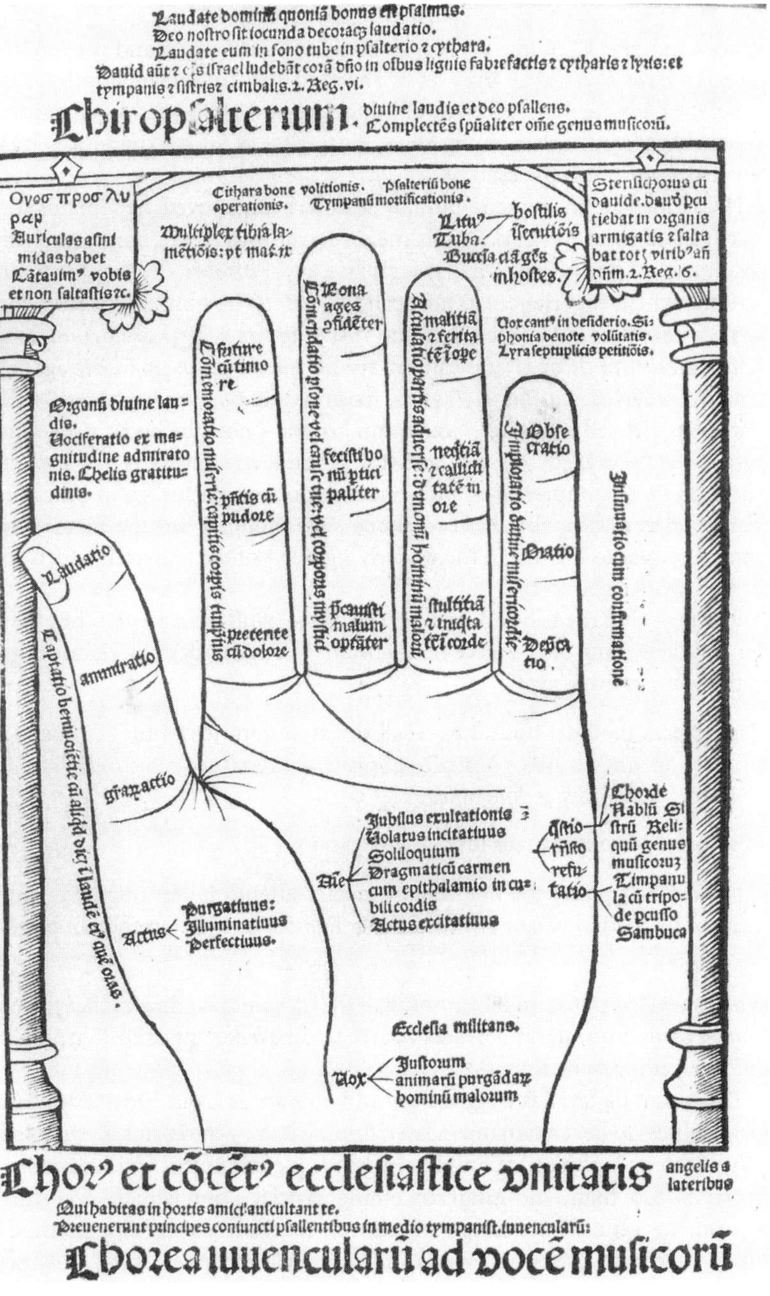

Figure 7.1. Diagram of the hand with artificial memory *loci* from Mombaer's *Rosetum exercitorum spiritualium et sacrum meditationum* (Paris 1510).

important material of his own which could support prayer and deepen his need? He may have been able truly to wish good for himself or another (is it the same?), or he has realised that, although he sincerely intends an action, he is never able to remember at the time. Awareness of such experiences includes a sense of scale and is the seed of prayer.

He is indeed in movement, but not flexible; being moved, he remains somehow inactive and inert. What does this mean? In the face of this constant change, the movement of becoming, what is his place and responsibility? He is the process and that which experiences it: how can this be? Yet he himself, his soul, is neither this nor that, but in between. Now he wishes to pray, to speak to God, as it were. While subject to disorder, he cannot, for he is lost, yet, if he forces against it, he cannot, for he loses stillness. Physical tensions and posture tell him that all that is being experienced is taking place within his body, now the body of his sensitivity. By what is he judged? 'Doing' something about his slavery is not the question. These processes, impressions and confrontations come and go in much less time than it takes to describe them with our slow thought, but the picture drawn is untrue neither to life nor to the underlying sense of the material, which concerns interior work *in extremis.*

It is clear that the use and significance of the hand exercise was the strengthening and deepening of the force of attention.[182] The Harderwijk manuscript refers to the hand in this way:

> at vespers thou art bound to recall thy attention three times in succession, firstly at the words, *Nisi Dominus edificaverit . . .* , secondly at *Beata mater . . .* , thirdly at *Magnificat . . .*

To sing the *Magnificat* calls for special devotion:

> from which place, for the sake of greater attention you ought to number devoutly the ten verses of this most delightful canticle on the ten fingers of your hand.

When speaking of the vital beginning of the day, this text directs that the *Benedictum* be said "from the innermost heart" upon awakening, and that the hand be unfolded at the same time.[183]

The extant material is fragmentary and uneven, as is our experience. Surviving forgetfulness to be written down later, finding its way into print, perhaps accidentally, it can only give an incomplete, external picture of this work. As instruction, it begins too high, omitting something crucial upon which everything else depends for genuine meaning.[184] Precise instructions concerning method would surely have been given orally and individually, perhaps in those 'collations' we know the Brethren to have adopted on the model of the Desert Fathers. When Gansfort describes a method to counter distraction in prayer by numbers, that is, by counting, he may well have been drawing on an oral source.[185] In other words, it is likely that we can know everything about the hand exercise except its kernel. That so many words are needed to interpret something so 'simple' is a paradigm of subsequent 'methodical' elaborations.[186] To understand would be the result, not of much explaining, but of persistently sincere trying, without reservation. Directions concerning the parts of the body, sensation and relaxation, are implied, rather than given explicitly in the texts known to us, but they do not conflict with what we know of the psychology of the New Devotion and their sources.

At a definite moment in the recitation of the psalms, by remembering to stroke his fingers in a particular sequence, he must needs become attentive to his hand and himself stroking it. Perhaps, until then, he had forgotten he had a hand, and a body, but now he remembers its presence and experiences his life more directly. Something strengthens in response to the shock. He wishes to remember what he has intended: when? It is *now*, connected somehow, with his hand, because he has made the connection artificially, but belongs properly to his inner life. Has he forgotten it, or—momentarily, he is in between—has it forgotten him? It is not a word he needs to remember, but that part which has tasted its meaning. Through a movement of attention which he initiates, directed towards himself, the intention present in him when he 'fixed' it in his hand earlier, is revived: now it is present again and true, and some part of him which was, as it were, absent, can participate. All this has happened with great speed and intensity. Just to have wished in his mind to remember was not sufficient: he had to connect the attention of his thought with his body through experiencing the flow of sensation as he relaxed, and only then, in silence, wish. Now, during the Office, he remembers this intention not merely with his mind, but with more force, because he is calling upon his body and its energy, through sensation, to support him. It is difficult to say whether he remembers his wish or his wish remembers him. He is able, suddenly, imperatively to feel, 'to sorrow for his sin.' This remembering is also associative, but not confined to one part, like usual remembering: because he has wished and more of him is participating, it does not happen without him. The injunction to sorrow for our sin, might thus be experienced—*obeyed*—with an intensity which it could not have had as a result of partial remembering, accidentally triggered from outside by the words of the psalm.

The key to this exercise is the effective connection between the attention of the mind and the sensation of the body, a connection which is ordinarily absent. As a result of this, he is more whole, in better order, however briefly; it is a question of a flux of energies of different qualities within him and of his relationship to them, of his self-awareness; and it is a mystery. This exercise is directed at an engagement in the Office from within as well as without; that is, in a completely new way. If he can be better placed in himself, he is no longer blindly reacting to the words reaching him from outside; if there is actually no room in him, how can these words find their echo? A different receiving, and thus giving, is at stake. By virtue of the relationship initiated with his body, he is able to feel as well as think his intention, *in the same moment*, more present, he receives the teaching of the liturgy proper to his need. Applied to the Eucharist, this exercise would be an approach to 'spiritual communion.'

This was, then, an exercise for the attention, sensation and feeling, which cut through habitual, automatic devotion by introducing a wholesome shock, the realisation of what *The Meditations of St. Bernard* called "remembering oneself."[187] In the psychological formulae of the *Rosetum*, based on Gansfort's *Scala Meditationis*, we find this:

| The seeking. | What anyone should seek, | What I think | The waking.[188] |
| | namely, from himself. | What I must think. | |

Behind the simple words of the Brethren's *Consuetudines*—"at the third hour you must prepare yourself for the reciting of vespers"—or the saying of Florence— "learn to understand what you are praying and thereby you will be driving away wandering thoughts,"[189]—lay a world of possible seeking.

The demand of medieval religious writings not to worship only outwardly seems comprehensible enough, but merely to oppose outer and inner is not to understand the significance of the situation, just to exchange one concept with another. The question is more interesting than this. The Brethren were trying to penetrate beyond mental concepts and imagined beliefs, and we must emulate them. The religious ideas embedded in the liturgy address the whole man: man as he could become. When not received directly as a call, they are arrogated, distorted and fixed by the isolated intellect, the partial emotion, by the ego, the 'old man,' and necessarily degenerate into slogans and ideals. The method of the New Devotion was a prophylactic against this. The demand to touch inwardly an echo of the word externally recited could give force to the great prayers of Christianity and corresponds to one of the purposes of the traditional liturgy, to awaken men between the outer and inner life, that they might receive a new truth. The New Devotion's method was a bridge between the traditional injunction to worship inwardly and the possibility of actually doing so.[190]

By taking into life a practical ascetic teaching based on systematic meditation and inner exercises, hitherto preserved under monastic discipline, the New Devotion was a vital link between the exclusive ideals of institutionalised monasticism and the Renaissance embrace of the Christian vocation in the world. Their experiment made possible the Society of Jesus. Between the outer and inner life of men, the 'mixed life' was a bridge, a search for free movement. During the critical period of the fifteenth century, when traditional forms were ossifying and dissolving, when religious thought had become divorced from the concerns of life and religious practice inseparable from social custom, the importance of the New

Devotion was that it embodied the daily work of turning towards the unknown, while accepting existing forms. The significance of their experience can be read everywhere in the religious literature of the sixteenth century, to which we must now turn.

EIGHT

The Ordering of Daily Life in England

> We drive over and pass our days by continual interchange . . .
> in continual commotion . . . never stable in one degree . . .
> there is no thing committed to the disposition of man more
> precious than is time. How be it that many waste their days?
>
> *Contemplacyon of Synners*, 1499

> Constrain yourself with the fear of death to spend your time at
> every hour to the most profit of your soul, offering your heart
> with your work both at the beginning and at the ending unto
> our Lord.
>
> *A dyurnall for devoute soules*, 1530?

> [F]irst gather yourself unto yourself.
>
> Richard Whytford, 1537

> [W]hile I am seeking or doing any thing outwardly, grant me
> grace to remember my self inwardly.
>
> William Peryn, 1557

> [I]t standeth us upon most watchfully to take heed to every
> thought, word and deed that passeth.
>
> Robert Southwell, 1598

These sayings refer to an inner turning in the midst of disorder, the experience of which was the foundation of the New Devotion. In traditional thought the idea of 'order' had an objective content related to levels of being and consciousness, justice and providence, ancient knowledge that antedates and transcends philosophy in the narrow sense of our current usage.[1] Order and disorder enter the most immediate experience of the common life:

And hardly do we divine the things that are on earth, and the things that are close at hand we find with labour; but the things that are in the heavens who ever yet traced out?[2]

What sunders 'heaven' and 'earth' and, consequently, us from our lives?

The order of the Brother's day, the round of prayer, manual work and meditation, laced with subjective exercises, was founded on principles discovered and communicated by monastic ascetics, applied, for pressing reasons, to life in the world. The significance of his search lay beyond the dullness of ordinary experience, in that place where, according to the vision of Christian spirituality, theology, metaphysics and practical devotion, above and below, were united. The teaching they earnestly studied needs always to be taken into life. Zerbolt's "spiritual ascendings" were movements of return, however relative, to man's rightful, that is, original, place in the universal order. Creation 'in the image of God' is meaningless without hierarchical order and levels of being. The call of the New Devotion was to find simplicity in front of these ideas. They present us with a question, therefore.

The English texts dealt with in this chapter concern the point of contact between such 'ideas' and all the sensations of daily life. In their homeliness, humility and simple truth, they represent the bridge made between the high spiritual teachings of the medieval mystics and the ground of everyman's life, at a critical moment in Western culture, when representatives of the Monastic Way, the virtual Christian tradition, could no longer command unconditional trust from those who sought meaning. Where but here-and-now, with "the things that are close at hand," should a beginning be made?

Tudor laymen were deeply preoccupied with religiously ordering their lives. It was the underlying question of the vernacular devotional treatises appearing on the eve of the Reformation, tugging on the sleeve of the impending, and became the main theme of the numerous guides of the later sixteenth century. Although continuity is more marked in Catholic writing, it is found in Protestant also, the sign of a common need: it was a territory through which the two sides marched more closely in step than their respective propaganda suggests. Taken as a whole, this literature implies the desire of innumerable men and women to order their lives outwardly and inwardly, for their own sakes. This aspiration was feeding on the practical religious teaching which the New Devotion had transmitted from their monastic sources. The quantity, and in some cases the quality, of this material authenticates the influence we have been discussing: the spiritual exercises which had informed the Brotherhouses and reformed congregations of the fifteenth century, were finding their way, in a modified form, into the consciousness of widening circles of laymen. In pre-Reformation England this literature is associated with the small Bridgettine and Carthusian communities. Just as there is a relationship between the New Devotion and the Society of Jesus in their spiritual teaching, so these early Tudor manuals anticipate the Ignatian *Exercises*. After the middle of the sixteenth century the Jesuit influence becomes overt, although the imprint of the New Devotion can still be discerned. The popularisation in these works is absent from New Devotional material. They are often opaque and verbose, coloured by contemporary preoccupations and lacking impartiality. Insofar as they have a place within a continuing transmission, the scale of which is inaccessible to our vision, they partake of a certain force and integrity, insofar as they seek to persuade through the repetition of methods incompletely experienced, they represent a diminishing of the original influence, an echo acquiring resonances extraneous to the original note. It is 'historically' interesting, but makes lesser demands on discernment than the study needed to penetrate its sources. Without attunement the sound at the echo's heart will not be revealed. Lay guidance by the monastic elite was established in the Middle Ages, and bridges the Reformation in these treatises, but the message is the 'mixed life' not the 'contemplative.' How intentional was this communication before monasticism was dissolved? How consciously farsighted was the formulation of a mixed life by Gerard's teachers at the end of the fourteenth century? We are questioning the existence of a more directed current within the common stream.

The mentioned strictures do not apply to the anonymous *A Dyurnall for devoute soules to ordre themselfe therafter* (1530?), through which sounds, with clarity and restraint, the tones of the "ghostly father," patiently communicating practical advice from personal experience. This little book contains nothing superfluous, no preaching, argumentation, speculation or sentiment. It encourages, but does not insist on, observance of the *horarium*; for practical purposes, the sevenfold monastic division of the day is replaced by a threefold, the early morning, at mealtimes and before retiring, undoubtedly more suitable for the 'active' man of business.

Like the Harderwijk manuscript, and unlike later works which merely give verbal prayers for the different actions of the day,[3] the *Dyurnall* addresses the inner life. Speaking to those who consider themselves to be on "the way of perfection," the author asks why they profit so little each day: and answers that they fail to take the necessary steps. We gain little because we continue to live as before, not acting on those "instructions . . . given us of our Lord God," which reach us in the midst of life, or through the agency of "secret inspiration." He says, truly, that these messages are never taken into "daily conversation . . . by perseverant exercise."[4] Why do we forget, and what would it mean to work with our remembering? Such moments may be infrequent and relatively shallow, but if we are closed to their special quality, "from God," we cannot help undervaluing them. These intimations have no power to stir us, indeed they cannot, and thus action is stillborn: what, then, must we exercise? Our inability to conform to these "instructions" is due, firstly to our negligence and lack of real, non-egoistic concern for our "soul's health," and secondly to our "oblivious memory," which forgets everything unless it has been "deeply written and graven in our stony hearts." This situation can only change when we become so aware, not negatively, of these weaknesses, that we sincerely wish to step into the unknown for the sake of what we lack, and then step, again and again:

Against the first the only remedy is a good will, the which with the help of grace (daily desiring by continual prayers to amend) shall at the last obtain that [which] it perseverantly desires. Against the second default the remedy is often times to read or hear those things the which would always be had in mind.[5]

We must give ourselves something real to remember.

"The way of perfection" was a conventional description of the monastic life. The atmosphere of the *Dyurnall* is of the monastery-in-life, focusing and proving faith within daily routine: our emotional life must be discovered, ordered and led towards an acknowledgement, without manipulation, of the truth and goodness of Christian values. These were not, nor could be, the aims of all laymen, nevertheless the *Dyurnall* was available to all who could read: the first presses enable us to eavesdrop on hitherto oral instruction. The author was speaking to a small group, perhaps 'middle class' London guild members, considered by historians to have been particularly devout and becoming increasingly literate, was writing down instructions for them, "according to your devout request." Such people figured large in early Lutheran circles and would have been drawn naturally to the idea of the 'mixed life.'[6]

As in the Brotherhouse, the day begins with the call to mark well what appears in the heart and mind: with the call to free 'our' attention and watch.[7] How else should a man learn what he truly is and measure his conformity with the teaching? To 'mark well' surpasses shallow noticing coloured by self-judgement. If what is observed is other than the "rule of perfection" requires, "the which is that our heart be at all times united and knitted unto God" through "actual love and contemplation of His Goodness," or through "continual prayer & confession," then this must be acknowledged. Absorption, as it may be, in aimless, egoistic thoughts and feelings so early in the day, is the inevitable result of the "want of diligent spiritual exercise in the time past," that is, of yesterday's heedlessness. A positive realisation of this (without self-pity, justification and guilt), in which a desire for something other than all this repetition is renewed, would correspond to the Brother's *intentio* for the day.

This process may bring him to a moment of silent prayer: he is directed to the Trinity, the symbol of unity and truth. His experience of the given prayer is the pivot of the subsequent day. When, during his affairs, he is particularly touched or feels delight, his *intentio* may be reawakened by turning to this prayer; being moved to self-pride in his work, he can remind himself of his wish by recalling this moment in the morning.[8] In this way a thread may be formed. It is important how he senses and pronounces the prayer. These instructions are very close to the spirit of the New Devotion.

"O blessed and glorious trinity, laud, glory and thanks be to thee of all thy creatures, world without any end, Amen." And when you say this prayer,

speak it not only with your tongue but of all your whole heart, most affectu-
ously desire that the praise, glory and thanks of all goodness that is or shall
be wrought by you or any other creature be returned all only to Him, the
which is the beginning, the midst & the end of all thing that is worthy any
praise. And accustom to rehearse this many times on the day, so oft as you
feel any spiritual or else corporal delectation of God or of his creatures, that
is to say whensoever you be touched with inward devotion or good thought,
when you consider the graces of saints, when you be delighted with the
beauty of any creature, when your meat & drink do content your appetite
and so of all other things that please you.[9]

If a benediction materially touches all, we could be reminded by everything. Preceding the sixteenth-century reaction against formal asceticism,[10] the records of
the New Devotion reveal a relation between the impulse of delight and the religious sense,[11] literally the wish to reunite and be reunited.

Whytford's *Werke for Householders*, contemporary with the *Dyurnall*, has a
similar exercise:

[A]s soon as you do awake in the morning . . . first suddenly turn your mind
and remembrance unto Almighty God.

There follows a prayer to the Trinity and a dedication of the day to the Three Persons, which recalls the consecration of the monk, but which he relates to the lay
baptismal vow.[12] Whytford was crossing the threshold by translating monastic
practices for laymen: Protestant and humanist reformers compared the monastic
vow with the baptismal, to prove its redundancy.[13]

And so the day begins to unfold. He dresses, breaks his fast and enters the life
around him. The *Dyurnall* bids him pause: as he dresses to thank God for providing his needs, as he takes food to remember others "much better" than himself
who are in need ("pray Him to move your heart and the hearts of others to relieve
His poor people"[14]) and, as he leaves the morning service, to be grateful to God
that he has "such leisure" to be able to attend church "without worldly let."

[T]hinking that many a one in the world that be compelled of need to apply
their bodily labours, if they might have such leisure as you have to follow the
spiritual life should much more profit in virtue than you do and be, peradventure, notwithstanding all their business, much more fervent in the love of
God. And then call to mind how many persons be let from the presence of
the church to provide for your need, meat, drink and clothing.[15]

It is a kind of circle which includes what is below and above: aware, even momentarily, of something other than our small selves, a return begins.

The *Dyurnall* insists every action be related to Christian values: easy to see,
but what does it mean? Through what can this new relationship be made? We

infer that the wished-for result is to do with the enlivening and redirecting of man's emotional life, but 'the result' of what? New Devotional sources indicate that it is associated with greater awareness of everyday actions, the black and the white. To mechanically remember the poor, to parrot prayers to the Trinity or thank God only passively were never the aims of this tradition, which points, on the contrary, to a subtle struggle for a different quality of attention in oneself. To 'remember God' sounds well, but what is able to remember, and where is God now? If, as New Devotional sources affirm, 'fallen man' is fragmented and unbalanced, lacking wholeness and right order, his functions dislocated, his energies degraded, and if, as a consequence, he has forfeited access to the higher levels, what is his movement of remembering God? This situation, deeply experienced, is the question.

Here we must enter a caveat. All the treatises examined in this chapter are written backwards. The source of their advice was the distilled experience of recollected people able to find support in outer life for an inner state of being in question: when formulated a reversal takes place, written down it becomes a 'should.' Why is this, and, if it is, what is being transmitted? We cannot step into the same stream twice. The *Dyurnall* tends towards the enthroning of virtuous results, a spirituality dependent on "leisure," the seeds of a conventional sixteenth-century Christian sentiment. The force of personal confrontation, felt in the New Devotional material, makes a weaker impression here. The urging on the reader of devout emotions, with only a hint that an inner life struggle might be necessary to sustain and give them meaning, is typical of the *Dyurnall*. It contains a call, but to what? Far more than the New Devotional texts, it is promoting a Christianity of imitation, focused on results, on what a man should feel rather than showing him the way to it. How conscious are these worthy emotions?

Before leaving his chamber in the morning, he is bidden to accept his station in life, to admit past failings and pledge himself to "begin a new life," with the help of grace. Realising his inability to order his life by his own efforts, he commits himself wholly to Providence.[16] This is expressed in three Latin prayers given in the vernacular. What is the sense of prayer at such a moment? It acknowledges that more can be involved in this sequence than wishful thinking, the mere desire to be good. There is a choice: he can emotionally repeat prayers, or strive for a more whole engagement, a confrontation with himself as he is. It is a question of two only because a third force hovers. Is it religious emotion that he seeks, in order to feel virtuous, or rather something else, a dimension almost unknown in his ordinary living, except for rare intimations? Does he wish to be uplifted on a wave of emotion, to escape from familiar reality, or to find a more real place in the present world, between 'heaven' and 'earth'? He cannot 'do,' so where is the choice? The *Dyurnall*'s prayer admitting past sins, used automatically or guiltily, may bring a certain release, but if he can revive his inner experience of moments of weakness (if it is there), and keep this before his eyes while praying, as the

Dyurnall suggests, a different contact may result: a genuine, less unconscious discomfort caused by an inkling of what he is and the threat this poses to all that he is accustomed to call 'himself,' accompanied by a strangely familiar sense of freedom ('I can know I am that, but I am not only that'). If he wishes to "begin a new life," he must become able to be free of the old: therefore, he must first study in order to know what he is, or his wish will be only a dream. In our view, this is the general sense of this exercise.

Similarly, we may question the meaning of the prayer submitting to Providence. The *Dyurnall* says that the Christian must acknowledge that he has no control over his life, but is this a received belief or an actual, verifiable fact? Who can bear this? Is our customary belief that we are masters of our life any different in quality from belief in the contrary, the plunge into guilt, or is it rather a question of experiencing and submitting to a higher level? What do we usually serve, in fact? Between what we like to believe and the sudden glimpse of the truth of what we are, free momentarily of the continual illusion that we are in control, we experience our need. A man's committing of himself to Providence must be accompanied, says the *Dyurnall*, by a resolve to offer himself "perpetually" in obedience to the "movings of the Holy Ghost," as far as he is able.[17] What can help him? He can try to experience deeply, attentively and often the fact of his own death, together with the prayer "into Thy hands.[18] The Holy Ghost is the bringer of reconciliation in Christian tradition, a potential force hardly ever received.

The active self-questioning implicit in the *Dyurnall*'s instructions is related to the New Devotion's striving to pay attention to oneself. They said it could lead to God. This is not the function of self-judgement arising from ordinary coloured thoughts about oneself, that absorbing commentary, but is rightly understood only in connection with the search for another quality of attention, the beginning and end of spiritual exercises and the ground of the interpretation of the religious life given here.

How then should we begin?

And when you come to church see that you do nothing only of custom, as if it were a thing that has no reason or understanding.[19]

'Spiritual exercises' are tools with which, by altering something, a man may begin to know himself in a new way. A spoke in the wheel, their use shows, beyond words, the slavery of habit. Having a real place only when religion becomes less habitual, before this becomes possible they reveal the nature of the difficulty. But, by themselves, they will not do it! What needs to be exercised in us?

The idea of religious psychology and method contradicts the idea of faith only if the latter means emotional belief and the former an academic discipline of the isolated intellect.[20] Such contradictions would have been considered the result of human ignorance and division—'sin'—by our subjects, who would have pointed to the possibility of new understanding arising from a different orientation. The need for heart, mind and body to be prepared for participation in the liturgy was at the heart of the New Devotion. Remembering God's Presence was an intentional action, supported by traditional forms.[21] The *Dyurnall* also teaches the maintenance of orthodoxy through inward effort: ceremonies are a means, to be able to make use of which one must prepare oneself.[22] This preparation is connected with freeing oneself from the conditioning of "custom," in order to become available to another influence:

> [I]n all things consider the presence of your lord God, having Him continually before the eye of your soul and so behave you in all things that your service may be pleasing to Him the which requires of us not only our corporal exercise but much more the exercise of our heart.[23]

It is a question of the quality of experiencing, or it is just a metaphor. The matter of "corporal exercise" is virtually passed over in favour of "the exercise of our heart," whereas in the writings of Gerard Groote there are definite indications that the service of God actually begins with finding a relationship to the body.[24] What is the Christian exercise of the heart, and does it exclude the body? What use is a temporary intensification of experience in one part, if the rest of ourselves, remaining untouched, continues as before? The emphasis on wholeness, characteristic of the New Devotion and early Jesuits, has become weaker here. What could relate us in the *normal* participation of which traditional sources speak? How many aberrations of Christian history have resulted from unbalanced application of discipline to our separated, disharmonised parts, albeit in the Name of God! Late medieval thought argued the precedence of knowing the Truth and loving the Good, but in this equation the third term is lacking.

These matters are closer to issues of the Reformation and Counter-Reformation than might appear. We are drawn to material evidence for the possibility of an inner, nonviolent revolution, the necessary conditions for 'conversion,' a complete turning on the scale of the individual. The focus is not on the faults of tradition and the sins of other men, but on the state of 'I myself' in the light of Christian teaching. It is naive to suppose that a search of this kind could ever have interested very many people, let alone motivate a mass movement, yet its seeds are in everyone: it cannot have been that the few who tried to find this way had no influence on those who came into direct contact with them. Kempis' first impressions of the Brethren, quoted above, illustrate this. Luther, Calvin and Ignatius all found their particular ground there, between the awe-inspiring commands of God and the facts of their own being. The later history of violence and intolerance, should not blind us to the origin of the reform movements of the sixteenth century in a common wish for conversion and purity of service. What happens when the individual forgets that his need for truth is greater than the need of others for the truth he can bring? According to the spiritual psychology of the New Devotion, the difficulty lies in being able to remember this need often and deeply enough with more than one part of oneself: if remembering is not a unifying action but a mechanical association in the mind or emotion, we are not penetrated by any impression of truth and there can be no conversion. What if we can remember nothing?

If there has been a real experience during the morning exercise from which an intention has arisen, then the question becomes how to remember its truth in the midst of the demands of life, how to carry it actively. After such a beginning, the *Dyurnall* implies, he is particularly vulnerable. He may, for example, be moved to release his gathered energies in a flood of unnecessary talking, but, remembering suddenly, is it possible to keep alive his meaning, to give his attention instead of helplessly letting it be dissipated, and with it everything? It is not a matter of outward silence at all costs in order to be 'good,' but of not being utterly taken by the tide, of including his intention whilst fulfilling his outer obligations, of the quality of his presence in his life. A renewal can be made, indeed, "after every work, before you divert to any other occupation."[25]

The *Dyurnall* gives times which can be doorways, when two worlds intersect and the questions of religion can sound. What would he wish to be doing were he to die this day?[26] Is he taking his food like a "reasonable man," or "like a beast, which in eating remembers nothing but his meat"?[27] Wishing for something different, he must experiment. The *Dyurnall* adopts the monastic practice of reading before meals, giving "for every day in the week one refection of our lord Jesu, that you may be accustomed to feed with Him."[28] He could pray that the Wisdom of God may "labour with me" when reading, and afterwards try to recall what he has read.[29] Is he a servant at his table, like Christ, or does he play the great lord? If he has received the grace of compunction before eating, his "sensual appetites" may naturally quieten.[30] Because he tends to eat "greedily, without consideration," can he try before each mouthful to lift his heart to God? Does he know whether his body needs more or has had enough, and how should he be in touch with this fine intelligence of his instinct? If he decides to eat less than he desires, it is his own affair, not something to display out of "singularity." Food is "sent of God," and so the remainder is "for the nourishing of charity." Leaving table a little hungry, where is his attention? While avoiding gossip he does not wish to be unnaturally silent, but if necessary must be available to speak.[31] In these ways he can reason with himself actively. His wish is to remember God in the heart, to be neither drawn blindly by 'life,' nor closed in preoccupation, to respond to what is really present.

In purpose and method the *Dyurnall*'s programme can be compared with the *Spiritual Exercises*. The intentional recollection of oneself, deriving from practical guides like the *Speculum Monachorum,* used by the Brethren,[32] appears in the *Dyurnall* and becomes a systematic exercise for the Jesuits. The Ignatian exercitant takes stock of himself in the morning, after the midday meal and supper ("the particular examination"), reviewing his intention ("that which he desires"), demanding an account from himself, recording his "falls" with a certain imperceptible movement when he becomes aware and noting them on the famous diagram. He compares one examination with another, the second day with the first, one week with another, resolving anew to amend.[33] This is an elaboration of the *Dyurnall*'s practice:

> [E]ndeavour yourself always to do better the afternoon than you did the forenoon, and the second day better than you did the first, and so forth to your lives' end.[34]

The *Dyurnall* ends the day with an effort to "imprint" the fact of heedlessness on the mind, to keep the heart occupied with remembrance of God's goodness and to conceive a strong desire to begin anew the next day. Ignatius says that a man should try when he has gone to bed and wishes to sleep, for a definite time to think of the hour he ought to arise and for what purpose, recapitulating the exercises he will then make, in order "to find more surely what he desires."[35]

What do these correspondences show? The Ignatian *Exercises* were unpublished in 1533, when the *Dyurnall* appeared, and there is no direct evidence for their English circulation in manuscript at that date, although it is possible. The first Englishman known to have followed the *Exercises*, John Helyar, joined Ignatius' circle in Paris.[36] *Spiritual exercises, whereby to conquer oneself, and order one's life, without being influenced in one's decision by any inordinate affection*[37] is the full title of the manual which bore Ignatius' name, the natural result of a long tradition of European spirituality and a radical reformulation of Christian asceticism for the new age, the fruit of his own search. He is reported to have said, "I can find God whenever I will."[38]

It is necessary to describe here, however briefly and inadequately, the sense of this powerful and influential work with which we are comparing these homely and forgotten English treatises. Underlying the famous "principle and foundation" of the *Exercises*—"man was created to praise, reverence, and serve God our Lord, and by this means to save his soul"[39]—is the essential question: where is the source of Christian action, from where can 'I do' without violence? The *Exercises* are concerned with fostering the experiences necessary for the discovery and establishment of outer and inner order in man, with the possibility of searching for active, free will through the renunciation of blind self-will, the purification of the emotional life and the intentional direction of thought in meditation, prayer and self-examination, and all this within the received framework of devotional values and traditional beliefs. They are concerned with nothing less than the possible inner transformation of man. His first annotation states:

> [A]ll methods of preparing and disposing the soul to rid itself of all inordinate affections, and, after it has rid itself of them, to seek and find the Divine Will in the ordering of one's life with a view to the salvation of one's soul, are called Spiritual Exercises.[40]

Wherever our texts speak of exercises, they speak of the search for order. The form in which they are given imply that our different functions might be united, the bodily senses participate in the common aim, thought operate without words and feeling be freed from egoistical desire and emotionality. Through faithful work a man may become able to be an instrument of God's Will, "like a cadaver."[41]

Ignatius had visited England in 1530, ostensibly to raise money for his studies, but little is known of his movements. Similarities between the *Exercises* and the works of Whytford have given rise to speculation that he visited Syon.[42] This is possible, even likely, but the relation of English devotion with Ignatian method was surely founded on the common influence of the followers of Gerard Groote.

The *Dyurnall* is trying to bring religion into life, for they are separated by a situation which a man only dimly, if at all, realises. This little book is not asking him to abandon his habits but to face them, not to escape 'daily reality' in the name of religion but to alter his attitude; to see directly what he is, and therefore is doing, and the gulf between this and the teaching, and then to seek a bridge through the force of his attention to himself (prayer and spiritual exercise). A quality needs to be found in daily life which renders him permeable to the action of Christianity.[43] If he could receive the teaching already, what would there be to seek? It is not knowledge of the ordinary mind that is missing. The *Dyurnall* transmits the Brethren's question: how to "put order in the heart by ascents of raising ourselves,"[44] how to make room for a finer influence from which our usual way of living separates us. In the search to know oneself in the Presence of God, at the heart of the New Devotion and the English mystical school, these questions had immense potency. Consider *The Cloud of Unknowing*:

> [T]herefore toil and sweat in all that you can and may, for to get you a true knowing and a feeling of yourself as you are; and then I believe that soon after that you shall have a true knowing and a feeling of God as He is . . . as it is possible, and as He vouchsafes to be known and felt of a meek soul living in this deadly body.[45]

The *Dyurnall*'s method, like the daily work of the New Devotion, aims at informing the lawfully 'worldly' conditions of our lives with states of being in which the subtle laws of grace can act: it is a response to the question, how can the aspiration towards God be given force and direction without entering the special environment of the monastery, for "we give no great force to our own profit."[46] With the degeneration of the religious orders and the impending revenge of society, this question had terrible urgency in the year of the *Dyurnall*'s publication. As to a monastic novice, it speaks of lifelong commitment,[47] "continue this order & cease not, but perseverantly enforce yourself to keep it to your lives end." It transmits practices of inner discipline, proper to the essential Monastic Way, contrary to the comfortable existence and lukewarm practice of the majority of contemporary abbeys.[48] In supporting the practical realisation of Christian teaching, given the individual's real wish, without requiring withdrawal from ordinary life, this forgotten book anticipates the central matter of sixteenth- and seventeenth-century religious experience and is related to the religious search of all times.

The Pomander of Prayer (1530), surely from the same circles as the *Dyurnall,* advises laymen on the difference between mental and vocal prayer and the significance of distraction. The author, a Shene Carthusian, says of his motives:

> of late time I have been instantly desired of certain spiritual friends to write some treatise that might be inductive and also demonstrative (to such devout persons as lack learning and knowledge of holy scripture) how and under what manner they might order themself in prayer.[49]

This preamble also well describes the writings of Richard Whytford, his neighbour across the Thames; the *Pomander* has, in fact, "an exhortation to the readers by a brother of Syon."[50] This little treatise, from an order which had preserved a tradition of contemplative prayer, is another example of the transmission of practical 'monastic' knowledge on the eve of the Dissolution, which was the particular work of the Bridgettines. We sense the hand of Colet and More in this process.

The maner to lyve well, devoutly and salutaryly every day for all persones of meane estate, translated from the French of Johan Quentin and inserted in some editions of the Salisbury Primer in the 1530s,[51] covers much the same ground as the *Dyurnall,* representing a further popularisation of approach, at once more formal and less demanding. Observance of the sevenfold monastic office is to be the core of the layman's day, beginning with Prime at six o"clock in the morning and working through the rest of the offices by suppertime.[52] The layman is to attend church before work ("if you have no needful business"), in order to meditate on God's Goodness and Power ("think what gift He has given to you to create you so nobly as to his Image and Likeness") and on his own death ("touching this death think often thereon"). Puritanical urges are warned against: he should eat "reasonably, without excess or overmuch forbearing . . . for there is as much danger in too little as in too much." A weekly fast is enough, but if even this is a strain, he should "do by counsel." Relaxing after food, he should pray that God "in that rest . . . will accept your health to the end that after it may serve Him the more devoutly." Passion meditation is to play an important part in his inner life:

> [C]onsider often, either by day or night when you do awake, what our Lord did at that hour the day of His Blessed Passion and where He was at that hour.

In this he would have turned to manuals like Fewterer of Syon's *Myrrour or Glasse of Christes Passion* (1534) or established favourites like the *Vita Christi* of Ludolph the Carthusian.[53] Regnault's 1534 *Prymer* also contains prayers for different times of the day: Latin meditations with English rubrics are given for the first hour, leaving the house, entering the church and for different parts of the Mass, where prayer is to be prefaced by a meditation beginning: "Depart from me, evil."[54]

The writings of Whytford deserve a separate monograph. Between 1525 and 1541, fifteen works were published under his name, the majority in the early thirties; in addition, there are three attributed titles, and four translations which have not survived.[55] Almost all the extant works, ranging from the terse formulae of the *Spiritual Glasse* to the polemical, discursive *Pype of Perfection*, were undertaken and published at the request of Syon's Abbess, his sisters or brethren,[56] signalling his obedience to the community's rule and the order's policy of education through the presses.[57] His manifest wish to share the monastic experience comprised a dual intention: to broadcast the discipline that had helped him ('transmission') and to recall the religious themselves to a commitment to their Rules ('observance'), that they might assist in the spread of the truths he had learned to value.[58] Because of this effort to convey monastic attitudes and spiritual exercises to laymen, directly in the *Werke*[59] and *Dialoge*,[60] and indirectly, through subsequent publication of material originally written for his monastic companions, in the *Dayly exercyse*[61] and *Pacience*,[62] he is central to the subject of this chapter. These four works are so complementary and cross-referenced that he surely conceived them as a whole.[63]

The popularity of *A Werke for Householders* shows that the rigours of strict enclosure had not isolated him psychologically from the outlook of his contemporaries. It is a mine of curious, colourful information on early Tudor social conditions and beliefs,[64] a corridor from which a motley procession of preliterate moral attitudes, priestly admonitions and popular practices from the medieval hinterland are seen emerging into the light of Renaissance England at the moment of their redefinition, under the influence of Whytford's Christian humanism,[65] Bridgettine spirituality and fear of heresy,[66] into the more familiar forms of Counter-Reformation Catholicism[67] and Puritanism.[68] The latter aspects have been most readily seized on by commentators anxious to augment an already conceived historical pattern, but it is the incompleteness and potentiality of the *Werke*, its uneven texture of sentimental and naive didacticism enlarged by a certain openheartedness and shot through with a spare monastic clarity, which holds our interest.

Reading was assuming a greater role in lay devotion.[69] The *Werke* and its companion volume the *Dialoge* (together with the writings of his peer, William Bonde) continued the attempt of the medieval clergy to convey Christian values to the unlearned,[70] intensified by the experience of Bridgettine discipline and the urgency of current need. Whytford's suggestion of a morning and evening exercise for laymen[71] (based on the traditional recognition of the possibilities of the early day, if our usual pattern is to be transcended, and of the night for silent reflection, if the sought-for-quality is not to remain unrecognised), and his whole preoccupation with finding order at all levels of life, beginning with inner orientation,[72] connects his thought with the strivings of generations of religious, especially Gerard's brethren, and anticipates the Ignatian exercises[73] and all the devotional guides of the sixteenth century. The systematic meditations of the *Dialoge* confirm the role of Whytford's order as a channel by which this practical spirituality entered the life of the time. The cumulative effect of these practices in the personal experience of subsequent generations of laymen was as profound and incalculable, in its way, as the spreading knowledge of translated Bible texts.[74]

Whytford's writing is more prodigal and comprehensive than the texts we have examined so far, but he confronts the participating reader in the same way with a potentially devastating question, intended to reorientate, to lead to the monastery within.[75] The "self-lesson" or counsel with oneself which opens the *Werke* is nothing less than a call to face one's death, the inevitable, the unknowable. To allow this is to be brought, unwillingly but in real need, to question one's life:

> sure we be that as we be found at that time so shall we be taken and without respite or delay, forthwith shall we be presented and brought before the high judge, that cannot be deceived.

Despite the proliferation of his instructions, Whytford retains a clear sense that it is a change of being ("the health of the soul") born of a different level of awareness, rather than an altered doing born of an accessible guilt, to which man is called.

> We have need, therefore, to be well aware how we spend our time, how we pass this life or rather how this life passes us. And much shall it avail and profit unto the health of our souls oft times for to remember our last end.[76]

How this might be remembered is the subject of his *Dayly exercyse*, based on Bridgettine practice. Such remembering, refined through the outer and inner discipline of the monastery, Brotherhouse or family may, in time, gradually alter the attunement of a life: it must disturb a man's calm and reveal his quality, evoking a meaningful intention to exercise spiritually, or its denial.

So familiar are such calls in the religious literature of all traditions and times, and so identified have they become with conventional moral attitudes, that we have become insensitive to their force; yet their persistence indicates a natural law buried in the hearts of men, on which a morality, both inward and common, could only be based. The action of this call, if admitted, can never be trite, for its aim is to breach the way men live and reach conscience. And if it has echoed down the ages, so also have men's defensive reactions at the prospect of a disturbance of their peace. Whytford's unsophisticated lay readers are not merely historical curiosities in their excuses:

> But yet some of you will say, "Sir, this work is good for religious persons and for such persons as be solitary and do lie alone by themself, but we do lie two

or three sometimes together and yet in one chamber diverse beds & so many in company: if we should use these things in presence of our fellows, some would laugh us to scorn & mock us."

The first obstacle is fear of what others will think of us. He answers that they daily accept greater risks for lesser ends: why is the thought of a 'daily exercise' so unpalatable?

Venture upon it, go forth withall. . . . Every beginning is hard and of great difficulty, but importunate labour does vanquish & overcome all things.[77]

The independence of the practical man was not to be harnessed exclusively to the radical heresies of the later Middle Ages, nor the Puritan sects of the new age. Whytford's vision is broad and deep:

to them that may not attend church every honest place of good & lawful occupation is their church, for God is there present, where He is duly and devoutly served.[78]

The family, workshop, market—truly, the place where one is—could become the ground of the mixed life. Order at all levels within the family or the practice of a craft, just as the disciplined round of the monastery or Brotherhouse, facilitates that confrontation with the unknown with which the "werke" begins, leading, in its turn, to the acknowledgement of, and submission to, a greater order.[79] The clarity of such a perspective engenders its own radicalism.

Trust them best to do for your soul not that do love, or say that they do love, but that you do perceive and conjecture do love their own soul . . . the most sure way to die well, is well to live.[80]

Whytford's writings, particularly the *Werke*, illustrate the nature of religion as a social cement, a series of moral injunctions and precepts designed to ensure a tolerably civilised life among people, which may then reveal, with help, the possibility of an individual and direct path to God and to the soul.[81]

The New Devotion was a bridge, for its time, between these two levels of religion, known and unknown, just as Syon was between monastic and lay Christianity, on the eve of the Reformation. His *Dialoge*, the companion to *Werke*,[82] aims at deepening lay participation in the sacraments, especially "this holy mystery of communion,"[83] by revealing a practical dimension: the introduction of exercises of attention and systematic meditations derived from Syon's discipline, closely related to the spiritual methods and insights of the New Devotion.[84] Christian ideals, alone and unsupported, are insufficient: how to prepare oneself to receive Spirit? In addressing himself to this, the central question of the *Dialoge*, he presents an outline of Christian asceticism, as it had reached him.

All that we have been discussing is summarised in this: the preparation necessary to receive what has been given in traditional religious teachings and, beyond these forms, what has been prepared for man by God, the image of Whose World man is, on his own scale. Preparation is the result of the persistently[85] renewed giving of something valuable, for which sacrifice is perhaps the only word. The Desert Fathers' saying was "give blood and receive spirit."[86] Whytford's instruction is simply to enter within oneself, as if life depended on it, in order to be able to submit: what a world is in this!

> [Y]ou should first gather yourself unto yourself, that is to say, your soul, heart, mind and will, inasmuch as you may, with all force and diligence, wholly and clearly, from all cures, cares, charges & business of the world & from all bodily matters & all cogitations and thoughts, that by any means might let & hinder you in this exercise and so to compel your spirit to labour alone herein. And then commend yourself wholly unto our Lord.[87]

This prayer of inner opening and commitment, sounding in a place of relative independence, is a lay version of the monastic vow, like that given at the beginning of the *Werke*.[88] Having gathered oneself, in honour of the biblical teaching that the Spirit cannot enter unless there is understanding and no deceit, the mind must be engaged unflaggingly to search and bring to light that which eludes usual perception, to remember all that is hidden within, forgotten.[89] (It is interesting that, in Whytford's English, 'conscience' has also the sense of 'full knowledge,' consciousness.)[90] This is *meditation*, which he describes as the action of separating in oneself 'earth' and 'heaven' through the light of reason: "that is to say, that every day of our life we should sometime be as well active as contemplative.[91] It is the formulation of the mixed life. In the great world what is below obeys what is higher (as it does not in man) for God is just.[92] In consciously accepting to be in between, he conforms to this order as the Image of God: only he who lives as Christ did is truly human.[93] The passage is all and everything.

Whytford is saying that it is necessary to see oneself as one is, to know one's 'earth' and 'heaven' for what they are. The pure in heart are able to see themselves.[94] It means experiencing, by moments, multiplicity, contradiction and disobedience, life "lacking His godly presence." Tradition speaks through Whytford of an inner process—the consciousness of meditation at all levels—subject to its own laws, in which self-knowledge reveals conscience, and leads to compunction and a new devotion:[95] perhaps even to remorse and the refining fire of the love of God.[96]

It is a far aim, but can be approached, he says, by paying attention to what one is saying, thinking and feeling during prayer at Mass.[97] So simple, to watch! To refine one's attendance at the service through an engagement in inner prayer sequentially with the movement of the liturgy, to find a vertical as well as a horizontal participation, to remember the Presence of God together with one's own, while outwardly conforming to the prescribed ritual, and to begin, according to Gerard, with an awareness of bodily posture in worship: such was the work of the New Devotion, and something very like this was Whytford's aspiration for his readers. The combination of an ultra-orthodox view of the sacraments with programmatic spiritual exercises of radical intention, marks the *Dialoge* as a true heir to the New Devotion, kindred to the Ignatian *Exercises*, and progenitor of the Counter-Reformation, a stable link between past and future through a time of great disturbance. He gives this prayer before communion:

> O lively flesh & blood of my loving Lord Jesu, the reviver & quickener of my death, O precious food immortal, the nourisher & standard of my life . . . I beseech Thy Goodness to work in me Thy Grace: that by the receiving of this glorious sacrament I may be transformed & changed into Thee (Lord) Thyself. . . . Thou alone to be sole object spiritual of all my wits. . . . And finally, good Lord, let the whole transformation and full exchange of both my soul & body be all in Thee.[98]

Is this the unnaturally heightened language of an emotionality born of exclusive concentration on religious symbols, or the only possible expression, given current terminology, of a more integrated experiencing? Are the remnants of a practical knowledge of human transformation preserved in such prayers? And if both views contain a truth, at what point has the imbalance begun? Whytford ends, as elsewhere, with a warning against heresy, also an imbalance: he points to a possibility within ordinary religious observance and 'ordinary life,' without either being changed.[99]

The teaching—or perhaps only its surviving language—which Whytford is transmitting, preserves the ancient idea of death-in-life. It is touched on in the *Dialoge*[100] and explored more fully in the *Dayly exercyse*, bringing again the question of different levels of understanding, and of the meaning of religion itself. Situated within the broad medieval tradition of the *ars moriendi*, the *Dayly exercyse* is related to ascetical teachings concerning the 'first' and 'second' deaths, the possibility spoken of in all religions of dying consciously ('liberation') before we die.[101] His aim is to destroy the childish fear of death,[102] founded on ignorance, self-neglect and the coarseness of popular art and piety,[103] in order to clear the ground for an impartial sensing of personal mortality—an "active knowledge of death," as he says[104]—able to evoke, by itself, a proper fear and the need for self-preparation. The monastic exercises of meditation and recollection of attention which form the second part of the treatise, are his answer to this need and invite comparison with the Ignatian *Exercises*,[105] which derive from the same tradition of practical spirituality. The fullness of this tradition calls into question the unreality of our fear, together with the virtual impossibility of consciously experiencing the inevitability of our own death.

By the "law of sin" man is always "in the first day of birth . . . the first day of life mortal," and hence subject to death, continuously dying and being born.[106] (Fortunately, as we are, nothing permanent can be formed in us.) To participate more consciously in this living and dying, then, is the challenge of Christianity. This religion concerns transformation.

> Every thing good that is ours . . . is mixed . . . with evil . . . which, notwithstanding, may (by the grace of the sacraments) be daily purged and so our life changed.[107]

Whytford is saying that, through the renunciation of spiritually exercising, in which a man faces death on his own level, and through submission in the sacraments, also a kind of death,[108] the balance in him—an imbalance?—can be altered. Calling on himself before he is called,[109] he precipitates a struggle in which he may participate more or less: he is challenging the Devil to face him now, as he surely will finally, in order to develop the "hardiness" of "a very man."[110] By practising "this death of contemplation," the possibility may already appear of separating the soul from its tomb, the body, a foretaste, as it may be, of his end.[111] To think what one feels is a step towards the unity by which this tradition of affective devotion was secretly sustained: it may yield a grain of new thought.

He gives two forms of exercise on the authority of Plato, Paul, Bridget and Catherine of Siena: they include homely and simple descriptions of mystical states[112] and have exact parallels in Bridgettine practice.[113] By emphasising the dangers of self-deception and "diseases of the head" in these states, while urging ordinary folk to search,[114] Whytford is defending the viability of the practical spirituality of Syon against the popular doubts raised by the current crop of politically suspect visionaries.[115]

The message of *Pacience,* Whytford's last work, is that life can become the teacher of a religious way only through inner detachment.[116] Reflecting the dilemma of the professional religious faced with Dissolution,[117] it continues his attempt to align Christian life in the world in a monastic direction, as his friend Erasmus had wished: with Syon's practical asceticism ever in mind, he addresses laymen:

> [A]ppoint yourself upon a certain exercise of lawful occupation: for every hour of the day, according unto the state and condition of your person, as if you be religious . . . and ever let prayer be one, and accompany every occupation.[118]

It is a description of the New Devotion. Among the works bound with *Pacience* was his translation of the *Synonyma* of Isidore of Seville, which has been described as advice to those aspiring to "live in the world a life of Christian perfection," "a seventh-century Imitation of Christ." Contrary to the later view,

Isidore considered the monastic life to be a union of action and contemplation.[119] Everyday conditions could also serve the inner work of the monk: these last writings were an urgent and timely call for an essential Christian practice independent of institutional forms, addressed equally to lay and religious.[120] The monastic teaching of the responsibility of all for each other in a common life was relevant to the family in the world.[121] How can parents, abbots and kings, learn to play a role outwardly while being inwardly free?[122] The imbalance of our bodily humours is the material basis of sin. He cites Christ's impeccable anger and inner detachment when expelling the moneylenders.[123]

And he speaks of the need for doing "violence" to oneself.[124] How can violence be connected with patience? What do these words mean? For us, patience inevitably involves suffering: it is the result of being "sinful." Everything we do is sin. God's Patience is passionless, without suffering, while ours is, and must be, a martyrdom of the passions.[125] What a man is able to bear depends on the "quantity of [his] love," thus its source is crucial: with help 'from Above'—which he may receive by doing what he can[126]—he is able to love what is beyond the grasp of desire and suffer what would be unbearable.[127] Ordinary patience is "sufferance"[128] in hope of eventual gratification, but the spiritual tradition enjoins submission, an impartial, unconditional suffering which grants body to the immaterial: suffer *now*, otherwise eternally without choice.[129] It is likened to the refining of precious metal in a furnace,[130] and concerns the purification of the emotions, the capacity to 'love God': "the persons that have God dwelling & abiding within them, be patient."[131] As we are, "violence" is necessary, but only to begin.

So the "disciple" must study patience exactly as a craft must be studied, for all work is essentially related: "he that will not labour, shall have no food."[132] This art of living can be learned only through the experience gained by exercise. To learn patience "you must love trouble," then everything can be a teacher.[133] To the layman's objections at the difficulty, his response is not to despair, only try.[134] Dissatisfied with what he has, why does he fear the unknown? Surely referring to monastic experience, yet equally to family and all human relations, he comments wryly that "few men can bear all persons."[135] But, if a man wishes to study, his weaknesses can be helpful.[136] The refining of his trying, the quality of his intelligence, is the point: "it is no shame to fall, but the shame is to lie thereby," "suffer and be still" if you would find will, "turn and apply your heart, mind and thought," "call yourself quickly home."[137] In learning how not to be attached to what happens within him, a man learns how not to consent to it.

In such practical work opposites come together: if Whytford was trying to bring the monastery into the world by revealing the needs of the layman's inner life and the relevance of traditional guidance, he was also trying to bring the world into the monastery, by restoring to a religious awareness expanded through crisis the sane practical valuation of the craftsman and householder.[138]

The expression of Christianity as a 'mixed life' was elaborated and formalised during the rest of the sixteenth century, but in the process means were confused with ends. The individual's exploration of his possibilities within a given discipline becomes a programme for imitation, the lawful result of the accumulated force of practice becomes a pattern to be imposed, something to 'do.' What the earlier sources of the New Devotion are pointing to is the preparation for religion, rather than religion itself. We are moving, relatively, from the oral to the literal, from the inner struggle to outer regulation and the preoccupation with results, from the kind of time in which men and women of different epochs and traditions are essentially related, to the sequential exclusive chronology of 'history,' a patchwork of accidental and ephemeral sociopolitical influences.[139]

The Brethren's "recollection" of themselves in the common life passed into the early-sixteenth-century Salisbury primers as the repetition of pious Latin phrases, which "ought for to be said," to become, in the popular Elizabethan and Stuart *Manuall of praiers,* sixty pages of sonorous and detailed meditations for different stages of the Mass and for the morning and night hours.[140] The *Manuall* retains a connection with traditional material, but tends to verbosity, and does not, despite indications,[141] squarely approach the crucial question of how to pray.

A *dayly Exercise privately of devoute persons to be used* (1576), is incomplete in the same way. Drawn from the *Officium Beatae Mariae* and thus a lineal descendant of the early Tudor primers, it was directed, like the *Dyurnall,* to laymen who shared the wish of the professional religious but not his leisure:

> if your worldly business suffer you not to spend much time in prayer, you may notwithstanding have wherewithal to occupy yourself aptly that little time you have permitted you.[142]

It gives prayers for different actions, a discipline of devotion. The Trinity is invoked on awakening,[143] prayers offered to the guardian angel and the saints and confession made; going out of the door, before and after food, entering church, the different stages of the service and laying down at night, all have an appropriate prayer or blessing: all, it is implied, could be experienced differently, perhaps more normally. The Brothers of the Common Life paused and prayed whenever they heard the church bell ring and this practice survives here.[144] The Brothers sought to "prevent" each activity with a brief prayer to clarify their direction; in the *dayly Exercise* this has become the enunciation of an elaborate pious sentiment:

> At the beginning of your work say: Prevent all our doings, we beseech Thee O Lord, with Thy favour and further them with Thy help, that all our prayers and practices may begin always of Thee, and by Thee begun, may be ended through Christ our Lord. Amen.[145]

We are on familiar territory, at last!

The life of the Dominican William Peryn spanned Reformation, Catholic reaction and Elizabethan Settlement, but his writings, while belonging unmistakably to their age, are grounded in the practical spiritual tradition of the medieval mystics and New Devotion. His *Spirituall Exercyses and goostly meditacions*, "a near way to come to perfection and life contemplative, very profitable for religious, and generally for all other that desire to come to the perfect love of God and to the contempt of the world" (1557), is modelled closely on the work of Nicholas van Ess (1507–78). Ess, a monastic reformer who had once considered becoming a Carthusian, protector of the local Beguine community and co-worker with the small group of Italian reforming humanists before and after the Council of Trent, had been in close contact with early Jesuit circles. He had studied at Louvain, in the college of Pope Adrian IV, another reformer who had been educated by the Zwolle and Deventer Brethren. His work shows a deep knowledge of the thought of Gerard Groote, Kempis and the German mystics.[146]

Peryn dedicated his *Spiritual Exercyses* to a Bridgettine nun, but was directed to the same circles as the works we have been discussing, as his subtitle suggests. Like them, he deals with the practical search for order and relationship with God, 'perfection,' within ordinary life, by showing how outer activity might be informed, and transformed, by an inward "intention" and self-denial arising from the discipline of meditation on the Passion. His use of systematic meditation, which relates him to the New Devotion and the Bridgettines, is not linked so formally with the daily routine of the exercitant; his tone is more emotionally intense, his exposition less simple. He is closer to the 'monastery.' He describes the possible results of striving to become indifferent to all desires and impressions not connected with his aim, by means of continuously focusing the attention of mind and heart on the Passion of Christ: only when God can truly be sought and remembered in everything, may Christ be recognised "in His members," a contemplative life be lived together with an active life. This means that, while God is being contemplated outwardly, inwardly "you do recollect yourself wholly," and, entering into the heart and searching its depths, "[you] do put yourself wholly in the hands of God."[147] This practice is directed towards, and begins anew from, that place in a man able to deeply realise "the knowledge of myself . . . that I am nought and nothing of myself."[148] Behind these meditations and prayers stands a psychology and a method,[149] inherited from the New Devotion and renewed by Ignatius. It distances Peryn somewhat from the earlier sixteenth-century English writers in this genre, saving Whytford and the *Dyurnall*.[150] He speaks of those actions of charity which do not hinder, but further, and even sometimes replace, contemplation, according to the CounterReformation creed,[151] yet his thought is permeated by older ideas of the *Imitatio Christi*, Passion meditation and the living awareness of God: "remember always, wherever you be, that you are in the Presence of God."[152] What, practically, did he mean by this?

When they speak of remembering God's Presence these treatises refer not to a different, as it were better, object for the awareness and memory which a man already has, but rather to the awakening of a different quality of perception, which he does not possess usually but which is possible and even natural for him, and upon which any new order depends. Phrases like "an exercise for reformation of the soul in the wit and senses," used by Peryn, indicate this. These writings are speaking, according to their lights, of the need for a radical inner transformation which must really begin if the Christian religion is to be lived rather than just imagined. The link made between self-knowledge and an awakening to God[153] is far from comprehensible to our ordinary thought (indeed, it is frankly suspicious), but Peryn does give practical exercises for approaching both the knowledge of God and "the consideration of yourself." The "practice" of the "exercise for reformation of the soul in the wit and senses," is expressed in this prayer:

> Grant me, sweet Jesu, that I may do and offer, all and everyone of my necessary works and deeds . . . with an actual and a new intent to the laud and praise of Thee, my lord God . . . and while I am seeking or doing anything outwardly, grant me grace to remember myself inwardly.[154]

This is an excellent description of the daily work of the Brothers of the Common Life. Similarly, Peryn's "aspirations," the part of each exercise designed to carry its meaning and results into the day, are equivalent to their "brief ejaculatory prayers."[155]

Like Whytford, Peryn fields the question: How can the layman with his daily commitments follow a time-consuming discipline derived from the practice of the full-time religious? His answer is to be flexible and practical, avoid overscrupulousness, seek the advice of a spiritual adviser when necessary, and, above all, exercise self-discretion: "you may not force yourself too vehemently, but mildly and gently do what you may."[156] In his account there is a sense[157] in which these exercises take place in another, inner, time, the time of the silent heart and mind not subject to external restraints and relatively slow, coarse energies, that they 'take' time only if they are deliberately 'done.'

Peryn refers to the adviser or "spiritual guide," "to whom you shall from time to time reveal and open how you do feel yourself in these exercises . . . that he may lead you by his discretion,"[158] an increasingly prominent figure in English religion, particularly Catholic, as the Reformation unfolded. In the Middle Ages, religiously inclined laymen might have taken their questions to the local monastery or hermitage and perhaps ended their days in a religious order; in the sixteenth century, "spiritual fathers" advertised their wares and published advice for those seeking to follow the religious path in life. Whytford and the authors of the *Dyurnall* and *Pomander* wrote in this spirit. Protestant experts also published guidance on ordering daily life which was less divergent from the spiritual tradition than might be expected: the degree of their concordance suggests that fifteenth-century experiments in religious method had become a common inheritance accessible to all confessional loyalties.

The martyr John Bradford's *Private prayers and meditations with other exercises* (1559), consists of a series of prayers for different daily actions.[159] The usual times are singled out: waking in the morning, the moment of beholding daylight, dressing, beginning the day, leaving the house, before, during and after eating and at the coming of sleep at night. Unlike the Catholic writers, he does not mention attending church before work. The pious Protestant is engaged, it would seem, in a lonely, stern struggle against the world, the flesh and the Devil, and the prayers Bradford provides are assertions and encouragements of his determination and nerve. As the Protestant reforms were consolidated, their prayers tended to become petitions for moral virtue or worldly success, or against natural disasters and personal enemies, to take four of the most common themes. Because of the prominence given to the doctrine of the godly vocation in the works of Luther, prayers for different trades and classes became very widespread. Their aim was still the ordering of daily life from within, or above, but their emphasis has become more active, so to speak, and less contemplative. Thomas Becon's *The Floure of godlye prayers* (1551), marks the beginning of this trend.[160] Something of the earlier approach survives in the form of brief prayers for morning, meal-times and night, but the volume and tone of the other material is such that their traditional significance hardly makes itself felt.

The conclusions reached by Thomas Keating, a modern student of prayer, about this change of traditional meaning in the sixteenth century, clarify the kind of influence we are trying to discover. The monastic practice of *lectio divina*, divine reading or the study of sacred writings, embodied their prayer, discipline and exercise.

> They would repeat the words of the sacred text with their lips so that the body itself entered into the process. . . . It was primarily an exercise in listening. Listening can be at different levels. It can be with the bodily ear, with the imagination, with the heart, or with the whole being. The monks sought to cultivate through *lectio divina* the capacity to listen at ever deepening levels.[161]

The theological schools of the twelfth and thirteenth centuries emphasised the analytical understanding of Christianity and intellectually systematised the spiritual life, yet a tradition of practical spirituality persisted in certain orders and heretical groups, to be rediscovered at the end of the fourteenth century by Gerard Groote and his friends. Their attitude to intellectual study corresponded exactly to the spirit of *lectio divina*. The Brotherhood's exercises belonged, as they claimed, to an older world, but were in their turn subsumed in organised systems of meditation. Amidst "a general decadence in morals and spirituality," prayer began to be used in the sixteenth century:

as a means of (moral) self-discipline in an age when institutions and structures of all kinds were crumbling. . . . While prayer can certainly be used for
this purpose, it is not its primary function. Prayer is response to God. It does
not come into being because we want to do things with it."[162]

This is the characteristic quality of sixteenth-century prayer books, particularly
the Protestant. The older idea of prayer as contemplative knowledge and love of
God involving the whole man moved into the background, but the influence of a
practical spirituality persisted insofar as these manuals were able to communicate
a way to search for wholeness in daily life. This influence underlay the Anglican
Church's attempts at the turn of the century to rediscover the inward dimension
of its tradition.

The ideal of the 'mixed life' influenced sixteenth-century devotion because it
was assimilated to the Protestant "godly vocation"[163] as if they were commensurate: were they? Those admitted to the Brotherhood sought their truth in life
through the guided practice of "recollection" and exercises of prayer, but they
accepted religious forms and never spoke of the unconditional 'godliness' of life
work and position. The 'common life' became a bridge for some to the special
conditions of Christian training which survived in certain monasteries. The
Devotion, a small-scale movement, embodied the idea of different levels of Christianity.[164] The godly vocation in the thought of Protestantism, which quickly
became a large-scale popular movement, was connected with the idea of 'the
priesthood of all believers,' that all men are equal, and equally poor, before God.
In reaction against the hypocrisy of an otherworldly piety and appalled at the
reality it masked, the sixteenth-century reformers asserted the rightness of the
collective social order: within that 'common life,' rather than in monastic separation, a man might more honestly find his religious duty. The 'mixed life' represented a balancing of the forces of outer and inner life, and was sustained by a
practical discipline leading to the threshold of a religious way, in the traditional
sense. The Brother's daily struggle was work to recollect himself in the midst of
his disordered energies, a preparation to face the call of Christianity. The significance of Protestantism, which aspired to bring the individual person into relation
with the Power and Mercy of God without intermediary, lay in its releasing and
channelling the energies of half of Europe at a time of vigorous expansion and
growing national assurance, energies that had been blocked and dissipated
amongst the impossibilities of late medieval religious culture. Here the godliness
of work had another sense.

Although the approach of the New Devotion tended to survive with more
integrity in Catholic literature, historians have remarked that the content of
devotional manuals was not markedly effected by the Reformation. In the second
half of the century there was mutual exchange: the Spanish schools of mysticism
and Jesuit methodology influenced Protestant devotion and renderings of *De*

Imitatione Christi were popular, while the Protestant emphasis on action, moral virtue and social conscience pervaded the reformed orders of Catholicism.[165] A comparison of the 1499 *Contemplacyon of Synners* with its Elizabethan version, *A dyall of dayly contemplacyon or devine exercise of the mind* (1578), shows the continuity and the divergence. Both present systematic meditations.

The *Contemplacyon* was compiled at the request of Richard Foxe, one-time Bishop of Durham and of Winchester, Lord Privy Seal and founder of Corpus Christi College Oxford, the first to incorporate the Renaissance study of Greek. He wrote to Wolsey in 1517,

> I have determined and, betwixt God and me, utterly renounced the meddling with worldly matters . . . whereof for the many intolerable enormities that I have seen ensue . . . in time past, I have no little remorse in my conscience.[166]

In old age, Foxe devoted himself to good works and private devotions. The introduction announces his intention to aid the sure search and true knowledge of the reader's conscience. Time, said St. Bernard, is the most precious gift given to man—perhaps the only one—and yet it is squandered without purpose on fantastic aims and goods without substance. Was 'the image of God,' intended to be so? According to this practical tradition, time escapes him because of his immersion in the constant flux within and without, and his consequent inability to find himself and be, independently of this disorder. And, with time, is stolen an unknown possibility: fragmented ("made narrower and, in all the energies and powers of an excellently ordered soul, deeply damaged," as Zerbolt put it), he becomes impervious to new impressions, let alone to those higher influences[167] of which religion speaks and about which he knows only by hearsay. For 'he,' read 'we.' "We drive over and pass our days by continual interchange," now well and now ill, now happy and now sad, no sooner despairing than consoled, an exchanging that takes place through what medium? Man resembles plants and lower life forms in his ephemerality and vulnerability to external conditions, to atmospheric and climatic changes. Time passes without profit, because he is "in continual commotion . . . never stable in one degree."[168]

Believing that time spent intentionally confronting this position was not wasted, he had compiled extracts from the Bible and Fathers for systematic daily meditation to support it. The Bible is a mirror in which a man can see his otherwise invisible 'face.' For each day there is "a new exercitation."[169] This sevenfold division of material for the week was an expansion, more geared to life in 'the world,' of the intensive monastic day of 'the seven hours.' Foxe had sponsored a vernacular translation or abstract of the *Regula Benedicti,* a sign of personal sympathies that may well have influenced his young chaplain (c. 1504–7), Whytford, who, upon joining the Bridgettines, was to translate their Augustinian rule and share monastic practices with lay Christians.[170]

Luther's protest coincided with the advent of mass propaganda: Tudor intelligentsia, sprung from an increasingly literate population, had an unbounded, naive confidence in the beneficent power of the printed word to inaugurate a new era, to instil faith, manners, social morality and political awareness. The *Contemplacyon* sounds a warning note: the author agrees that it is "right speedful" for all estates to read, or hear read, "diverse scriptures . . . in which are contained noble histories, moral teachings & real examples of men of virtue by the which we may eschew vice & choose virtue," but he insists on the importance of discriminating among the flood of moral literature. Who chooses? Just as we can distinguish quality in food, drink and clothing, which protects and sustains the physical body, so we can regard what we take into ourselves through reading as a matter of "spiritual nourishing."[171] Impressions are food, but for whom? The *Contemplacyon's* texts resembles the *rapiaria* of the Brethren, who also adopted a weekly framework for meditation and regarded the process of study as analogous to the digestion of physical food. Whytford's *Dialoge* is also kindred.

Monday's theme for meditation was "the wretchedness of this world," Tuesday's "the sure state of innocency," Wednesday's "the damage of deadly sin," Thursday's "the general judgement," Friday's "the passion," Saturday's the "pains of hell" and Sunday's "the joys of heaven."[172] Related quotations from the whole of Western thought recognised as orthodox in medieval Christendom follow, and demonstrate its unity regarding man's inner life and its rightful orientation; they are interspersed with a commentary of English verses. For example, Monday's meditation has a fragment of Psalm 119, "they are troubled and moved unto mischief as a drunken man," followed by Augustine, "the thing that you desire to enjoy is like unto a mousetrap, for while you seek to catch your desire, you yourself are snared," and then Bernard: "what does God punish. or what does He hate, but a man's self-will in sinfulness. Let self-will in sinfulness cease, and there shall be no hell ordained for you." Next come verses on the "misrule" of man's inner world, governed by a self-will he is unable to "wrest . . . inward." The foolishness of this world is the Wisdom of God (*1 Cor.* 3:18–19), but people are bewitched and cannot obey the truth (*Gal.* 3:1–4), as Terence says, "even seeing it with my eyes, myself wittingly and willingly do perish, and am undone." Augustine said that those who love the world, go to war with themselves.[173] These quotations are from the Elizabethan version; the 1499 text has the same material in general, the verses in English but the extracts in Latin, "mixing the Latin with the English . . . so that who so likes not to read the Latin may find the English whole & complete by itself," a balance English primers began to adopt thirty years later.[174]

The tradition we are examining returns often to the question of food. What is food! There is a mystery of scale here. The underlying question concerns the right food for those higher parts, called the soul and the spirit, proper to every man. How can they grow unless they are fed, and what is our part in the reception and digestion of this fine food, whose source, we are told, is from Above. That "new intelligence," which must appear in us for Christian teachings to take on living meaning, needs a more subtle "nourishing" than we allow. The Word speaks, but who is there to listen? Echoing a thousand years of monastic *lectio divina*, the *Contemplacyon* affirms that its collected texts require "more digested reading & profound intelligence":

> For right as cinnamon or ginger or other spices give not sharp taste to him that only looks upon them or to him that bears them in his hand, but he that will put them in his mouth & bray them small with his teeth, he may perceive of them a good wholesome gust & a comfortable taste. Right so, sententious compilations daily read & lightly overseen, to the reader or to the hearer give but a savourless sound, which & if they were profoundly considered might be found both pleasant and profitable and, with often reading of misty matters, might follow a new intelligence & a more clear understanding.[175]

Within the field of a better attention, more, qualitatively, of oneself appears. The introduction to the Bridgettine *Myroure of Oure Ladye* has a similar passage,[176] both works inheriting from the New Devotion and the preceding tradition the exercise of Passion meditation, which they present as a method of feeding the understanding. The *Contemplacyon* says it is like a lost treasure—lost only because we do not search for it—and should be used in conjunction with the "inward thought" of hell as a "spiritual medicine," to help us understand the contradictions of inner and outer life, to "mix the wine of temporal prosperity with the water of penance and adversity."[177]

The tumultuous eighty years separating the two editions of this work did not greatly effect the text: the Elizabethan *Dyall* is more explicit on Bible reading but less instructive on how to read; the editor reduced, updated and polished the doggerel, but doggerel it remains; some of the alterations illustrate a fine Elizabethan optimism, not to say smugness, while an original verse exhorting kings to reexamine their responsibilities is wisely omitted.[178] The greater sophistication of presentation probably reflects Jesuit influence. The *Contemplacyon* started each day of meditation with a brief statement of theme, such as "Remember the wretchedness of this world." The *Dyall* starts with two verses, one addressing the reader, the other commemorative, and "the translator's application," which relates the days of the week to the Days of Creation. Three associated ideas from Christian tradition preface the texts and verses: for example, we are wretched in this world, God divided light from darkness when creating heaven and earth, eschew the darkness of this world and "walk in light, O man!"[179] The reader was left to make his own connections before he began to ponder the texts. This kind of elaboration is typical of later sixteenth-century devotion. As methodical techniques spread, they became more complicated: the more that is explained, the more remains to be sought.

Figure 8.1.   Frontispiece from *A dyall of dayly contemplacyon* (London 1578)

To see how these practices of daily meditation were effected by the emergence of the Jesuits as a spiritual force in the latter half of the sixteenth century, we must turn to Robert Southwell's *A Short Rule of good life to direct the devout christian in a regular and orderly course*, part religious manual for Counter-Reformation Catholics and part secular monastic rule, published in 1598 after years of private circulation. Based on the Ignatian *Exercises* and the *Regulae* of the Society of Jesus adapted for lay use, it is a Jesuit version of the 'mixed life,' as the introduction makes plain.[180] The *Regula Benedicti* remained the means for the professional religious to find God, but the layman who followed Southwell's instructions, "in what estate soever he lived in this world," also "ran the way of Christian perfection."[181] The monastic and secular rule have the same goal and are based on the same truths and sense of search. The antithesis between the Christian life in 'the world' and withdrawal was very stark in sixteenth-century thought, perhaps because of Protestant pressure to level the distinction: the early Jesuits tried to unite these two lines of search for their time, as the New Devotion had done.

In both cases, the importance of active self-questioning was emphasised at the outset. The famous "Principle and Foundation" of the Ignatian *Exercises* is echoed in Southwell's "foundations of a good life," the first of which was to consider often and deeply:

for what end and purpose I was created and what God's design was when He made me of nothing, and that not to have a being only as a stone, nor withal a bare kind of life or growing as a plant or tree, nor moreover a power of sense or feeling only as a brute beast, but a creature to His own likeness, imbued with reason, understanding and free will.[182]

It is a man's own reality that is in question. Between the distant call of his higher nature and his deeply buried sense of nothingness, his poverty of being, this question can, and—if he has ears to hear—must, sound in him. Spiritual exercises help him to hear by supporting a quality of inner attention: it is as if the question remembers him, for it does not come from his ordinary thought or feeling and cannot be answered, only devalued, by them. His awareness of its presence is "the foundation of a good life." There are lawful gradations of being: minerals, plants, animals and men, and higher intelligences also, according to tradition. What is the level of being proper to man, who was intended by his Maker to surpass "a bare kind of life," and what kind of work is necessary to develop and nourish it? On what does his usual low level of being depend? What can feed him actually, in this sense?

The source of the remarkable similarity between Southwell's *Short Rule* and the exercises of the Brotherhood must be sought in his Jesuit training. If the world was to be the abbey of the layman, then his own house was a cell. The details of internal monastic organisation in the Rules are mirrored in his discussions of household management and the upbringing of children. His advice develops the lines laid down over sixty years earlier in the *Werke for householders*.[183] Whytford had written, in the spirit of his order and the New Devotion, of the layman's daily dedication to God; Southwell concurs, adding that the day of one's conversion should be celebrated solemnly every year, as an opportunity to recall the first fervour.[184] Like the monastic Rules, the *Short Rule* was to be read regularly, beginning anew each month.[185] In all our material the great evil is forgetfulness, for, traditionally, memory is the root of redemption, just as oblivion is the root of perdition and exile. No vow is involved in following this rule (the 'mixed life' admitted no external authority): a man's pact with himself to remember his intention amidst the conflicting demands of life had to be renewed as often as he forgot, as the Brethren had well understood. 'His' awareness was the authority. A measure of order must be found

> because confusion and an unsettled kind of life is the cause of many sins. . . .
> I must set down with myself some certain order in spending my time, allotting to every hour in the day some certain thing to be done in the same, so near as possibly I may, or at least to have some times in the morning, evening & afternoon, certainly devoted to some good exercise, which I must (though not by vow) after a sort bind myself unto, when things of greater weight do not call me from them. Also to keep due times of rising, meals and going to bed and all other ordinary times.[186]

Is he expressing the bourgeois morality of the Elizabethan middle classes, a prescription for pious rigor mortis, or formulating a realistic framework for an inner search in life? Both vie, as they must.

Whatever he made of his material, Southwell the Jesuit wrote in the spirit of the New Devotion. His understanding of the *intentio* is that of Gerard Groote and Florence Radewijns. Having touched his need, the layman who wishes to follow Christian teachings must try to remember more often and deeply what he has been given to experience: he defines his "intention" as he can and wishes to recall it at certain times in the day, in order to renew it and support his watching. He asks for grace that his effort should become neither stale nor repetitious. He expresses this as follows:

> First to appoint and set down with myself, that every morning one of my first thoughts shall be of the good purposes I have made, which must not be many, but some one or two particular and principal points that I see most necessary for me, and to set down also in the morning, at what times in the day I will remember the same, as at service, at dinner, at evensong . . . for the care to remember them at some certain times, will make me still mindful of them, and so readier to perform them. . . . Secondly to examine myself twice in a day, whether I have broken them since the morning or no. . . . Thirdly because I can never go on in virtue without falling, I must every morning, or

at least every holiday, think with myself that hitherto I have done nothing, and that, by God's grace, that day I will begin afresh as though it were the first day that ever I began to do any good thing.[187]

He himself has to know what is "most necessary for me." In an "order how to spend every day," he says that the "intention" links the morning effort with those at mealtimes and evensong. As in earlier sources, the apprentice Christian is advised not to begin talking immediately he gets out of bed, but to pray and meditate in silence for at least fifteen minutes. He dresses ("neatly and handsomely . . . agreeably to my calling"), and then, in his prayers, "for the better procuring of attention, to take my good Angel or some other saint, as it were, to say with me." He meditates on the Passion, the Life of Christ or his sins, "as the book of meditation gives notice."[188]

The keys to the teaching of the *Short Rule* are the formulation and recollection of the "intention" and the call to watchfulness of oneself. As if speaking to himself, Southwell returns to these again and again, often writing in the first person. The traditional warning, 'take heed of idleness, the mother of all vices,' becomes an intention. I wish to work, "directing mine intention in all my exercises to this end, that I may avoid idleness and bestow my time in good sort to God's Glory,"[189] the Jesuit aim to live "to the greater glory of God" thus combining with the practical endeavour of an earlier tradition. And again: "in the beginning of every chief action, directing therein our intention and action to God's glory and service and our good," for every task could serve the common aim.[190] At night, "my intention must not be so much for sloth and contentment of the body, as for necessity of keeping my health & that I may rise fitter to serve God."[191] At eleven o'clock he pauses, to say his beads and remember how the morning has been spent. Before the midday meal, he stops again: "and when I am set, before I lay my hand to my trencher, I may pause a while, and in my mind desire God to give me temperance and mindfulness of His Presence."[192] Meals are preceded by systematic reading and are opportunities to remember the poor and hungry, as in the *Dyurnall*.[193]

All this will necessarily provoke conflicts of all kinds at every level, but the essence of work must be sought before its form: it may be that when I wish to read silently before eating, my place as host requires me to attend to my guests, but why does what I feel to be important sever me from my fellows? What divides the life in me from the life around me?

In such occurrences, instead of what I should have done, I must seek to make my conversation meritorious by having a good intention and often renewing the same & by watchfulness to avoid all offence of God, leaving Him in one exercise to serve Him in another, as He appoints occasions to fall out.[194]

A mobility of attention, actively submissive to the changing inner and outer situation, can dissolve any tendency to self-importance and 'singularity': to be able to move freely with the movement of life without being swallowed is an approach to the 'mixed life,' to being in the world but not of it. There are many coded descriptions of this flexibility in the literature of the New Devotion.[195]

At the end of the day, Southwell continues, I examine myself, "especially concerning the purposes that I have made in the morning." After my devotions, I try to direct the mind to a picture of myself at the foot of the cross or in the manger as a witness, after the manner of the Ignatian *Exercises*. Before I sleep, I establish with myself "whereupon I will think as soon as I awake, that God may have the first fruits of my thoughts, for which the Devil lays great wait."[196] These exercises are, in a sense, artificial, but necessary, for man's very nature has become unnatural. "Better is art than evil strength."

> Man's nature being so corrupted, that without continual violence & force, it cannot attain to virtue, or leave vice, whereunto it is much inclined, I must assure myself that care and watchfulness is ever necessary: and because I am apt to fall, I must often renew my good purposes.[197]

The idea of violence is often found in this practical literature and has a specific meaning connected with breaking habitual patterns.[198] Consider the strange saying in *Matthew* 11:12, "from the days of John the Baptist until now the Kingdom of Heaven suffreth violence, and the violent take it by force."

The renewal of intention was intimately associated with prayer. Southwell's "short and sweet prayers, which are the fuel of devotion," correspond to Peryn's "aspirations" and the "brief ejaculatory prayers" of the New Devotion. Southwell maintained, like the Brethren of the Common Life, that it was a man's duty to God to "bear always in mind His Presence." The Presence pervaded and supported all and everything, although men lived oblivious of it, otherwise they would not behave as they do.[199] He relates the remembrance of personal intention directly to this greater awareness. An example of the short prayers he gives for renewing intention:

> Jesu be my sun in the day, my food at the table, my repose in the night, my clothing in nakedness & my succour in all my needs. . . . Gracious Lord & sweet Saviour, give me a pure intention, a clean heart, and a regard to Thy Glory in all mine actions.[200]

The prayer which arises in the awareness of the Presence of God,—"in Him I live, move and I am . . . and should He withdraw Himself from me but one moment, I should forthwith turn into nothing,"[201]—and is the means by which his being is fed,—"short prayers are fuel of devotion, causes of attention, food of the soul, preparations against temptations and assured helps to attain any virtues,"[202]— that prayer will not be a mere outer form of words and cannot but support his intention. This prayer is not the projection of the ordinary self.

Without the search for attention in the activities of ordinary life, the instructions given in the *Short Rule* amount to little more than a catalogue of invented aims and pious hopes, meaninglessness. In the section entitled, "Of the watchfulness and attention required in the care of our soul," he says that, due to the great dangers and difficulties which beset anyone concerned with this "weighty affair":

> it standeth us upon most watchfully to take heed to every thought, word and deed that passeth, lest through the number & subtlety of our enemy's trains, we be often entrapped, for it is hard to touch pitch, & not to be defiled, to live in flesh a spiritual life, to converse in the world, without worldly affections.[203]

It is an invitation *to be* in between our two natures. Only the new experience is unable to be conveyed in known words. He understood the urge to judge what was seen and the temptation to despondency. Unless the next step can be found, a worse fall will result than before he tried to pick himself up.

> Neither the multitude, continuance, nor badness of any thought, must breed any scruple or disquiet in me. For not to have them, is not in my power, but only not to consent unto them: and so long as with deliberation I have not consented, not willingly or with delight stayed in them, I have not sinned any more than if I had only had them in a dream.[204]

This touches on the difference between morality and conscience. The flame of watchfulness withers automatic self-accusation, and a powerful question concerning one's present state surfaces, the dream being interrupted: actively refusing the passive resistance, which continually asserts itself in my name, non-desires momentarily predominate over desires.

The direct observation of the associative flow of undiscriminating thought and exaggerated emotion throws new light on the idea of 'sin.' What is sin? There is what happens automatically in us, truly in our absence, under those influences which prey on diminished consciousness, and there is the possibility to know instantly and impartially that it is taking place: joining with 'my life,' I discover another, more abundant. Southwell is implying that a man who is completely absorbed in this automatism, who only dreams and never suspects his passivity, cannot be said to commit anything as significant as a sin: a man's responsibility begins when he begins to see himself, when he awakens. If he sees his position of estrangement, but even then consents to stay in it, then he commits sin. It is the indifference to the truth about oneself, at those moments when one is able to receive it, which constitute sin, which keep one enslaved when there is a germ of choice. The practice of watchfulness, therefore, can lead at last to real difficulties. This is the sense 'in translation' of Southwell's religious language.

The precious thread of awareness, once found, is fragile:

[We] ought to be very wary, even in our least thoughts & deeds, for fear that we offend the Presence of God and give occasion of triumph & victory to our deadly foes. And for this says the Scripture, keep thyself very watchfully . . . to attain this diligent & attentive care to all our actions let us consider what men use to do, that carry great treasure by places haunted by thieves . . . how warily he walks & how careful he is never to stumble nor fall that carries in each hand a thin glass of liquor very precious, through stony and rough places . . . let us remember that much more respect is necessary in us, whose treasure is more precious than any worldly jewels, & yet do we carry it in earthen & frail vessels, in the midst of so many thieves, as there are passions and disordered appetites in us.[205]

What does this mean? Is the "diligent & attentive care" of oneself a capacity which emerges gradually with the practice of these exercises, or a 'self-conscious' external watching imposed by the desire of the mind: or is it a question? He is speaking of a kind of love. Care is not necessarily the child of fear. Does care appear because we begin to be aware of something very valuable within ourselves, or are we already able to start a religious life with care as our guide? Can care evolve? What is worth caring for in ourselves? For Southwell, care has meaning only in proportion to the awareness of the Presence of God: this awareness, if real, is the touchstone of understanding ('wisdom'). In contact with this "treasure," the question of "disordered appetites" and our relationship to them takes on new meaning. Without that treasure, the interest we take in ourselves tends towards the self-indulgently introspective and this is very far from the call of religion as it is being presented here.

One of the Masters of Desert asceticism, a continuing influence on this medieval tradition, wrote:

If there is any monk who wishes to take the measure of some of the more fierce demons so as to gain experience in his monastic art, then let him keep careful watch over his thoughts. Let him observe their intensity, their periods of decline, and follow them as they rise and fall. Let him note well the complexity of his thoughts, their periodicity, the demons which cause them, with the order of their succession and the nature of their associations. Then let him ask from Christ the explanations of these data he has observed.[206]

What is the measure of this science? What does it mean to be free to know myself, identified with these passions and separated from them? In Southwell's response to the basic question of 'how,' the methods of the Brethren (which they considered early monastic) reappear. What, precisely, is missing?

To procure this attention the most effectual helps are these. First to think how careful we should be to do all things well, if this present day were the last that ever we should live in this world (as peradventure it may be). . . .

Secondly to remember that God is in His Own Substance, Power & True Presence in every place and sees both our outward and inward actions. . . . [T]hirdly we must consider the carelessness of our life past, remembering how often we have fought against God with His Own weapons and abused the force that He has afforded in every part of our body & mind. . . . Fourthly, to procure this attention, it is good oftentimes in the day when we are about our ordinary actions, to use some short prayers or some one verse of a psalm, or any other short petition of God's Grace, Aid and Assistance. For these short prayers are fuel of devotion, causes of attention, food of the soul, preparations against temptations and assured helps to attain any virtues.[207]

Prayer, attention, the soul: in this tradition, the power of attention was regarded as the function of the soul. To speak of feeding the soul is to recognise the possibility of different qualities of attention. It follows that the growth of the soul and the development of attention, that is, presence, are intimately related.[208] In all our material, awareness of the Presence of God is the key, the threshold of the truth, and the fundamental movement associated with it is self-recollection, total attention to oneself: this is the movement towards order in the midst of disorder ("so many thieves as there are passions and disordered appetites in us") with which this chapter began. And, if we persist to ask, what precisely is recollected at this moment, this is the question of the soul.

The *Short Rule* was Jesuit inspired but transmits an older tradition of practical spirituality whose origins were the origins of the New Devotion. Social, religious and intellectual forms had undergone many changes since the late fourteenth century, but this tradition had retained, and even increased, its relevance. In the work of introducing prayer and watchfulness into life, existing conditions had to be used, rather than evaded or changed (as if they could be). There is a clue here to the persistence and invisibility of the tradition. The demand received by a man has to be joined, he has to 'make a demand' on himself: the help given serves to increase his need *and* his strength. Our texts were vehicles for these teachings and products of their time: Peryn's exercises, appearing during the Marian reaction, had a monastic basis; Whytford administered Bridgettine doctrines as an uncompromising yet kindly confessor; Southwell, writing for the Elizabethan bourgeoisie, emphasised prudent book-keeping of the soul and household cleanliness. Without its subjective colour each work would have had no place or recognition in its day, yet without its traditional content it would have had no meaning. From its source and from its renewal in men's lives, tradition derives a quality less subject to the passage of time.

We sense two histories: the religious partisanship, unbalanced polemic and official shifts that crowd the sixteenth-century stage are the type of one, while the other, the life of such a tradition and of men's search for the truth of the heart, remains almost completely unseen. Providentially, they are not mutually exclusive. "Thus, in the torrential stream of human history, two currents meet and mix," wrote Augustine, referring to 'good' and 'evil.'[209] Our interest has been magnetised by the evidence of this meeting and the traces it has left. The ground of difficulty in facing the greater reality of a teaching and the sincere self-questioning arising from its experience, becomes the link between the two histories: acknowledgment of the common ground relates us to the accumulated intelligence of the past—for all men are brothers in this poverty—and supports the continued life of a tradition to help our search. "Perseverance of all other things is most necessary in this business."[210] From persistence in the kind of trying advocated by Southwell, Whytford and the others, our deeply buried need for the meeting of 'heaven' and 'earth' enters the common life. The question of order and level, with which this chapter opened, is given back to us in another form at its close.

NINE

The Place of the Monastery

Keep your heart with all diligence, for thereof comes your life.
Myroure of Oure ladye, c. 1415–50

S acred tradition affirms three outstanding things: the unique role in creation intended for man as a being formed in the image of God; his actual, unnatural position due to the consequences of an ancient calamity, the memory of which is preserved in the story of the Fall, and to a manner of living which has further diminished his original possibilities;[1] the existence of a reconciling knowledge, providential for those who seek to understand their position, whose expression for our time and culture has been the teaching of Christianity and whose purpose is the restoration of man to his rightful place. The true scale of these ideas is virtually beyond our comprehension; we must remember them, nevertheless.

The monastic way of life arose out of a renewed search for this knowledge, and was a training[2] for the real life to which we are called. Early monastic records speak unequivocally of "inner work" and "spiritual doing," of the community as "school" or "workshop."[3] Historical records show, regardless of all special pleading, that the monasticism of the ensuing thousand years curved always further from this aim: from being a path to a threshold, it became through repetition only the exclusive property of an ever-growing, institutionalised class of professionals, who claimed thereby to interpret Christian truth.

However, the note that had been struck continued to echo in conscientious renewals of direction throughout the Middle Ages, for not only the memory but direct knowledge of the original ascetic exercises had been transmitted from generation to generation among those who still sought. In the late fourteenth century, the enigmatic, perhaps heretical, 'Friends of God,' certain Carthusian houses and the circles around John Ruysbroeck, supported Gerard's search. This quality of relationship is hidden from the historian's view, but secretly imprints the records left by the Brotherhood.

If the work of restoration *(re-ligio)* to which Christianity recalls men is an objective necessity, the form of the search has always to be renewed as conditions change, and thus 'new' attitudes appear with the power to influence the orientation of popular religion. The 'mixed life' was just such a vehicle. In this sense the New Devotion was an antenna, a foreseeing adaptation of traditional values for the needs of the coming time. Zerbolt's emphasis on the need for a "great labour" to "put order in the heart by ascents of raising ourselves," renewed the understanding of Christian duty "without vows."[4]

The real Christian monastery, then, is a place where there is a living knowledge of how to be a Christian, a special place free from the influence of worldly care, where a man can be worked on according to his understanding, for the sake of the realisation of this knowledge in practice. It is as a lawful result of this, rather than through deliberate persuasion, that the monastery can become a source of reconciling influence for the relatively unenlightened surrounding community, the 'body' that bears it. The monastery is a symbol and has been a fact. For our theme, the Bridgettine house of Syon, with their study of how to "keep the heart," most closely corresponds to this meaning. In what follows we will be examining their role in transmitting religious attitudes to laymen on the eve of the Reformation, especially where they touch on the practices of the 'mixed life.'

On the scale of the individual, 'the monastery' is a special place of experiencing within and the purpose of spiritual exercises is just to make contact with that place, where the knowledge of how to "keep the heart" could be received actively. The question then becomes how this new understanding could be transmitted to all the other parts of the body of man, that is, how it could be lived.[5] For free movement between action and contemplation ('the mixed life'), the outer monastery was unnecessary: wherever a man found himself, there must he find his freedom from 'the world.'[6]

The Order of St. Saviour, or Bridgettines after Bridget of Sweden (d. 1373), had come to England with royal patronage in 1415.[7] Their unique foundation, Syon, on the Thames between Isleworth and Brentford, was formally enclosed in 1420, and, with the Carthusian monastery of Jesus of Bethlehem at Shene, nearby physically and spiritually and also a new royal foundation (1415), was effectively the last monastery established in medieval England.[8]

The life at Syon was austere in the eremitical tradition, yet based on a relationship between the sexes. Like the houses of the contemporary Windesheim congregation, also Augustinian canons, they aimed at the strict observance of the Augustinian Rule, supplemented by their own *Constitutiones* modelled on the dictated writings of Bridget; it was said that contemplation and obedience were one, and that this was the meaning of being at Syon.[9] John Vos of Heusden's words apply to them, when he said that the Windesheimer's life was the maintenance of the rule and the perpetual striving after observance.[10] The first two Bridgettine Confessors joined them from hermitages, and their first Abbess left to become a recluse. The spirit of the hermit Rolle presided here.[11] The Abbess was responsible for the "temporals," the outward organisation of the religious life and its relationship with the world, the male Confessor General for the "spirituals."[12] The twenty-five brethren acted as manual helpers, chaplains, spiritual directors and liturgical celebrants for the sixty sisters. Despite the rigours of the life, recruitment was steady and these numbers were maintained throughout a century of existence;[13] the Benedictine letter to Wolsey in 1521, warning him that, if observant reform was introduced to their order after the customs of the Bridgettines, a wholesale exodus would terminate what remained of English monasticism,[14] reflected a majority view. According to the *Addiciones*, or local usages, the numbers of men and women, their differentiated functions and distinctive costumes had a complex analogical significance connected with the practices of remembering the Passion, which was as central to Syon's devotional life as it was to the New Devotion.[15] Bridget had not been a professed religious, and accounts of her work as mother and wife, establishing and maintaining a hospice with the help of her husband, suggests the discipline and imperatives of the mixed life. She was a type of her age, like Catherine of Genoa.[16] The Bridgettines were the only late medieval religious order to return formally to the early idea of the mutual relationship of the sexes in monastic conditions,[17] found among the Desert Fathers and in English 'Double Houses' before the Norman Conquest.

Syon was outstanding among contemporary monasteries. Her relationship with distinguished, cultured and powerful families was maintained throughout her life. A comprehensive collection of theological and mystical writings, augmented by the fruits of new humanist scholarship, stocked a library unparalleled in England. Like her Swedish mother house, Vadstena,[18] her resources made her a centre of learning, piety and literary activity, receptive of the very currents to which the establishment remained resolutely closed. Noble and intellectual affiliations gave them an international outlook within the bounds of their strict enclosure. They were one of the few houses to oppose the Royal Divorce without subterfuge from the outset.[19] With the Shene Carthusians, they were the only English order to survive as a community after the Dissolution had severed them from their original home.[20] They held, indeed, "a key position in the religious life of the country."[21]

To follow these aristocratic connections a little way is revealing. Sir Hugh Fitzhugh, Baron of Ravensworth and nephew of Archbishop Scrope, the Constable of England at the time of Henry V's accession and later his Chamberlain, who had arranged the original transplantation from Sweden and who was described in Syon's *Martiloge* as "the first who introduced this religion into the Kingdom of England,"[22] was a Yorkshire man who owned a copy, perhaps a holograph, of his countryman Rolle's *Incendium Amoris*. Actually, almost all those involved in Syon's foundation were Northerners with a common interest in Rolle, the English mystics and monastic reform.[23]

Syon's relations with Lady Margaret Beaufort, Countess of Richmond and Derby and mother of Henry VII, have been emphasised in a recent study.[24] Lady Margaret sponsored translations of Hylton and Kempis, made her own translation of the fourth book of *De Imitatione Christi*, endowed Divinity chairs at both universities, founded St. John's College, Cambridge and was a friend and patron to humanist scholars. Her later years conformed to the pattern of the mixed life, at least externally: separating from her husband before his death in 1504, she took monastic vows but lived 'in the world' on her manor at Woking, Surrey.[25] Details of her devotional life given in the *Mornynge Remembrance* of John Fisher, her confessor, contain the earliest definitive example of the rosary recitation which came to be known as 'Bridgettine';[26] her practice of the *ars moriendi* parallels New Devotional and Syon usage and her name was associated with the English version of Bridget's prayer, popularly called the "fifteen Oes."[27] Sir Richard Sutton, educated in Lady Margaret's household, became Syon's steward, and the dedicatee of the *Orcharde of Syon* (1519), based on the writings of Catherine of Siena.[28] His contemporary, Sir John Hussey, the Comptroller of the Royal Household, was the patron of *The Myroure or Glasse of Christes Passion* (1534), a translation by Syon's Confessor General.[29]

Bridgettine name lists from 1518 and 1539 disclose "a strangely complete epitome of recusant lists of a succeeding age," indicating a current of aristocratic piety which was a European phenomenon.[30] The Prioress at this time was the sister of Lord Windsor; Elizabeth Urswycke, a Bridgettine in 1518, was related to the Dean of Windsor, Christopher Urswycke, chaplain and confessor to Lady Margaret and executor of her will, and a friend of More, Erasmus and Tunstall.[31] Lest our account be deflected by the covert snobbery of past English Catholic historiography, we must weigh these connections.

Syon's literary production bears witness to her special relationship with laymen. Just because the place of the layman was a fundamental issue underlying the sixteenth-century revolt, care is needed in order not to confuse our own possible understanding with the mere restatement of contemporary argument. The 'layman,' the ordinary person who does not know anything particularly, separated from the Christian Mystery through ignorance and unpreparedness, should be distinguished from the lay brother, who, trying to associate himself with the religious work from where he found himself in life, was called *conversus*, one who was turning or wished to be able to turn, and who, meanwhile, served his helpers to the best of his abilities as part of their 'body.' The significance of the lay brother's position depended on the quality of the religious life with which a connection was being sought. In this sense, a 'monk' could be a layman, and a 'layman' could be a *conversus*, or even a monk.

Although the number of official *conversi* in the older orders was declining from the mid-fourteenth century[32] and hermits and ascetics were increasingly looked to for spiritual guidance,[33] the austerity of the life at Syon retained the respect of laymen.[34] The Bridgettines had recognised from the start the importance of the lay-brother,[35] as well as their special need and the demand they made on the regulars, and provision was made for them at Syon.

The relationship of laymen to the committed study of Christianity and the place this study occupies in ordinary life, are two ends of the same question, whose resolution during this historical period can be glimpsed in the 'mixed life' of the Brotherhood of the Common Life. These men, learning how to turn in life,[36] were the true *conversi* of the fifteenth century.

The traditional relationship of layman and monk, as expressed in the *conversi* who reconciled them, was breaking down during our period. The reality of an individual monk's aspiration had been a beacon for laymen who sought a different orientation, as many traditional stories attest. Gradually, lay-devotion had become a reflection of monastic method, however indirectly: lay Books of Hours, for example, contained the additions to monastic services which had been introduced from the ninth to the eleventh centuries,[37] and the popular lay devotion known as 'Our ladyes Psalter' had been devised in the fourteenth century for the nonlatinate laity who wished to follow monastic usages. Relationships tend always to become a repetition of forms. If, as the weight of evidence suggests, the quality of monastic search had utterly deteriorated, so then would the kind of influence transmitted by the monks.

Syon appears to have been an exception to this general involution. She was transitional, in the sense that her brethren acted as tutors in religious values to laymen while, at the same time, educating their co-religious in an increasingly vernacular devotion. Bridgettines were often given 'Our ladyes Psalter' in lieu of the full liturgical programme.[38] An undated Norfolk guild document associates the devotion of Syon and the Carthusians of Shene and Mountgrace with the religious aspirations of laymen.[39] Whytford translated the Bridgettine Rule and Martyrology and some writings of Kempis into English for his sisters, while in the *Werke for Householders*, *A dayly exercyse and experyence of dethe* and the *Dialoge* adapting monastic exercises for layman. Thomas Prestius, a Syon deacon (*fl.* 1537), translated the *Formula Noviciorum* for other religious,[40] and William Bonde dedicated to the sisters of Denney Abbey a vernacular guide for the over scrupulous conscience.

The relationship of monk and layman was mirrored in the relationship between Latin and the vernaculars: an understood difference of levels between the 'sacred' and 'profane' had involved into a matter of convention and degrees of intellectuality by the sixteenth century. The respective place of these languages was changing. European vernaculars had been emerging from a multiplicity of dialects to become national tongues since the fourteenth century, with the assistance of poets and mystics who turned to living forms to correspond to the immediacy of their experience. Although Latin was to issue from its confrontation with humanist philology refined of medieval impurities, it was the vernacu-

lars, flexible and organic, expressing an intelligence at once older and more contemporary than the late medieval church, which were to become the true bearers
of new cultural vigour.

During our period a religion framed in an ancient language was giving way to
forms tied to the quite different nuances and expressiveness of vernaculars which
were themselves in great flux. The main significance of this change is usually
taken as an access of popular comprehension. In Christian tradition there is the
Word and there is 'Babel.' What does language serve? Surely the quality of comprehension demanded by religion ranks before the quantitative availability of its
truths, if we are trying to gauge the force of a teaching to change men. Is it self-
evident that all languages are equally objective? Who listens? An ancient, still verifiable, tradition maintains that the native language of religion is silence.
Descendants of the Reformation parties continue to argue whether these changes
resulted in religion being assimilated to the standards of 'the world,' or whether,
for the first time since the early church, ordinary life was, so to speak, given access
to the 'higher' level of religion by the removal of artificial barriers: but for us,
these dualities point to the reconciling possibility of a 'mixed' life, whose communication was indeed silence in the midst of work.[41]

Latin, the priestly language of medieval learning which had given the religious
orders keys to the culture of the ancient world, was being supplanted by English
dialects in the monasteries long before the Reformation. Since 1343, statutes had
been promulgated to preserve Latin and ban English "in the dining room and other
places of ease, and even in the chapter house . . . and in other conversations."[42]
Ignorance of Latin was equally common in continental houses and is often mentioned by Observant reformers.[43] Humanist scholars with their passionate conviction in the moral efficacy of pure Latinity scorned this situation, yet its significance
lay in the fact that the teaching which the monks claimed to be following had been
largely transmitted and was commonly expressed in a language which fewer and
fewer of them understood, even literally. The Abbot of Malmesbury was censured in
1527 for holding a chapter "in the mother tongue and not in the Roman tongue,"
but injunctions delivered to Leicester Abbey in 1528 and Missenden in 1530 were
partly in English so that those concerned could not plead ignorance of the authorities' wishes.[44] We hear of daily readings of the Rule in a forgotten language and of
"singers knowing not what they sing and bellowing forth un-understood psalms."[45]
The translation of monastic rules and liturgical texts was one response to this

At Syon the vernacular had been encouraged from the beginning, intentionally.
Bridget required its use in conversation and even penalised the use of Latin in her
foundations.[46] The Bridgettine order, rooted in a vernacular devotional mysticism, was able to develop more in tune with the religious needs of the laity: Vadstena became, like Syon, a centre of vernacular literary production in the fifteenth
and early sixteenth centuries.[47] The original supporters of Syon shared an interest
in the fourteenth-century English mystics, especially Rolle, who wrote extensively

in the vernacular. The author of the *Myroure of Oure ladye* (1415-50), translated these liturgical usages of Syon "that you should have some manner of understanding of your service," that the unlettered sister might be able, by referring to the English version during the Office, to "feed her mind therewith."[48] In this and later Bridgettine translations, the use of the vernacular and the ideals of the Observance movement join.[49]

The association increasingly made between heresy and the vernacular in early Tudor England was driven by traditional ecclesiastical suspicion of unbalanced extremes and the establishment's fear for their own security, as well as by a real intuition, in some quarters, of the tide of events. The scriptural translations used in the *Myroure* were made independently of existing English primers with Episcopal permission.[50] A copy of Purvey's Lollard translation of the New Testament was presented to Syon in 1517 by Anne Danvers, while a certain London draper, being examined for heresy in 1528 revealed that he had passed on works by Luther and Tyndale and an English paternoster to the Confessor General of Syon. In neither of these cases do we know why the books were required.[51] Sixty copies of the Observant Friar Ryckes' *Ymage of love*, written for the Bridgettine nuns but considered heretical, were delivered to Syon in 1525 by Wynkyn de Worde.[52] The Syon brothers' library had at one time several works by Wycliffe which are not known from any other source; the fact that they were indexed but not mentioned in the early-sixteenth-century Catalogue suggests they had been disposed of, or lent out and never returned, by the time the Lollard scare was intensifying.[53] There were twenty six-English works in the brothers' library, mostly small theological and devotional tracts.[54] If the Catalogue of the sisters' books was extant, it might well have shown a larger number of vernacular works, for it was they who had little Latin; there are provisions in the *Addiciones* for "the service of sisters unlettered" and it was for them that Whytford and the others made translations.[55] The order's origin in fourteenth-century vernacular spirituality accounts for the persistent association of Syon with English; the contemporary continental houses of the New Devotion shared similar roots and orientation.[56]

The atmosphere of the religious life at Syon is indicated by the range and quality of the brothers' library, by the 1520s probably the finest collection of early printed books in the country.[57] In addition to patristic and medieval works of theology and devotion, the number of Renaissance writers,[58] surely unknown to the majority of Tudor religious, reflect the taste of that exceptional group of Cambridge educated priests—Reynolds, Westhawe, Fewterer, Copynger, Bonde, Lacke and Whytford—drawn to Syon in the last thirty years of its existence.[59] The presence of the basic texts of Italian Neoplatonism and Hermeticism[60] after the dispersal of the library in the 1530s, bore rich fruit in the intellectual life of Elizabethan England.

Works by the Victorines, Bernard, Bonaventure, Suso, Ludolph, Catherine of Siena, Bridget of Sweden and the English mystics,[61] often donated by the same group, round out the impression given in the works of Whytford, Bonde and Fewterer, in the *Myroure of Oure ladye* and the *Orcharde of Syon*, that the Bridgettines, together with the Carthusians and the continental houses of the New Devotional Observant reform, were heirs to the practical spirituality of the Middle Ages. David Knowles, referring to Rolle, Hylton and *The Cloud of Unknowing*, writes, "it is remarkable that, with few exceptions, all the surviving manuscripts of these authors come either from the libraries of the Carthusians and Bridgettines or from the collections of devout lay folk."[62] Among the brothers' books was a holograph of Rolle's *Melos Contemplacionis* and many other of his writings.[63] Vadstena possessed a unique copy of Thomas Basset's *Defence against the Detractors of Richard*, almost certainly sent from Syon.[64] The *Myroure of Oure ladye* assumes a close familiarity with Rolle in its audience.[65] Moreover, a manuscript of the *Incendium Amoris*, now in Emmanuel College, Cambridge, contains the monograms of Joanna Sewell, a Syon nun of the early sixteenth century, and James Greenhalgh, a contemporary Carthusian of Shene, witnessing a close relationship of some kind. Sewell also owned a manuscript of Hylton's *Scala Perfectionis* annotated by Greenhalgh.[66]

William Bonde expresses their attitude towards traditional writings: "the unspeakable works that holy doctors have written and left for our comfort."[67] Catherine Palmer of Syon was the dedicatee of Peryn's *Spirituall Exercyses* (1557), which synthesised current meditation practices and the approach of the Society of Jesus. Ignatius may well have visited Whytford at Syon in 1530.[68] Whytford made two translations of Kempis, *De Imitatione Christi* and *Alphabetum Religiosorum* (*Crossrowe*). The library owned several copies of *De Imitatione* and a volume of Kempis' minor works may have been donated by Reynolds.[69] Whytford translated Hugh of St. Victor and co-operated with Fewterer on a version of that summary of the ascetic wisdom of the Desert, the *Scala Spiritualis* of John Climachus, a basic source of the New Devotion.[70] Fewterer's translation, *The Myroure of Christes Passion*, owes much to another seminal contemporary work which developed methodically the meditation exercises of the New Devotion, the *Ejercitatorio* of Abbot Cisneros of Montserrrat. The brother John Selby (*fl.* 1537) gave a copy of *De Ornatu Spiritualium Nuptciarum*, by the mentor of Gerard Groote, John Ruysbroeck.[71]

The Bridgettines' connection with the English and Flemish mystical schools and the New Devotion cannot be discussed without mention of the Carthusians and Observant Friars, for these three orders were closely related as results of, and sources for, the same quality of spiritual influence.[72] Carthusian booklists parallel Bridgettine in depth of subject matter.[73] From the remote Yorkshire Charterhouse of Mountgrace, founded in 1397 at the time of the first expansion of the New Devotion into monastic life and a notable centre in the assimilation and transmission of these influences in the fifteenth century,[74] came the basis for the library of the new Charterhouse at Shene, founded contemporaneously with

Syon. Seven of the original Shene brethren were sent from the Low Countries, where their order had a close relationship with the New Devotion.[75] There, and in adjacent parts of Germany, the same patron would often favour both Carthusians and Bridgettines, and their houses were frequently neighbours:[76] the closeness of Syon's connection with Shene[77] was not an English peculiarity.

The liturgical indications of the *Myroure of Oure ladye* point to their shared understanding of the impersonality of worship: the Bridgettines' attention is drawn to

> the song of them that are called Charterhouse, whose psalmody savours more the sweetness of the soul, and meekness & devotion, than any vain showing outward. For the heart is not clean from sin, when the song delights more the singer than the thing that is sung.[78]

The two houses may have sung the liturgy in intentional concert, as adjacent Bridgettine convents and Charterhouses are reported to have done on the continent. The waspish comments of Tyndale support this. Henry V had established Syon and Shene as neighbours, he said, "that lip labour may never cease."

> For when the friars of Syon ring out, the nuns begin; and when the nuns ring out of service, the monks on the other side begin; and when they ring out, the friars begin again, and vex themselves night and day and take pain for God's sake; for which God must give them heaven.[79]

Remarking on the volumes of the influential Dutch Carthusian, Dionysius de Leewis, in Syon's library, one scholar has wondered whether Shene and Syon co-operated in collecting and transcribing books.[80] A Syon brother wrote the introduction to the *Pomander of Prayer* by a Shene monk.[81] Syon possessed three copies of the *Speculum Spiritualium*, by Adam the Carthusian, "from the compilation of Dom Henry, monk of the Carthusian house of Bethlehem [Shene]."[82] It was quoted in the *Myroure of Oure ladye* and by Whytford[83] and, containing many references to Rolle and Hylton, with a set of rubrics by Dom Henry, was printed in Paris in 1510 at the expense of William Bretton, citizen of London. This commitment to the heritage of practical mysticism had to be shared with all Christians.[84]

The *Speculum Spiritualium* includes much material on the cult of the Holy Name, discussed above in connection with the Observant Friars, Syon and the publication of Ryckes' *Ymage of Love*.[85] The Observant Friars at Richmond were neighbours of Syon and Shene and in close contact with them.[86] Pole's *Defensio Ecclesiasticae Unitatis* (1536) linked them in the sense of faithfulness to their origins:

> [W]hom will you find to compare with these three? Or rather, when you exclude these three, whom can you find who have not utterly degenerated from the founders of their orders?[87]

Likewise Whytford, when speaking of the secrecy about the contents of their rules which unobservant houses maintained, compares them with:

> such persons as do keep their rules & ordinances, as the reverend fathers, Friars Observants, Charterhouses . . . they be not loath to show their rule but rather would they be glad their rule were unto all persons commonly known in most clear & open manner, for the edification of all Christians.[88]

Syon's relations with the London Charterhouse were close during the final crisis. Sebastian Newdigate, one of the martyrs, had a sister at Syon,[89] and a series of letters survives between Fewterer and members of the London house concerning the policy to adopt over the Oath of Supremacy.[90] We may speculate on a connection between the Confessor General's acquiescence in the Oath, after initial resistance, and the inner freedom to act, obey and serve within changing outward circumstances upon which the work of the New Devotion turned: if the bones of the teaching are to assume flesh, how else should that which is 'Caesar's' and that which is 'God's' be distinguished, except in a moment of action free from the influence of inordinate affection? 'Good' and 'evil' dance together at such times. His letter of January 1536 to the London Charterhouse, explains his resolution to recognise Henry as "the prior" of the church as the result of an "informed and ordered charity" working in him, although he ends by admitting his present poor health and his inability to "write my full mind unto you."[91]

In order to enter more deeply the life of this monastery, let us take this phrase, an "informed and ordered charity," as a starting point. What does it mean, and in relation to what?

A Christian tradition, often taken for granted, identifies disorganised emotion as the fundamental feature of that wrong or displaced living which is mans' predicament. Augustine prayed, "order love in me," and defined virtue as "the order of love"; "impurity of heart," maintained by the way we live, keeps us in the "city of the moon," said Zerbolt.[92] Texts dealing with actual Christian practice—from the Desert Fathers' strivings for *apatheia*, emotionlessness, onwards—focus on this disorganisation and confirm that the work of the monk was understood to be the acquisition of will over the heart: the purification and transformation of the emotions, their unification and submission to faith. Hence the saying of Abba Alonius in the *Apophthegmata Patrum*, "if only a man desired it for a single day from morning till night, he would be able to come to the measure of God."[93]

If it is not realised that to love like a Christian, according to Christ's directions, is impossible as we are—*even if* we sincerely wished it, as we understand wishing—then the idea that it is necessary to work on the emotions will mean nothing, or worse. In the absence of the glimmerings of impartial self-knowledge, the practical force of this tradition has evaporated. To love like a Christian, in freedom not slavery, could only be a result, perhaps a distant result, of this same work, a final fruit of that "spiritual doing" which was the goal of the early monks.[94] Such love includes, as well as the 'being able' to love, the 'being able' to wish. A twelfth-century Augustinian canon expressed this succinctly:

The being able, the wisdom, the goodness or charity. Image of Trinity.

And again:

Happy is he to whom it is given to collect the fragmentations of the heart into unity.[95]

These texts indicate that Christian love is not emotion as we experience it, nor its intensification: it is not 'in part,' but is connected, as Paul says, with being "face to face," with knowing "even as also I am known," with the possibility of becoming "a man" (*1 Cor.* 9-12). To quote is reassuring, but it must be admitted that the individual's starting point, as well as the actual sense and direction of this work on emotion remains unclear. The loss of the starting point results in the corruption of the tradition, hence the importance of the Brotherhood's renewals: yet it can never be ultimately defined, for we are in flux.

It was expressed in terms of 'devotion' in the fifteenth century, and thus statements concerning emotional work must be referred to the meaning of devotional practices. The medieval form of the religious life was the round of regular observance and liturgical prayer, its challenge the confrontation with oneself through the friction of obedience. The material of this life was the demand of prayer and the resistance to it, the recognition of fragmentation, seeking and submission: its purpose was nothing less than to change the being of men, that they might also serve God, willingly, in accordance with their possibility and His Wish. What was the place of devotion in this, and, indeed, what is devotion?

Our study indicates that when 'devotion' is used in these sources it has a definite content, unlike current usage. Words can have precise meaning only in a practical context. We are told that "devotion is nothing other than the desire of the soul for God," and that it is man's duty.[96] Such desire can be weighed. 'Devotion' is not the outcome of dispersed emotional yearning, nor a fascinated collapse before unattainable beauty, but a *wishing*, religious in the real sense, born of the acknowledgement of personal nothingness, the separation from the God's Being which is deeply buried in all men according to traditional psychologies. The result of spiritual exercising, it is proper to the soul, the highest part of man, that which is able to know itself impartially. Within a monastic tradition whose aim was to purify the emotional life, the developed wish to turn from multiplicity and fragmentation towards unity was expressed as 'devotion.' If true piety is continual mindfulness of God, as the Brotherhood's sources affirm, then 'devotion' was the power generated.[97]

The *Myroure of Oure ladye*, written between 1415 and 1450 and published in 1530,[98] says:

though it be not in our power to have devotion at our will, for it is the free gift of God, yet it is in our power by grace to do that [which] is in us to dispose ourselves to devotion.[99]

Devotion is given from above, but what is our part, how can we "dispose" ourselves and why? This is never directly stated, nor can it be, for it touches the individual's case: it is different for different people at different times. It is generally described as 'conversion.' In New Devotional sources 'our part' is an inner movement towards order connected with the renewal of the power of attention, its gathering, containment and intentional direction within. The Bridgettine Bonde wrote, after Augustine:

He that hath made thee without thee, will not justify thee without thee, that is except you help thereto thyself.[100]

'Our part' is just the above-mentioned elusive starting point. The Bridgettine treatises examined below seek to deepen participation in the form of the religious life, to sharpen its challenge and enrich its material by calling for the strengthening and deepening of attention together with the "stabling" of the heart. (Although the force of these practices was essentially independent of formal monasticism, they may well have contributed indirectly to its weakening.) The instruction given on the inner discipline of Passion meditation, intended to touch a vein of purer feeling within the traditional religious framework, is the contribution of these treatises to 'our part.' Reading them, we face again and again the question of the emotional life and its real content.

The *Myroure of Oure ladye* and the *Glasse of Christes Passion* reveal a devotional life centred on the Passion and the honour of the Virgin,[101] conducted in a strict conventual atmosphere imbued with the principles of the New Devotion. The last monastery founded in medieval England became a crucible where the intelligence of contemporary European spirituality blended with the native mystical tradition. In this way English religion was prepared for the impact of the Ignatian *Exercises* and Syon became a bridge between the most vital late medieval conceptions of the religious life and the devotional values of all parties after the Reformation. We must now turn to the evidence of the Bridgettine texts.

The *Myroure* was a handbook explaining the meaning of the liturgical and devotional usages of the new order.[102] It emphasises throughout the necessity of finding an inner meaning to these forms and indicates how this might be approached: the place of the monastery is also within. Before the Virgin can be honoured she must be *seen*, and this means "sight . . . by inward understanding": eventually they "may see her face to face without any mirror."[103] The mere repetition of devotional forms is therefore unworthy; more, qualitatively, of our faculties must be engaged, and firstly awakened. All who call themselves Christians must intend this, but the religious, having assumed special obligations, have greater responsibilities to come to this vision, to become spiritual as well as bodily "daughters of Syon." And this more subtle seeing *must* include themselves as they are: their "unkindness against God" and His Benevolence, their psychological instability and the inevitability of death with bitter prospects thereafter unless real change can begin in this life.[104]

The liturgical *opus dei* summarised Christian tradition: mans' place in the universe, his relation to God, heaven, earth, hell and all beings, his primal innocence, fall and sin, his objective possibilities, his continual descending and ascending, his hindering and assisting of nature and the divine maintenance of creation, the salvation and damnation of the world, the meaning of Christ's life, of the soul and love. All and everything was contemplated symbolically therein, *sub specie eternitatis*. By participating in its ritual repetition, this material in all the immensity and intimacy of its true scale might enter the feelings and evoke a confrontation: to support and deepen this indispensable experience, the *Myroure* translates the Bridgettine service into English[105] and harps on exercises for the participation of "attention of the heart" ("entendaunce in the heart").[106] "I counsel you that in simpleness seek your soul's food."[107]

The recitation of the Office (*opus dei*, work for God), based on the traditional sevenfold division of the day, was intended to "feed the soul"—a simple phrase which echoes throughout this material with profound meaning. Unlike the instinctive digestion of physical food, the absorption and transformation of the Word by a man's finer parts cannot be left 'to nature.' Because of our great need for this daily bread, the *Myroure* speaks of special inner efforts.[108] The aphorism "God likes not to hear his prayer that hears not himself," associated with *The Meditations of Saint Bernard*,[109] indicates that the elusive beginnings of real participation lay in the opening of self-awareness. Traditionally, these first steps are a kind of remembering, an intentional inner and outer listening,[110] a deepening and refining of attention: awakening, literally. The inner and outer life of man must be brought into active relationship:[111]

[W]hen you praise God or pray with psalms or hymns, think in your heart on that same thing that you say with your mouth.[112]

The focus of effort is internal: a part of the attention usually drawn outward, or absorbed within, must be intentionally redirected.[113] The traditional injunction *laborare est orare* is directly relevant here,[114] and also the proverb quoted by Whytford, "Be as thou seemest, or else seem as thou art."[115] It would have been known by the Bridgettines and their mentors that among the Fathers of the Desert prayer and work were conjoined in silence.[116] The continued influence of Desert asceticism indicates the presence of the lost Celtic Church, like a submerged continent, in the English consciousness of religion.

We are again in the territory of the New Devotion. In the manner of Gerard Zerbolt, the *Myroure* describes an inner chaos inevitably revealed by sincere attempts to pray and work in the way indicated: man is "bound and borne down" by the weight of "long and evil custom," the result of continual "reckless . . . wandering of mind"; his body and spirit at loggerheads, he is lopsided, full of contradictory moods, thoughts and emotions, truly "diverse in himself."[117] Religion points in a new direction. The "Divine Office" has many purposes and is perhaps firstly a call to arise from this multiplicity: its action depends on

the stable keeping of the heart and of the mind . . . so that you give all your attendance thereto, and to none other thing for that time.[118]

This "simple" injunction raises the question of payment,[119] even sacrifice.

The New Devotionalists spoke of different kinds of attention,[120] because they experienced degrees of unconsciousness: to worship relatively unconsciously, when we have the possibility to do otherwise, is to be asking something for nothing. It is clearly useless "to sing only with the voice . . . without attention of the heart," but how can a divided, partial being do otherwise? Undoubtedly, "God takes heed to the heart, not to the words," but is this not because the words are not ours? What responsibility can we realistically claim for the life of our heart? Perhaps at the deepest level of a man's life there is indeed a debt, and a question, but can a dispersed consciousness understand it? It may well be, that

they that say their service and occupy their mind the while on other things are like to a man that pays his debt with false money, that seems gold or silver without, and is copper or brass within, which contents not his lord that he pays it to.[121]

But can we afford what we are barely aware we need? Who can discriminate what is valuable and worthless in this situation?

Persisting, the realisation dawns that, although distractions cannot be abolished, it is possible not to stay "wilfully" in them, to return again and again.[122] Hence the *Myroure* refers to the "full great need" to "give battle" with "great inward labour," in a sense doing "violence to ourselves" in order to "gather the mind," so that the Office may be experienced more completely.[123] 'Violence' had a special meaning among the New Devotion's heirs: an intentional denial of 'nature,' as it has become unnaturally adapted in us, an upsetting of automatic patterns of thinking, feeling and sensing, for the sake of growth. If artifice were unnecessary, there would indeed be no problem. The idea reached Luther, who once wrote that "study is violence."[124]

True to the type of this material, the *Myroure* assumes the first step[125] and repeats the tradition of subsequent practice. Once "violence" had opened an experience of a new order, everything is seen to depend on the attempt to renew this relationship, called here the "keeping of the heart" or the "keeping of yourself."[126] Assuming the first step, the religious is told to be "full ware of all occasions that might cause any scattering" during the service:[127] impartial observation of oneself was study. What could be understood in action of the obstacles to the more complete participation in the Office which he desires: what hinders the reception of the Word? Is he sufficiently free from previous occupation to be available 'now'? Free or unfree, is it all of himself? An attentive self-cognisance reveals the restless turning of imagination, driven by blind emotional currents senselessly repeating what has been, in which state he remains oblivious of his prayer.[128] In this watching, the traditional teaching concerning man's 'free will' and 'sin,' comes alive with a meaning beyond words.

The *Myroure* understood preparation for prayer to be a gathering of attention, an inner movement towards the unknown, a freeing of the heart and an opening to a greater presence.[129] If the religious cannot actively assist this quickening, he will leave the church no better than he came, "cold and dull," fragmented and "dissolute"; if he has "received . . . grace," then let him take especial care how he re-enters life.[130] Like the Brotherhood, and citing the same Desert sources, the *Myroure* emphasises preparation for the day begins the previous night, for tomorrow depends on today as today on yesterday: the only time for action is the present if the future is to have hope. In the monastic context, wakefulness and "keeping of yourself," "inward strength" and stability are interrelated.[131]

The fundamental question of self-study, the intentional investigation of the causes of dispersion ("scattering") and the corresponding struggle for unity (*"religio"*), is touched on in the *Myroure*, as it is everywhere in the writings of the later Bridgettine, Richard Whytford:

> You are poured out and shed as water, and therefore you may not increase, nor grow neither go forward. The natural disposition of water . . . is to flow and run abroad here and there, and so to be dispersed and divided insunder, so is it of that mind that is dispersed and divided into many occupations. . . . [Y]ou must gather in your heart and fix your mind wholly and fully in our Lord God.[132]

Although conventional conclusions tend to be repeated, we can recognise the truth of the experience. Dullness, boredom and listlessness are causes and results of dispersion, directly connected with lack of preparation—without which they cannot be seen. They arise from and are sustained by a kind of self-negligence "rooted by long and evil custom,"[133] which draws negative strength from habitual inattention to ordinary activities. Here is the *accidie* of the Desert Fathers, an untranslatable technical term which could be rendered as "the desire to give up."[134]

Clearly, it is only the reality of an aim, the presence of a wish, that gives these states of resistance meaning. Where God is, there also is the Devil. He is seen in the *Myroure* as that which is wounded by sincere devotion. Because there is usually no need to exert an evil influence, the Devil is quiescent, but when a man tries to pray, He is alerted and attempts to "scatter the heart" by his deceits.[135] In other words, the more a man is able to make special efforts in a new direction, the more he exposes himself to unexpected and dangerous forces of implacable power,[136] forces, moreover, which he needs to face.[137]

Equally clearly, it is the quality of his engagement in everyday work, which serves as preparation for those special times when he is called upon. Speaking of this engagement as the "study" of gathering together the heart and mind, the *Myroure* says:

> this spiritual study may not be done shortly, nor now done and now left; but it must be continued full busily and abidingly, every day and every hour and time of the day. For he that in other time lets his heart run where it will and believes that he shall keep his mind upon his prayer or service when he comes thereto, he shall find that it is not in his power.[138]

Among other things, this interesting text shows the spiritual life to be a process obeying certain laws.

The point is to be willing—and able—to call upon ourselves before we are called. A man's lack of availability to the continued calls of life upon his attention is revealed at every turn. He also knows, however partial his acknowledgement, that the ultimate call will be made at his death, the 'presentation to judgement' of Christian tradition. This material implies that preparedness, even on this level, is a result of being able to hear a call within the ordinary routine of life,[139] at "every hour and time of the day," turning towards God volitionally, before he is choicelessly summoned at the end. Whytford wrote *A dayly exercyse and experyence of dethe*, because exercises to remember one's death were central to Syon's work. He describes the intentional experiencing of these exercises as "the active knowledge of death."[140] The *Myroure* relates this to an effort (*fac quod in se est*) to speed up, to become more active within, having recognised that in listlessness one waits passively to be moved from without: to turn from the heaviness of boredom through "sharpness of dread or quickness of hope," thus making room for "grace."[141] This directional use of the mind to awaken the sense of one's death in the rest of oneself is very close to the practice of the Brethren of the Common Life:

> beholding therewith what peril he stands in if he continue recklessly in such wandering of mind unto his death. . . . This dreadful beholding often and deeply used and continued [may make him] by grace . . . to gather his flowing thoughts.[142]

Here is an approach to that work on emotions spoken of above.

"Keeping the heart" was an ancient discipline. The *Myroure* calls the Desert Fathers to witness,[143] and their *Apophthegmata* and the writings of the spiritual masters of the early church refer constantly to it in different ways as the fundamental preparatory action of the would-be Christian, the purification of the emotions.[144] But merely reading about these practices, however absorbing, reveals nothing of their meaning or necessity. What is one reading? These early texts, accessible in modern languages ill-adapted in expressiveness to the original, relate to different levels of questioning,[145] and this, with the confusion of transmission, accounts for the apparently indiscriminate use of the terms "heart," "soul" and "mind," an impression utterly at odds with the clarity of experience mirrored in the thought.[146] A living understanding of the traditional psychospiritual categories had perhaps disappeared by the time of the *Myroure*, but their insistent injunction—awaken, be watchful both inwardly and outwardly, be attentive to yourself, keep attention inside, tend your lamp[147]—was renewed in our period by the New Devotion.

Where and what is the 'heart' that is to be kept? The *Myroure* says that our heart is our life, the cause and result of what we actually are.[148] Tradition concurs. Hence the saying of Augustine that the being of every man is according to his love, that a man's weight is his love.[149] If the 'heart' is an organ other than the seat of partial, egoistic emotion, then it has first to be discovered, the lamp unearthed.[150] We always overlook this. The *Myroure* speaks of turning from multiplicity ("scatterings") towards unity ("God is one"). It says that "keeping the heart" is synonymous with this inner movement:

> the heart may never be kept but only in God. For there is nothing that may fill the soul but God alone. For God is one, in whom is all: therefore all scatterings of the mind may be oned in Him. And for He only is more than the soul, therefore alonely in Him the heart and soul is rested on each side.[151]

We recall again the formulations of Augustine, normative for medieval spirituality:

> You have made us for Yourself, Lord, and our heart is unquiet until it may rest in You.[152]

A Desert Father said, "do not give your heart to that which does not satisfy your heart."[153] We glimpse here the experiential basis of metaphysics, discounted by our culture since the discipline was lost.

The experiences mediated by 'the senses of the flesh,' *which include* the thought and emotion of our ordinary level of being,[154] are indeed partial:

> whatever [you receive] through these senses is partial; and you do not know the whole of which these are parts; yet it delights you.[155]

It is surely not the partial thought, the relatively coarse and immobile attention of the ordinary mind which shall keep the heart, for that way lies rigidity and hypocrisy: thought, failing to alter or cast out emotion, can only pretend or repress. But the *Myroure* is speaking of unity, a higher level of feeling, the heart which can love God. The text continues:

Therefore be aware that you live not recklessly, go day, come evening, and so spend your time in vain and your labour without fruit, but inwardly and busily and continually travail in this spiritual study to stable the heart in God, namely in time of this holy service.

The attention of the heart must be gathered by "study," "a labour amongst all labours."[156] It is perhaps the threshold of real religion, the door to another life.

The seeds of unity may be within, but the beginning is everywhere. What is not touched by the question? The *Myroure* focuses on outer observance for the sake of what it contains.[157] Gerard Groote had found within himself the interdependence of inner and outer experience.[158] That strain of religious thought which exclusively emphasises higher possibilities holds no sway here: heedfulness begins with the physical body, for 'asceticism' is only an acknowledgement that unity is created within the body. If the tradition does not serve the restoration of the whole, it is antireligious. Bridget wrote:

I am bound to serve Him with all my strength and all the parts of my body and I am bounden also to remove all my desire from me.

And William Bonde:

honour thy Lord God with thine own substance & steal not from thy body that [which] is due to it.[159]

What is the meaning of Christian denial? The records of the monastic seekers of the Desert, besides many incomprehensible stories, contain profound indications about the redirection of the senses (not their obliteration), the attunement of the body to receive finer impressions and the development of the will.[160] The *Myroure* insists on an "aware" keeping of the body during ritual.[161] Self-cognisance within a traditional religious framework, according to the exemplary conduct of the Desert Masters, links the New Devotion and the Bridgettines in liturgical observance, reading and meditation:[162] the outer and inner life of man must come together in a new and inconceivable way.[163] This fundamental purpose underlay the Bridgettine's practice of systematic meditation,[164] intentional remembrance of death[165] and use of the hand in prayer,[166] all of which are mentioned in New Devotional sources.

At the heart of the *Myroure* is the urgent "keeping of your self."[167] It is for us to gauge the sense of these words, considering the subtlety of the tradition which Syon inherited but questioning how much, qualitatively, had reached them. Everything is two-edged. What informed this 'self-protection'? Which self? Such questions lead beyond the narrow brief of historians, but are legitimately evoked by the material. Self-deception is the rule not the exception in these matters. If the *Myroure* is trying to support the striving always and in everything to keep the mind in God,[168] where is God now?[169] The text concerns how to worship, but what was being worshipped at Syon? A Desert Father wrote that "what the mind constantly looks upon during prayer should rightly be acknowledged as its God."[170]

The continuity of Syon's inner life is demonstrated in the *Glasse of Christes Passion*, written a century later but published four years after the *Myroure* in 1534. It was a meditation manual translated by John Fewterer, another product of that concentrated literary activity dedicated to spreading monastic techniques on the brink of the revolution.[171]

Fewterer is something of a mystery. A graduate of Pembroke College, Cambridge, associated with the circle of Fisher and More and a friend to the distinguished Prior of the London Carthusians, John Houghton,[172] by 1524 he had become Confessor General of Syon. He oversaw the Will of Sir Richard Sutton, friend of the Bridgettines and patron of the *Orchard of Syon* (1519), pious diplomat and one of the chief movers in the foundation of Brasenose College, Oxford, together with Lord Hussey, the patron of the *Glasse*.[173] We know from a letter dated 1536 that he still held office and therefore was the confessor referred to by Cromwell's agent Bedyll in 1535 as "conformable to his duty" and "well contented" with the king's newly assumed ecclesiastical title.[174] John Copynger had replaced him by August 1537, whether due to his death, removal or departure, we cannot know.[175]

The number and variety of Fewterer's bequests to the Syon library reveal his inclinations. Apart from editions of medieval theology, history and devotional classics, there are several books on medicine (a fitting interest in a confessor of souls), sermons of controversial modern preachers like Raulyn and Bernardino of Siena, Renaissance editions of classical and patristic texts, original works by seminal figures like Poggio, Bruni and the learned and independent Reuchlin, Ficino's comprehensive edition of Dionysius the Areopagite and collections of writings from the Victorine school of mystical theology.[176]

There was great interest at Syon in the practical teachings of the mystics, at a time when they were being studied more outside the religious orders than within.[177] Hugh of St. Victor would have been familiar through Whytford's translation of his annotations on Augustine's Rule, which the Bridgettines followed, and was often cited in the works of Whytford and Bonde. Whytford completed the translation of the classic of Desert asceticism, the *Scala Spiritualis* by John Climachus, which Fewterer began.[178] Climachus was a favourite source of the Brotherhood. Fewterer also donated a copy of Mombaer's *Rosetum exercitiorum spiritualium et sacrarum meditacionum,* a compendium of devotional exercises and technique closely associated with the foundations of the Windesheim congregation and hence with the tradition on which Gerard had drawn. The other copy in Syon's library was given by Whytford.[179] Ludolph of Saxony's *De Vita Jesu*, an

influential collection of meditations on the Passion which bears a close relationship to the *Glasse* and the works of Cisneros, is also in the *Catalogue* in Fewterer's
name.[180] Although he gave no works by Erasmus, apart from patristic editions,
"the Confessor of Syon" who received books by Tyndale, including a translation of
the *Enchiridion*, from a London draper before 1528 may have been Fewterer. This
confessor also took an English paternoster and Luther's *De Libertate Christiana*.[181]

The *Glasse* is the most comprehensive and interesting vernacular exposition of
Passion meditation that has come to light in early Tudor England. Its teaching
and method has antecedents in Bernardine and Franciscan devotion, and was
developed among the Carthusians whence it passed into the New Devotion.
Fewterer's translation corroborates Syon's place in this lineage and anticipates the
Ignatian exercises, which were beginning to make their influence felt in the 1530s.
The *Glasse* presents meditation on the Passion as the central exercise of the spiritual life.[182] If it could become "continual," touching all sides of a man's life, it
would enable him to "obtain the love of God." The aim must "ever to be in
prayer," to become able to move from one "exercise"—as he begins to fail—to
another, so that his consciousness, fed by meaning, may be "ever renewed."[183]

For whom was it written? Material originating in the monastic experience of
another time is here translated into English at a layman's request. By all accounts,
Tudor monastic Latinity was so poor and their relation with traditional monastic
spirituality worn so thin, that he may have been addressing contemporary monks
in search of their roots. On the other hand, the Syon Fathers were producing
works during these years equally relevant to layman and religious, and their order
was *ab origine* sympathetically inclined to the spiritual aspirations of laymen: that
the *Glasse* does not specifically target the religious implies an intention to reach a
wider audience. Questions of intention fascinate, but the words must speak for
themselves. The *Glasse* is making available technical exercises arising from knowledge gathered and studied in the past, at a time when even the shadow of those
endeavours had faded and the institutional fabric left behind by them was about
to be swept aside as obsolete: thus Fewterer's work can take its place among the
early-sixteenth-century treatises examined above as a vehicle of the same transmission. The sevenfold monastic *horarium* lies at the basis of what the *Glasse* pro-
poses for all Christians:

> I shall show you how we should use and exercise our self in the Passion of
> Christ . . . vii times in the day at the least, every Christian should exercise
> himself accordingly to the . . . mind of St. Bernard saying: the continual or
> daily lesson of a Christian should be the remembrance of the Passion.[184]

The incorporation of monastic exercises in the life of "every Christian" would be
the 'mixed life.' This is the relation of the *Glasse* to the New Devotion. The work is
addressed essentially neither to layman nor monk per se, but to those who wished
to become Christians by imitating Christ.

This is easy to extrapolate from the text, but how does it aid our understanding? The *Glasse* was addressed to a minority who felt the need for a practical spiritual discipline in order to progress. If they were laymen they would once have entered religion, but if the orders had sold their inheritance where should they turn? In the eleventh century it was remembered that religious ritual had been instituted "by men who grasped the sublimity of those mysteries to the fullest extent," as instruments for transforming the quality of experience: but without the search for conscious participation it could never have been this. How it was approached was crucial, then as now. This text affirms that "we should lovingly cultivate the gift of fully understanding what we are actually saying when we pray and sing psalms."[185] The importance of preparation runs through all the material connected with the New Devotion. The *Glasse* offers a programme of meditation, but what is meditation? The traditional understanding of the psychological obstacles to new experience on which it draws, is buried in conventional late medieval religious language. If it were not for the difficulties, a discipline would be unnecessary.

The *Glasse* says that meditation which reinforces the blind attachment of attention to thought is useless, even if thought is revolving around 'holy' subjects like the Passion: a deeper quality of feeling needs to be awakened (or rather the path to it reopened, for it is there), that it may participate in the general life. Meditation can take place without thought, said Bonde, for it is "a free opening of the eye of the soul, for to look on such things that be necessary for our salvation."[186] The *Glasse* often speaks of feeling ("affection") in a way which implies its connection, through compunction, with what we would call conscience: the reestablishing of this connection is the purpose of meditation ("remembrance").

A man desires to weep for his sins, for he knows that Christ has bidden it and has been told that it will serve his salvation, yet he is *sincerely* unable to do it. The *Glasse* tells that deep "remembrance" of the Passion is a "means to prick him forward to his intent." Persevering, he may begin to feel what had previously been only thought, namely that God is merciful and he himself unworthy, and as he becomes able to include the conflict and contradiction inherent in this, the teaching that Christ was a sacrifice for humanity can enter with the new force, without the interference of the 'religion' of his ordinary thought and emotionality. This may bring him to an inner frontier, to the very action of compunction, that is, he "may find how to weep and mourn for his sins."[187] We can recall the traditional saying here, "when the heart weeps for what it has lost, the Spirit laughs for what it has found."[188] Like the rest of our material, the instruction of the *Glasse* is directed to opening a closed door, to evoking a certain quality of feeling normally inaccessible and the more subtle energy proper to it, by means of which a deeper knowing of one's place in relation to what is higher and lower—'heaven and hell'—is made possible.

These manuals of spiritual exercise arose out of practical study undertaken by serious Christians wishing to understand the teaching of human—that is their own—disunity in its relation to the traditional monastic aim of purifying emotion. We even know something of where this study took place and with whom it was connected during our period. This is the context within which the *Glasse* speaks of how a man might "exercise himself in his own knowledge and so come to meekness," within which it calls him to face his nothingness before God "as every man may daily see in himself."[189]

Meditation, sincerely and intelligently practised, reveals a man to himself, for it is a state of real self-observation. He is a slave: the same habitual thoughts revolve continually in his own absence, his emotions, alternately denied and indulged, remain primitive, chaotic and bound, in a certain way, to the coarser energies of the body.[190] Seeing this, it is not quite as it was when he was blind. Connection with the intelligence of deeper states of feeling and more conscious thought is not easily made, yet it is just these states, beyond the desire and fear of the ego, to which the masters of Christian spirituality refer when they wrote of the objective meaning of religion.[191] It is the passage, the finding, losing and refinding of this connection which is the most important "study."

Hence the *Glasse* says that in meditation the functions of thought and feeling need to be reunited and reformed in a new relationship to what is higher. In order for remembering to be in all of a man, he must first forget.[192] This means that attention be less passive during meditation, thought deeper and longer, less subject to distraction and deflection. The chapter "How we should feel the Passion of Christ in our understanding and reason," describes mental pondering as endeavouring to "diligently and with attention, form our thoughts accordingly unto the pains and passion of Christ." The tendency to pass imperceptibly into habitual thoughts and images is resisted; attention repeatedly recalled is refined; the subject, less thought about than dwelt with, "ceases to be a picture and becomes a window."[193] He must stay, his attention must "abide," for a movement to inform him:

> this Passion which hitherto has been only remembered in our thoughts and understanding, if we will profit, it must proceed into our affection, so that it be not only remembered in our thoughts, but that also the devotion of the rememberer be inflamed by love in his will. And surely if our understanding do his diligence in the remembrance of the said Passion, it shall surely move our affection.[194]

Ordinarily, movements take him. While speaking of what a man must do, the *Glasse* emphasises, like the *Myroure*, that "devotion is only of the special grace of God which is not in our power."[195]

This view of meditation as a process drawing together all the fragmented parts of man, links the Christian mystics of the Middle Ages through the New Devotion with the Jesuit writers of the next generation. Consider a late-sixteenth-century commentary on *Luke* 10:42, "But one thing is needful":

Thou art troubled and perplexed with many thoughts, affections and cares, but the most necessary point is that thy soul be one, that is to say, united and recollected within itself: one in her sensual affections, reducing them to union with the spirit . . . one in her will, referring her whole will entirely to the Will of Almighty God . . . one in her cares, abridging them all in one, to become agreeable to the Divine Bounty . . . one in her thoughts, gathering them all together . . . one finally in love, placing it wholly in one only infinite good.[196]

The thought is more elegantly expressed, the psychology more systematic, but the direction is the same. The quality of meditation depends on our ability to follow an inner movement, on the wholeness within which 'it is experienced,' because God is One and man is legion. "Devotion" arises from a new relation between thought, emotion and the senses:

if this most sweet and pleasant tree of the cross be not affectionately and lovingly chewed with the teeth of fervent devotion, the savour thereof . . . shall never move you.[197]

More whole for a moment, a man may be able to digest what has never before been his food, be moved by forces that have never been able to reach him. The *Glasse* is a relatively scrambled expression of a tradition which held that the levels of consciousness and purpose which sustain the greater world are reflected in man, the lesser world, depending on his relation to God, the Unique and Common source. The idea of different materialities of food is directly connected with the mystery of the soul's growth.[198]

Like all the manuals of "remembering" derived from the practical spirituality of the New Devotion, the *Glasse* focuses on the 'imitation of Christ.' Gansfort wrote in *De Sacramento Eucharistiae*:

"He that says he abides in Christ, ought himself to walk even as He walked." For it is only through frequent and pious remembrance that we fully achieve these results in Him.[199]

The analogy of the holy mountain unites ancient and medieval spirituality: "Ascend the mountain, learn to know thyself."[200] The *Glasse's* prologue begins with a quotation from *Exodus* 25:40, *Inspice et fac secundum exemplar quod tibi monstratum est in monte*:

"Behold and work accordingly to the exemplar that is shewed unto thee in the mount." Christ . . . oftimes in scripture be compared to a mount . . . for the excellency of His most high perfection, yet most specially in that He was exalted on the cross in the mount of Calvary, He may be called a mount for the excellent merit of his most bitter and sacred Passion. In this mount (that is in Christ crucified) is this day (that is by all the time of our life) shewed unto us a glass or an exemplar, whom we should not only behold, but also with most diligence follow His steps: for it is not sufficient to a Christian to behold Christ crucified, for so did the Jews and also the Gentiles, his cruci-fiers, but it is required of a Christian that he live and work accordingly to the exemplar shewed to him in the mount, that is, Christ crucified.[201]

What does the 'imitation of Christ' mean in these manuals?

The arrow of attention has properly two heads, directed away from and back to oneself. Through intense systematic pondering, both on the biblical details of Christ's life and the objective results of a man's own self-cognisance, this teaching intended to evoke a fundamental initiatory experience: an active realisation of the gulf between Christ, the manifestation of God in this world, and our personal nonbeing. Thus the 'imitation of Christ' is not merely a chapter in the history of religious thought but the form in which a practical teaching sought expression during a particular historical period.[202] Only he who lives as Christ did has the right to call himself a Christian: if a man could ponder and weigh "the order of his whole life" together with the 'labour and life' of Christ,[203] he will recognise the force of its extraordinary challenge. This devotional Christianity, rooted in the perennial search, giving birth to the uncompromising Ignatian method and an influence that reached into the seventeenth century, was epitomised by inner con-frontation supported by systematic meditation, prayer and spiritual exercise. Fur-thermore, and in common with other religious traditions of practical prayer,[204] the sources speak of this confrontation and remembering, having been initiated and deepened, becoming virtually continuous. These were the Brotherhood of the Common Life's "renewals":

> Without ceasing I will strive to be inwardly renewed before the Face of the Lord.[205]

The Psalmist's call, "seek His Face evermore," rings throughout this teaching.[206]

Syon's place within this movement is demonstrated by further correspon-dences. There is the dedication to a Bridgettine of William Peryn's synthesis of Bernardine, Carthusian, New Devotional and Jesuit devotional techniques in the *Spirituall Exercyses* (1557). Abbot Cisneros of Montserrat, through whom the influence of the New Devotion touched Ignatius at a critical time, summarised his practical training in *Ejercitatorio de la Vida Espiritual*, parts of which Fewterer borrows. Compare this from the chapter "That the Passion of the Lord has in itself all the perfection that is possible to a man in this life" with the *Glasse*'s pro-logue quoted above:

> Do therefore that which is commanded by God in the book of Exodus, in these words: *Inspice et fac secundum exemplar quod tibi in monte monstratum est.* Which is to say, "See, and do according to the example that has been shown thee in the mount." And as Christ our Redeemer is continually called the mount in holy scripture, by reason of the loftiness of His most excellent

perfection, so also above all He is so called from His having been lifted up on the cross, in the exceeding loftiness of His most sacred Passion—that is to say, in Christ crucified there is set before us an example, that we may diligently consider it and effectively imitate it.[207]

Each of the six ways to meditate given in chapter 57 of the *Ejercitatorio* become separate chapters in the *Glasse*:[208] their programme is identical here (both echo the Carthusian Ludolph of Saxony), the difference being only in the penetration of expression; Fewterer's characteristic early Tudor prolixity and frequent quotations from scholastic theologians set against Cisneros' clarity of diction and a psychological acuity and fineness of feeling not apparent in the *Glasse*. We should note among other parallels those anticipating the Ignatian exercises.[209] Catherine of Aragon is known to have been a frequent visitor at Syon and Whytford may well have acted as her spiritual adviser;[210] among the Spanish train of this pious lady must have been those familiar with the spirit and aims of the reforms of Montserrat, whose Abbot came from a noble and currently politically powerful family. The prologue of the *Orcharde of Syon* (1519) prints a letter to an Aragonese Observant Friar.[211]

Beyond the affirmation of the *imitatio Christi* in Ludolph, Fewterer, Cisneros and Peryn lies the strange territory of the *conformitas Christi*, the literal incorporation of the Lord's sufferings, psychophysical results of continuous intensive meditation on the Passion: the sensing of His wounds, tasting gall and vinegar, assumption of the way of blame.[212] The aim of meditation is to "alienate and change the heart," says Fewterer.[213] These methods open a known path into the unknown.

> whosoever wholly fixes the eye of his mind on the mysteries of the Passion and on all things concerning our Lord, will, by thus meditating, be brought as it were, into quite a new state.[214]

This is the "union of thy senses in God," in which awareness of the cross is maintained in all experience:

> in all things [thou] seekest purely not thyself but only thy Lord God, and dost use the creatures in God and for God, with fear and reverence, to thy bare need.[215]

Seeking in this way the religious man becomes "wholly abstracted from all things," "truly dissolved in Christ," "wholly converted to Christ," intentionally suffering with and "transformed into his suffering Lord," so that freed from attachments he "sees nothing within himself except Christ crucified, mocked, reviled and suffering."[216] He becomes able, "in a manner," to forget himself: "he that continueth . . . seeth not himself, because he always and only beholdeth his saviour Christ crucified." He sees Him "in his members."[217]

This forgetting makes possible a new remembering.[218] Who is present?

If a man does not say in his heart, in the world there is only myself and God, he will not gain peace.

[I]n your outward doings you have contemplation spiritual of God and find Him everywhere, and in every thing specially you do recollect yourself wholly and do enter into your heart.[219]

Not only are these words like the instruction given in the *Philokalia* for entering the heart by means of attention and constant invocation of the Name of Christ ("the prayer of the heart" or "Jesus prayer"), "until the name of the Lord becomes rooted in the heart and it ceases to think of anything else,"[220] but the aim is the same: to reduce the restlessness of habitually associative thought by intentionally giving it work, to free the attention, to open oneself to an active inner silence, to awaken. When Fewterer says that a man who continues meditating does not see "himself," it is that self (ego) maintained by all the habitual associations and reactions of ordinary thought and emotion: meditation helps to loosen the grip of this self by freeing the energy of attention which is 'normally' stolen and consumed by it. All that we read of unity and contemplation within action ('the mixed life' exemplified by Christ) are descriptions of a human possibility which depends on a prior liberation, however momentary, from the "old man."[221]

The *Glasse* describes this meditation as contacting a source of strength not 'his own,' through the action of which outer and inner life may be reconciled 'from Above.'

this person [who meditates rightly] would bear the cross of Christ with him and he also beareth in his heart Him which sustains both heaven and earth, with Whom he may easily sustain and bear all heavy burdens and pains.[222]

Our suffering can be very different to what we know. By the struggles of self-denial:

though we be in a manner consumed and lost through hunger and penury . . . we satisfy partly to our Lord for His Passion.[223]

If the "sensual nature" is "overcome for God . . . our inward man is daily reformed into the Image of God with new visitations of grace."[224] The 'sensual nature' is 'the flesh' or 'carnal body' of traditional Christian psychology, all that complex of functioning within which we experience ourselves 'normally' (insofar as we do), including ordinary partial thought and emotion.[225] These systematic meditations are a tool for mortification, by altering the psychophysical state (particularly the emotion) in such a way that a certain confrontation can take place, the necessary friction between our two natures. It is just before this point is reached that the Tudor material tends to become vague, but the fact of it is implied time and again, and especially in the earlier New Devotional sources.[226] A sensitive modern student of medieval mysticism, Evelyn Underhill, has written of the process of mortification:

> [It] is necessary, not because the legitimate exercise of the senses is opposed to Divine Reality, but because those senses have usurped a place beyond their station; become the focus of energy, steadily drained the vitality of the self. *"The dogs have taken the children's meat."* The senses have grown stronger than their masters, monopolised the field of perception, dominated an organism which was made for greater activities, and built up . . . barriers of individuality. It is thanks to this wrong distribution of energy . . . that "in order to approach the Absolute, mystics must withdraw from everything, even themselves."[227]

The whole process with which these treatises deal is "the work of our redemption," "the spiritual creation and renewing of the lesser world, that is man" according to "the science of the saints":[228] it is described variously as the great battle "to build the house of conscience and to order our senses,"[229] the gathering together of the soul and the preparation of an "upper chamber" within which Christ may eventually be received.[230] The appearance of these formulations throughout our material indicate the coherence of the tradition at an essential level.

We conflate texts through the consonance of words, but when questions of meaning arise their imprecision and subjectivity becomes poignant. 'Soul,' 'spirit,' 'body,' 'passions' and 'self' had an exact experiential content from Anthony through Augustine to Bernard, Eckhart and Ruysbroeck—this is the meaning of tradition—but they have ceased to have this in our understanding, in contemporary psychology which has virtually dispensed with them, and perhaps in these late medieval translations into the newly forming English language. For example, 'heart' once meant the centre of a man's being, the place in himself which he sought to discover through prayer, from which he could speak to and hear God, the 'monastery' or 'cell' within.[231]

How exactly does the language of the *Glasse* convey meaning, how practical is its guidance? Only experience of such a discipline could discriminate. Descriptions of the *conformitas Christi* occur in the context of exercises, prayer and fasting,[232] practised originally under guidance by a minority who had sought out life in a monastery or in specially created and maintained conditions: nevertheless, at this time, information about the significance of this experience was being broadcast as never before. The dangers inherent in this—comparable in some ways to the permeation of contemporary Western culture by spiritual teachings and methods divorced from their context in the Eastern traditions—may be inferred from Cisneros' warning to a fellow monk: "it behoves not, brother, that thou undertake lightly any exercises soever."[233] The danger is heightened if the Bridgettine treatises are merely repeating received information about spiritual exercises, although it is likely that they represent Syon's practice.[234] With what other currents would the *Glasse*'s influence have become mixed on entering life? The strong Christocentricity of the meditations,[235] together with the disturbing initial effect of personal discipline, may have created favourable conditions for the reception of Protestant attitudes.

The states described in the *Glasse*, and in much of our material, are not only beyond the criteria of ordinary experience but suspicious, unnecessary and disabling from that standpoint. The categories of modern psychology which buttress these criteria, are biased towards identifying and rectifying mental and emotional states regarded by definition as pathological and abnormal. However, we meet here a still traditional psychology in the service of a possible human development with quite other horizons. Contemporary psychotherapy seeks to improve the self according to the valuation of that same self: the religious tradition underlying our material understood why—and how—that self must be weakened.[236] The state of 'normality,' in which men have been, throughout history, content to deceive each other and themselves, is the question.

Modern psychology has tended to indict Christianity for encouraging a harmful attitude towards the body. But whose Christianity has done this? How are the Pauline strictures on the sins of the flesh to be understood? We are told that a struggle with oneself is necessary, but who must struggle and for what? There is an asceticism the obverse of hedonism, arising from fear of gratification rather than fear of its absence: the ego, motivated by fear and the literal understanding associated with it, attempts to dominate the body in order to maintain its usurped sense of identity.[237] Protestant reformers revolted against this distorted asceticism of self-calming, divorced from the intelligence of a living tradition of search and study. Modern psychotherapy addresses itself to the results of this distortion and revolt.

But historical sources indicate the existence of another understanding, an asceticism in the service of self-change and self-study, based on a more just and balanced attitude towards the body and its needs and supported by a practical psychology and metaphysics. We have specially stressed this different attitude wherever it has appeared, however slightly, in the material. In the Christian tradition, and the other great religions, the body is seen as a servant who, in the absence of its real master, has usurped control. The functions of the body are not the enemy but our wrong, 'passionate' relationship to them: that which was destined to rule has been overwhelmed by and become subservient to that which was designed to serve.[238] The ego, the false 'persona' unconsciously projecting our significance and worth is a consequence of this whole slavery, is 'of the flesh.' It is not a question of 'morals' as ordinarily understood. Living in ignorance of this disorganisation we are unconcerned by it, but ascetic practices can awaken an internal vigilance which feeds on the truth. The real ascetic was struggling not against the body but *for* a truer relationship with himself and his functions:

not the destruction of the body but a natural relationship to it, a relationship corresponding to the structure of universal creation itself, in which consciousness and intelligence determine the operation of the physical world.[239]

The life of the heart is determining. The real ascetic struggled for freedom from ordinary emotion (*apatheia* means 'without emotion,' passionlessness), for the transformation of his love, that the 'love of God' (*agape*) might be born in him.[240] "We have not been taught to kill our bodies, but to kill our passions."[241] Hence Anthony, the father of monastic asceticism, said:

> I believe that the body possesses a natural movement, to which it is adapted, but which it cannot follow without the consent of the soul; it only signifies in the body a movement without passion."

He discusses two other bodily movements, arising from indulgence in physical food which "causes the heat of the blood to stir up the body to work" (cf. *Luke* 21:34–35) and "yet another movement which afflicts those who fight, and that comes from the wiles and jealousy of the demons."

You must understand what these three bodily movements are.[242]

The answer to 'who can struggle,' is he who sees his situation and its consequences, and is able to care.

The reflection of this confrontation gives reality to the treatises we are examining. Alert to the pull of self-deception, we recognise the meaning of the *Glasse*'s instructions: the need to experience new feeling in the body, the joining of thought and feeling with instinct and sensation. Unless what the mind knows and the heart loves can live in the body, it has no ableness.[243] The striving for a unity including the senses underlies the Ignatian system. Descriptions of the material results of spiritual exercising challenge not only the division we think we experience between mind and body, but also scientific assumptions of a psychophysical continuum which can only legitimately be studied through the natural sciences. The Presence of Christ is spoken of as an objective material reality in the consciousness of the seeker: guided meditation is a means to awaken this, with grace. For Christ to be manifested in man, what disruptions of the known, what earthquakes must not take place!

The remarkable *Pilgrymage of perfeccyon* (1526), in which William Bonde makes available what he had received at Syon of "the science of the saints," completes our view of the role of this monastery in the transmission of medieval teachings on the inner life.[244] Originally compiled in the manner of the Brotherhood as a self-reminder,[245] Bonde chose to present his *rapiaria* of texts in English, so that

it might be the more acceptable to many, and specially to such that understand no Latin . . . to make you partners in the same.[246]

The harvest of medieval spirituality reaped by Tudor Bridgettines[247] was garnered
during the Counter-Reformation and passed into the storerooms of Anglicanism.
The *Pilgrymage* was transmission at a time of compelling urgency. The aspirations, methodology and intelligence of the last monastic renewal are epitomised
in a treatise comparable with Mombaer's *Rosetum* and counting only Whytford's
Pype of perfection as an English rival. Bonde's work is, however, broader in scope
than his brother's apologia for the monastic ideal, surpassing it in intellectual
vigour, emotional clarity and freedom from polemic.

In Bonde our themes find their latest expression: the relationship between the
Bridgettines and the New Devotion;[248] the pervading model of the Desert;[249] the
persistent vigour of a current of feeling, observation and technique associated
with Augustine, Bernard, the Victorines and the Franciscans; a traditional diagnosis of man's condition sufficiently merciless to destroy illusion and bring about,
with help, extraordinary responsibility; the emphasis on awakening from sleep
and the refining of attention as the first step towards the possibility, providentially
given, of new order and relationship, of knowing oneself as the image of God in
this life.

Bonde's wish is to lead men to the "perfection of the Kingdom": "the presence
of the Trinity, in a purified soul by grace." The unobstructed and undistorted
action of the universal law of the Trinity within man would be "service to God."[250]
For this, indeed, the heart must be "clean":

> it pertains only to a clean heart to see God; for this we labour, for this we sow
> our seed, we weed our land, that is our hearts.[251]

On the brink of the Reformation, the *Pilgrymage* is dealing with the possible birth
of new feeling, with work to transform emotion according to traditional methods, 'exercises' and 'prayer.' It is a repository of medieval devotion, drawing copi-
ously from

> the sentences of illumined doctors concerning perfection . . . joining also
> thereto the spiritual exercise and experience of holy fathers,[252]

but founded on "the counsels of our Lord and specially in the sermon that He
made in the mount."[253]

The life of "every Christian" is, more or less knowingly, a pilgrimage. Upon
reaching responsible age, "the years of discretion," the way divides and there can
be a choice. Bonde addresses himself to those who have experienced this choice,
those who seek to become knowing "pilgrims of the way of religion" on their
journey through this life, although he acknowledges in words reminiscent of
Rolle that

"God has made and ordained sufficient provision and safeguard in every state or degree, if man will put to his good will to bring him safe to the end of his said journey."[254]

It is a question of finding 'our part.'

The three books of the *Pilgrymage* are intended to embody the Trinity. The third, "the principal purpose of our intent," describes a journey of seven days, after the archetypal making and perfecting of the "great world": just so, it takes seven days for the "lesser world, that is man" to be made, "in which man is renewed and in manner created again, by the vii fold graces of the Holy Ghost."[255] This refers to the universal laws originally taught by Christianity, to the relation between three and seven, creation and completion, which was reflected in the practice of meditation and the liturgy.[256]

What does transmission mean? We must look for a beginning which is *ab origine* outside time, beyond common experiencing. What was the nature of the transaction between Gerard and Ruysbroeck in the forest of Groenendaal? Transmission, as it concerns us here, begins with the reception of the influence of a teaching being wholly lived. This quality becomes mixed in the course of time with other matters 'of the world,' influences generated in the vortex of ordinary living, thinking and feeling; it needs to be always renewed because it is continually being fragmented as it passes through our lives.[257] If transmission concerns the revelation of the hitherto unknown or inaccessible, then the receptivity and conductivity of the individual is of paramount importance.

Now we are looking at a book which is, however cogent and sensitive, only an arrangement of the words of long dead men about the kinds of experience they believed to be involved in living a teaching. This compilation arises, however, from a monastic life dedicated to following these indications. While invoking the reader's prayer for his ability to "weave and work in mine own life these instructions that I have gathered and written for you," Bonde says that he is actually beating the bush so that we may catch the bird.[258] He is attempting to convey the "secret doctrine of perfection," but insists,

as much as in me, I forbid all singular persons from the studying of this treatise and all such curious persons that desire more to know secrets than to ensue or follow perfection.[259]

Guiding a search, his writing becomes a vehicle for one kind of influence, feeding curiosity, for another: in the first case a line may continue its completing process, in the second it curves into 'the world.'[260] The eve of the Reformation was a crucial interval in the transmission of Christianity in the West. At such a time, what is withheld is as significant as what is made available.[261] That the "secret" impregnate the world and man find his rightful place between action and contemplation, was the meaning of 'the mixed life.' Is it not here, between the opposing forces of a man's outer and inner lives not sleeping, that 'the place of religion' may be found, the reconciliation ('forgiveness') of the Holy Spirit received?

To illustrate the nature of the difficulty and draw together what has gone before, let us follow one theme in the *Pilgrymage*, the disorder within man, the condition of his sleep. If it were not so, there would be no need for religion; if it remains utterly so, religion will feed only our dreams. By assigning a limited 'historical interest' to these traditional formulations and remaining unwilling to prove their verity, we continue impervious not only to their real meaning but also to the available help.

In relation to the level in himself capable of receiving the Word, man is asleep, metaphorically and literally. Moreover, the tragicomic examples quoted by Bonde when discussing the different degrees of attention show man to be, in fact, so deeply asleep for so much of the time that even the fulfilling of his ordinary life obligations frequently eludes him.[262]

An experiential understanding of the consequences of the Fall as presently verifiable inner chaos, characterises all the sources associated with the New Devotion and the *Pilgrymage* is no exception. The three powers in man, represented by his thinking, emotional and sensual-instinctive functions, have been "wounded": his thought—"scantly it has light," his emotions regard only themselves and his senses seek always the gratification of their own comfort, so that the order of "original justice," relating him to God, has no place. Because he hardly cognises this upside-down position, ruled by that which is lowest in him, and, even realising it, being virtually unable to bear anything that will help, the "health of the soul" languishes.[263] Unless this is known, he cannot care. What can care?

Great emphasis is laid by Bonde upon the struggle to awaken with all of oneself to this reality, to "exercise" oneself intentionally in order to be closer to it:

watch well and have ever your eyes open and look on the sure custody or keeping of your own soul at all times. . . . He that keeps Israel, never sleeps.[264]

From his sources, confirmed as they may have been in his own trials, Bonde had found that the practice of spiritual exercises was synonymous with the struggle to be more wholly awake.[265] The flash of this different state, the fruit of a new yet unmistakable inner relationship confirming the mystery of other levels, allows momentarily an order which must be reflected in action: or, as he says, through the "light" gathered we can "lift our self above our self."[266] The struggle for this is the threshold of that great battle to which the real documents of our spiritual tradition refer, "to build the house of conscience and to order our senses."[267] Being as we are, this involves "bitter tears."

Speaking of the degenerated presences of contemporary men, he associates their inaptitude for this exercising with unbalanced mental and physical health, a lack of proportion and discretion in the bodily humours, and by implication, the unbecoming conditions of common life which they themselves have created.[268]

No one's life "is worthy to bear the name of the life of man: for the life that pertains to man as man is only founded in virtues."[269] All conventional ideas about virtue are inadequate to convey what is meant here: the manifestation of "original justice" in man. It is interesting that Bonde also uses the word "virtue" in the old sense of force, that which can carry through to completion.[270]

Analogies and symbols of man's condition, their origin lost in the remote past, have been handed down in all religious and philosophical traditions: inaccessible to the isolated intellect and thus escaping distortion, they retain their power to challenge us impartially, to call our reason. Bonde is mining this vein when he speaks of man as a city in such disorder and dissension that he is unable to hear that which is summoning him in his depths. Man is a "lesser world" and necessarily partakes of all the substances from mineral to angel; he embodies a trinity as the image of God, but, as he is, without grace, his powers have been disharmonised and he is effectively ruled from below. In him "be diverse manner of people . . . all out of good order and each will have his own will, against reason." Religious tradition seeks to guide from multiplicity to unity, from fragmentation to wholeness. If the hubbub of this throng of "people"—who claim to represent the whole man, the 'I'—abates, then, at such an extraordinary moment, some message from another level of order may be received, called here "the voice of God," "none other but the inspiration of the Holy Ghost in the . . . city of man's soul."

> Therefore if we will hear clearly the voice of God, we must first subdue and put to silence the unruly people.[271]

It is the undeveloped lower functions, the thought, desires and sensations "of the flesh," which interfere with this precious awakening: "the dogs have taken the children's meat." "Spiritual exercising" and "mortification of the senses," described externally in Bonde and our sources as literally breast beating,[272] actually and essentially concern a refining and developing of these lower functions that they may take a place proper to them in "the city," cooperate harmoniously in "the lesser world," as Providence originally intended them to do. Christian teaching affirms that this is still possible.

Following Aquinas and Gerson, Bonde distinguishes three degree of attention, "actual," "virtual" and "habitual."[273] "Actual" attention, arising in a "whole" and "mortified heart" when the "household of the soul" is in a state of peace, he considers virtually unknown to us and almost impossible in its fullness: it is the attention of the angels. It has nothing in common with mental concentration or any intensification thereof. For the whole man to be able to pay attention to each word and sound of the prayer *as he is praying*, receiving their resonance and discerning meaning while sensing his own subjectivity, seeking to understand objectively, being sought, then this would be "actual attention."[274] He points out the extraordinary fact that we men believe ourselves to have such attention *already*.

only sincere pracical experiments can disabuse us of this illusion, as the story of the ploughman shows:

> This was well proved on a time when (as Master Gerson says) a ploughman all uplandish and rude, reproved an holy father, saying that he could say all his prayers with a whole heart and sound memory, never thinking on any [other] thing. To whom the father said, "Say one *Pater Noster* and think on none other thing, but only on that [which] you say and I shall give you my horse." And anon as he had begun to say his *Pater Noster* for the horse his thoughts moved him to ask, whether he should have also the saddle and bridle with the horse. And so he was convicted.[275]

"Habitual" attention is acting, thinking and feeling in "sleep," without "for that time the actual use and deliberation of reason."[276] The many direct and indirect references to sleep in our sources suggest that without undertaking the supremely difficult work of actually experiencing oneself in these continually shifting states of hypnotic partiality ('normality'), they cannot truly be evaluated, let alone overcome.

"Virtual" attention, which the religious man is bound to seek, is the key to understanding. Bonde describes a quality of attention which includes supplication and one's own intention, on which it is necessary to call at the beginning of a prayer or action. Despite, or perhaps because of, this demand, a man almost immediately loses his attention, becoming "alienated and abstracted or withdrawn"; but "the virtue of the first preparation remains unto the end." We are again in the territory of the New Devotion and their struggle to find and renew.[277] He likens "virtual" attention to an archer whose action is to loose his arrow, bringing together senses, wish and thought one-pointedly in the present moment.[278]

Such distinctions as these three attentions are grist to the mill of the academic study of spirituality, yet they bid us stop, for their true meaning is inaccessible to this kind of enquiry. Academic knowledge is the accumulation of information in one part of a man, the exercising of a partial attention, useful when fulfilling its role within a larger range of perception. The knowledge which Bonde intended to convey, the "science of the saints," is of another order: "it shows to man or woman themselves, and makes them to know what they be.[279] Reliance on the isolated intellect is harmful: thought, being too slow, distorts. It is always a finer attention that is being indicated however enwrapped in religious phraseology, always another quality of experiencing which can harmonise reason, feeling and instinct towards which we are being directed, however circuitously. One of the Desert Fathers said, "when words and life correspond to one another they are together the whole of philosophy."[280] Hence traditional sources emphasise the possibility of different qualities of attention.

The way represented by the sayings of the saints is opposed to all that takes place by itself in the lives of those who are rich 'of the world': "which forgetting themselves and sleeping at their death, find nothing but vanity in the purse of their conscience."[281] How can conscience be reached in this life?

The active, contemplative and mixed lives were based on the same truths and directed to the same goal. We have been attempting to discover their common principles from sources appearing during a particular historical period, an interval of disturbance and renewal, infused with the hope of a new devotion, in which the principles of a way in life were displayed in the borrowed clothes of the monastic experience. When writing of the "unspeakable" aim of religion and of the struggle to cleanse the heart between the knowledge of oneself and the experience of God, an authority on the medieval spiritual life concluded that the truth lies in a man's "cell," that "on the forehead of his conscience he may have this title written: 'My secret is to myself, my secret is to myself'" (*secretum meum mihi*).

> Thou hast one cell without, another within. The outward cell is the house wherein thy soul and thy body dwell together; the inward is thy conscience, which ought to be dwelt in by God (Who is more inward than all thine inward parts) and by thy spirit. . . . Wherefore love thou thine inward cell, and love the outward; and give unto each its proper service . . . and get for thyself the lordship therein.[282]

Sacred tradition, transmitted actively, brings knowledge and hope to the gulf between what man is and what he was intended to be, and can be received by him to the degree to which he can inhabit that place—it is the place of religion—between his two natures: then may 'the three lives' become one.

Notes

ABBREVIATIONS

AHSI   *Archivum Historicum Societatis Iesu* (Rome 1932–).

Allen   H. E. Allen, *Writings ascribed to Richard Rolle . . .* (*PMLA* Monograph Series 3, New York/London/Oxford 1927).

Aungier   G. J. Aungier, *The History and Antiquities of Syon Monastery . . .* (London 1840).

BL   British Library Catalogue, British Museum, London.

Bateson   *Catalogue of the Library of Syon Monastery . . .* , ed. M. Bateson (Cambridge 1898).

Blunt   *The Myroure of Oure ladye 1530,* ed. J. H. Blunt (*EETS* extra series 19, London 1873).

CF   *Consuetudines fratrum vitae communis* in *Fontes Minores Medii Aevii,* vol. 8, ed. W. Jappe Alberts (Groningen 1959).

D   Richard Whytford, *A dialoge or communication between the curate or ghostly father and the parochiane or ghostly chylde for a due preparacion unto howselynge* (London 1537, J. Waylande, *STC* 25413.5, *BL* 4402aaa58 [1]).

DE   *Ibid., A dayly exercyse and experyence of dethe . . .* (London 1537, J. Waylande, *STC* 25414, *BL* 4402aaa58 [2]).

Dumbar   *Gerhardi Dumbar, Reipublicae Daventriensi ab Actis, Analecta seu Vetera aliquot Scripta inedita . . .* , 3 vols. (*Daventriae* 1719–22), vol. 1.

EETS   *Early English Text Society* (London 1864–).

ER   Richard Whytford, *Saynt Augustyn's Rule in englysshe alone . . .* (London 1525, W. de Worde, *STC* 922.3, Bodleian Douce A277).

Gem   S. H. Gem, *Hidden Saints* (London 1907).

HI   Richard Whytford, *Dyvers holy instruccyons,* including *a devoute work of patience* (1^r–48^v), *a work of dyvers impediments and lets of perfection* (49^r–60^v), *a little lesson of iiii virtues . . .* (60^v–65^v), *an instructyon to avoyde*

	and eschewe vices . . . (66$^\text{V}$–85$^\text{V}$), *of detraction* (86$^\text{r}$–90$^\text{V}$) (London 1541, W. Myddylton, *STC* 25420, *BL* 4408cc27).
JEH	*Journal of Ecclesiastical History* (London 1950–).
JHI	*Journal of the History of Ideas* (Lancaster, Penn. 1940–).
LER	Richard Whytford, *The rule of saynt Augustyne bothe in latyn and englysshe* . . . (London 1525, W. de Worde, *STC* 922.3, Bodleian Douce A277).
LP	*Letters and Papers of the Reign of Henry VIII*, ed. J. S. Brewer, J. Gairdner and others, 22 vols. (London 1862–1932).
MBE	*The Meditations of Saint Bernard* (Westminster 1496, W. de Worde, *STC* 1917, *BL* C11a22).
MBL	*Divi Bernardi abbatis ad humana conditionis cognitionem meditationes* in *Meditationes S. Augustini et S. Bernardi* . . . (*Lugduni* 1564, *BL* 3670a6).
OED	*Oxford English Dictionary.*
Parabola	*Parabola, The Magazine of Myth and Tradition* (New York 1975–).
PBA	*Proceedings of the British Academy* (London 1905–).
PL	*Patrologiae* . . . *Latina*, ed. J.-P. Migne (Paris 1844–90).
PMLA	*Publications of the Modern Language Association of America.*
Post	R. R. Post, *The Modern Devotion* (Studies in Medieval and Reformation Thought, ed. H. A. Obermann, vol. 3, Leiden 1968).
P	Richard Whytford, *The Pype or Tonne of the lyfe of perfection* (London 1532, R. Redman, *STC* 25421, *BL* C69e1).
PP	William Bonde, *The Pilgrymage of perfeccyon* (London 1531, W. de Worde, *STC* 3278, *BL* 223k1).
RO1, 2, 3	David Knowles, *The Religious Orders in England*, 3 vols. (Cambridge 1948–59, 2nd ed. 1979).
SA	Gerard Zerbolt, *De Spiritualibus Ascensionibus* in M. de la Bigne, *Magna Bibliotheca Veterum Patrum et Antiquorum Scriptorum Ecclesiasticorum*, 17 vols. (Paris 1654), vol. 5, cols. 879–936.
STC	*A Short Title Catalogue of Books printed in England, Scotland and Ireland 1496–1640*, ed. A. W. Pollard, G. R. Redgrave and others (London 1926, revised 1976–)
T2, 3	*Thomae a Kempis* . . . *Opera Omnia*, ed. H. Sommalius S.J., 3 vols. (Antwerp 1601), vols. 2 & 3.
Trinkaus	C. E. Trinkaus, *In Our Image and Likeness, humanity and divinity in Italian humanist thought*, 2 vols. (London 1970).
W	Richard Whytford, *A Werke for Householders* . . . (London 1537, J. Waylande, *STC* 25425.5, *BL* 4402aaa58 [1&2]).
Ward	*The Sayings of the Desert Fathers, the alphabetical collection*, ed. B. Ward (Cistercian Studies Series 59, Oxford 1975, 1981 rev. ed.).

Wessel 1, 2   *Wessel Gansfort, Life and Writings*, ed. E. W. Miller and J. W. Scudder, 2 vols. (American Society of Church History 1, New York 1917).

YARS   *Yorkshire Archaeological Society Record Series.*

INTRODUCTION

1. *[The] Rule [of Saint Benedict*, ed. J. McCann (London 1952)] vii–x.

2. Ibid. 61 and below, 1, chap. 9 n. 15, 241.

3. Ibid. 68–69, eight times including the night office; cf. below, 190–91, 223, 228–29, 230–31.

4. Cf. Index: *lecteo divina.*

5. Cf. Index: manual work.

6. Quoted in ["Gregorian Chant in context,"] *Material For Thought* [no. 13 (San Francisco 1992)], 17, 23; cf. "To speak of God is to be of the most extreme quiet and freedom of mind. For the tongue is well directed in speech when the inner mind has been quieted in secure tranquillity" (ibid. 17) and for the search for balance between action and contemplation, ibid. 18; cf. also below, chaps. 7–9 passim.

7. Cf. *Rule* 32–33, "and almost in the same moment of time that the master's order is issued, is the disciples' work completed, in the swiftness of the fear of the Lord; the two things being rapidly accomplished together by those who are impelled by the desire of attaining life everlasting," and cf. Index: purification of emotion.

8. *Rule* 32–33, and below, 12, 55, 193, chap. 9 n. 2 and Index: craft.

9. *Rule* 8–9, 49.

10. Ibid. 30–31.

11. Ibid. 28–29.

12. *Ward* 145–46 and cf. 74 no. 2, 67 no. 1, 179 no. 85, 102 no. 2, 224 no. 11 and passim.

13. *Rule* 39, 13, 9.

14. *Early Fathers [from the] Philokalia*, [ed. E. Kadloubovsky and G. E. H. Palmer (London 1954)] 82 nos. 58–59, 90 no. 104.

15. *Rule* 13.

16. Ibid. 38–39.

17. Ibid 7, 33–35.

18. Ibid 7.

19. Ibid 161–63.

20. Cf. Index: religion; Way of the Monk.

21. C. Bamford, review art. *The Plan of St. Gall*, W. Horn and E. Born (Berkeley 1979) in *Parabola*, vol. 7, no. 2 (May 1982), 99.

22. Cf. below, 100–101, 107, 111–12, 220ff. and Index: duality, and Meister Eckhart: "A man should not escape from, nor evade nor deny his inner life, but he must learn to work

in God, with God and from God, in order to allow the inner to emerge into activity and lead the activity into the inner, eventually becoming accustomed to act without constraint. He must direct his attention onto the inner work and act from it, either by reading, prayer, or when appropriate, by outer action. When the outer threatens to destroy the inner, then follow the inner. But it is best if both be in unity, so that a man thereby may receive the participation of God," *Tractates from Meister Eckhart*, 11 (privately printed At the Press of Pembridge Design Studio, London 1982), based on [*Meister Eckehart, Deutsche Predigten und Traktate*, J.] Quint [(Munich 1969)], 94.

23. Cf. [D.] Knowles, [*The Monastic Order in England, 940–1216* (Cambridge 1963)], 679–82; *RO3* 457–68.

24. *RO2* 219–22.

25. Cf. below, 34ff.

26. Cf. below, 54–55, 106.

27. Cf. below, chap. 8 n. 58.

28. Cf. below, 150, 211–12 and n. 2, 221, 227, 236–37 and Index: asceticism; attention; self, man's lower.

29. The main historical source for these ideas in the Middle Ages was Dionysius the Areopagite.

30. Cf. below, 150–51, 227 and Index: "I am"; "remembering."

31. Cf. Index: Platonists, Renaissance.

32. *MBE* sig Ev^V; the spelling, word order and punctuation of early English texts have been modernised and every Latin passage translated for this edition; folio references have been given without abbreviation, and all biblical citations are to the authorised version unless otherwise stated; double quotation marks indicate textual references.

33. Paul Ricouer, quoted by T. Buckley in *Parabola*, vol. 9, no. 3 (August 1984), 64.

34. Metropolitan Anthony quoted in [J.] Needleman, [*Lost Christianity* (New York 1980)], 37: it may be that "it is for just this world of personal inner experience that the Fathers provide an objective language" (*Material for Thought* 15).

35. Ruth Steiner quoted in *Material for Thought*, 11.

CHAPTER ONE

1. Cf. *PL* 159:679; it has become a shadow in Luther, as R. Bainton, *Here I Stand* (New York 1950), 182.

2. [P.] Pourrat, [*Christian Spirituality* (London 1922–27)], vol. 3, 9–11: medieval thought persistently related seven and three, as *Blunt* 99, and above xv, below, 241, Index: seven; three.

3. Cf. Index: 'Image of God'; The Trinity.

4. *PL* 41:227–29, 647–48; cf. Thomas Aquinas, *Summa Theologica*, ed. T. Gilby (London/New York 1964–), vol. 46, 90–102, 117–19.

5. Cf. [G.] Constable, [*Religious Life and Thought (11th and 12th Centuries)* (London

1979),] I:31–32, 39–40, XV:27–60, XVI:5–28; [A.]Squire, ["Aelred of Rievaulx and the monastic tradition concerning action and contemplation," in *Downside Review*, vol. 72 (1954)] 290, 297ff.; and Index: *imitatio christi*; 'mixed life.'

6. [R.] Parkyn, [*Tudor Treatises*, ed. A. G. Dickens (YARS 125, Wakefield 1959)], 23, 59, and cf. C. S. Lewis, *The Allegory of Love* (Oxford 1958), 265.

7. *Ward*, 122 no. 1, 188 no. 152, 103 no. 6, and cf. 95 no. 44.

8. Cf. below, 8–9, 166–67, 175–76, 211–12, 241 and Index: Desert Fathers; 'mixed life'; psychology, traditional; spiritual exercises, transmission of.

9. Cf. J. Lawson, *A Town Grammar School through Six Centuries* (London 1963), 3, 21–36; [E. M.] Nugent, [*The Thought and Culture of the English Renaissance* (Cambridge 1956)] 326–27; and *Genesis* 19:17.

10. Cf. *Nugent*, 332, Erasmus, *The Praise of Folie*, tr. Chaloner (London 1549), sigs Piii^v–iv^r; Erasmus, *Colloquiorum Familiarum opus* (Antwerp 1564), 234–41; [E. M.] Thompson, [*The Carthusian Order in England* (Church Historical Society Publications, new series 3, London 1930)], 375, *RO2* 132, 134; *RO3* 224 189; *LP* 7, pt. 2, no. 1090, 421–22.

11. *Constable*, XV:40–41.

12. *Nugent* 328; cf. Matt. 5:1, *Ps.* 67:16–17 (Vulg.) and William [of] St. Thierry, [*The Golden Epistle*, tr. W. Shewring (London 1980)], 9–10; *Post* 639; below, 35 and Index: mountain.

13. *Nugent* 328; cf. Thompson 519.

14. Cf. Index: *lectio divina*.

15. *Nugent* 328; cf. *Isa* 2:3.

16. *Nugent* 329–30, 680: to show the equivalence of the monastic vow with the obedience Christ taught, he cites Ambrose, "I, having so good a lord, I fear not to die," and inserts with neither acknowledgement nor grammatical sense, "and be obedient to my superior."

17. *Blunt* 12–13.

18. *Ampleforth and its origins*, ed. J. McCann and C. Cary Elwes (London 1952), 75.

19. *Nugent*, 332; cf. *John* 10:34, *Ps.* 81:6 (Vulg.), also W. A. Pantin in *Medieval Studies presented to Rose Graham*, ed. V. Ruffer and A. J. Taylor (Oxford 1950), 201–2, 208, and in *Studies in Medieval History presented to F. M. Powicke*, ed. R. W. Hunt, W. A. Pantin and R. W. Southern (Oxford 1948), 368–85.

20. As Latimer in *LP* 12, pt. 2, no. 1259, 442.

21. *Nugent*, 330, 332; cf. [J. K.] McConica, [*English Humanists and Reformation Politics* (Oxford 1965)], 83, 178, 198, 204, 251; the first fifteenth-century English translation from Greek was of a Chrysostom sermon (*RO3* 89); for Jerome on the imitation of Christ, frequently noted by humanists; cf. *Post* 41.

22. *Nugent* 332 and cf. Index: observant reform.

23. Cf. [*The*] *Incendium Amoris* [*of Richard Rolle*, ed. M. Deanesley, University of Manchester Historical Series, 26 (Manchester 1915)], 48.

24. *Pourrat* 77–78; on the criterion of usefulness, cf. [The Cell of Self Knowledge, ed.] E. G. Gardner [The Medieval Library 9 (London 1925)], 81–2, [Thomas] Aquinas, *[Summa Theologica*, tr. English Dominican Fathers (London 1911–22)], vol. 14, 162–67 [J. L.] Connolly, *[John Gerson* (Louvain 1928)], 187–88.

25. [M.] Aston [*The Fifteenth Century* (London 1968)], 155–56; cf. Index: 'mixed life'; Gerson considered the contemplation practiced in many monasteries dangerous ([J.] Huizinga [*The Waning of the Middle Ages*, Harmondsworth 1965], 187, 189).

26. *Aston* 157; cf. below, chap. 5.

27. *Aston* 158.

28. Cf. Index: urban culture.

29. *Enchiridion* sig Civ^v (London 1544).

30. *Pourrat* 78.

31. Cf. below, 100–101, 102.

32. [H. C.] White, *Social Criticism [in popular religious literature* (New York 1944)], 1–40; *RO2*, chap. 7.

33. See below, chap. 8.

34. *Allen* 4; cf. 416 and appendix [G. R.] Owst [*Preaching in Medieval England* (Cambridge 1926)], 116–17; [*Yorkshire Writers*, ed. C.] Horstmann [2 vols. (London/Leipzig 1895], prints many tracts circulating in Rolle's name.

35. *RO2* 132–34, 219–26; *Owst* 112–13.

36. *Cf.* below, 28, 34–52, 103.

37. *Horstmann* vol. 2, 101–2; cf. [W. Hylton,] *Medylde lyfe* [(London 1516)], sigs Avii^v–viii^r; idem, *Scala [Perfectionis* (London 1533)], sigs Eiiii^{r-v}, Pvi^r; H. Gardner [in *Essays and Studies* (Oxford 1937), vol. 22], 112: "For the apostle says, let each man remain in that calling in which he is called; only let each man know his calling that it is of God and then persevere in it. I know that solitude is not for all but I know also that to some the common life is not suited. And therefore you must be prepared, and all other men, to obey the divine call"; cf. also *P* xix^r, *ER* sig Aiii^r..

38. *Allen* 405–6, 337; *Horstmann* vol. 1, 321–2; the *Abbaye* was printed by Wynkyn de Worde in 1496 and 1500 *(STC* 13609,13610) and was attributed to Alcock (*BL* 1A55232). See also Index: conscience.

39. Cf. Index: the heart; love, ordering of. Bernardino of Siena said, "a man knows as much as he loves" *(Constable* XV:28).

40. *Incendium Amoris* 44.

41. Cf. Index: Holy Name, cult of.

42. *Allen* 263–64.

43. Ibid. 255; cf. 266.

44. Cf. above, xvii–xix, 43–52 and Index: monastic ideal; scale; 'the world.'

45. *Allen* 267.

46. Ibid. 252; cf. 275.

47. Ibid. 264; cf. *H. Gardner* 104.

48. *Incendium Amoris* 267; cf. above xv–xix, below 227–45 and Index: love; manual work; sleep.

49. [E. J.] Arnould [*The Melos Amoris* (Oxford 1957)], xlix.

50. G. Hodgson, *Some Minor Works of Richard Rolle* (London 1923), 153.

51. *Arnould* xlviii.

52. For another example, see *Allen* 328; cf. 161.

53. F. M. Comper, *The Life of Richard Rolle* (London 1928), 45–49 and passim.

54. *Allen* 335.

55. Ibid 252–53.

56. *Owst* 280, "the vigorous unsacerdotalism of Rolle, coupled with the strict religious discipline for the household which he handed on from St. Edmund Rich . . . re-emerges in the sturdy sixteenth and seventeenth century yeoman of England. . . . [Its] influence stalks on silent, but wonderfully real . . . troubling little about the noisy clash of theologians. . . . [R]ound the family board and in the hearts of the peasantry, the Reformation meant no such break with the past as many would have us believe," and cf. 33–34, 43, 92–95, 116, 126, 157–58; for Edmund's *Myrrour*, see Bibliography.

57. [H. C.] White, [*The Tudor Books of] Private Devotion* [(Madison, Wisconsin 1951)], 3, 181, 231–32.

58. *Allen* 4, 90 n. 1 and cf. 266; for the *Psalter* see below, chap. 8 n. 67.

59. Cf. Index: 'godly vocation', W. Haller, *The Rise of Puritanism* (New York 1957), 124–27: Rolle reflects the ancient idea that all Creation exists on different levels of Being in relation to its Source, while the Puritans tended to use the idea of 'a calling' in the sense of a trade or occupation.

60. *Incendium Amoris* 45–46; cf. below, 90–91, 93–97 and Index: wisdom.

61. *Allen* 275.

62. Ibid. 364–65 and cf. *Scala* sigs. tviii^v–uii^r.

63. *Medylde lyfe* sig Bvii^v, quoting Gregory the Great, and cf. D. M. Jones, *Minor Works of Walter Hylton* (London 1929), xxxiv on Protestant interest.

64. Ibid. xi–xvi, xx; D. Knowles, *The English Mystical Tradition* (London 1960), 117; [H. S.] Bennett [*English Books and Readers 1475–1557* (Cambridge 1969)], xiii; *H. Gardner* 107–8; *Incendium Amoris*, intro.; *RO2* 219, 223–24; *Allen* 3–4, 49, 311, 407ff., 416, 521ff.; *Bateson* M24, 25, 43, 97.

65. See *STC* 14042–45, 4602 pt. 2, 14041, in order of citation; the Old English 'medylde' means 'mixed.'

66. Cf. H. Gardner 103–28; also *E. G. Gardner* 61–73.

67. *Medylde lyfe* sigs.Aiii^{r-v}; cf. *Scala* sigs.tii^r–v^r.

68. *Matt.* 22:37–39, *Mark* 12:30–31, *Luke* 10:27.

69. *Scala* sig. fiii^r.

70. Cf. *Squire* 297; *Constable* I:31–32, XV:41–44; above, xvii, below 241–42, 244–45 and Index: contemplation; duality.

71. And the same men at different times, *Medylde lyfe* sig. Aiiii^{r-v}.

72. Ibid. sig. Av^r; only if a man were without all temporal and spiritual responsibility would the contemplative life be unconditionally more suitable.

73. Ibid. sigs Bii^v–iii^r; the *BL* copy has this last phrase underlined.

74. *Constable* I:39, XV:31–32, 41:2, XVI:20–21 and cf. Index: *vita apostolica*.

75. *Medylde lyfe* sig. Aiiii^v.

76. P. E. Heath, *English Parish Clergy on the eve of the Reformation* (London 1969), 71; and cf. *Scala* sig. Pvi^r; *Owst* 113; [A. G.] Dickens [*The English Reformation* (London 1967)], 73.

77. Cf. *HI* 25^v–6^v, *P* lxi^v 25^v–6^v, Plxi^v and Index: craft.

78. *Ward* 185 no. 128; the view that monasticism degenerated into a craft (*RO3 461*) respects neither its historical origins nor the tradition of craftsmanship; *cf.* also [E.] Under-hill [*Mysticism* (London 1961)], 173.

79. *Medylde lyfe* sigs.Aiii^v–iiii^r.

80. Cf. above xvii, below 241–42, 244–45 and Index: 'mixed life.'

81. *Medylde lyfe* sigs. Aiii^v–iiii^r.

82. *Thrupp* 174–75.

83. *The Scale of Perfection*, ed. G. Sitwell (London 1953) xiii; White, *Social Criticism*, 89.

84. Cf. below, 79–80.

85. *Medylde lyfe* sigs. Av^v–vi^r.

86. *Enchiridion* (1544) sig. biv^{r-v}; cf. above, 1 and Index: Halton, Walter.

87. *Medylde lyfe* sig. Avi^v and cf. H. Gardner 109.

88. *Medylde lyfe* sig. Aiiii^r and cf. above 1–2, Index: *vita apoltolica* and [A. G. Dickens, in] *Christian Spirituality* [ed. P. N. Brooks (London 1975)], 160.

89. *Scala* sig. fi^r.

90. *Medylde lyfe* sig. Biii^r and cf. Index: order of daily life.

91. *The Third Spiritual Alphabet*, tr. by A Stanbrook Benedictine (London 1931), 139 and cf. 138–43.

92. Cf. Index: "recollection."

93. *Medylde lyfe* sig. Biii^v: I have transliterated 'antidote' and 'medicine' for Hylton's 'trya-cle,' an alexipharmic, for example a treatment for viper bite containing the flesh of that snake; for a later use in the same tradition; cf. Luis of Granada, *An excellent treatise . . .* (London 1599), 116.

94. *Medylde lyfe* sig. Bvi^r.

95. Cf. E. G. Gardner 28, 90 and Index: "art is better than evil strength."

96. *Medylde lyfe* sig. Bi^V.

97. Cf. chap 9 n. 273 and Index: *intentio.*

98. *Medylde lyfe* sig. Bii^{r-v}; on the place of the heart, *cf.* below, 227–29 and Index: the heart.

99. *Medylde lyfe* sig. Bii^V; cf. below, 169–70, chap. 8 n. 118, 252, below, 137–38, chap. 8 n. 118, 205–6.

CHAPTER TWO

1. [E.] Garin, [*Science and Civic Life in the Italian Renaissance* (New York 1969)], xiii–iv, 2, 14–20; Pico [della Mirandola, *On the Dignity of Man, On Being and the One, Heptaplus,* tr. C. G. Wallis, P. J. W. Miller, D. Carmichael (New York 1965)], vii.

2. [E.] Panofsky [*Renaissance and Renascences in Western Art* (London 1970)], 10.

3. Cf. W. Ferguson in *JHI*, vol. 15, no. 4 (October 1954), 501–8.

4. *Garin* 27–32; cf. 18–19.

5. Or 'sacred antiquity'; cf. *Panofsky* 8.

6. *Pico* xxv, 29.

7. Ficino and Pomponazzi, the most incompatible of philosophers, share this vision; see [P. O. Kristeller,] *Renaissance Thought* II [(New York 1965)], 107–8.

8. Drawn from *Pico* 5–7, 10 and *[The] Renaissance Philosophy of Man* [ed. E. Cassirer, P. O. Kristeller, J. H. Randall Jr. (Chicago 1956)] 224–25; cf. Garin 150–51; *The Letters [of Marsilio Ficino,* ed. the School of Economic Science, vol. 1 (London 1975)], 164–66, no. 110; for the cosmological-metaphysical tradition expounded by Pico, in which the three interpenetrating worlds (angelic/intellectual, celestial/rational and sublunary animal and plant/sensory) are contained within the fourth world, man himself, cf. Pico 75–82.

9. Ibid. ix–xi, 68 and cf. 147–74.

10. Ibid. 10–2, 60–62, xxvii; cf. his saying "philosophy seeks truth, theology discovers it, religion possesses it" (P. O. Kristeller, *L'Opera e il Pensiero di Giovanni Pico della Mirandola nella Storia dell' Umanesimo* [Florence 1965], 78); [P. O. Kristeller,] *Eight Philosophers [of the Italian Renaissance* (Stanford 1964), 68–69; *The Letters* 187; above, 1 and Index: philosophy.

11. *The Letters* 187.

12. *Pico* 10–11; cf. 136; chap. 6 below.

13. *Pico* xxvi–ii and cf. *Eight Philosophers* 58–59.

14. Cf. *Eight Philosophers* 50–53, 69–71.

15. *Garin* passim, a view strongly contested by some.

16. *Eight Philosophers* 69 and cf. F. Yates, *Giordano Bruno and the Hermetic Tradition* (London 1964) and D. P. Walker, *The Ancient Theology* (London 1972), passim.

17. Cf. [J.] Burckhardt [*The Civilisation of the Renaissance in Italy* (London 1965)], 341; *Eight Philosophers* 43–45, 69; *Pico* 49–53; *Renaissance Thought II* 94.

18. *Renaissance Thought II* 37, 40; *Eight Philosophers* 38–39, 49, 60–63, 69, 156; *Pico* vii–xxviii.

19. *Burckhardt* 85; cf. Garin xiv–xv, 18, "philology . . . a study so rich and complex that it includes a complete critical survey of the totality of man.".

20. *Renaissance Thought II* 29–30, 50; *Eight Philosophers* 155–56.

21. *Renaissance Thought II* 65–66.

22. Cf. above xix–xx, below 80–82, 98, 154, 244–45, for example.

23. Petrarch, *Opera* (Basle 1581) 1039, *fulgida vincula,* "splendid fetters"; and cf. [E. F.] Rice [Jr., *The Renaissance Idea of Wisdom* (Cambridge, Mass. 1958)], 35.

24. [G. de] Santillana [*The Age of Adventure* (New York 1956)], 12 and cf. [G.] Holmes [*The Florentine Enlightenment* (London 1969)], 2.

25. Ibid. 31 and cf. [G. G.] Coulton [*Five Centuries of Religion* (Cambridge 1950)], vol. 4, 236.

26. *Holmes* 118.

27. Cf. below, chap. 8.

28. Cf. *Renaissance Thought II* 42.

29. [T.] Elyot [*The Governour,* ed. S. E. Lehmberg (London 1962)], 231; cf. 190.

30. *Rice* 8, 38–40; *Holmes* 111.

31. Ibid. 109–11.

32. Ibid. 33.

33. Ibid. 113.

34. *De Voluptate* (1431) mocks the use of pagan philosophy in a Christian context; *De Libero Arbitrio* (1435) denies free will as usually understood and attacks the seminal medieval text, the *Consolation of Philosophy; Dialecticae Disputationes* (1439) attacks Aristotle philologically; *De Professione Religiosorum* (c. 1441) undermines the monastic ideal, and is discussed below, 43–6, 140–1; *Encomium Sancti Thomae Aquinatis,* given before the Dominican Congregation, pillories Thomist dialectic and praises the Fathers.

35. His *Novum Testamentum Adnotationes,* edited and published by Erasmus in 1505, is a clear forerunner of the latter's *Novum Instrumentum* (1516); cf. Trinkaus 681; *Renaissance Philosophy of Man* 150–54.

36. [E.] Wind [*Pagan Mysteries in the Renaissance* (London 1967)], 81–82.

37. *Rice* 68–71.

38. *Wind* 82 and cf. *Trinkaus* 707–10.

39. Cf. *Holmes* 144–67; *Rice* 74–77.

40. Cf. *Garin* xv n. 7; *Renaissance Thought II* 43; and Index: urban culture.

41. Cf. Index: 'godly vocation.'

42. Cf. *Rice* 46–47, 38–40.

43. Cf. *Renaissance Thought* II 21–24; *Trinkaus* xvii–xxiii and passim; [D.] Bush [*The*

Renaissance and English Humanism (Toronto 1939)], 13–38, 54–57.

44. *Bush* 55.

45. *Elyot* 227; *Rice* 39, 48; and cf. L. Bruni, *Humanistisch-philosophische Schriften*, ed. H. Baron (Leipzig 1928), 113–15.

46. *Rice* 52–53.

47. Cf. Index: spiritual work.

48. *Santillana* 12.

49. *Rice* 37–38 and cf. *Trinkaus* 68 on the difference between contemplation and speculation.

50. *Rice* 41–42.

51. "As the Pythagoreans and Platonists believe, during the whole time the sublime soul lives in this base body, our mind, as though it were ill, is thrown into continual disquiet— here and there, up and down—and is always asleep and delirious; and the individual movements, actions and passions of men are nothing but vertigos of the sick, dreams of the sleeping, deliriums of the insane, so that Euripides rightly called this life the dream of a shadow. But while all are deceived, usually those are less deceived who at some time, as happens occasionally during sleep, become suspicious and say to themselves: 'Perhaps those things are not true which now appear to us; perhaps we are now dreaming'" ([P. O. Kristeller, *The Philosophy of Marsilio] Ficino*, [New York 1943], 208–9).

52. *Ficino* 292–93, 356, 357, 294 and cf. 239, 361; for Erasmus' view, *Adages*, ed. M. M. Phillips (Cambridge 1967), 84–85, 92–93.

53. His considered view, *Renaissance Thought II* 56; cf. above, n. 47, below, chaps. 6 and 7 and Index: will.

54. Cf. *The Letters* 19–24 and above 24, below 31–34.

55. Cf. *Trinkaus* 645, 647; L. Spitz, *The Religious Renaissance of the German Humanists* (Cambridge, Mass. 1963), 268–69.

56. Thomas a Kempis, *The Imitation of Christ* (London 1960), 1, 3, 5.

57. *Renaissance Philosophy of Man* 105.

58. Gerard quoted in Thomas [a Kempis, *The Founders of the New Devotion*, tr. J. P. Arthur (London 1905)], 57; *T3* 30; and cf. below, 93–97.

59. *Trinkaus* 629–33, 647–50.

60. Ibid. 628.

61. *Studies in Renaissance Thought and Letters*, ed. P. O. Kristeller (Rome 1956), 99–121; *The Letters* 20–21; *Eight Philosophers* 40–41; *Renaissance Thought II* 91–4; *Trinkaus* 638, 644.

62. *Eight Philosophers* 52.

63. *Ficino* 321; *The Letters* 127–29, 40.

64. *Theologie Platonicienne*, ed. R. Marcel (Paris 1964), vol. 1, 36; *Ficino* 25–27, 321; *The Letters* 127–29, 40.

65. *Ficino* 28–29, 322.

66. Ibid. 292.

67. Cf. above, xvii, xviii–xx, 22–24.

68. Cf. Index: order; religious method; scale.

69. Cf. Plotinus: "it is necessary to . . . detach ourselves in so far as we may from the body to which we are fettered, in order that with the whole of ourselves, we may fold ourselves about Divinity and have no part void of contact with Him"; "they have not ascended in the pure integrity of their being, but are burdened with that which keeps them apart. They are not yet made one within" (*Underhill* 93, 207); cf. below, 226–29, 236–39 and Index: order; scale.

70. Cf. below, chap. 6 and Index: Zerbolt, Gerard.

71. Cf. Plotinus: "There are . . . different roads by which this end [of union] may be reached. The love of beauty which exalts the poet; that devotion to the One and that ascent of science which makes the ambition of the philosopher, and that love and the prayers by which some devout and ardent soul tends its moral purity towards perfection. These are the great highways conducting to that height above the actual and the particular, where we stand in the immediate presence of the Infinite, who shines out as from the deeps of the soul." ([K.] Walker [*The Conscious Mind* (London 1962)], 101–2; and [L.] Miles [*John Colet and the Platonic Tradition* (London 1962)] 23–24.

72. Plotinus spoke of finding "the pathway to reality" through "the love of the intellect for God" (*amor intellectualis Dei*), "the flame of love for what is there to know" (*Walker* 91; *Underhill* 86).

73. *The Letters* 78.

74. *Ficino* 295; *The Letters* 93–94; *Renaissance Thought II* 42.

75. *Ficino* 296; *The Letters* 130–31.

76. *The Letters* 40.

77. Ibid. 134; *Miles* 126–27; and below, chap. 9 n. 165.

78. [N.] Robb [*Neoplatonism of the Italian Renaissance* (London 1935)], 97, 126; cf. *Rice* 68–71, 48.

79. Cf. Index: Platonists, Renaissance; purification of emotion.

80. Cf. above, xxiii.

81. *Otiosum non est vacare Deo, sed negotium negotiorum omnium*, Bernard; cf. H. B. Workman, *The Evolution of the Monastic Ideal* (London 1913), 1.

82. *Knowles* 221; and cf. below, 48.

83. Cf. *Trinkaus* 654–56; *LER* sig. Bi^{r-v}; *ER* sig. Aiii^v; J. Fewterer, *The Myrour* . . . (London 1534), x^r; *T3* 61, 66; *Blunt* 72; W. Bonde, *the consolatori* (London 1534?) xi^v, xix^v–xx^r.

84. [Erasmus, *The Lives of Johan Vitrier and John Colet*, ed. J. M.] Lupton [(London 1883)], 43; cf. Lupton, *A Life of Dean Colet* (London 1909), 297.

85. [M. M.] Phillips [*Erasmus and the Northern Renaissance* (London 1949)], 46 [*The Essential Erasmus*, ed. J. P.] Dolan [(New York 1964)], 28–29.

86. *Dolan* 54–55; cf. above Introduction; Index: 'mixed life'; 'the way in life.'

87. [T.] More, [*The*] *English Works,* [ed. W. E. Campbell and A. W. Reed (London 1927–31)], vol. 1, 381–88.

88. *W* sig. Bii^V; cf. *HI* 47^{r-v}.

89. For example, R. Baxter, *The Saint's Everlasting Rest* (London 1653), pt. 4, 118; [R.] Southwell, [*A Short Rule of Good Life* (London 1622)], 20–21, 22, 135; L. B. Wright, *Middle Class Culture in Elizabethan England* (Chapel Hill 1935), 228–96; and Index: the Christian; order of daily life.

90. *BL* Sloane MS 1037 (1536), 5^V–6^r.

91. Cf. C. S. Lewis, *The Allegory of Love* (Oxford 1958), 66–73; *HI* 1^r–48^V.

92. Cf. Index: monastery, the medieval; religion.

93. *Coulton* 688–89.

94. *Trinkaus,* 676; cf. 675.

95. Ibid. 680–81; *Renaissance Philosophy of Man* 151. Valla's thought, even expression, is strangely similar to certain twelfth-century writers: cf. his words quoted in our text, 44–45, with these passages (*Constable* XV:41–42), "To flee the world from the middle of Babylon and to be saved is as much safer as it is easier; but to be crowned victor in the middle of Babylon is as much grander as it is harder; so that monastic perfection, although commendable for merit, is considered as much lower as it is easier than clerical" (Premonstratensian canon, Philip of Harvengt); "the laurel of victory is given not to him who flees, but to him who remains, not to him who falls but to him who resists, not to him who submits but to him who conquers" (Peter the Venerable writing to persuade his secretary to become a hermit, not in body but in heart, with which cf. above, 8, 11, below 245.

96. *Trinkaus* 674–75.

97. Cf. J. H. Rieger in *Studies in the Renaissance,* vol. 9 (New York 1962), 187–94; *Nugent* 37–41.

98. Cf. *Trinkaus* 682, 674–75.

99. Ibid. 674–75.

100. Ibid. 676; cf. [Erasmus], *Enchiridion* [(1544)], sig. Uvi^V: "The order of monkship is not piety but a kind of living, to every man after the disposition of his body and his mind also, either profitable or unprofitable."

101. See Index: faith; submission.

102. *Trinkaus* 677.

103. Cf. Index: urban culture.

104. *Trinkaus* 676.

105. Cf. *Dolan* 55; [Erasmus,] *De Contemptu Mundi* [(1533)], 88^V, "nor you should not think that there wants anything for you to vow if you fulfil the vow that you made to Christ at your christening"; also H. Denifle, *Luther et le Lutheranisme* (Paris 1914), vol. 2, 20–39; W. A. Pantin in *Studies in Medieval History presented to F. M. Powicke,* ed. R. W. Hunt, W. A. Pantin and R. W. Southern (Oxford 1948), 383; and Index: baptismal vow.

106. *Trinkaus* 677.

107. Ibid. 678.

108. Ibid. 679; cf. below, 113.

109. Cf. C. Hill, *Society and Puritanism* (London 1969), 429–66; all this is conjured in the subtitle to Coverdale's *The Christian Rule* (1547), which concerned the "state of all the world from the highest to the lowest: and how every man should live to please God in his calling . . . the Christian state of matrimony and how man and wife should keep house together with love."

110. *Trinkaus* 679–80; cf. *Enchiridion* sig. Uvi^V on a monasticism which taught men "to tremble and fear, but not to love," *Post* 475.

111. Implicit in all our material; cf. above, chap. 1 n. 59; below, 118–19 and Index: being, and chaps. 6–9 passim.

112. *Trinkaus* 654–55, 661–62.

113. Ibid. 661; cf. [P.] Brown [*Augustine of Hippo* (London 1969)], 101–27.

114. *Phillips* 16, *voluptas* is 'pleasure'; the debate in Valla's *De Voluptate* is resolved through the idea that Epicurean *voluptas* is more Christian than Stoic 'virtue' (*Holmes* 130).

115. *Post* 667–68.

116. *De Contemptu Mundi* 73^r–74^r.

117. *Post* 667–68.

118. *De Contemptu Mundi* 74^r.

119. See below, 51.

120. *Post* 596–98; and cf. *Wessel* 2, 330–31.

121. More, *English Works*, vol. 1, 370.

122. *RO3* 101–7, 87–90, 95.

123. [T.] Starkey [*A Dialoge*, ed. K. M. Burton (London 1948)], 53; cf. ibid. 140 and *Owst* 50.

124. *Starkey* 79–80; cf. ibid. 145 and S. Fish, *A Supplicacyon for the Beggers* (1529?, *STC* 10883, *BL* C21b45).

125. See above, 26–27.

126. *Holmes* 147, cf. ibid. 119–20, and *Holinshed's Chronicles* (London 1807), vol. 3, 617; *Ampleforth and its Origins*, ed. J. McCann and C. Cary Elwes (London 1952), 58.

127. *Trinkaus* 665.

128. Cf. [E.] Male [*The Gothic Image* (London 1961)], 355–56; *Owst* 135; E. L. Tuveson, *Millenium and Utopia* (Berkeley 1949), 22–70; T. Sampson, *A Sermo . . . of pacience* (London 1550), sig. Aiii$^{r–v}$; R. Barckley, *A Discourse of the Felicitie of Man* (London 1603), 315–16.

129. *Trinkaus* 668.

130. Ibid. 668; he touches the concept of *adiaphora*, for which see W. G. Zeeveld, *Foundations of Tudor Policy* (London 1969), 137–41.

131. *McConica* 255.

132. Cf. White, *Social Criticism*, 268–70.

133. Cf. below, 164–65, 228–29.

134. [*Opus Epistolarum*, ed.] P. S. Allen [(Oxford 1906–)], vol. 3, 375, tr. in [*Christian Humanism and the Reformation*, ed. J. C.] Olin [(New York 1965)], 129; cf. *De Contemptu Mundi* 84^v–5^r, "in old time . . . a monk was none other thing than a pure Christian man . . . a monastery was none other thing than a flock or company, which had conspired or consented together to follow the most pure doctrine of Christ"; also *P. S. Allen*, vol. 1, 296; vol. 8, 406–10; *Trinkaus* 680.

135. *The fyrste sermon* (London 1549), sig. Cii^v.

136. *Ymage [of love]* (London 1532?), sig. Cii^r; and cf. *The Foundacyon of Christendome* (see Bibliography), sigs. Hi^r–iiii^v.

137. [*Concilia Magnae Brittaniae*, ed. D.] Wilkins [(London 1737)], vol. 3, 732; the first monks were said to have been Helias and Helizeus, sons of Jonadas (Elijah and Elisha); on the freedom of the early monks; cf. *Ward* 226, no. 3, 217 no.21, "I eat when the need arises."

138. *Ymage* sig. Cii^r; cf. *Coulton* 284, 179–81; *Enchiridion*, sig. Ciii^v; *P. S. Allen*, vol. 3, 374–75.

139. *Thrupp* 180–89, 174–75; *RO3* 233–34; *Thompson* 494.

140. Cf. Index: monastic rules.

141. *RO3* 338.

142. *Documents illustrating the activities of the General and Provincial Chapters of the English Black Monks 1215–1540*, ed. W. A. Pantin (Camden Third Series 45, 47, 54, London 1931–37), vol. 54, 123–24, document no. 283; within a few years Puritan writers were to use the same arguments to explain their own lack of public support.

143. *Coulton* 194.

144. *Thompson* 426.

145. [A.] Boorde [*The Fyrste Boke of the Introduction to Knowledge*, ed. F. J. Furnivall (London 1870)], 47; cf. 53, 57; however, he was to write later that the banishment of fasting by the new religious authorities was one of the seven (medical) evils of England (ibid. 82).

146. *Thompson* 391–92; cf. 29, 34–35; the Carthusians had been accused of murdering their sick since the thirteenth century, T. D. Fosbroke, *British Monachism* (London 1843), 65; cf. also *LER* sig. Oi^{r-v}.

147. *Thompson* 39.

148. Cf. Index: asceticism; body, the physical.

149. Cf. *De Contemptu Mundi* 2^{r-v}.

150. Cf. Index: body, the physical; spiritual work.

151. *McConica* 118; cf. *Coulton* 697.

152. *William of St. Thierry* 38.

153. *Trinkaus* 678; and cf. *Enchiridion*, sig. Niii^v.

154. *Boorde* 66 n. 3; cf. *Coulton* 313, quoting Pius II, "for weighty reasons marriage was taken from the priests: for weightier it ought to be restored."

155. *Wilkins*, vol. 3, 733, part of a commentary on *1 Cor.*7 which continues, "all other evils may be suffered with a merry conscience, this cannot so be endured"; and cf. 730.

156. *Wessel 1* 244–45, continuing in her language of affective devotion: "Through desire for Christ and pious meditation upon him it is within our power to have righteousness and purity of heart if we but wish it. These things are obtained not by struggle and conflict, but by quiet longing, by sweet tears, by faithful kisses upon the feet of Jesus. There is no necessity for severe fasts or the wearing of a rough goat's hair garment. The worthy fruit of repentance requires no bodily severity, but only that which is necessary for us all, the piety that availeth for all things."

157. Cf. above, n. 148.

158. [A.] Hyma [*The Christian Renaissance* (New York 1925)], 33–34; *Gem* 52; and cf. Index: Gerard Groote, personal life; spiritual exercises.

159. Cf. above, 35.

160. *Wessel 2* 69–70.

161. Cf. Index: Wessel Gansfort.

162. [M.] Foss, [*The Founding of the Jesuits* (London 1969)], 71, 74: his wish was great, for he wrote "Lord, show me where to find help, because, even though I had to follow a little dog in order to find a remedy, I would do it" (ibid. 74).

163. *Christian Spirituality* 166.

164. *Parkyn* 69–70.

165. *Incendium Amoris* 47.

166. *E. G. Gardner* 81–82.

167. Ibid. 82.

168. *Scala*, sig. Iiiii^V and cf. *Medylde lyfe*, sig. Biii^V; *E. G. Gardner* 95; H. E. Allen, *English Writings of Richard Rolle* (Oxford 1931), 86.

169. Cf. W. Hilton, *The Scale of Perfection*, ed. G. Sitwell (London 1953), xiii; W. Allen, *A Briefe Historie*, ed. J. H. Pollen (London 1908), 83.

170. *The Works of Hugh Latimer*, ed. G. E. Corrie (Cambridge 1844–45), vol. 2, 94.

171. *P* xix$^{r–v}$; cf. xii^v–iii^r and for a more usual view ccxxxv^v–vi^r; cf. Index: 'Christ, mystical body of.

172. *Enchiridion*, sigs. Ciiii^r–v^r; *P. S. Allen*, vol. 3, 376; and cf. *De Contemptu Mundi* 88^V. On compulsion, cf. *Trinkaus* 677; *Thompson* 422; *Ymage*, sigs. Ci^v–ii^r; *Aquinas*, vol. 11, 116–19; and below, 101–13.

173. Cf. D. Chitty, *The Desert a City* (Oxford 1966), passim.

174. Cf. [P.] Villari [*The Life and Times of Girolamo Savonarola* (London 1888–89)], vol. 1, 338; F. Yates, *Giordano Bruno and the Hermetic Tradition* (London 1964), 55–56, 367–73; *Garin* 21–48.

175. Cf. *RO3* 145–47.

176. *Phillips* 82 and cf. *Paraclesis* [Basle 1519], 12; on the Brotherhood's understanding of the restoration of the image of God, see Index: 'Image of God'; 'regeneration of man.'

177. Cf. below, 102–3, chaps. 4–7 passim.

CHAPTER THREE

1. *Miles* vii; *RO3* 152–53; *McConica* 24, 36, 42, 45, 46–48; [F.] Seebohm, [*The Oxford Reformers* (London 1914)], 90 and passim.

2. *Miles* ix, 19–20; *RO3* 153; *Seebohm* 97, 258, 293–94; [St. Thomas] More [*Selected] Letters* [ed. E. F. Rogers (New Haven 1961)], xiii–xiv.

3. *Miles* 172–73.

4. *McConica* 119–20.

5. *Seebohm* 90, 156; *Miles* x.

6. Cf. *Miles* 180–81.

7. Ibid. vii; *Seebohm* 90.

8. *McConica* 47–48; cf. Miles 177, 179–80, 181; *Seebohm* 313.

9. *Miles* 173; cf. *Seebohm* 70–73.

10. *Miles* 141–50, 166; cf. *McConica* 25, 47.

11. *Miles* 179–81; *Seebohm* 289–90, 292.

12. *Miles* 171–72.

13. Ibid. 182–86, 214, *McConica* 47; and cf. *Seebohm* 73–75; *ER* sig. Aii^{r-v}.

14. *Seebohm* 289–91.

15. *RO3* 237; *Seebohm* 190.

16. *Lupton* 34.

17. *P. S. Allen*, vol. 4, 521 n. 455.

18. *Lupton* 28, 34–35; and cf. *HI* 51^v.

19. *Miles* 141–47; cf. Index: 'being in, but not of, the world'; 'mixed life.'

20. *Lupton* 46; cf. *Miles* 207–8; *HI* 47^v–8^r; *W* sigs. Bi^v–ii^r; Colet [*A ryght frutefull monycion* (London 1534)], passim.

21. Cf. 22^r–25^v; *P* lxxxv^v; *DE* sigs. Aii^v, fi^v–fii^v; fii^v; Index: craft, and [J.] Lacarriere [*The God Possessed* (London 1963)], 28–29.

22. *DE* sig. fii^r; cf. Erasmus, "everyone must be given a target toward which he must strive" (*Olin* 121); and Index: *intentio*; will.

23. *HI* 22^v; and cf. below, 236–37 and Index: *fac quod in se est.*

24. [R. W.] Chambers [*Thomas More* (London 1963)], 72; [*Lives of Saint Thomas More by W. Roper and N. Harpsfield*, ed. E. E.] Reynolds [(London 1963)] 5, 62.

25. *Seebohm* 90, 98; *Miles* 211.

26. *Seebohm* 92–98; *Chambers* 169–82; *Reynolds* 14–16, 63, 89–91; and cf. *D* sig. Cvii^{r-v}.

27. *Miles* 210; *McConica* 19, Index: 'the city as monastery'; Erasmus, Desiderius.

28. *Miles* 209, 115–16, 119; cf. Index: priesthood.

29. *Miles* 83, 85–86, 96, 103–4, 110, 117–18, 124–26, 128–29.

30. Ibid. 201, 207–8.

31. Ibid. 200, 202–3 and n. 124, 206–8.

32. *Seebohm* 157.

33. Ibid. 203–6.

34. *McConica* 24.

35. *Enchiridion*, sigs. Aviii^r–Bi^r.

36. *McConica* 25, 47.

37. *Enchiridion*, sigs. Aviii^r–Bi^r.

38. *De Contemptu Mundi* 87^v, 88^{r-v}.

39. *W* sig. Dviii^r; cf. LER sig. Dvi^r; *MBE* sig. Cii^r; *Blunt* 74.

40. *Ymage*, sig. Bv^r; cf. Cvi^{r}ff.

41. [G.] Leff [*Heresy in the Later Middle Ages* (Manchester 1967)], vol. 2, 577; cf. *Wilkins*, vol. 3, 730.

42. Cf. Index: mystical tradition, medieval.

43. Cf. Index: 'the monastery within'; orthodoxy & unorthodoxy; 'the way in life.'

44. [A. W.] Reed [*Early Tudor Drama* (London 1926)], 166–68; *STC* 21471.5.

45. *Bennett* 163.

46. Cf. Bateson ix, xv, C15, 224, O49, K37, N28, O36; *The Cambridge History of the Bible*, ed. G. W. H. Lampe (Cambridge 1969), vol. 2, 414; and below, 74–75, 213, 217–19, 229–30.

47. See below, 62–64, 66, 71–72, 74–78.

48. *Reed* 166–68.

49. *Dickens* 123–25.

50. *STC* 21801, attr. to A. Savorine O.P.

51. More, *English Works*, vol. 2, 15–16, 18; *Miles* 204–5; cf. *Ymage*, sigs. Biii^r–vi^r.

52. Ibid. sigs. Ai^v–ii^v; and cf. *Wind* 63 for Ficino's reformulation of this traditional idea.

53. *Ymage*, sigs. Aiii^v–v^r and cf. [F.] Yates [*The Art of Memory* (London 1969)], passim.

54. *Ymage*, sig. Av^{r-v}, vii^r, viii^{r-v}.

55. Ibid. sigs. Av^v–vi^r; cf. Cv^r–vi^r; and Index: 'Image of God'; The Trinity.

56. *Ymage*, sigs. Bi^v–ii^r; cf. above, 11–12.

57. *Ymage*, sig. Bii^r; cf. above, 14–15.

58. Cf. White, *Social Criticism*, 89; above, 12–15 and Index: 'the world.'

59. *Ymage*, sig. Bii^v.

60. Ibid. sig. Biii^r.

61. Ibid. sig. Biii^r–iv^r; cf. *Owst* 142, 144.

62. *Ymage*, sig. Biv^{r-v}; cf. Ci^v–ii^r, Bv^v–vi^r, 'treen'—wooden.

63. Cf. below, 68, 74–75, 77–80.

64. "[I]n the primitive church, the chalices were of wood, the prelates of gold. In these days the church hath chalices of gold and prelates of wood," *Villari*, vol. 1, 182–84; cf. ibid. 113; *Aston* 126; *Trinkaus* 656–57 [L. L.] Martz [*The Poetry of Meditation* (New Haven 1954)] 284–85; D. and G. Mathew [*The Reformation and the Contemplative Life* (London 1934)], 196.

65. *Villari*, vol. 2, 87, 391; *McConica* 65, 71, 94, 98–99, 100–101, 168, 189, 195–96, 278, 283–84; *Bateson* R51; White, *Private Devotion*, 52, 79, 96, 100–101; J. H. Lupton *A Life of Dean Colet* (London 1909), 52.

66. *Villari*, vol. 2, 383, 385, 387–88; *McConica* 168, 196.

67. *Hos.* 4:9; cf. Colet quoted in *Nugent* 361; and proverbial in medieval preaching, as in *Owst* 35, *Villari*, vol. 2, 98.

68. *Ymage*, sigs. Biv^v–v^r; above, 57.

69. Ibid. sigs. Bv^r–vi^r; cf. *Villari*, vol. 1, 113.

70. *Ymage*, sig. Bvi^{r-v}; and on the "actual" attention of angels; cf. below, 243–44.

71. *Ymage*, sig. Bvi^v.

72. *Ps.* 45:9–15 and cf. Whytford's use of the same imagery in *P* ccvi^r.

73. Cf. Index: Bridgettines of Syon.

74. *Blunt* 1–2.

75. Cf. Index: Victorine school.

76. *LER*, passim.

77. *Rule* 7.

78. *Ymage*, sig. Bvii^r.

79. Ibid. sig. Bvii^{r-v}; he writes in the tradition of male spiritual advisers to the Bridgettine nuns, as in Civ^v–v^r; *Incendium Amoris* 79–83; *Allen* 50, 216, 321; below, 213.

80. Cf. below, 189–91 and Index: meditation.

81. Cf. *LER* sigs. Li^v–ii^v, Aii^{r-v}, Tiv^v; *Blunt* 130, 140; *Bonde* 2^v.

82. Ibid. sigs. Diii^{r-v}; the queen's dress "in gold of Ophir" symbolises the qualities of contemplative love, as did the Bridgettine nun's, *Aungier* 22–24, 314–15.

83. *Ymage*, sigs. Div^v–v^r (*John* 4:23); cf. Dvi^v (*John* 4:24); the most 'spiritual' of the synoptic gospels was held in particular reverence at Syon (*Blunt* 102).

84. Cf. *Enchiridion*, sig. Niii^{r-v} and *Ymage* Dv^r–vi^r; Erasmus quotes the same psalm at sig. Niv^r.

85. *Enchiridion*, sig. Niii^v; cf. *Enchiridion* (Antwerp 1523), sig. il^r; and Index: 'the monastery within'.

86. Cf. Index: Franciscans, observant.

87. Cf. below, chap. 7 passim.

88. Cf. N. Cohn, *The Pursuit of the Millennium* (London 1962), 251.

89. Cf. Lefevre d'Etaples in H. A. Obermann, *Forerunners of the Reformation* (London 1967), 302–5; Index: listening.

90. *Ymage*, sigs. Dvi^{r-v}; cf. *Luke* 11:28; *Matt.* 23:3; and *Enchiridion*, sigs. Niii^{v}–iv.

91. *Needleman* 129; cf. *Material for Thought* 17–25; Index: *lectio divina*.

92. F. L. Weis, *The Life, Teachings and Works of Johannes Denck* (Strasbourg 1924), 23–24, 71, 24–25; cf. 72: "if all ceremonies were lost, little harm would come of it."

93. *Ymage*, sigs. Bvii^{v}–viii^{r}; cf. Civ^{r-v}, 1 *Cor.* 13:9–13; and R. Fox, *Contemplacyon of Synners* (London 1499), sig. Aiii^{v}.

94. *Ymage*, sigs. Bviii^{r}–Ci^{r}.

95. Ibid.; cf. *Post* 514; *Coulton* 161, 414; *Aungier* 320; *Blunt* 56–60; *RO3* 20; but also *Blunt* 32–3, 37; it was a Carthusian characteristic too, *Blunt* 59–60, *RO3* 20.

96. *LER* sigs. Aiii^{r}–iv^{r}; *The folowyng . . .* is a translation of Kempis' *De Imitatione Christi*.

97. Cf. above, 43, 57, below 102–3; and the vernacular heretical sources in *Wilkins*, vol. 3, 729–31.

98. *Ymage*, sigs. Ci^{v}–ii^{r}; cf. *Romans* 12:2; and above, 51.

99. Cf. Index: "delight" in work.

100. Cf. Index: psyche, human.

101. *Ymage*, sigs. Cii^{r-v}.

102. For the contemporary significance of 'new' and 'old,' cf. Urbanus Rhegius, *The olde Learnyng and the new* (London 1548), "The Preface of the Translator" and the 1536 edition of Rolle cited in *Allen* 13.

103. *Ymage*, sig. Ci^{v}.

104. Ibid. sigs. Ciii^{v}–iv^{r}.

105. Ibid. sig. Civ^{r}.

106. Ibid. sig. Cvii^{r}.

107. *Ymage*, sigs. Cv^{r}–vii^{r}; cf. *Col.* 3:10, 1 *John* 2:10–1, 3:14, 4:16; Richard of St. Victor in [*Late Medieval Mysticism*, ed. R. C.] Petry [(London 1957)], 110–11; Ficino in *Trinkaus* 464–65.

108. *Ymage*, sigs. Cvii^{v}–Dii^{v}, citing Bernard.

109. Cf. Index: body, the physical; chaos in man; "the dogs have taken the children's meat."

110. For the emotional life as 'of the flesh' cf. Index: emotional life.

111. *Ymage*, sigs. Di^{v}–ii^{v}; cf. Index: love; self, man's lower; watching.

112. *Ymage*, sig. Diii^{r}.

113. Ibid. sig. Dii^{v}.

114. Cf below, 314 n. 181.

115. *Ymage*, sigs. Eii^{r-v}; cf. Eiii^r [*Four revelations of Saint] Birget* [(London 1531?)], sigs. Biii^v, Ciii^r.

116. *Ymage*, sig. Eviii^v; cf. Index: the soul.

117. *Ymage*, sigs. Dviii^r–Ei^r; cf. Index: love.

118. Cf. above, 33; below, 116.

119. *Ymage*, sig. Ei^v, quoting Bernard.

120. Ibid. sigs. Eii^v–iii^r; cf. below, 2193.

121. Cf. Index: spiritual exercises.

122. Cf. below, 129, 184–85 and Index: Ignatius Loyola.

123. *Ymage*, sigs. Eiii^r–v^r; cf. *HI* 5^v–7^r.

124. White, *Private Devotion* 226–27.

125. *LER* and cf. *Bateson* which includes over thirty entries for Hugh.

126. Cf. *Allen* 139, 341; *Petry* 96.

127. Cf. below, 167–72 and Index: Momtaer, John.

128. Cf. below, 229.

129. *Ymage*, sigs. Ev^v–vi^r.

130. Ibid. sig. Evi^r.

131. Ibid. sigs. Dvii^{r-v}; cf. Index: 'the monastery within.'

132. *Ymage*, sigs. Evi^{v-r}; cf. below, 241–42.

133. Cf. above 65, below 223, 228, 245.

134. *Birget*, sigs. Bi^{r-v}, Bii^r; cf. below, 213.

135. *Birget*, sig. Ci^v.

136. Cf. below, 207, 224, 238–39, 242–43.

137. *Birget*, sigs. Bii^v–v^r; cf. Ciii^r.

138. Cf. above, xvii, xix, 13, 27–28; below, 241–42, 245.

139. *Birget*, sigs. Bv^v–vi^r; cf. v^r; Rolle also spoke much of "fire."

140. Cf. Index: compunction; *conformitas Christi;* suffering.

141. *Birget*, sig. Bvi^{r-v}.

142. Ibid. sigs. Bvii^r, vi^v; cf. above, 17.

143. *Ymage*, sig. Eviii^v, cf. below, below, 122–28, and Index: love; The Trinity.

144. Cf. Index: the New Devotion.

145. Hylton's *Scala*, bk. 1, examines the "image of sin" and bk. 2, the reform of the soul and the restoration of the "image of Christ," the passage from outer devotion to images to the inner devotion, Paul being drawn on throughout (cf. *Scala*, sig. Fi^r); cf. also *Allen* 139, 341; *Petry* 96.

146. *RO2* 219, 343–44, 347; cf. Index: mystical tr5adition, medieval and Index: Bridgettines of Syon.

147. Cf. *RO2* 344, 348; *Bateson* B27, 55, C2, 3, 4, 5, 5, 6, 7, D118, O17, 41, 42; and below, 272.

148. Cf. [A. G.] Little [in *PBA* 10] (1923), 455–66; *RO2* 207; R. Pole *Pro Ecclesiasticae Unitatis Defensione* (Rome 1538) 103; *ER* sig. Ai^v; below, 273–75; the Richmond Observants were close neighbours of Syon.

149. *Little (1923)*, 465–66.

150. Cf. *Allen* 37, 65, 74, 314–17, 522; and, for Bernardino in England, *STC* 1966–67.

151. *Allen* 315.

152. Ibid. 317.

153. Cf. [A. G.] Little [in *PBA* 27] (1941), 155–61.

154. Cf. below, 83, 88–89.

155. *Thomas* 177–78; *T3* 84; cf. *Tractatus de cotidiano holocausto* [*spiritualis exercitii*, ed. C. Hirsche in *Prolegomena zu einer neuen Ausgabe der Imitatio Christi* (Berlin 1873)], vol. 1, 499–501.

156. *Allen* 349 [E. F.] Jacob [in *JEH*, vol. 3, 1 (1952)] 43, 48–49; *Owst* 286 n. 2; cf. *STC* 5065; *Scala*, sig. Evii^r.

157. *Allen* 10, 349; cf. 128.

158. *Incendium Amoris* 78; *Allen* 49, 50, 133, 411–12, 414, 416, 528; *Bateson* 226; and for their relationship with the Carthusians in this, *Incendium Amoris* 79–83.

159. Cf. below, chap. 8 n. 67; and echoes of Rolle's alliterative style in Whytford's translation of Kempis, *The folowyng of Christe* [(London 1535?)] at clxvii^v.

160. Cf. [A. C.] Southern [*Elizabethan Recusant Prose 1559–82* (London 1950)] 226–27, 374–75.

161. *Post* 310–13.

162. Ibid. 311, quoting John Busch.

163. Ibid. 514.

164. Cf. ibid. 312; and for Beguines, *Leff*, vol. 1, 18–22, 198.

165. *Aungier* 26–27.

166. Cf. below, 199.

167. *Little (1941)* 156, 158–59.

168. *STC* 4815.

169. Cf. Index: the vernacular.

170. Cf. below, 90–91, 93–97 and Index: the Bible.

171. Cf. Index: Bridgettines of Syon; Brotherhood of the Common Life; lay devotion.

172. Cf. Index: grace.

173. Cf. Index: meditation.

174. For the New Devotion as forerunners, *Post* chaps. 14, 15.

175. Cf. *LER* sig. Tiv^v; *Bonde* ii^r–iii^v; *ER* sigs Cv^v–vi^r; above, 66–67.

176. Cf. Richardinus [*Commentary on the Rule of St. Augustine*, ed. G. G. Coulton (Scottish Historical Society 3rd. series, 26, Edinburgh 1935)], 74–76; and [W.] Tyndale [*Expositions and Notes*, ed. H. Walter, Parker Society (London 1849)], 80.

177. Cf. *BL* Sloane MS. 1037 (1536) 31^{r-v} with the Protestant tone of its introduction and the characteristic pruning of saint's days in the biblical-based calendar: Ryckes translates from Otto Brunfelsius.

178. Cf. [P. J.] Caraman [in *The Clergy Review*, vol. 28, no. 1 (1947)], 5–6; Whytford translated parts of Erasmus' *Enchiridion* in *P* ccxxi^v–ccxxviiii^v (properly ccxxiii^v) and in *ER* sig. Aiv^r supported the general availability of the Bible as well as monastic rules, "after natural learning and reason . . . some things . . . are not good except they be known and common, as Holy Scripture," also [*The*] *Martiloge* [(London 1526)], xlii^r, marginal note; his inclusion of a Chrysostom sermon almost verbatim in one of his own public sermons (*HI* 86^r–90^v) reveals the young humanist and his use of English proverbs and epigrams is reminiscent of Erasmus (cf. *LER* sigs. Eiv^r, Civ^v, Oiii^v, *P* vii^r, lxxvii^v, lxxix^v, lxxxi^v, lxxxv^v, xcvi^v, ccxiiii^r, ccix^r, ccxi^r, ccxx^r, ccxxxvi^v, *W* sigs. *iiii^r, Avii^{r-v}, Bii^v, Giii^r, Hiii^v, Hiiii^v, a small selection); Index: Whytford, Richard.

179. *Ymage*, sigs. Av^{r-v}, vii^r; cf. 1 *John* 2:15; he also calls this "carnal love."

180. Ibid. sigs. Av^v–vi^r; cf. Cv^r–vi^r.

181. Cf. above, 23.

182. Cf. Index: justice.

183. Cf. *Pico* 123–26; *Trinkaus* 213.

184. *The Workes of Sir Thomas More* [ed. W. Rastell (1557)], vol. 1, 11 A–B; cf. *Enchiridion*, sig. Li^v.

185. Cf. *Male* 378–79.

186. *P* ccix^v (properly ccxix^v)–ccxxi^v, xl^v–xli^r; cf. below, 275ff.

187. *Pico* 117–18; cf. 123 "that saying of the Chaldeans, 'the beasts of the earth dwell in your body'" and *Song of Sol.* 1:7–8.

188. *Pico* 118.

189. *Colet*, sigs. (Aii^v–iii^r).

190. Cf. below, chaps. 6–9 passim; *MBE* sigs. Diii^v–iiii^r; *MBL* 335.

191. *Pico* 136.

CHAPTER FOUR

1. *PL* 34:39, 40:231–32, 41:160, 436; Gerard in *Hyma* 34.

2. *T3* 78.

3. [*The Imitation of Christ*, ed. B. I.] Knott [(London 1963)], 14; *T3* 81; *Gem* 188; *Post* 76; *Jacob* 44, 54; *Brown* 143, 160, 193, 198, 293–94; *CF* 25; John Climachus, *Scala Spiritualis* (Toletana 1505), vii^v, viii^r; Augustine and John were among the Brethren's favourite sources.

4. *Gem* 96.

5. For example, Luther, Cusanus, Ignatius, Gansfort, Standonck, Cisneros, Agricola, Pupper, Biel, Hegius, Erasmus and Adrian IV.

6. Cf. [L.] Spitz [*The Religious Renaissance of the German Humanists* (Cambridge, Mass. 1963)], 8, 199, 236, 238–39, 268.

7. *Hyma* passim.

8. *Post* 17; cf. 49.

9. Cf. below, 87–88, 109.

10. Cf. Index: Gerard Groote, personal life; Mommickhuizer, Charterhouse of; Ruysbroeck, John; on the relationship between the New Devotion and the Carthusians, cf. *Jacob* 43, 47, 48, 51; *Post* 56, 60, 78, 97; *T3* 7–8 [E. F. Jacob,] *Essays [in the Conciliar Epoch* (Manchester 1953)], 123; [T. P.] Van Zijl, [*Gerard Groote, Ascetic and Reformer* (Catholic University of America Studies in Medieval History, new ser. 18, Washington, D.C. 1963)], 112–16; [H.] Jedin [*A History of the Council of Trent*, tr. E. Graf (London 1957)], vol. 1, 144–45; the *Epistola ad fratres de monte Dei*, dealing with Carthusian exercises of prayer and meditation, was studied intensively at Deventer and attributed to Bernard (*T3* 73); Kempis wrote that the "light of heavenly life" had survived hidden among the Carthusians (ibid. 7; *Thomas* 9).

11. Cf. below, 110–11, 163–65.

12. *Jacob* 48; *T3* 18, 27–28, 32.

13. *Knott* 235; *Gem* 29, 40; *Dumbar* 163; *Jacob* 43; *T3* 84; *Post* 277–81; at this time 'lollard' was coming into indiscriminate use in England.

14. *Spitz* 8.

15. Cf. Florence [Radewijns, *Multum Valet*, ed. H. Nolte (Friburg 1862)], the full title of which simply relates their priorities: *Tractatulus devotus de exstirpatione vitiorum et passionum et acquisitione verarum virtutum et maxime caritatis dei et proximi et verae unionis cum Deo et proximi.*

16. *T3* 106; cf. David of Augsburg's placing of this in the context of the habitual waste of attention, in G. G. Coulton, *Ten Medieval Studies* (Cambridge 1930) 70: "Beware lest thou regard or scrutinise curiously other men's persons, faces, dispositions, dress, gestures, deeds, words or duties. So far as it pertaineth not to thee to scrutinise these things for the sake of spiritual profit, pass them by and think no more thereon than if they were sheep or other beasts; let them claim no more either of thine eyes or of thine heart."

17. *Gem* 50.

18. *Post* 431; *Gem* 141 quoting Amilius of Buren; cf. above, 4, 109, 177–78.

19. *T3* 20, 26; *Jacob* 44–45, 47.

20. They ran hostels for poor scholars and many Brethren were school teachers (*Dumbar* 184); historians disagree on the extent and nature of their influence on their boarders, but "there was among them a remarkable silence and discipline" (*Gem* 105).

21. *Gem* 163; *Dumbar* 163.

22. *Gem* 164; *Dumbar* 165.

23. As did Gerson's sisters, cf. above, 4.

24. *Gem* 164; *Dumbar* 165; cf. below, 121.

25. *Dumbar* 166.

26. Cf. *Jacob* 43.

27. *Hyma* 38–39; *T3* 46.

28. *T3* 23.

29. Ibid. 7; [R.] Jones [*The Flowering of Mysticism* (New York 1939)], 236–37.

30. The sources, all much later, mention the Prior of Monnickhuizen, Henry Egher, a canon of St. Peter's Utrecht, and an unknown priest (*Jacob* 46–47).

31. *Hyma* 12; cf. *T3* 14.

32. *Jacob* 43, 48.

33. Ibid. 48–49; *T3* 14.

34. *Jacob* 51; *Post* 57–58, cf. 56, 58–59.

35. *Gem* 89; cf. Gerard's note to his third person self in the *Conclusa* that, "he will always look forward more to eternal glory than fear Gehenna" (*T3* 36); and *De materiis meditandi* from Deventer in *Hyma* 442–43.

36. *T3* 24; cf. *Thomas* 23–25; *Jones* 238; Groenendaal was the first Augustinian house in Belgium to join the Windesheim congregation (1413) and became the head of the Belgian congregation, [E. P.] Goldschmidt [*Gothic and Renaissance Bookbinding* (London 1928)], vol. 1, 198.

37. For his translations, *Ornatus Spiritualium Nuptiarum* and *De Septem Gradibus Amoris*; and for John of Leeuwen, cf. *Post* 105, 118–20, 167, 179; and *Gem* 52–53; Post considers his suggestion of deletions in the published edition to have come from his fear of their being misunderstood rather than from lack of sympathy, for he wanted Ruysbroeck's thought, which he "entirely accepted," to be transmitted accurately (*Post* 119–20). Ruysbroeck influenced also the Windesheimers Peters and Mande (ibid. 319, 335, 338–39).

38. *Van Zijl* 123; on "spiritual doing," cf. Index: spiritual work.

39. Cf. *Jacob* 48; *Hyma* 11, 12; *Thomas* 13–17, 23–25; *T3* 9–10, 13–14.

40. *Thomas* 13, 17; *T3* 9, 11; cf. *Dumbar* 190; *Gem* 177.

41. *Jones* 246; and for his preaching, *T3* 11–13, 21–23; monks composed songs slandering him and his associates, he was forbidden to preach in 1383 and his death was announced as a matter for public congratulation from the Zutphen pulpit (*Hyma* 48; *Jacob* 55; *Knott* 13).

42. *Thomas* 143; *T3* 69–70: "In Holland there flourished certain famous priests, learned in the law of the Lord and notable for their words and deeds, some of whom were fellow soldiers with Master Gerard Groote and very dear to Florentius…it were a lengthy task to mention by name each one of those devout fathers who began to flourish in the time of Gerard and were contemporary with Florentius."

43. *Post* 51–66; *Hyma* 26–27.

44. *Post* 54–55.

45. Ibid. 77, 197, 198; and for the *spirituales* 76, 198.

46. *Knott* 15–16.

47. *Thomas* 42; *T3* 22.

48. Cf. *Jacob* 51ff.; *Essays* 123ff.; *Post* 74–80, 197–222.

49. *Knott* 17.

50. *Post* 631, 555; *Essays* 134–37; and below, 110–11.

51. Gerard also referred to them as "lay and clerical servants" and the first Kampen and Zwolle groups included married couples (*Post* 76–77, 200, 204–5); although the priestly element came to predominate in time, in the early days there were some remarkable lay brethren (below, 109–10).

52. *T3* 49.

53. Lay mendicants, slightly predating the Franciscans, with a strong female following, founded by a certain Lambert le Begue, the Stammerer ('lollard' derives etymologically from the word 'to mumble, stammer,' 'a state of astonishment, bewilderment'); they took no vows, were denounced by the fourteenth–century church and persecuted by the Inquisition (H. Grundmann, *Religiose Bewegungen im Mittelalter*, Historische Studien Hft. 267, Berlin 1935, passim); for their association with the Devotion, cf. *Post* 78, 200; *Jacob* 52.

54. Cf. Index: *rapiaria*.

55. *Thomas* 126; *T3* 61.

56. *Essays* 125–26; cf. *Hyma* 442; *Jacob* 56; and the view of the early-sixteenth–century reformer, Badius Ascensius, in *Foss* 86.

57. *T3* 33; cf. *Thomas* 66.

58. *Thomas* 63; *T3* 32; he adduced the rule of the early church against pluralism, for example (*Thomas* 54; *T3* 28).

59. For the lists, *Thomas* 53, 63; *T3* 27–28, 32; for the importance of Augustine and Bernard, *Jacob* 45–46; *Thomas* 47, 49, 59; *T3* 24, 25, 30; and for Bernard, *Thomas* 135, 151–52, 225; *T3* 66, 73, 108 (neither the *Speculum Monachorum*, *De Conscientia Aedificanda*, nor *Epistola ad Fratres de Monte Dei*, ascribed to Bernard by the Brethren and at Syon, are now believed to have been his, *Thomas* 63, 151; *Bateson* N15); for the Victorines, *Essays* 123; *Post* 319, 328; and cf. Kempis' verse in *Essays* 151–52.

60. *Post* 380–81.

61. *Gem* 80–81; cf. *Post* 283; on connection with the heart; cf. below, 227–29 and Index: the heart.

62. Cf. *T3* 88; *Post* 40; *Hyma* 443; *T3* 117; Index: Desert Fathers.

63. *Gem* 85.

64. *Dumbar* 6–7.

65. *T3* 35.

66. *Post* 316–17.

67. *T3* 19.

68. *Post* 321–22; cf. *Select Library of Nicene and post Nicene Fathers*, ed. H. Wace and P. Schaff (Oxford 1890–1900), vol. 11, 339–51.

69. *Gem* 81–82, 173; cf. *T2* 288; *Knott* 49.

70. Cf. Index: Cisneros Abbot Garcia; Desert Fathers; Ignatius Loyola; John Climachus.

71. Cf. *Spitz* 268–69; Index: the New Devotion.

72. *Van Zijl* 242; cf. *Jacob* 46, 56; *Essays* 123; *Gem* 190–91; *Post* 551–53; as well as Breviaries and Lives of the Saints, they printed Martial, The Four Fathers, Athanasius, Cassian, Chrysostom, Bonaventure, Bernard, Gerson, Poggio, Lefevre d'Etaples and the *Vitae Patrum*.

73. *Post* 304–8; *Gem* 121–22; A. Hyma *The Youth of Erasmus* (Ann Arbor, Michigan 1930), 125; Gerard had been a textual scholar (*Jacob* 46).

74. *Renaissance Philosophy of Man* 105–6; cf. Augustine "it is impossible to love what is entirely unknown, but when what is known, if even so little, is loved, this very capacity for love makes it better and more fully known" (*Brown* 279); also W. Hilton *The Scale of Perfection*, ed. G. Sitwell (London 1953), 247; M. Nicoll *The New Man* (London 1967), 38–56; and above, 30–31; below, 129 and Index: will.

75. Cf. above, 30; *Jacob* 46; *Post* 10, 61, 84; *T3* 29–30; *Gem* 78; *Spitz* 33.

76. *Post* 55–56, 82, 169.

77. Ibid. 82.

78. *Gem* 183.

79. *Rice* 31–32; used earlier, by Abelard for example, but originally patristic (*Spitz* 204).

80. *Post* 379; *Rice* 31; the latter was a compendium of Petrarch and Cusanus.

81. Florence Radewijns quoted in *Thomas* 159, 160; *T3* 77.

82. Henry Mande quoted in *Post* 43; cf. *Ecclus.* 1:16; *Prov.* 1:7; *Ps.* 111:10.

83. *Post* 316–17, 62–63; cf. 55; he was described as "a man sated with knowledge, as it were, in all branches of study" (*Jacob* 44).

84. *Thomas* 7; *T3* 7; cf. *Knott* 150; *PL* 183:133.

85. Cf. *Jacob* 46; *Goldschmidt*, vol. 1, 5–12 (I owe this reference to Hannah Bensley).

86. *T3* 107; cf. the very similar view of the Carthusian *Consuetudines*; *Thompson* 34–35.

87. *Thomas* 72; *T3* 36.

88. *Jacob* 49.

89. *Thomas* 35; *T3* 19; a brother who desired a psalter asked Francis' permission, and he said, "'When you have a psalter you will begin to long for a breviary, and when you have a breviary you will sit on a throne like a great prelate and say to your brother, "Fetch me my breviary."' And speaking thus with great fervour of the spirit, he took some ash with his hand and put it on his head, rubbing his hand around his head as if he was washing it, and saying to himself, 'I a breviary! I a breviary,' repeating his words over and over again. . . . And the brother was astonished" (quoted in R. H. C. Davis, *A History of Medieval Europe* [London 1963], 365–66).

90. *Van Zijl* 188.

91. *Post* 163–64.

92. Alexander Hegius to Wessel Gansfort, in *Wessel 1* 333.

93. *Post* 58.

94. *Thomas* 221; *T3* 106.

95. Wessel, quoted in *Essays* 131.

96. *T3* 29.

97. *Tractatus de cotidiano holocausto* 503; cf. "for it is more effective if a man begins with one virtue and exercises himself in that, such as humility, obedience, patience etc., than if he studies four thousand and lives without fruit. Just as the religious renounces delicate food, study nothing except that by which you may live well" (ibid.).

98. *Gem* 94–95.

99. Cf. below, 141, 237.

100. *T3* 101; cf. *Wessel 1* 251; Index: the soul.

101. Cf. Index: attention.

102. *Post* 323; cf. above, xvi; *T3* 88.

CHAPTER FIVE

1. *Matt.* 12:43–45; *Luke* 11:24–26.

2. *Post* 59–60, 64; *Jacob* 51; *Van Zijl* 211.

3. *Gem* 50.

4. *Post* 58–59.

5. Ibid.

6. Ibid. 61.

7. *Post* 60.

8. Ibid. 57; *votum* was the monastic vow.

9. *Van Zijl* 210.

10. Cf. Index: asceticism; freedom; 'mixed life.'

11. *Aquinas,* vol. 11, 116–19.

12. Cf. above, 40; *ER* sig. Cv^v–vi^r; *LER* Tiv^{r-v}.

13. *Trinkaus* 671.

14. *P. S. Allen,* vol. 1, 226.

15. P cciii^v–iiii^r; cf. clxxv^r, xxv^{v}ff.; *LER* sigs. Lii^v–iii^r; cf. Bii^{v}ff.; Bv^{v}ff.

16. [H. A.] Obermann [*The Harvest of Medieval Theology* (Cambridge, Mass. 1963)], 343–44.

17. *Obermann* 345; cf. *Coulton* 82 "[the Brotherhood were] a definite link between monas-

ticism and ordinary life."

18. Many Tertiaries in the Low Countries were drawn into the Devotion in the early fifteenth century, *Post* 312–13; above, 76; Index: *vita apostolica.*

19. E. M. Jung in *JHI* 14, no. 4 (October 1953), 525.

20. Ibid.; I owe this translation to Alexandra Dobbs.

21. *Hyma* 243–45, 249–50; *Coulton* 365–66; cf. Index: "collations"; *sapiaria;* self-examination.

22. See Index: spiritual exercises, transmission of; cf. *Essays* 139–40; *Jedin* 145ff.; *Van Zijl* 113–14.

23. [W.] Peryn [*Spirituall Exercyses* (London 1557)], sigs. Ivi^{r-v}.

24. Ibid. sigs. Ovii^{r-v}; cf. above, 14–15, 230–39 and Index: *conformitas Christi;* contemplation & contemplative life; "recollection."

25. As he admits in the introductory "Epystle" (no sig.).

26. *Hyma* 33; cf. above, 55–56; below, 165 and Index: 'mixed life.'

27. Cf. J. Needleman, *The New Religions* (New York 1977), 128; Index: religious method.

28. *Wessel 2* 16; for "ordinary men" meaning laymen; cf. *Wessel 1* 195.

29. *Wessel 2* 34, 67 art. 21; and cf. 85–86.

30. Ibid. 34–35.

31. Ibid. 35, 43; cf. Gerson's similar distinctions in *Connolly* 297–98.

32. *Wessel 2* 43.

33. Ibid. 17: "remembering" can lead to "rumination," the function of a "discerning" and "strengthened" heart (cf. 27, 31 on the spiritual communion of the desert monk), while "the degrees of increasing affection" (remembering, considering, pondering, discerning, ruminating, tasting, desiring, hungering, panting and loving, ibid.) relate to the "formation of Christ in us" (ibid. 38); for the technical use of such terms; cf. above, 97, below, 141 and Index: Martha & Mary; "remembering"; *ruminatio.*

34. *Wessel 2* 6–7, 13–14; cf. Index: "remembering."

35. *Wessel 2* 69–70; above, 47–48 and Index: food; scale; cf. *Wessel 2* 30.

36. Ibid. 57.

37. Ibid. 42, 48–49; cf. 28–29: "The inner man, that is, the memory, intellect and will, should be occupied with the Word that became flesh, with God who became man, with his times, desires, doctrines, examples, precepts, benefits and promises, just as the mouth, throat and stomach of the outer man are employed with a feast. Even as the latter take, eat, taste, chew, delight in, prove, approve, accept and transmit to the belly and are thereby nourished, strengthened and invigorated for life's work; so with regard to that flesh which was assumed in oneness of person by the eternal Word, as embodying his works and desires, his doctrines and examples, his precepts, sacraments, gifts and promises, we with unremitting thought in the inner man must meditate, reflect, consider, compare, ponder and keep in our hearts. By the exercise of our intellect, we must discern, value, raise and exalt it in accordance with its dignity and sublimity. With all our will we must desire it, long

for it, pant for it, esteem it, love it, pine for it, and in love seek and evoke its presence"; such passages (cf. above, n. 33) mark the emergence of methodical meditation, and relate to Renaissance philology ("a study . . . of the totality of man," *Garin* 18); cf. also *Post* 538; Index: food; meditation; scale; the word.

38. *Wessel 2* 66 art. 11, 68 arts. 37–40.

39. Ibid. 50–52; cf. 29, 31, 61.

40. Ibid. 27.

41. Ibid. 44; cf. 5, 21–23, 50; *Wessel 1* 123; his aphorism, "to love is to live," is from Lull.

42. *Wessel 2* 44–45; cf. 326 on Wessel and Luther, and H. A. Obermann, *Forerunners of the Reformation* (London 1967) 18.

43. Ibid. 99.

44. *Post* 293–95; cf. 200–201; *Van Zijl* 324–28.

45. *Gem* 62.

46. *Dumbar* 60.

47. Late 1390s, *Post* 286–87.

48. Cf. *Van Zijl* 240; *Tractatus de cotidiano holocausto*, passim; Index: "perfecftion, states of."

49. *Post* 316.

50. *Gem* 133.

51. Ibid. 199, *T2* 583; cf. Florence, quoting Augustine, "understanding without action is like wisdom without fear, while fear is yet the beginning of wisdom" (*Post* 323).

52. *Jacob* 43–44, 55.

53. *Gem* 146: "My Brothers, we have left parents, relatives and country and other desirable things of the world, and have, for God's sake, undertaken to live together; if, therefore, we are captious and spiteful and discordant, we are more miserable than other men."

54. *T3* 80.

55. *Coulton* 94.

56. *Gem* 148.

57. Ibid. 150–51; cf. *Coulton* 95–97, 100; below, 214–17; Index: Brotherhood of the Common Life; lay devotion.

58. *Essays* 134–35.

59. *Post* 467, 555, 631, changes which facilitated their post–Reformation change into secular vicars or canons enjoying their own income.

60. Ibid. 430–31; he acknowledged the influence of Biel on these views.

61. *T3* 28; cf. *Van Zijl* 105.

62. *Post* 39–40.

63. *T2* 574–75.

64. *T2* 572.

65. *Dumbar* 180–81; cf. *Gem* 171.

66. *Post* 586–87; cf. *P* ix^v–x^r.

67. *T3* 28.

68. Cf. below, chap. 7 n. 111, chap. 8 n. 124 and Index: freedom; violence.

69. *T2* 349; cf. Index: mastery.

CHAPTER SIX

1. *PL* 40:232; *Rice* 8.

2. *Hyma* 257.

3. Zerbolt, *De Reformatione virium animae* quoted in [Garcia Jimenez de] Cisneros [*Obras Completas* (Montserrat 1965)], vol. 2, 98 n. 4: "A certain man went down from Jerusalem to Jericho [*Luke* 10:30]. In these mystical words the fall of humankind is described; under the signification of Jerusalem and Jericho the passage from the state of being right to its overthrow and our eviction is designated. . . . Jerusalem, it is said, is the seeing of peace, Jericho is truly interpreted as the moon, because mutability is implied. Then indeed, that man, said rightly to have been in Jerusalem . . . wholly possessed by peace and tranquillity . . . yet refused to submit to God, when he alone owed that submission, just his lowest force making rebellion by itself . . . and necessarily, according to various movements of concupiscence and suggestions of desire, changing like the moon and never remaining in one state, he was finally reduced to that state whence, by this wretched mutability, he has fallen into ruin"; for these traditional etymologies, cf. *Male* 196 and the patristic sources given by Cisneros' editors, *PL* 15:1805–6, 36:728, 734, 37:1065–66, 1624, 1755, 75:885–86, 76:857, 1113.

4. *SA* 882E; [Gerard] Zerbolt [*The Spiritual Ascent*, tr. J. P. Arthur (London 1908)], 11.

5. *SA* 882B–C.

6. Ibid. 881D; Luther said, "Nowhere have I found such a clear explanation of original sin as is in the treatise of Gerard Groote, *Blessed is the man*" (*Hyma* 220), referring to the *incipit* of *SA*; cf. also *De Reformatione virium animae* [in M. De la Bigne, *Magna Bibliotheca veterum Patrum* (Paris 1654), vol. 5], 839–41.

7. *SA* 880C–D, 881A–B, B–C: "Diligently, therefore, give heed, that the Lord God, who created you in His Image and likeness, formerly set you in such sublime dignity, established you on such a high mountain of natural gifts and graces, that unless you had attained to the essential vision of God you could scarcely have been able to ascend higher. You were indeed set in a paradise of delight, replete inwardly and outwardly with all good things. . . . He ordained your energies within you in the best way, so that the lower would obey the higher without contradiction, without even wishing for anything contrary . . . and just this way of peaceful harmony and concord of the energies and affections was called 'obedience,' and is termed by the saints 'natural justice.'"

8. Ibid. 881E.

9. Cf. Index: "collations."

10. Cf. *SA* 880C, although he loved the "sacred codices" (above, 93–94).

11. *Foss* 89; cf. *Squire* 295–96.

12. *SA* 881E–2A; at 880C–81C their proper work is discussed.

13. Cf. Index: attention; self-knowledge.

14. *SA* 882A–B; cf. Jacob Boehme: "It appeareth that it is not so easy a matter to be a Christian and that Christianity doth not consist in the mere knowing of the history and applying the knowledge thereof to ourselves, saying that, 'Christ died for us, and hath destroyed death and turned it into life in us, and He hath paid the ransom for us so that we need do nothing but comfort ourselves therewith and steadfastly believe that it is so.' A Christian should therefore consider why he calleth himself a Christian and examine truly whether he be one or not. For surely by learning to know and confess that I am a sinner and that Christ hath destroyed my sins on the cross and shed His blood for me, doth not make me a Christian. . . . All Christian religion wholly consisteth in this, to learn to know ourselves; whence we are come and what we are" (quoted in A. Gage, *The One Work* (London 1961), 12, 14).

15. Cf. *Eckhart* 73–74, "How the inclination to sin is helpful to men"; *Ward* 102 no. 3.

16. *SA* 882B; cf. Index: "spiritual ascents."

17. *SA* 882E: "For just as, in nature, things are called and made impure by the admixture of baser things—for gold is made impure if it is mixed with silver, and silver if mixed with lead, so O man, your rational soul, which is more worthy than all temporal creatures, incurs impurity and uncleanness, if it becomes subject to temporal things through its love, and hence is unclean and impure by the adherence of the affections and desires fixed, habituated and joined to them."

18. *PL* 41:467 (virtue is *ordo amoris*, "the ordering of love"), 38:144; *Song of Sol.* 2:4 (Septuagint); cf. [*J.*] Mombaer [*Rosetum exercitiorum spiritualium* (Paris 1510)], sig. eiii^{r}L; *W* Av^v; Augustine follows Origen here ([J.] Burnaby, [*Amor Dei* (London 1938)], 106–7); for Lazarus, *Brown* 149, 177, 325.

19. *SA* 882D–83A.

20. Ibid. 883A–B: "When everything he had had been wasted with harlots, he came into the land of estrangement, where he subjected himself to one of the citizens of that land, who set him to feed his pigs. . . . Behold, O man, where you have now come, into the land of estrangement" (*Luke* 15:11–32); cf. Augustine, "One way or another, therefore, the human soul approaches the inner man who is recreated in the image of God, because it was created in the image of God, and has been distanced insofar as it inheres in unlikeness. For one does not come closer to God, or further from Him, because of physical distance: having become unlike, you have receded a long way; having been made like, you are brought near" (*Corpus Christianorum*, Series Latina [Turnholti 1953–], vol. 39, 1956, 1395) and cf. [A.] Louth [*The Origins of the Christian Mystical Tradition* (Oxford 1983)], 42–43, 117–18.

21. *PP* i^v, ii^r, clxix^r; cf. clxxvi^r–vii^v.

22. Cf. chap. 8 below; on the immediate origins of methodical meditation cf. Index: meditation; H. Watrigant in *Revue* [*d'ascetique et de mystique*] ([Toulouse]1922), vol. 3, 134–35, ibid. in *Revue* (1923), vol. 4, 13–29 [H. O.] Evenett [and J. Bossy, *The Spirit of the Counter-Reformation* (Cambridge 1968)], 32–36, 51–66, 126–28.

23. *Cisneros* 99–101, echoing *Ps.* 76:7 (Vulgate), *Wisdom of Sol.* 1:4 (Vulgate) and *Song of Sol.* 6:3; cf. also above, 84.

24. *Hyma* 420; *Post* 543.

25. *Evenett* 35 n. 2.

26. The *Directorium* was largely based on Mombaer's *Chiropsalterium*, a section of the *Rosetum* (*Post* 548; *Hyma* 267–68, who cites Watrigant, "almost all the practical hints and nearly everything relating to the general method are extracts from the *Rosary*"); cf. also *CF* 14–31.

27. Cf. Index: religious method.

28. Cf. Index: practicality in religion.

29. *Trinkaus* 213, 383; cf. 301, 518, 527; *PL* 42:971ff.

30. Ibid., and cf. *Wind* 41–52, 241–55 for the Renaissance belief in the antiquity of the teaching of the Trinity.

31. *Itinerarium* [*mentis in Deum*, ed. Father James (London 1937)], 14ff.; cf. 43; it has the same *incipit* as *SA* (*Ps.* 83:6 Vulgate).

32. Cf. *Wind* 41–52, 241–55 and Valla, quoted in *Trinkaus* 156, 382–83, comparing the soul with the sun as an image of the Trinity, its three qualities of "vibration," "light" and "heat" representing "Father," "Son" and "Holy Ghost" respectively: "In the sun or substance of the sun . . . are present vibration, light and heat, so in the soul or substance of the soul there are three perpetual qualities: memory, which is the life of the soul, intellect, which is the same as reason and which always is born from memory, and love, which also emanates from the memory into the intellect, while the intellect is being generated . . . just as the sun emitting vibrating and burning rays enters into exterior things by vibration, illuminates by light, warms by heat, which are its actions, so the soul comprehends and retains other things by memory, examines and judges by the intellect whether they are and what kind they are and embraces them or rejects them by the effect."

33. Cf. Index: The Trinity.

34. *Nugent* 393–94; cf. above, 79–80 and Index: memory; reason, the soul; will.

35. *T3* 32, the "Fathers" being the Desert Fathers.

36. 1496 *STC* 1916, 1499? 1917, 1525 1918, 1608 1919, 1614 1919a, 1626 1920, 1631–32 1921; for Syon's many copies, cf. *Bateson* 217.

37. *MBE* sig. Ev[v]; he says that, before he had corrected his MS, "devout persons . . . I do not know how often against my will" had made and circulated inaccurate copies, and tells how these "doubtful" versions may be recognised (ibid. Ai[v]–ii[r]).

38. Ibid. sig. Aiii[r] (wrongly paginated Bi); cf. *MBL* 298, *De Reformatione virium animae*, 841; *Louth* 40–43; Index: self-knowledge.

39. *MBE* sig. Av[r]; *MBL* 302; *Louth* 40; cf. *Itinerarium* 41–42.

40. *MBE* sigs. Aiii[v]–iiii[r]; *MBL* 300: "It therefore behoves that which has been made in the image, to befit that image and not to participate in the name of the image emptily . . . for, in fact, our mind is His Image insofar as it has capacity and is able to be a participant."

41. *MBE* sigs. Aiiii^v–v^r; *MBL* 300–2.

42. *MBE* sigs. Aiii^{r-v}; *MBL* 300–1.

43. *MBE* sigs. Diiii^v–iiii^r: "Those things that annoyed me or displeased, I have desired their destruction & yet I knew that they were good in their nature & kind & made of a good maker, but they were noisome to me because I was evil and used them evilly. For there is no thing contrary to me but I myself. It is mine, whatsoever may annoy me, and I am a burden to myself," *MBL* 335 and cf. above, 79–80, below 175.

44. *MBE* sigs. Ciiii^v–Di^v; *MBL* 329–31; and cf. [E.] Rich, [*Myrrour of the chyrche* (London 1527)], sig. Diiii^r, "wisely to sing is this: that what a man says with his mouth he should prudently think it in his heart, for if your body be in the choir or church, & your lips in the psalter & your heart in the market or the fair, then are you wretchedly disposed in yourself and are not graciously heard of our lord God."

45. *MBE* sig. Di^v: "like as a mill runs about swiftly & forsakes no thing but grinds whatsoever is put therein, and if there be nought put therein it consumes & wastes itself, so is mine heart always moving & never rests, but whether I sleep or wake it is always dreaming & thinking on whatsoever comes thereto. And like as gravel or sand if it be put into a mill hurts & wastes it & pitch makes it foul & chaff occupies it in vain, so bitter thoughts trouble mine heart, make it foul and unclean, change it, disquiet it & make it weary"; cf. *MBL* 331; *SA* 913B; *PP* lxxv^r; *P* ccxx^v–ccxxi^v; Index: emotional life; thinking.

46. *MBE* sig Di^r; *MBL* 330; cf. "therefore it is great perversity & forwardness, yes and very foolish and greatly to be loathed, when we presume to speak with the lord of majesty in prayer, and, like as we had no wit or understanding, we turn away our ears and turn our heart and mind to unbecoming fables and trifles. For it is outrageous folly & grievously to be punished when most vile & filthy dust disdains to hear the maker of heaven & earth speaking to him" (*MBE* sigs. Ciiii^v–Di^r; *MBL* 329–30); and "when thou enter in to the church to pray & to worship God, leave without the heap of flowing thoughts and forget utterly cure and charge of all outward things that thou may take heed to God only. For it may not be that a man speak any time with God that talks or chatters softly with all the world. Therefore give attendance and take heed to Him that gives attendance & takes heed to thee. Hear when He speaks to you, that He may graciously hear when thou speaks to Him" (*MBE* sig. Bviii^v; *MBL* 321–22; cf. *Horstmann*, vol. 1, 301–2; *LER* sig. Dvii^v; *Richardinus* 74–76).

47. *MBE* sig. Di^r.

48. *MBL* 330; cf. Augustine quoted in *Brown* 155, "our prayers are, sometimes, so lukewarm, stone cold, indeed, and hardly prayers at all: they are so distant in our thoughts that we do not even notice this fact with pain—for if we were even to feel the pain, we would be praying again," and Index: "remembering"; self-knowledge.

49. *MBE* sigs. Bviii^{r-v}, *MBL* 321.

50. *MBE* sigs. Avii^r–viii^r; *MBL* 307.

51. *MBE* sigs. Eiiii^{r-v}; *MBL* 347–49.

52. *MBE* sigs. Dii^{r-v}; *MBL* 332.

53. *MBE* sig. Ev^v; *MBL* 350; cf. above, xx.

54. *MBE* sig. Ev^r; *MBL* 349–50.

55. Cf. below, chap. 8 and Index: spiritual exercises, transmission of.

56. Cf. Index: "recollection."

57. Cf. *The Spiritual Exercises of Saint Ignatius Loyola*, ed. J. Rickaby (London 1915), 24, 26, 209, 213, 215.

58. Ibid. 38, "so that I may feel the disorder of my doings: so that, loathing, I may amend and order myself."

59. Cf. *Martz* 34–35, 70.

60. Cf. below 272 n. 74 and Index: understanding; will.

61. Luis [of Granada, *An excellent Teatise of Consideration and Prayer* (London 1599)], 115–16, 118, 120–21: "The second advice is that he labour to eschew in this exercise of meditation the superfluous speculation of the Understanding, and endeavour to use this matter rather with affections, and feelings of the Will . . . the understanding on the one side helps, and on the other side it may hinder the operation of the Will, to wit, the love and feeling of divine things. For as it is necessary that the understanding do go before the Will to guide it and give it knowledge what it ought to love; so when the speculation of the understanding is overmuch, then it hinders this operation of the Will; forasmuch as it suffers it not to have place and time to work . . . the Patriarch Jacob was made lame of one of his feet at that time he received the blessing: for, whereas our soul has two feet wherewith to go unto Almighty God, which be the Understanding and the Will, it is requisite that the one foot be weakened, to wit, the Understanding in his speculation, if the Will (which is the other foot) shall enjoy Almighty God in the rest and quietness of contemplation . . . all this business of meditation consists in speaking little and in loving much, and in giving place to the Will, that it may join itself with all his forces unto Almighty God . . . you go in a Chariot drawn with two horses, whereof the one is very forward and quick, and the other very slow and dull: and you must bear the bridles in your hand with such dexterity, that the one you must hasten forward, and hold the other back, that so they may go together, the one by the other"; cf. *Scala*, sigs. tvi^v–vii^r and Augustine, quoted in *Brown* 373, "the understanding flies on ahead, and there follows, oh so slowly, and sometimes not at all, our weakened human capacity for feeling."

62. *Luis* 116–17.

63. Ibid. 105–6, 107–8, 119; cf. below, 243 adn Index: the soul.

64. *Martz* 114–15.

65. *MBE* sig. Cii^v, *MBL* 325–26; for this inner room, cf. John of Heusden, second prior of Windesheim, who "withdrew from the world and crept by himself into the inmost recesses of his heart; and there he made unto Christ a large upper chamber for supper, dwelling with Him therein" (*Coulton* 91); *Wessel 1* 244; *Fewterer* fo. i$^{r–v}$; *Knott* 170; Index: 'the monastery within'.

66. *Gem* 155; *Dumbar* 135; cf. *CF* 30, 23.

67. *De Oratione [et Modo Orandi* (Zwolle 1520?)], vii^v–viii^r; if the inner man, made in God's image is alive only when conforming thereto (through "imitating" Him and being influenced, moved and enkindled by His love, *Wessel 2* 20–23), the outer man corresponds

to the "old man" in *MBE* sigs. Eiiii^r–v^r and above, n. 40, 127–28, Index: 'regeneration of man.'

68. *Gem* 97; [Gerlach] Peters, [*The Divine Soliloquies*, tr. "Monialis" (London 1920)], 74.

69. *Blunt* 63–65.

CHAPTER SEVEN

1. *T3* 113–14.

2. Cf. Index: John Ketel.

3. Cf. Index: spiritual work.

4. D. Knowles, *The Evolution of Medieval Thought* (London 1965), 100–1; cf. below 272 n. 74 and Index: faith.

5. *T3* 120, 121; cf. 119.

6. *Post* 56.

7. *Thomas* 159; above 81 and cf. *W* sig. (H10^v): "Trust those to do the best for your soul, not who love, or say they love your soul, but who you perceive and guess do love their own soul."

8. *T3* 22.

9. *Post* 546.

10. *MBE* sig. Cii^v.

11. *T3* 53–54.

12. Ibid. 76; cf. 77, "never be idle, but involve yourself chiefly in holy tasks, directing your emotions and all your working towards God," and 53–54.

13. *SA* 931D; cf. *Horstmann* vol. 1, 313–16.

14. *Coulton* 155, quoting Busch on his own reforms.

15. *RO3* 200.

16. *T3* 54 ("the blessed Paul" was perhaps Paul the Hermit, the teacher of Antony in Jerome's account); Mombaer is quoted in *Hyma* 420, and cf. Biel quoted in *Obermann* 345 "[idleness] which of all the seeds of evil is the most pernicious."

17. *SA* 931B–C: "And so, since you are a weak man, do not suppose yourself an angel, who always makes use of spiritual food; of this you know nothing; so that even you might be willing always to keep close to spiritual things, at certain times exercise yourself in manual work in many different ways, primarily so that you may not succumb to boredom and entirely forsake exercising the spirit. . . . This is what Cassian means when he says that he who is not content to do some manual work every day, is not able to persevere in his cell to the end"; cf. also *Squire* 298–99.

18. *SA* 931B–C: "and do not consider yourself more fervent and more spiritual than was the great Antony, who, had he not learnt from the angel this kind of ascent and descent between manual and spiritual work, would have succumbed to tedium and returned to the world"; cf. *CF* 20–21, "Concerning this work of writing, note that the work of the hands

ought to be ordered to this, that it may conduce to the purity of the heart, because you are frail and cannot always apply yourself to spiritual things; it is for this reason that manual work was instituted"; cf. also *SA* 912E–13A; *Hyma* 256; *PP* cxxxix^r, clxvi^{r-v}.

19. *T3* 54: "For manual work is a holy work, most useful to all progress of the spirit; through which the lasciviousness of the flesh is tamed and the mind, loosened by frivolous dispersal, is more quickly curbed. Through this activity harmful forms of idleness are lifted, and frivolous conversation arising from inactivity is more easily curtailed. For when the occasion of talking is taken away, work may progress by the hands, and will always enrich with good things he who has been a faithful workman"; cf. *CF* 20.

20. *SA* 931C–D: "your heart is intensely unstable and thus, like a boat on the waves of the flowing sea, it is agitated by different emotions and thoughts. Therefore, as Cassian says, you must make fast your heart as with an anchor, namely by pondering and by some occupation of manual work."

21. Ibid. 932C; cf. *Isa* 30:15; *2 Thess* 3:12.

22. On this and silence; cf. above, 96–97, 120–21, 123–27 adn Index: "remembering"; self-knowledge; silence.

23. Cf. Index: energies in man; manual work.

24. *SA* 931C.

25. Ibid. 931A–B: "rather, you should certainly order your exercise so that you may engage yourself everyday in manual work at certain times, and again, in its time, you may progress in raisings of the heart, and yet, perhaps the work of the hands might not hinder the progress of the heart. For even in the midst of [literally, beneath] your work you can pray, meditate and exercise yourself in fear and wishing. Our holy fathers had this for a rule that the more faithfully they undertook manual work, the more they hoped to attain greater heights of purity and charity and progress of the spirit"; cf. 932B, "when you work with your hands, you must certainly not allow your mind to be inactive; rather, exercise yourself in the duty of the heart by some prayers or meditation, or certainly by pondering quietly upon what you are writing"; and *Post* 96.

26. *SA* 913A; cf. [*An Augustine Synthesis*, ed. E.] Przywara [(London 1936)], 447 and *Brown* 154–55, quoting Augustine on the "unconscious" processes enabling the heart to take "delight" in God.

27. *CF* 31, the last words of the manuscript.

28. *T3* 36.

29. Ibid. 121; cf. *SA* 913E–14A; his recording of failures after reviewing the day anticipates Ignatius, but is referred to the Bernardine/Carthusian tradition at *T3* 73; for the mental review cf. also ibid. 123; *CF* 30.

30. *Florence* 20–21: "it seems useful that a man might, at some hour of the day and especially at night, before he goes to bed, because that hour is more appropriate for the purpose, meditate or read some passage concerning the death or passion of Christ or about hell etc., and exercise himself in such matters, so that, being occupied with this, he may have purer dreams. On arising or awakening, let him fall in with what he had been thinking

in the evening, so that he may more easily cast aside the strange and wandering thoughts, which infest the heart of a man most at that time,"; and cf. *Post* 324.

31. *CF* 14.

32. Cf. *Hyma* 259, quoting Mombaer.

33. *SA* 913D; although meditation must permeate the whole day, the morning hours should especially be set aside, "in which he may uniquely exercise his soul [*anima*], searching somehow his spirit and enkindling it to spiritual desire," studying to seek devotion from the Lord, or to produce it in his heart by the methods known to him (ibid. 913D–E); cf. Mombaer, sigs. Eiii^{v}O–v^{v}X; *Luis* 84; Index: order of Daily Life.

34. *Post* 354–55.

35. *T3* 73, the teaching of Bernard according to Florence; cf. also *PP* clxii^v–iii^r.

36. *Post* 539, quoting *Tractatus de cohibendis cogitationibus*.

37. *T3* 100.

38. Cf. Index: "art is better than evil strength."

39. *Hyma* 258.

40. For example, "in order to be reverent, be both attentive and devout during the hours" (*Post* 545), echoed by Cisneros, "during the triple prayer that begins the office and in our mental preparation, we must firmly believe that we are in the presence of God and strive to be there with reverence, attention and devotion" (Cisneros [*A Book of Spiritual Exercises and a*] *Directory* [*for the Canonical Hours*, ed. a monk of St. Augustine's monastery Ramsgate, London 1876], 18) and cf. *Hyma* 420 n. 49.

41. *CF* 11, "When we look back at the intention whereby we came to live in a community, we find that God is the cause, together with humble obedience and a life of love on account of the health of our souls."

42. Cf. Index: sin, and the instructive story in *Ward* 102 no. 3.

43. *T3* 89–90: "When he was reading at the table, he sometimes knowingly stumbled, so as to be corrected by the corrector, and occasionally he pretended not to hear, in order to be corrected again, wishing to be confounded and to have it considered that he did not know how to read any better. . . . But he had a virile voice, like a trumpet, and read extremely well"; Zerbolt, the corrector on this occasion, refrained from further admonition when he understood what was taking place.

44. Ibid. 100.

45. *T3* 101, 122; cf. 77.

46. Ibid. 101, "always think of some virtue in anyone you are with, and of your vice, to humiliate yourself inwardly because of the inner vices known to God, the angels and yourself"; cf. Gerard, "you should always strive to observe and consider some good in another person" (ibid. 36).

47. *Dumbar* 8–9; *Post* 182; cf. Gerard's letter to Ruysbroeck, above, 117; he held a chapter of faults with his close friends, when they examined their consciences together (*Dumbar* 6–7; *Post* 182).

48. *Gem* 53, 78; *Post* 167, 182; *Dumbar* 6.

49. Cf. below, 72 and Index: talking.

50. Cf. above, 123–25 and Index: self-knowledge.

51. *T3* 75; below, n. 55; Index: attention; habits.

52. Cf. Index: Brotherhood of the Common Life; the heart; prayer.

53. *T3* 37; cf. Florence, "we must raise our hearts to heaven without ceasing . . . do all things with attentive thought and not out of habit" (ibid. 75), "have the heart always above" (ibid. 74); cf. *HI* 51^v.

54. *Tractatus de cotidiano holocausto,* 498; on the *Conclusa, cf. Van Zijl* 105.

55. *T3* 120: "I shall also try to read my prayer attentively and without haste, and during my labours and work to bend the knees often and to pray by moments, briefly and with attention. . . . In amongst your labours and work you should often kneel and pray briefly with attention, especially at the sign of the bell, and when it is rung in church at the elevation of the sacred body of our Lord Jesus Christ"; cf. Arnold of Schoonhoven, of whom it was said "before beginning to read in the book or to write, he prayed briefly, lifting his mind to God; he did the same at the end of the work he had done, giving thanks. As he left the house or returned to his room he knelt in the presence of the statue of Christ, and approached his work with prayer and inclination of the body" (ibid. 126) and the practice of Lubbert ten Bosch quoted in *Post* 241. Haste was considered the antithesis of attentive, balanced work, as *T3* 75 "haste greatly squanders devotion. Therefore beware importunity, and do everything with attention and not habitually."

56. Cf. *The Way of a Pilgrim,* ed. R. M. French (New York 1965), 198–99.

57. *MBE* sig. Cii^r.

58. J. Crehan in *AHSI,* anno. 25, fasc. 49 (Rome 1956), 79–80.

59. *T3* 119: "What should I repay to you, Eternal God, for the sake of all that you have restored to me? Oh, beloved John, have pity on your own self (*miserere tui ipsius*) and think with great conscientiousness and all your energy about your past life, what you were in the world, what you still are and what you have earned. Think of the immeasurable goodness of our beloved Lord Jesus Christ, which He has shown to you above so many men, think how much more gravely He will judge you than others, if you do not reform yourself. Stand in fear, and think that He who has spared you with such generosity is perhaps unwilling to spare you any longer. Set in your heart that today, or tomorrow at the latest, you will die, and go on to where? Woe to me, eternal God, where shall I flee from the face of your wrath, for my sins are more than the sands of the sea? Nevertheless I know most truly that nothing displeases You like despair, and that You do not wish the death of a sinner, but repentance. Speak therefore to Him in the sighing of your heart: 'Look upon me, a wretched sinner, immense mercy of god; turn back towards me, a wicked man, in pity. Behold, I come desolate to the Almighty; wounded, I run to the physician'"; on the remembrance of one's death, a fundamental practice of the New Devotion, cf. *T3* 117 (Ketel's wearing of his own shroud, as the poet John Donne did two hundred years later); *Coulton* 90; *CF* 24; and for Syon, cf. *Aungier* 245; *Blunt* xxxviii–ix; and below, 237–38, 282, 284.

60. *T3* 119; Index: order of daily life; self-examination; on the "sayings of the saints," cf. above, 89–91, below, 237, 239–45.

61. Cf. Index: purification of emotion; Way of the Monk.

62. *T3* 120.

63. Ibid. 115, "a master of cooking," 116–17 and cf. *Dumbar* 12, 22–23, 56, 57; *Post* 241–42, *Gem* 26–27.

64. *T3* 114: "For he was often found on bended knee praying by the fire, and while with his hand he filled the pot, with his mouth he chanted faithfully. He made his cooking a prayer, knowing God to be everywhere; he summoned spiritual heat from the material fire"; cf. Biel on the Brethren, in *Obermann* 345, "in truth, they could readily sing sacred songs while working with their hands," and *Tractatus de cotidiano holocausto* 494, " . . . and if perhaps you often fall in such things, then draw together your ass, saying, 'Truly, if you do not guard against this or that, and do not say with deliberation and usefully one psalm, you will gather any accident occuring to you due to changing conditions.'"

65. *T3* 114–15, and cf. above, 111–12 and Index: freedom; meditation.

66. *T3* 31.

67. Ibid. 78.

68. *T3* 74.

69. *Tractatus de cotidiano holocausto,* 496.

70. Cf. Index: food; *masticatio;* scale; the soul.

71. Cf. Francois de Sales quoted in *Pourrat* 7, "To meditate is the same as to masticate . . . we must take the meat that nourishes the soul and masticate it, that is, meditate on it to swallow it and transform it into ourselves"; cf. ibid. 6–7, quoting the twelfth–century Carthusian *Scala Paradisi, Fewterer* fo. iiii^v; Richard Baxter in *Martz* 169–70; Luis of Granada, *Of Prayer and Meditation* (London 1599), sigs. A5^v–6^r.

72. Cf. below, 266, also *William St. Thierry* xlix–l; cf. below, 212, aslo *William of St. Thierry* xiix–1; Index: the soul.

73. Cf. Index: "remembering"; the soul, and Gregory the Great, "[It is said in Ezekiel that] their belly devours the sacred volume and the bowels are filled, because those precepts of life which the inner mind is able to grasp, the memory will not turn loose" (quoted in *Material for Thought,* 20).

74. *SA* 912E: "Therefore so that you may more immediately restore reading to purity you must always draw forth something from reading that combines with your purpose, something that may occupy your memory and bring to your remembrance that you must go forward, that you may be like a clean animal that is used to ruminate."

75. Cf. above, 125–26 and Index: The Word.

76. Cf. above, 97, n. 70 above and Index: *lectio divina;* Gerlach Peters is said to have masticated his food at table as if he were drawing devotion from his plate (*Gem* 95); Lubert Berner considered that only if he were able to eat differently could he listen properly at table and thus masticate a finer food, "during meals beware of greed and hasty eating; rather restrain your appetite, in order that your blind and disorderly concupiscence may be

illuminated by compunction and a hunger for what is being read; and masticate something from the reading in quietness" (*T3* 101).

77. Ibid.: "the fruit of study is the fortitude of the soul and the consequent acquisition of virtues. To study in order to know, and consequently to teach others, or for any other purpose that has been said, does not nourish the soul but renders it insane, like the superfluous humours of the body, and generates vainglory, a proud heart, disorderly manners, empty thoughts, mental instability, forgetfulness and contempt of God, the applause of men, a troubled conscience and a darkened understanding, and it leads rather to the pillaging and crippling of the soul than to its restoraton."

78. Ibid.

79. Cf. Florence quoted in *Post* 323 and *Material for Thought* 19–21.

80. *CF* 30; *Beatus Vir* being the *incipit* of Psalm 1 and Zerbolt's *De Spiritualibus Ascensionibus*; cf. John Ketel, "and if you have time, study a little in your excerpts" (*T3* 121), and Gerard Groote, "allow yourself time to read through what you have written in this book, because this orders your state" (ibid. 35), referring to their *rapiaria*; cf. also below, 177–78 and Index: *rapiaria*.

81. *Coulton* 106–7: "When, during my noviciate, I sang in the service . . . then I thought within myself, 'Our lay folk in the nave, prostrate on their knees, are thinking with admiration, "How good and pure a voice hath our brother John!"' When another novice sang any part, then I murmured within myself, 'Now the lay folk are thinking, "That sounds like a rasp!"' Rarely did one of our brethren leave the choir or do anything, but that I had various suspicions of him, thinking within myself, 'He cannot stay longer in the choir, he goeth forth because he would go hither or thither.' One was wont to spit frequently in the choir; and I thought that he had many temptations which he drove forth by this continual voiding of his rheum. . . . I had most frequent suspicions of many others; for a novice is as full of suspicions as an egg is full of meat. . . . Whensoever after this I felt inclinations or movements to fault or sin, or when I was offended by others, I conceived certain remedies thereunto, which I had found by experience of myself or by study from the Holy Scriptures, which I collected into a certain little book that I might have them at hand; whereby I brought myself back little by little to peace of mind and withstood such evil inclinations"; cf. *Dumbar* 9–10 for Gerard Groote's notebook.

82. For instance, Florence Radewijn's *Multum Valet* and *Omnes Inquit Artes*, the collections of sayings included in Kempis' *Lives* of the early Brothers and Windesheimers and perhaps also *De Imitatione Christi* and *SA* (cf. *Gem* 61); Erasmus' *De Contemptu Mundi*, written during his stay at a monastery of the Windesheim Observance, was described by him in the preface to the 1521 edition as "a collection of common sayings" (A. Hyma, *The Youth of Erasmus* [Ann Arbor, Michigan 1930], 173).

83. *Florence* 17: "we ought always to direct our meditations towards purging ourselves of vices and concupiscence and the acquisition of virtues, as was pre–eminently laid down in the collation of Abbot Moses. Hence Augustine also says in his book on true innocence: 'It is useless for him who works to meditate upon the law of God to hold in his memory what he does not fulfil in action'"; ibid. 20 "by meditation a man ought to quicken the prick of conscience in his self–examination"; cf. *Post* 324; above, 136; below, 191, 288ff.

84. Cf Index: attention; emotional life; food; meditation; *masticatio; ruminatio;* scale; thinking.

85. Cf. Index: 'the fresh.'

86. Cf. Index: being; self-knowledge.

87. Cf. Index: wisdom; hence Gerard, "the scriptures are to be masticated and ruminated upon" (*Post* 108).

88. Cf. above, 127–28, 138–39.

89. Cf. Index: knowledge & being.

90. Cf. Index: understanding.

91. Cf. above, 137–38 and Index: meditation.

92. Its reference to the *horarium* suggests the assimilation of this Brotherhouse to the conventional monastery or house of canons; cf. above, 83, 110–11.

93. *CF* 14–15.

94. Ibid. 15; cf. Dumbar 198–99.

95. Cf. 16–17.

96. *Post* 543–44.

97. Cisneros, *Directory*, 17; cf. [*Writings from the*] *Philokalia on Prayer of the Heart* [ed. E. Kadloubovsky and G. E. H. Palmer (London 1954)], 152–61; Index: attention.

98. Cf. Index: devotion; spiritual exercises.

99. *T3* 32.

100. Ibid. 117; cf. 120.

101. *Trinkaus* 311, 451; cf. 317, 647; and Index: *imitatio Christi.*

102. *Trinkaus* 647; cf. 631, 633, 645; for the influence of their translated works on the lay gilds, ibid. 638, 644; Index: the New Devotion.

103. Cf. R. Bainton, *Studies on the Reformation* (London 1964), 51–61.

104. Quoted above, 82 and Index: 'regeneration of man.'

105. The Bridgettines of Syon were encouraged to meditate on the Passion during each of the seven hours, "as your best quiet spirit shall or may minister to you at the said time" (*PP* ccxlix^r).

106. *Coulton* 90; cf. Index: compunction.

107. Cf. Pourrat 14, 17–22; *Hyma* 442–43; *Florence* 17–25, 49–56; *Post* 318, 322, 542; *SA* 898A–911A; Cisneros, *[Book of] Exercises [for the Spiritual life,* ed. E. Allison Peers (Montserrat 1929)], 223–87; *Tractatus de cotidiano holocausto,* 500–1; *PP* ccxlviii^r–cclxi^v, cclxv^{r-v}, ccxcviii^r–cccviii^r.

108. Cf. Index: balance.

109. *De materiis meditandi* from the constitution of the Deventer Brotherhouse, in *Hyma* 442–43: "Because it is necessary that the fear of the Lord profit those who are willing—for he who is without fear is not able to be justified—for this reason it behoves each of us to

ponder tirelessly material which calls a man to the fear of God, that is, material concerning sin, death, judgement and hell. But lest uninterrupted fear overthrow the mind and give rise to desperation if he does not breathe again in the hope of divine mercy, it is necessary to intermix material that calls him to hope and the love of God, namely concerning the Kingdom of Heaven, the divine gifts, the life of Jesus Christ and His Passion. We are used so to divide and alternate this material, that on Saturday we meditate on sins, Sunday on the Kingdom of Heaven, Monday on death, Tuesday on the gifts of God, Wednesday on the Judgement, Thursday on the pains of Hell, Friday on the Passion of our Lord, concerning which we assemble to meditate every day during Mass, beginning on Sunday with the life of our Lord, and subsequently on each day some subject of the Passion, according to what has been indicated. But on the principal festivals we conform to the practice of the Catholic Church, forming our meditations and exercises according to the material of the feast. For the renewal of memory, we are used to read some short passage from this material morning, evening and night"; cf. Bonaventure, in *Martz* 74, "I think it is delightful to meditate thus, whatever the facts may have been."

110. Cf. Gerard Groote, in *Gem* 54: "We must take heed that we are not overcome by sadness, nor cast down and destroyed thereby, lest instead of being led on by it to hope, as the Apostle desires, we should be brought down into cowardice and despair. 'God is our Refuge and Strength, therefore we will not fear though the earth be removed and the mountains be carried into the midst of the sea'" (*Ps.* 46:1–2); cf. Index: fear.

111. Cf. Gerardi Magni Epistolae, ed. W. Mulder (Antwerp 1933), 283–93, no. 70, "A letter sent to a certain brother Carthusian who was infirm in the head," above, 45–47, *Hyma* 256; Gerard's *Conclusa* consider habits of eating and sleeping conducive to bodily and mental health (*T3* 34–60) and the *Tractatus de cotidiano holocausto*, attributed to his friend Henry Egher the Carthusian, pleads eloquently for a sense of balance in the work of realigning our inner architecture, 483, 489, 498: "however, let the mean not be exceeded in excessive sadness of heart because of madness, which can happen often to those with a weak head . . . just as it is in the building of bridges: over the stone foundations of divine love, he should lay down prepared timbers, namely the continual remembrance of sin and its sorrow; but rarely, once a week or now and then, gently, lest he injure his brain . . . and lest our head suffers harm through thinking, as some would say, let us treat ourselves sensitively"; cf. also Cisneros *Exercises*, 31–32 and *Peryn*, sig. Aiii[r], "you may not force yourself too vehemently, but mildly and gently do what you may without great violence."

112. Cf. *Bonde* passim.

113. Cf. Index: "delight" in work.

114. *Wessel 2* 11.

115. Ibid. 86; cf. *De Oratione* ii[v]–vi[r]; the method of meditation aimed at focusing the mind and then developing its activity in a particular direction, according to *Post* 544.

116. Cf. *Van Zijl* 114; Gerard Groote's *Tractatus de quatuor generibus meditationum*, ed. A. Hyma (Utrecht 1924), 297–326, contains frequent warnings against imaginative delusions arising from attempts to think oneself present to the events of Christ's life.

117. The tradition of meditation on which the Brethren drew can be found in earlier writers like Bernard, William of St. Thierry, Bonaventure and David of Augsburg (*Post* 328), for

example: "Be present, then, in spirit at all He does . . . look at Him and at the disciples and endeavour to reconstruct the scene. . . . For if you wish to gather fruit from these things, imagine that you are actually present when the Lord Jesus says or does them; as if you heard with your own ears, and saw with your own eyes and attend with your whole mind and heart, intently and joyfully, putting aside for the moment all other cares" (*Meditations on the Life of Christ*, attr. Bonaventure, in *Martz* 73); the Carthusian text is in *Allen* 365.

118. Cf. Index: Ignatius Loyola, and above 129.

119. *SA* 897E; cf. *Wessel 2* 82–83.

120. Cf. Index: *Fac quod in se est.*

121. Cf. *Tractatus de cotidiano holocausto*, 499–500: "Wishing therefore that he might accustom himself to live thus by God before all things, let him think that, as often as he is able, the Lord Jesus is present to and perceiving his acts, and let him stand upright [or still] near Him . . . weighing each word and act and even thought. . . . O let the thoughts of this presence of Jesus be powerful, because He is indeed present . . . if he is asked a question or must speak, let him have the Lord Jesus always in his mouth every fifth word and accustom himself to this and seek the same in his mind"; also below, 162 and Index: Christ.

122. Quoted by F. Schuon in *The Sword of Gnosis*, ed. J. Needleman (Baltimore 1974), 27.

123. *MBE* sigs Cii^v–iii^r; *MBL* 326.

124. *Post* 108; cf. *Tractatus de cotidiano holocausto* 494; Index: meditation.

125. *Tractatus de cotidiano holocausto*, 497126: "And if this [thought of God] is perhaps too difficult, because he does not have the way of it and the Devil obstructs, certainly it is so much the more meritorious, because he is crucified with Christ"; cf. Gerard Groote, "A little confusion suffered patiently here abolishes eternal confusion in the Presence of God and all the saints" (*T3* 36).

126. *Tractatus de cotidiano holocausto*, 491.

127. *MBE* sigs. Eiiii^v–v^r; cf. below, 230–39 and Index: "the old man."

128. *Gem* 54–55; cf. *Luke* 24:46; *2 Cor.* 4:11.

129. *T3* 36.

130. *Van Zijl* 115; *Gem* 53.

131. Cf. Hyma 442; Gerard Groote quoted in *T3* 32, also 27–28; on the Mass, *Dumbar* 4 and *Essays* 140; and on the high place of the priest, *Post* 89, *T3* 85, *Gem* 145–46.

132. *Jacob* 56, they neither expended themselves attacking the Curia, nor championed it; cf. Gerard's letter quoted in *Gem* 88: "We are suffering above, all in our head, the Pope; and, according to . . . Gallienus [Galen], mischief in the head is a symptom of a grave malady, and the effect of a fever which is ravaging the whole organism. We all, like inexperienced doctors, perceive only the actual signs of the evil, without paying heed to the older symptoms, that are not less important . . . the present suffering is not the chief cause of the degeneration."

133. Cf. *Post* 463–64, 484, 544, 548.

134. Cf. Index: *fac quod in se ets* and *Obermann* 468, 342: often called nominalist, this aphorism was used by the medieval mystics to indicate a fundamental movement, as *Blunt*

21, "although it is not in our power to have devotion at will, for it is the free gift of God, yet it is in our power, by grace, to do that which is in us to dispose ourselves to devotion," and *Luis* 106, "doing on his part so much as lies in him, which is the thing that almighty God requires principally of us," cf. 127; Gansfort brings it down to earth, "although God is the source of all things, still he wishes the farmer to labour . . . and this to such an extent that, although God Himself does it all, no blessing, no fruit will attend a lazy, snoring farmer" (*Wessel 2* 82–83); cf. also below, 277.

135. *T3* 33: "Let them hear with attention the word [of the Gospel] and worship faithfully, that is, let them venerate through the orderly arrangement of the body . . . such humble adoration and bowing of the body is proper for God, and is in every way conformable to the mind as a help to devotion; or rather, it is most suitable to incline the head over the elbow, as you know. For a servant is very much bound to show reverence to the Lord in the presence of the Lord. Bending is wonderfully conformable to the devotion of the mind, on account of the proportional movement of the imagination"; cf. Gregory the Great's instruction, eight hundred years earlier, to study Scripture with "the inner mind," "examine the meaning of things with more acute perception," in doing which we find significance in "the position of the place . . . the posture of the body . . . the temperature of the air" (*Material for Thought* 20).

136. Cf. *Ward* 95–96 no. 46; below 279, 283, 284, 303.

137. *Early Fathers Philokalia* 124, quoted below, 228–29.

138. *T3* 32–33: "Chanting is a help to our earthly nature in devotion, as you know from experience. . . . And so when the Gospel is read the mind ought not to set before itself any other prayer or any other reading to which it owes attention. For the powers of perception are less when they are intent on many things than on one thing. It is enjoined that the words of the Gospel and the writings of the Apostles are attended to during the solemnities. . . . 'It is useless to listen unless we pay attention.' And so we should read nothing, meditate on nothing, because we owe attention to the present, or we owe to the gospel, from which we withdraw all that we say and pass through in our meditating. And so our bowing at these words [Jesus and Mary] and the veneration of the body, are signs of our mental veneration. The signs are false, unless what they stand for corresponds. And these external attitudes induce states of mind: they are vain if there is no correspondence. And so it is better to worship with the voice and the mind, than with the voice or mind alone. And so I will hear by lowering the hood, I will hear with the ear and I will hear with the mind; Otherwise it is just like tinkling cymbals and sounding brass. No voices or words are my own whose sound is not received by me."

139. Ibid. 34.

140. *CF* 23.

141. *Knott* 235; the last book is in the tradition of Bernard's *Sermones super Cantica Canticorum* (cf. *Essays* 145); cf. also *Wessel 2* 56, 58–59; Index: 'the monastery within'; "spiritual communion."

142. Gerard quoted in *Gem* 52.

143. *Knott* 235.

144. Cf. *Aston* 164–66; *Pourrat*, vol. 2, chap. 14.

145. Gararde published 1532, *STC* 11549; for *Dialoge*; cf. below, 189–91.

146. Cf. Index: morality, outer & inner.

147. *Wessel 1* 245.

148. Mande quoted in *Post* 40: only the "intention" underlying works matters, as Cassian taught.

149. *Obermann* 345, "from this root, with the accruing of God's favour, will have sprung forth the universal fruit of reformation, not only of this order [Windesheim] but actually of very many other orders besides . . . many of these which have newly arisen are the successors of fathers now dead, even if they have not responded with due gratitude."

150. *Gem* 146; cf. Cisneros, *Directory* 10–11: "It is . . . the greatest rashness to go before so great a majesty utterly unprepared. For the whole fruit of both day and night office depends on our foregoing preparation, according as the Prophet says: Thy ear hath heard the preparation of my heart."

151. Quoted above, 117.

152. *Post* 320; *Dumbar* 117; cf. *Gem* 147.

153. *Essays* 141; he deplored the neglect of works like David of Augsburg's *Profectus Religiosorum* and Suso's *Horologium Eternae Sapientiae*.

154. *Dumbar* 134.

155. *Post* 635–56; cf. above, 110–11.

156. *Gem* 175, 177, 179; *Dumbar* 187, 190, 194–95.

157. *Gem* 175, *Dumbar* 187.

158. *Hyma* 33–34: "Asceticism is often very harmful, for the devil will frequently use it as a tool, telling the person in question that it is a very helpful method for the religious student, and yet all this watching, praying and fasting will often cause mental diseases, anger or pride. Man is prone to think that he can do good on his own initiative, thus taking too much pride in his own work, which if really good, is not his own work, but that of God. Hence there are many people who pray much and inflict physical hardship upon themselves, while within they are unrighteous and avaricious."

159. Erasmus, quoted in *Essays* 134–35.

160. *SA* 932C; cf. above, 50 and Index: 'godly vocation'; Thomas Sampson's identical interpretation of Christ's injunction to "watch" in *A Sermon . . . of pacience* (London 1550), sigs. Aii^v–iii^r, suggests that Protestant writers accepted the godliness of vocation as unconditionally as medieval doctors had accepted the holiness of the monastic state, Christ's call being identified with the night vigils of the established orders.

161. *Wilkins*, vol. 3, 728.

162. Ibid. 734; above, 106; cf. *Wilkins*, vol. 3, 730, "Christ forbade that one place should be taken as holy and another profane, but that all places should be indifferent," with Meister Eckhart's "abgeschiedenheit," loosely translatable as 'indifference,' with *MBE* quoted above, 129, 145 and *Ymage of love* quoted above, 57; the Lollard asscoiations of these Tudor pamphlets remind us that the Brethren were originally labelled as Lollards and Beguines, above, 75, 83, 88–89.

163. [*The Spiritual Exercises of Saint Ignatius Loyola*, ed. W. H.] Longridge [(London 1950)], 53–54, 304–5, 337–38.

164. Cf. the following descriptions of the "composition": "contemplate the vast surface of the world and windows fashioned in the sky, that I may more conveniently be able to look on, and let me also construct mentally the house of the virgin Mary, as an architect is wont to do" (John Helyar's early version of the Ignatian exercises, quoted in H. Thurston, *The Month*, vol. 142, no. 712, Oct. 1923, 345–46); "We must see the places where the things we meditate on were wrought, by imagining ourselves to be really present at those places, which we must endeavour to represent so lively, as though we saw them indeed, with out corporal eyes; which to perform well, it will help us much to behold beforehand some image wherein that mystery is well represented and to have read or heard what good authors write of those places and to have noted well the distance from one place to another, the height of the hills and the situation of the towns and villages. And the diligence we employ herein is not lost, for on the well making of this preludium depends both the understanding of the mystery and attention in our meditation" (Richard Gibbons S.J., *Practical Method of Meditation*, 1614, quoted in *Martz* 27), and cf. *Southwell* 162–67 for his method of peopling all the rooms of one's house with imaginary images of the saints "to help my memory" (R. Freeman, *English Emblem Books* [London 1948], 173; cf. 26), *Martz* and *Yates* passim, nn. 172, 173, 182 below. All these techniques relate to the *ars memorativa*, for which see Index.

165. *Post* 548.

166. Cf. above, 82, 120, 128–30.

167. Cf. Index: religious method.

168. Cf. Index: craft.

169. Cf. Index: psychology, traditional; worship.

170. Cf. Index: 'mixed life'; 'the way in life'; Ways, the traditional.

171. Cf. *Rom.* 7:18: "For I know that in me (that is, in my flesh) dwelleth no good thing: for to will is present with me; but how to perform that which is good I find not."

172. *Hyma* 259; in 1486 Mombaer submitted the *Chiropsalterium* to Gansfort, whose *Tractatus de cohibendis cogitationibus*, dedicated to St. Agnietenberg, the house of Mombaer and Kempis, contains methods closely related to the *Rosetum's* "ladder of meditation," includes an artificial memory system and cites Climachus, the Desert Fathers and Lull as its authorities (Gansfort taught Lull's "art" to his circle, and it was with Lullism that the Renaissance revival of "the art of memory" was connected); cf. Post 544, 480, 537, 539; *Wessel 1* 123, 208; *Wessel 2* 342; *De Oratione* ix^r (citing Lull on the unification of the three parts of the soul in attentive prayer); *Yates* 175–96, 206ff., above, n. 164; Gansfort, like Lull, studied the sacred writings of other religious traditions (cf. *Wessel 1* 123).

173. *Post* 544; the *Chiropsalterium* is prefaced by the illustration of a hand divided into corresponding intentions and placed within an architectural doorway between two columns, recalling a "memory *locus*" as described by Yates; similar hands, associated with the examination of conscience, are found in later editions of the Ignatian *Exercises* (*Mombaer* sig. kiiii^v; *Exercitia Spiritualia S. P. Ignatii loyolae*, Antwerp 1689, 72, and cf. above, n. 164).

174. Cf. Index: "remembering."

175. Cf. Index: "art is better than evil strength."

176. Thomas Sampson, *A Warning to take heed of Fowler's Psalter* (London 1578), 22.

177. Cf. above, 123–31, 143–44 and Index: man.

178. Cf. Index: liturgy; New Devotion; religion.

179. Above 125–26 and Index: chaos in man.

180. Cf. Index: attention.

181. Cf. Index: body, the physical.

182. Cf. Cisneros, *Directory* 19–20: "follow the psalms of the first Noctum, wherein a monk must keep his mind in some fixed place and set down a number of these resting places, lest it should wander hither and thither. As far as he can, he should adapt the meaning of the psalms to the scenes he has in his mind; and can thus go through the whole of the Office, reckoning, for example, all the psalms of matins on the joints of the four fingers of his left hand after this fashion: let him place the tip of his thumb on the first joint of his forefinger and first meditate on the annunciation . . . as if he saw the angel going into our Lady's poor dwelling. . . . The first psalm being ended (placing his thumb at the second joint of his forefinger) let him now see in his mind's eye the city of Bethlehem and behold the new born child laid in the crib, listen to the angels' and shepherds' hymns of praise and with them let him recite the second psalm, adapting, where he can, its meaning to the things that pass before his mind; and should his thoughts wander he may easily recall them by pressing his finger with his thumb nail"; are these "resting places" equivalent to the memory *loci* mentioned by Yates?.

183. *CF* 28; cf. *Ps.* 126:1 (Vulgate); *Luke* 1:46ff.; and *CF* 14, which has the marginal note "open the hand" opposite the directions for the morning *Benedictum*.

184. Cf. Index: religion.

185. *De Oratione* v^{r}ff.

186. Early editions of the *Rosetum* have only a few intentions associated with the hand, but later seven were associated with each finger (*Post* 544), while Dirk of Herxen, the Zwolle Brotherhouse rector who directed Gansfort's early studies (ibid. 478–79), in his work on Passion meditation, divided each consideration into seven articles, each of which was subdivided into four points, which were to be "drawn on the hand" (*in manu depictu*), thus constituting "the beginning of methodical meditation," according to scholars (ibid. 378–79).

187. Cf. above, 155.

188. The arrangement given is that on the page, *Post* 544–46; cf. Hyma 420 n. 49; Index: sleep.

189. *CF* 27; *T3* 74; cf. *CF* 21: "in writing you ought to pay attention to three things, namely that you make your letters perfectly and in due manner, that you write correctly, and that you understand the sense of what you are writing and bring back wandering thoughts and emotions to one of these matters," and above, n. 25 and Index: prayer; search, man's; understanding.

190. Cf. Blosius, writing c. 1551, quoted in *Pourrat* 21–22: "Good no doubt and well pleasing to God are such exterior exercises as the devout chanting of the divine praises, the recitation of long vocal prayers, continued kneeling, the giving of outward signs of devotion, fasting, watching etc.; but infinitely superior to them are spiritual exercises whereby man through ardent desires, not by senses and images but in a supernatural manner, rises unto God to be united with Him."

CHAPTER EIGHT

1. Cf. J. Needleman, *Consciousness and Tradition* (New York 1982) 12–22.

2. *Wisdom of Solomon* 9:16 (Revised Version); cf. Index: Heaven & Earth; order.

3. Cf. *[A] Manuall [of praiers* (Calice 1599)], 3–69, 27 editions between 1583 and 1640 (A. F. Allison and D. M. Rogers, *A Catalogue of Catholic Books in English 1558–1640* [Bognor Regis 1956], 92–95).

4. *Dyurnall* [(London 1530?)], sig. aii^r.

5. Ibid. sig. aii^{r-v}.

6. Ibid. sig. aii^v; cf. J. W. Adamson in *Transactions of the Bibliographical Society*, 2nd series, 10 (1930), 163–94; J. Simon *Education and Society in Tudor England* (Cambridge 1966), passim, *Dickens* 49–52, 102–6; and Index: lay devotion; 'mixed life.'

7. *Dyurnall* sigs. aii^v–iii^r.

8. Ibid. sig. aiii^v.

9. Ibid. sig. aiii^{r-v}; cf. *Peryn* sig. aiii^v.

10. Cf. above, 43–52.

11. Cf. Index: "delight" in work; religion.

12. *W* sigs. aiii^r–vi^v; cf. *DE* fii^v–iii^r.

13. Cf. above, 36, 38, 51.

14. *Dyurnall*, sigs. aiii^v, biv^r, ci^v; cf. *Colet* (Avi^r); *The Workes of Sir Thomas More*, vol. 1, 13B–C.

15. *Dyurnall*, sig. bi^v.

16. *Dyurnall*, sigs. aiii^v–iiii^v; cf. *Colet* (Aiii^r) (Aiii^v–iiii^r).

17. *Dyurnall*, sigs. aiiii^v–bi^r.

18. Ibid. sig. bi^r; this prayer was used by Whytford in his writings on the ordering of lay life; cf. *D* sig. Av^v.

19. *Dyurnall*, sig. bi^{r-v}.

20. Cf. J. Needleman, *Lost Christianity* (New York 1980), 37–42.

21. Cf. Index: liturgy.

22. *Dyurnall*, sig. bi^{r-v}, for orthodoxy cf. aiiii^v–iiii^r, bii^r, bii^v, ci^v.

23. Ibid. sig. bi^{r-v}; cf. DE Bv^r, *The Workes of Sir Thomas More* vol. 1, 20C; Luis of Granada, *Of Prayer and Meditation* (London 1599), sigs. A5^v–6^r.

6 NOTES TO CHAPTER EIGHT

24. Cf. Index: body, the physical; Gerard Groote.

25. *Dyurnall*, sigs. bi^v–ii^r; cf. biiii^r, biiii^v; and above, 136.

26. *Dyurnall*, sig. bii^r–v; cf. Index: death, remembrance of; *Longridge* 132; *Colet* (A3^v).

27. Ibid. (A6^r); cf. (A2^v–3^r).

28. *Dyurnall*, sig. bii^v; he gives seven chapters of *Vita Christi secundum Bonaventuram* to be read through the week; cf. above, 154–55.

29. *Dyurnall*, sig. biiii^r.

30. Cf. *The Workes of Sir Thomas More*, vol. 1, 11A–B; above, 95, *LER* sigs. fiiii^r–vi^v; see Index: compunction.

31. *Dyurnall*, sigs. biiii^v–iiii^v; cf. *Parkyn* 69–70; *Longridge* 145–47.

32. Cf. below, 272 n. 59.

33. *Longridge* 44–51.

34. *Dyurnall*, sigs. biiii^v–cii^r.

35. Ibid. sigs. ci^v–ii^r, *Longridge* 69; cf. *PP* cxxxiii^r for the "Puritan" image of the "spiritual merchant" casting his book of conscience every night to see if he has gained that day.

36. H. Thurston in *The Month*, vol. 142, no. 712 (Oct. 1923), 343–44.

37. *Longridge* 24.

38. Quoted in [A. G. Dickens, *The*] *Counter-Reformation* [(London 1968)], 80.

39. *Longridge* 26.

40. Ibid. 4.

41. *Counter-Reformation* 82.

42. Cf. [W. A. M.] Peters [in *AHSI*, anno 25, fasc. 49 (1956)], 328–50, whose argument, based on the Spanish affiliations of Whytford's circle and textual similarities between the *Spiritual Exercises* and the *Dayly Exercyse* and *Dialoge*, is intriguing, but not conclusive.

43. Cf. above, 127–28 and Index: religion.

44. Cf. Index: "spiritual ascents."

45. Transliterated from *The Cloud of Unknowing*, ed. E. Underhill (London 1956), 103–4; and cf. Index: self-knowledge.

46. *Dyurnall*, sig. aii^r.

47. Ibid. sigs. bi^r, ci^r, cii^r.

48. White, *Private Devotion* 160–61; *Dyurnall*, sigs. bi^r (the morning dedication), biii^v (the body as "continual enemy"), biiii^r ("singularity"), ci^v (exercises at "compline"); and Index: Way of the Monk.

49. White, *Private Devotion* 153–54.

50. Ibid. 153.

51. Ibid. 150–53, 261; *This prymer* [*of Salysbury use* (Paris 1538)], after the calendar, and the Bodleian Salysbury primers of 1532 and 1534; the 1538 reforming primer, *Thys prymer in Englyshe and in laten*, *STC* 16005, omits it.

52. *Thys prymer*, sigs. Bvii^v–viii^v; he is also to say the *Dirige* and *Commendationes* for all Christians on holy days, and every other day if he can.

53. Ibid.; cf. *The Workes of Sir Thomas More*, vol. 1, 21B–22B, 27B, 31B–C, 7H–8A; and below, 229–39.

54. *This Prymer of Salysbury use* (Paris 1534), sigs. ciiii^v–vi^r; cf. *This prymer*, sigs. ci^r–iiii^r, which includes a short translation from Gerson.

55. Translations of Climachus with Fewterer (*HI* 47^r), of Gerson on contemplation (*P* ccxxxvii^v), of Syon's Statutes (*P* cxciii^r) and Mafeo Vegio's *De Perseverantia Religione* (*P* lxxxvi^v); the three attributions were *The fruyte of Redempcyon* (by Symon Anker, see chap. 9, n. 11), *The Pomander of Prayer* (by a Shene Carthusian, 1st. ed. 1530; cf. [*Typographical Antiquities*, ed. T. F.] Dibdin [London 1810–19], vol. 3, 115) and *Jesus Psalter* (cf. below, n. 67).

56. Cf. *ER* sig. Aii^r; *LER* Aiv^v; *D* Aii^r, Cvi^v, Diii^v; *DE* Aiv^v; *HI* Aii^r, 49^r, 66^r, 86^r: conventional phrases, but not necessarily untrue.

57. Cf. above, xx, 77, below, 213–18, 230, 329–40.

58. *ER* sig. Aiv^{r-v}; for monastic ignorance of their Rules, cf. ibid. Aiii^r, iv^r; *P* lxii^v; *Martiloge* "Unto the devout readers . . . "; *LER* Dii^{r-v}, Oiv^{r-v}, Si^v ("and so as they professed they knew not what, so they keep it they know not how"), Tiv^v–v^r ("as others lived there before they follow without rule, for they be clean out of rule"); *Coulton* passim; Index: monastic rules.

59. 1530? R. Redman *STC* 25421.8 (formerly 25426), 1530 W. de Worde *STC* 25422, 1531? P. Treveris *STC* 25422.3 (formerly 25424), 1531 Redman *STC* 25422.5 (pt. 2 of 25412), 1533 W. de Worde *STC* 25423, 1537 Redman *STC* 25425 (pt. 3 of 25413), 1537 J. Waylande *STC* 25425.5 (pt. 3 of 25413.5).

60. 1531? Redman *STC* 25412, 1537? Redman *STC* 25413, 1537 Waylande *STC* 25413.5 (formerly 25416).

61. 1537? Redman *STC* 25413, 1537 Waylande *STC* 25414 (pt. 2 of 25413.5), 1538? Redman *STC* 25415.

62. 1541 W. Myddlyton *STC* 25420.

63. Cf. *D* sigs. Aiii^v–iv^r, Av^r, Bii^{r-v}, Bvii^r, Ii^v; *DE* Diii^v, Dvi^v, Dviii^v, Fi^r; *HI* 19^r, 49^r, 55^v; *P* lxxxviii^v.

64. Cf. *W* sigs. Bii^r, Biii^{r-v}, Bviii^r, Civ^{r-v}, Cvii^v–Diii^r, Dv^{r-v}, Dviii^v–Ei^r, Eiii^r, for example.

65. His humanist status is equivocal, although his friendship with Erasmus and More is well authenticated: cf. above, 55, 77, 102, 192, *Caraman* 5–6; *McConica* 115–16; [C.] Hill [*Society and Puritanism in Pre-Revolutionary England* (London 1969)], 432; also his inclusion of part of Erasmus' *Enchiridion* in *P* ccxxi^v–ccxxviii^v, his reference to Christ the teacher in *D* sig. Evi^r (a humanist concept according to *Trinkaus* 644–45, G. F. Nuttall, *The Puritan Spirit* [London 1957], 51). This 'humanism' tends to dissolve under examination: his avowed concern for textual accuracy (cf. *The Folowyng of Christe*, sig. Aii^{r-v}; *ER* Aii^r–iii^r; *LER* Ai^v) is belied by humanist standards (cf. *Martiloge* passim, *Golden Pystle* [London 1530], sig. Aii^r); although frequently citing the classics, especially Cicero and

Seneca, biblical and patristic wisdom always holds the ring (cf. *DE* sigs. Aiii^r, Bi^{r-v}, *HI* 12^v, 15^v, 16^{r-v}, 21^v, 41^v, 49^v, 59^v, 73^r, 79^r; *P* lx^r; *LER* kiii^r); Vegio's work (cf. above, n. 55) was an essay in traditional piety of the kind often produced by Italian humanists (cf. above, 30–31), Vegio himself becoming an Augustinian canon and thus a close monastic relative of Whytford; although a collector of proverbs like Erasmus, Whytford gave English versions, whereas Erasmus deliberately omitted the common sayings of the people, as did the contemporary humanist monk of Evesham, Robert Joseph, who even censured the writing of English (*RO3* 102–3). Whytford's earlier work is touched by a humanist spirit, but his later work, like More's, reveals the depth of his commitment to the English and European devotional and spiritual tradition, strengthened by his experience of monastic discipline: humanism was a diffuse, subtle and contradictory presence in England at this date, too easily anticipated.

66. Cf. *P* iii^{r}ff. and passim; *HI* "A Preface," sigs. Ai^v–ii^r; *W* *iii^r–iiii^r.

67. Syon writers held a key position in the transition between late medieval and Counter–Reformation devotion in England in their emphasis on the ordering of daily life, the role of the spiritual adviser, the subjective state of the worshipper, the importance of the sacraments, the use of methodical spiritual techniques and examination of conscience: cf. *D* passim; *Bonde* xiii^{r-v}, xvi^r, xxii^{r-v}, xxvii^v; *HI* 54^{r-v}, for example; the popularity of Whytford's translation of *De Imitatione Christi* (*The Folowyng of Christe*, 1531? R. Wyer *STC* 23961, 1531? Wyer *STC* 23962, 1531? T. Godfray *STC* 23963, 1531? R. Redman *STC* 23964, 1531? Redman *STC* 23964.3, 1535? Redman *STC* 23964.7, 1545? W. Myddlyton *STC* 23965, 1556 J. Cawood *STC* 23967, 1566 Cawood *STC* 23967.5, 1585 G. L'Oyselet *STC* 23968, extracts 1533? Wyer *STC* 23968.5) and of the *Jesus Psalter*, persistently attributed to Whytford, but surely older and rooted in the tradition on which Syon's practice was based (cf. *STC* 14563–70, editions from 1529–1640; White, *Private Devotion*; S. H. Sole, *Jesus Psalter* [London 1888]); *Southern* 533 quotes a prayer by Whytford (actually from *W* sigs. Aiii^v–iiii^r) borrowed in Vaux's 1581? *Catechisme*, while *Bonde* chap. 15, xvii^v–xviii^v, is transplanted in *Iesus Psalter* (Antwerp 1575), sigs. Dv^v–viii^v; Whytford's translation of the Syon martyrology for private reading anticipates a Counter–Reformation trend ([*The*] *Martiloge* [ed. F.] Proctor and [E. S.] Dewick [London 1893], vi–viii); cf. below, n. 71.

68. Cf. *P* xxxv^r–vi^r (the "secret surety" in the soul validating God's calling also recalls Ignatius); *HI* 7^v–8^r, 72^v, 84^r; *Bonde* xii^r; *D* sigs. fvi^r, hvi^r; *LER* Lii^r; *W* Aviii^{r-v}, Biii^r, Cvii^r–viii^v, Diii^v–iiii^r, Dvii^v–Eii^r; *Golden Pystle* Aiv^r; his observantism is often reminiscent of puritanism, as *LER* sigs. Dii^r, Gii^r; *P* ccxxxii^v, ccix^v; cf. *Aungier* 320; M. M. Knappen, *Tudor Puritanism* (Chicago 1965), ix, 425, 436, 451. *The Werke* anticipates a whole genre of puritan manuals for householders; cf. *Hill* 146, 432, chap. 13 passim; L. B. Wright, *Middle Class Culture in Eizabethan England* (Chapel Hill 1935), 201–96, for although referring to priest and confession (cf. sigs. Aviii^v), its tendency, like the Puritan guides (and also the medieval *ars moriendi*, orthodox in intention but often circumventing the priest; cf. [M.] O'Connor, [*The Art of Dying Well*, New York 1942], 6), is to underline the authority of the father (cf. Avii^r–viii^r), who, by setting himself in order with God, rules his house.

69. Cf. *Aston* 160–73; *Reed* 180; below, 71, 215–17; and cf. *W* sigs. Bvi^{r-v}, Eii^v with *Owst* 274 and White, *Private Devotion* 119, 227.

70. *Owst* 296–308; Pecham's *Ignorantia Sacerdotum* (cf. D. L. Douie, *Archbishop Pecham*

[Oxford 1952], 134–35, 138–42) is bound with *W* in Bodleian *Ash 1215,* inviting a comparison which reveals Whytford's greater concern with inner life, the influence of the New Devotion?; cf. *W* sig. Biiii^v with *Owst* 283, Rolle quoted in *Horstmann,* vol. 1, 261–64, *Rich* chap. 18; cf. *W* Dv^{r}ff. with *Owst* 272; [F.] Gasquet [*The Eve of the Reformation* (London 1919)], 248–49; cf. *W* Dvii^v–viii^v with Myrc, *Instructions for Parish Priests,* ed. F. Peacock (London 1868), 11; cf. *W* Ei^v with *Aston* 170, *Gasquet* 250–51, *RO3* 135.

71. *W* sigs. Aiii^r–vi^v, "First then . . . begin with yourself. And as soon as you do awake in the morning to arise for all day, first suddenly turn your mind and remembrance unto Almighty God" (cf. above, 179 and the following account of putting on the "badge of Christ"—also in *HI* 39^v—with the monastic practice in *Aungier* 23–24, 313–15); *W* sigs. Avii$^{r–v}$, "make every day once your said account by yourself . . . at night after all your occupations before your bed; there kneel down & there begin to remember whither you went & what you did immediately after your morning exercise & in what company you were & what was there your behaviour and demeanour in work, word or thought" (cf. *Longridge* 44–51, 17), also *Golden Pystle* Bii^v–iii^r, *Crossrowe* [(London 1537)], Iviii$^{r–v}$; *DE* Cvi–ii^{v}ff., Diii^v–iiii^r. For examples in later works; cf. *The Psalter of Sainct Hierome* (Antwerp 1576), sigs. Cv^r–Dviii^v; *A Manuall of praiers* (Rouen 1583), 2^{v}ff.; *A Manuall or meditation* (no place or date, Bodleian 8°M37Th) fi^{r}ff, *Southern* 226–27.

72. *A Werke* (London 1537, R. Redman), sig. Aii^r, "the matter is directed principally unto householders or unto them that have guiding and governance of any company for an order to be kept both in themself & in them that they rule and charge"; *W* sig. Av^v, "and having unto Thee ever a reverend dread, I may love Thee for Thyself & all other in Thee (Lord) and for Thee, so that, according unto the spiritual strength and knowledge that Thou hast given me, I may apply my will wholly unto Thy Will, so that I have no will proper unto myself, but that my will be all Thy Will and both (as much as may be possible) one will. And so I may here in this life order my love and come unto such perfection of fervent charity that (by the grace) I may attain unto the fruition of everlasting charity in Thy Joyfull Presence" (part of a long prayer for a different orientation, a new and free will); cf. Index: love; will; from this viewpoint the "Jesus Psalter," attributed to Whytford, was an instrument for volitionally ordering each day, outwardly and inwardly, "Jesu give me grace to order my life and the works of my body and soul with actual intent, finally to Thee" (*Iesus Psalter* [Antwerp 1575], sig. Dii^v).

73. *Peters* 328ff.; cf. *Golden Pystle,* sig. Biii^r with *Longridge* 100–108.

74. Cf. *Martz* passim; *Dickens* 192–96.

75. Cf. Index: 'the monastery within.'

76. *W* sigs. Ai^v–ii^r; cf. Avii^r.

77. *A Werke* (London 1537, R. Redman), sig. Aviii$^{r–v}$, part of the exercise cited above, n. 72.

78. *W* sig. Dviii^r; cf. above, 57, 61, 144–45.

79. Cf. Index: craft; order.

80. *W* sig (Hx$^{r–v}$); cf. above, 81, 136 and Index: death, remembrance of.

81. Cf. J. Needleman, *A Sense of the Cosmos* (New York 1975), 159–62.

82. Cf. *D* sigs. Aiii^{v}–iiii^{r}, Bii^{r-v}, Bvii^{r}.

83. Ibid. sig. Bii^{r}.

84. On the eight works, eight days of Creation, eight Beatitudes and eight kinds of knowledge arising from meditation; *D* sig. Bvii^{r}·

85. Cf. *D* sig. Ev^{v}, "you must . . . chew your cud again" ("mastication," cf. Index: *masticatio;* preparation); "perseverance" was one of his favourite words; cf. *HI* 46^{v}.

86. *Early Fathers Philokalia,* 171; for other parallels with Desert asceticism; cf. Index: Desert Fathers and cf. *Iesus Psalter* (Antwerp 1575), sigs. Dv^{v}–vii^{r} with *Philokalia on Prayer of the Heart,* 143ff.; Whytford's "additions" to the Syon martyrology are preponderantly saints of the 'desert,' English, Gallic, Celtic and, especially, the Desert Fathers of the Near East, *Martiloge Proctor and Dewick,* xiii–iv; cf. folios vi^{v}, xxxvii^{v}, xli^{r}, lxxii^{v}, ciii^{r}, cvii^{r}, cxvii^{v}, cxxi^{v}, cxxxiii^{r}).

87. *D* sigs. Aiv^{v}–vi^{r}, quoted at Av^{v}; for the subsequent prayer, "into Your hands," cf. *DE* fii^{v}–iii^{r}, *W* Aiii^{v}, above, 179; on "attendance in the heart," cf. *Blunt* 49–50, below, 122, 223–24, 228.

88. Cf. *W* sigs. Aiii^{v}–vi^{r} and above, n. 72.

89. *D* sigs. Bi^{v}–ii^{r}.

90. Cf. ibid. sig. fi^{r}; below, n. 95.

91. *D* sigs. Cvii^{r}–viii^{v}, quoted at Cvii^{v}; cf. Index: contemplation & contemplative life.

92. *D* sig. Cviii^{r}; cf. Dvi^{r}; cf. above, 96–97, chap. 6 passim.

93. *D* sig. Dii^{v}; cf. Index: *imitatio Christi.*

94. *D* sig. Eiiii^{v}, "the most high & most profitable science . . . is self–knowledge, which is . . . when a person by diligent & oft used meditation is illumined & lightened unto the very perceiving & knowledge of himself," citing Augustine as authority; for the pure in heart; cf. Ei^{v}.

95. Ibid. sigs. Evii^{v}–fii^{r}, defining compunction as "a joined pricking or striking," and devotion as "a religious, faithfull & meek affection inwardly & perfectly unto God . . . meek and lowly by the conscience and full knowledge of our proper infirmity . . . religious and faithfull by the consideration of the . . . merciful gentleness of our Lord," drawing on Isidore, Augustine and Hugh of St. Victor; cf. *HI* 58^{v}; *Longridge* 45 for the secret striking of the breast to mark a moment of self–awareness and compunction; also Index: compunction; conscience; devotion.

96. Cf. above, 156–59 and Index: the heart; love.

97. *D* sigs. fii^{v}–iii^{r}: "Surely to say or read alone without thought is little worth. To think alone is very good: but both is best . . . [the purpose of the *confiteor* is to] stir up your mind . . . that you understand and perceive well what you say or think"; cf. J. A. Jungmann, *The Mass of the Roman Rite* (New York 1951–55), vol. 1, 298–311, and on the influence of the New Devotion, 275–76; *cf.* also below, 243–44 and Index: attention; liturgy.

98. *D* sigs. hi^{r}–ii^{r}; cf. *Wessel 2* 3–70; above, 105–8 and Index: *conformitas Christi.*

99. *D* sigs. Gvi^{v}ff.; cf. *DE* Evi^{v}–fiii^{v}; Index: 'the way in life.'

100. *D* sigs Ci^v–ii^r.

101. Cf. Francis of Assisi, "our sister, the death of the body, which no living man can escape; doomed are they only who die in a state of mortal sin, while blessed are they who have done God's holy will, for no harm shall be done them by the second death" ([G.] Duby, [*The Age of the Cathedrals*, London 1981], 164); Anthony the Great, "let us awake from sleep while we are still in the body" (*Early Fathers Philokalia*, 54); the saying of Mohammed, "die before you die" ([S. H.] Nasr [*Living Sufism*, London 1980,] 35).

102. *DE* sig. Aii^v and passim.

103. Cf. *Duby* 239–48; *Huizinga* 134–46; L. P. Kurtz, *The Dance of Death* (New York 1934), passim.

104. *DE* sigs. Ciiii^v, Aii^r, Aiii^v, Bv^{r-v}; cf. *Bonde*, passim on "servile fear."

105. Above, n. 42; Whytford is less systematic and more affective, less ruthlessly concerned with wholeness.

106. *DE* sigs. Bvii^v–viii^r.

107. Ibid. sig. Cvi^r, quoting the *Hermetica*; cf. above, 74–75, below, 217.

108. *DE* sigs. Cv^v–vi^r; cf. *D* Ci^v–ii^r.

109. *DE* sigs. Cvii^{r-v}; cf. *Nasr* 23.

110. *DE* sigs. Dii^v–iiii^r, quoted at Diiii^r.

111. Ibid. sigs. Diiii^r–vi^v, Eiiii^{r-v}, echoing Neoplatonic ideas: "To depart then the soul from the body and to render and put either unto his proper and natural place is the very practise of death . . . this exercise stands all in contemplation . . . for between natural death and this death of contemplation, is little difference" (Diiii^v–v^v); cf. *D* Cvii^v; Evagrius [Ponticus, *The Praktikos & Chapters on Prayer*, tr. J. E. Bamberger (Kalamazoo 1981)], 30:52: "To separate the body from the soul is the privilege only of the One who has joined them together. But to separate the soul from the body lies as well in the power of the man who pursues virtue. For our Fathers gave to the meditation of death and to the flight from the body a special name: *anachoresis* (literally withdrawal, but very early a technical description of the monastic life).

112. Cf. *DE* sigs. Cviii^v–Evi^r.

113. Below, 214, 226, 228 and Index: death, remembrance of; cf. *DE* sigs Diiii^{r}ff. and the third method in Ludolph [of Saxony, *The Hours of the Passion*, ed H. J. C. (London 1887)], 24–25; also the monastic prayer, *DE* sigs. Diii^v, fiii^{r-v}.

114. Ibid. sig. fi^r.

115. Ibid. sigs. Evi^v–fiii^v; More conversed with Elizabeth Barton at Syon, *More Letters* 197–99; *Reynolds* 140.

116. Cf. *HI* 3^r, 16^v ("the right possession of his heart and mind," the mind being "at home," cf. *Luke* 21:19), 18^{r-v}, 19^v, 21^r, 42^v, 47^v–8^v (connected specifically with the exercise of Passion meditation, "in this life if you in all . . . troubles turn & apply your heart, mind & thought unto the . . . example of our Saviour Jesu"); on life as teacher, cf. Index: 'the way in life.'

117. Cf. *HI* 44^r–5^r, a barely veiled reference to the persecution of the religious and their

betrayal by their fellows; *Pacience*, although written earlier (cf. sig. Aii^r), was quite possibly revised for publication in 1541, by which time he was under the protection of his old patrons, the Mountjoys (*RO3* 221; *McConica* 205, 266); the signature at 48^V ("a late brother") may as well refer to his departure thence as to his death; cf. also *Caraman* 5 n. 3; *Martiloge Proctor and Dewick*, xxiii.

118. *HI* 51^{r-v}; cf. 69^r for the mingling of prayer, labour, reading, meditation and contemplation—"use them interchangeable, now from one unto another, and so without weariness you shall go forth with great ease, pleasure and profit in all of them"—which might have come from the writings of the Brotherhood; cf. Index: prayer.

119. *HI* 66^r–85^V; P. J. Mullins *The Spiritual Life according to St. Isidore of Seville* (Washington, D.C. 1940), 169–72, 191; cf. Index: contemplation & contemplative life.

120. Cf. *HI* 47^{r-v}; *W* sigs. Bi^V–ii^r; of his audience he says (*HI* 35^V) "I presuppose that you be the lovers of Christ" and wear His livery (ibid. 39^V; cf. 43^V–44^r).

121. *HI* 20^r, "every brother and faithful Christian has cure and charge of other"; cf. 18^r; above, 81, 136 and Index: 'the common life.'

122. *HI* 18^r–21^V, a division of oneself which is the opposite of hypocrisy (ibid. 23^V–24^r); the head of a household is being tacitly referred to the obligations of the abbot and at 24^V the opening words of the *Regula Benedicti* are echoed; cf. also above, n. 68.

123. *HI* 1^r–3^r, 15^V, 21^r.

124. Ibid. 3^V, 62^r; cf. 47^V "importunate labour does vanquish & overcome all things" (also *W* sig. Bii^V; above, 235); cf. also *LER* sig. Diiii^{r-v}; *P* xli^V, cxcvi^V–viii^V; [R.] Baxter, [*The Saints Everlasting Rest* (London 1653)], 116–17; Index: "violence"; *Ward* 67 no. 1.

125. *HI* 26^V–29^r, 40^r–42^r, 46^r; on the *apatheia* (passionlessness) of the Desert Fathers, see Index: *apatneia*, and the revealing story from the Desert quoted in *HI* 8^r.

126. Ibid. 22^V, 24^V, 47^V; cf. Index: *fac quod in se est.*

127. *HI* 26^{V}ff.

128. Ibid. 28^r.

129. Ibid. 41^{r-v}; cf. 51^{r-v} on not acting for results.

130. Ibid. 23^V, 25^r; cf. above, 190–91.

131. Ibid. 42^V; cf. Index: purification of emotion.

132. *HI* 22^r; cf. *2 Thess.* 3:10; he talks throughout of the "school of patience"; cf. above, xiv and Index: craft.

133. Ibid. 22^V–25^r; cf. *Crossrowe* sig. Iv^{r-v}.

134. *HI* 47^{r-v}.

135. Ibid. 18^r, "some can bear their sovereigns and superiors, but not their equals or inferiors; and some can suffer or bear their friends, but not their foes or enemies; and yet some can better bear their enemies than any other persons; and few men can bear all persons."

136. Cf. Index: sin.

137. *HI* 48^{r-v}, 16^V; cf. 8^r; below, 207.

138. *HI* 25^V–26^V (cf. *Luke* 16:8), 7^V–8^r, 21^V–26^V; and Index: craft.

139. Cf. Index: duality; the New Devotion.

140. Above n. 3; the *Manuall* has the same shape and similar prayers to the *Dyurnall*, but is more elaborate (cf. *Manuall* 9–10; *Dyurnall*, sig. aiiii^r); cf. *[The Psalter of Sainct] Hierome* [(Antwerp 1576)], sig. Di^{r-v}.

141. *Manuall* 4–5: [upon awakening in the morning] "'Lighten mine eyes O Lord, lest at any time I oversleep in sin and lest mine enemies do say, I have prevailed against him' . . . when you are apparelled, give not yourself presently to babbling or jangling, or to vain fancies: but lift up your heart unto God in silence and prepare yourself to say these prayers . . . [after prayer corresponding to the Brethren's *intentio*] you shall purpose firmly and constantly in yourself, not to commit willingly that day anything whereby God or your neighbour might be offended . . . it shall be very necessary besides these aforesaid, to call to mind your affairs & with quickness of spirit set down with yourself how to spend the day to come."

142. *Hierome* sig. Ai^V (*A dayly Exercise* occupies Cv^r–Dviii^V).

143. *Hierome* sig. Cv^r; cf. *Dyurnall* aiii^r; *Manuall* 8–9; *This Prymer of Salysbury use* (Paris 1534), ciiii^V; *Peryn* Avi^V–vii^r.

144. *Hierome* sigs. Cvii^V–viii^r, "when in the morning, at noon, or at night the bell tolls to the saying of the angelical salutation say . . ."; cf. above, 140, 146.

145. *Hierome* sig. Cviii^V; cf. *T3* 73; above, 142; cf. also the prayer for the end of work, *Hierome* Cviii^V–Di^r.

146. *New Catholic Encyclopaedia* (New York 1967), vol. 5, 523.

147. *Peryn* sig. Ovii^{r-v}; cf. above, 105.

148. C. Kirchberger, *The Spiritual Exercises of a Dominican Friar* (London 1957), 15, 66.

149. Cf. ibid. 86–87, 9.

150. Cf. *Peryn* sigs. ki^r–iv^V with *D* Bvii^r–viii^r and *Longridge* 57–58, 63.

151. *Peryn* sig. Aii^r.

152. Ibid. sig. Rv^r.

153. Cf. Index: self-knowledge.

154. *Peryn* sig. Dviii^V.

155. Cf. Index: prayer.

156. *Peryn* sigs. Aiii^r, Aiv^V–v^r; cf. above, 17–18, 46–50.

157. Cf. *Peryn* sig. Aiii^V.

158. Ibid. sig. Aii^V.

159. *The Writings of John Bradford*, ed. A. Townsend (Cambridge 1848–53), vol. 1, 221–47, based on the *Excitationes animi in Deum* by the humanist Vives.

160. *Prayers and other pieces of Thomas Becon*, ed. J. Ayre (Cambridge 1844), 1–70.

161. Quoted in [J.] Needleman [*Lost Christianity* (New York 1980)], 129; cf. Index: listening; *lectio divine*.

162. *Needleman* 129–30.

163. Cf. Index: 'godly vocation.'

164. Cf. above, 127–28, 138–39 and Index: Christianity; consciousness.

165. Cf. [P.] Janelle [*Robert Southwell the Writer* (London 1935)], 252–53, 284–85; *Counter-Reformation* 63–90, 185–88, 200; *Martz* 122–23.

166. *D[ictionary of] N[ational] B[iography]*, vol. 20, 150–55; [R. Fox], *Contemplacyon [of Synners* (London 1499)], sig. Aii^r; *Letters of Richard Fox*, ed. P. S. and H. M. Allen (Oxford 1929), 93; he refers perhaps to the French war, with the outbreak of which he had been diplomatically involved.

167. Cf. above, 116–17, 126 and Index: "I am."

168. *Contemplacyon*, sigs. Aii^r–iii^r.

169. Ibid. sig. Aiii^v, Aiiii^v; cf. above, 66.

170. Cf. above, n. 58; for Foxe's translation, see Bibliography.

171. *Contemplacyon*, sigs. Aiii^r–iiii^v ("spedeful" is almost impossible to transliterate: conducive to success and prosperity, is etymologically closest); a long passage recommending "scripture" in general, refers finally to the special "prerogative" of Holy Scripture, but Bible reading had become so widespread by 1578 that the Elizabethan version makes almost all this refer to Holy Scripture by judicial insertion (*A dyall [of dayly contemplacyon*, London 1578], 4–5).

172. *Contemplacyon*, sigs. Av^r–vi^r, Bi^r, Diiii^r, Fiiii^r, Giiii^r, Ivi^r, Mii^r, Oi^r; cf. above, 189–90.

173. *A dyall*, sigs. Cvi^r–vii^r; cf. *Contemplacyon*, Dii$^{r–v}$.

174. *Contemplacyon*, sigs. Aiiii^v–v^r; White, *Private Devotion*, 60, 67, 86.

175. *Contemplacyon*, sig. Avi$^{r–v}$, a paragraph omitted from *A dyall*.

176. *Blunt* 40.

177. *Contemplacyon*, sigs. Av^v–vi^r; cf. Jvi^r–Mi^r on Passion meditation and Index: meditation.

178. Cf. *Contemplacyon*, sigs. Ciii^v–iiii^r; *A dyall*, Cii^r; the "instruction for kings" is at Biiii^v of *Contemplacyon*, while *A dyall* has only general classical texts illustrating the point.

179. *A dyall*, sig. Ai^r; meditations on the Days of Creation through the week are also given in *D* Cvii^r–Diii^v.

180. *Janelle* 151–52, 155: completed before 1592, *A Short Rule* was intended for the Countess of Arundel, who was in his spiritual care, but was revised for general use and published after his death.

181. [R.] Southwell, [*A Short Rule* (London 1622)], "The Preface to the Reader," 3–7.

182. Ibid. 15–16; cf. *Longridge* 26; man's true purpose according to the New Devotion and the Jesuits was just to serve God.

183. *Southwell* 90–91, 95–97, 98–105, on education 101–3.

184. Ibid. 67–68.

185. Ibid. 91; cf. *Aungier* 375; *Rule* xxiv.

186. *Southwell* 62–63; cf. the 'puritanical' instructions at 54–55 with *Aungier* 297–99, and above, n. 68.

187. *Southwell* 65–67.

188. Ibid. 71–73; he particularly recommends, 13–14, Parson's *The Exercise of a Christian Life.*

189. *Southwell* 76.

190. Ibid. 144–45; cf. above, 133.

191. Ibid. 81; cf. William of St. Thierry quoted above, 46.

192. *Southwell* 74.

193. Ibid. 75–76; cf. above, 179, 183.

194. *Southwell* 78–79.

195. Cf., for example, above, n. 118 and Index: attention; manual work; prayer.

196. *Southwell* 80–82; cf. Index: order of daily life, and *Thomas* 258, speaking of Arnold of Schoonhoven, "he awoke instantly and arose with alacrity and then, before the bed on bended knees, he said a short prayer, fervently pouring forth the first fruits of his mouth to the Lord."

197. For the proverb, cf. above, 20; *Southwell* 65; cf. *Blunt* 63.

198. Cf. Index: "violence."

199. *Southwell* 28–31; cf. Index: Christ; meditation.

200. *Southwell* 172, 170; cf. Index: *conformitas Christi.*

201. Ibid. 29.

202. Ibid. 144; cf. Index: prayer.

203. *Southwell* 139.

204. Ibid. 112–13; cf. *Bonde* xvii[r–v] where "sin" is consenting inwardly to that which automatically moves our "corrupt nature," and not consenting involves an inward disengagement, with results described as "pain" and "merit": "wisely and discreetly we must resist them, but in no wise wrestle with them . . . reason not . . . but use this medicine. Suspend your reason, restrain all your senses and pluck up all your spirits, and as the motion comes, so let it pass without without strife." Opposition to the use of "reason" in this situation suggests the emotional nature of the Monastic Way; cf. Index: the heart; Way of the Monk.

205. *Southwell* 140–42.

206. *Evagrius* 29–30, and for his influence on the Middle Ages, xiii–ix.

207. *Southwell* 140–42.

208. *Needleman* 156, 167.

209. *PL* 41:788–92 and cf. Index: duality.

210. *Southwell* 145; cf. Index: perseverance; search, man's.

CHAPTER NINE

1. Cf. Index: "Fall of man."

2. *Askesis* (exercises, gymnastics) translated as asceticism, has the sense of training for self–control in art, craft, trade or athletics (*Lacarriere* 28–29; *Early Fathers Philokalia* 18; and *Evagrius* lxxxi–vii, where it refers to "the spiritual method whose aim it is to purify the part of the soul that is the seat of the passions," 70 "train yourself like a skilled athlete," 3–4, where it is defined as the method of the *active life*, as below, n. 255); cf. Index: asceticism; craft; monastery, the medieval.

3. Cf. above, n. 2, Index: spiritual work and *Early Fathers Philokalia*, 71, 171, 210 and passim.

4. Cf. Index: monastic vow; "spiritual ascents."

5. Cf. above, 133, 148; and *William of St. Thierry*, xlix–l.

6. Cf. Index: 'the monastery within'; 'the way in life'; 'the world' ; Jacobus de Voragine *The Golden Legend*, ed. F. S Ellis (London 1892), vol. 1, 333, "a man demanded of Saint Anthony what he might do to please God, and he answered over all where you shall be, or shall go, have God before your eyes & the holy scripture, and hold yourself in one place all still."

7. *RO2* 175–82; *Incendium Amoris*, 91–130; *Aungier* 25–30.

8. *RO2* 175; cf. *PP* xxvi^v–vii^r: "now in the last end of the world, when man is most weak & the world, the flesh & the devil most mighty & strong, He [Christ] has added to all these foresaid graces [the established religious orders] . . . this holy religion of men & women, under one rule, of one religion, of one concord & love, & of one life & heart, but distinct or dissevered into divers companies, daily labouring in the holy pilgrimage of perfection, for to come to the high Jerusalem. . . . No religion is founded hitherto, that so near represents the primitive church of Christ . . . what may all this represent . . . but the congregation of the holy apostles, which after the ascension of our Lord were with the mother of God & the other holy women, in one parlour continually persevering in prayer, unto the coming of the Holy Ghost"; and cf. cclix^r.

9. *Blunt* 1–2; cf. 147–48.

10. *Post* 311; cf. Index: observant reform.

11. *RO2* 179–80, 220, 222, 367–68; *Incendium Amoris* 118–24; R. M. Clay *The Hermits and Anchorites of England* (London 1914), 144, 112; *Martiloge Proctor and Dewick*, xxx–xxxi; *Allen passim*; cf. Symon Anker, *The Fruyte of redempcyon* (London 1532, eds. 1514, 1517, 1530, STC 2257–59), attributed to Whytford, which deals with Passon meditation and refers frequently to Bridget's works; for the influence of Rolle, cf. Index: Rolle, Richard.

12. *Incendium Amoris*, 110; *RO2* 261, 347; *RO3* 213; *Aungier* 26–27.

13. Cf. *Aungier* 301, 24–25, 318; *RO2* 261; *RO3* 212.

14. Quoted above, 44–45, linking the Observant Franciscans and Carthusians with Syon.

15. *Aungier* 21–24, 312–16; on other symbolisms, cf. *Blunt* 11, 14–15, 99ff., 147, 206, 303–5; on Passion meditation, Index: Brigettines; meditation, *Pourrat*, vol. 2, 319.

16. *Aungier* 17–20; *RO2* 175–76, *PP* xxi^v, "although she were not in the professed habit of religion, yet in heart & work she was all religious, for all her life was poverty, chastity & obedience" (cf. cli^v–ii^r); *Petry* 392.

17. *New Catholic Encyclopaedia* (New York 1967), vol. 9, 1021; cf. above, 85, 88.

18. *Incendium Amoris* 81; *Bateson* ix.

19. Cf. *Aungier* 435–38, 85, 87, 430–33, *D. & G. Mathew* 299; *LP* 7, pt. 2, 421–22, no. 1090; *LP* 8, 25–27, no. 78; *LP* 9, 332, no. 986; *RO3* 216–21.

20. *RO2* 181.

21. *RO3* 215.

22. *Incendium Amoris* 95, 101.

23. Ibid. 51–54, 78, 95–105; *Allen* 411–12, 414, 416; *RO2* 176–77; the first two confessors general of Syon were Northern hermits, *RO2* 179–80.

24. *McConica* 55–56, 63, 67, 81; cf. *Aungier* 74–76.

25. *DNB*, vol. 4, 48–49, *McConica* 55; W. E. Axon in *The Library*, new series 8 (1907), 34–41.

26. Cf. H. Thurston in *The Month*, vol. 100, no. 458 (1902), 189–203.

27. *O'Connor* 19 n. 39; *Aungier* 245; White, *Private Devotion*, 216.

28. Cf. above, 77, below 218, 229, 235, *McConica* 56, 65, 81; Sutton co–founded Brasenose College, Oxford.

29. Ibid. 56, 81 and above, 186, below, 222, 229–39.

30. *RO3* 212, recording the likes of Scrope, Campion, Strickland, Windsor, Nevill, Brereton, Conyers, Vaux, Fitzherbert, Bourchier, Newdigate and Montague; cf. also *Aungier* 81, 89–90; cf. 80.

31. Ibid. 81; *DNB*, vol. 58, 55–56.

32. *RO2* 125–26.

33. Ibid. 130, 219–22.

34. *Owst* 52 n. 2; *Aungier* 421–22, 426, 530; *Bateson* C39, O79–87, xxiv; *LP* 7, pt. 2, 421–22, no. 1090.

35. *Aungier* 24; out of the twenty-five male Bridgettines, eight were lay–brethren.

36. Cf. above, 110 and Index: Brotherhood of the Common Life.

37. R. W. Southern, *The Making of the Middle ages* (London 1959) 165–66.

38. *Pourrat*, vol. 2, 330 n. 2; *Aungier* 273–74, 364–65, 422.

39. Ibid. 426 n. 1; cf. 422; *Owst* 52 n. 2.

40. Cf. *Aungier* 90, 527; *Bateson* xxvi.

41. Cf. Index: silence.

42. *RO2* 245 n. 6; cf. *RO3* 92, quoting Abbot Kidderminster of Winchcombe in 1523, "it was a fine sight to see how the brethren devoted themselves to sacred learning, how they

made use of Latin even in their familiar conversations"; Winchcombe made a translation of the *Regula Benedicti* (ibid.).

43. Cf. *Coulton* 145, 212, 334.

44. *RO2* 245 n. 6; *RO3* 67–68, 85.

45. R. Fox, *Rule of seynt Benet* (London 1516?), sig. Aii^r; *Richardinus* 28; cf. 74; *Coulton* 409–22, 608; *LER* sig. Aiii^r, iv^r; cf. Index: monastic rules.

46. *Bateson* ix and n. 1, but cf. *Aungier* 388.

47. *Bateson* ix; *Incendium Amoris*, 81.

48. *Blunt* 49, 71; there was a mid–fourteenth–century processionale in Syon's library with English rubrics (ibid. xl); cf. Rolle's views on translation in his introduction to the *English Psalter*, "in this work I seek no strange English, but lightest and commonest," *English Writings of Richard Rolle*, ed. H. E. Allen (Oxford 1931), 7, and Whytford's in *HI* 81^r, *ER* sigs. Aii^v–iii^r, P ccxx^v.

49. But cf. *Blunt* 71, "looking on the English while the Latin is read, is to be understood of them that have said their matins or read their legend before . . . else I would not counsel them to leave the hearing of the Latin for attendance of the English"; cf. also [*The Cambridge History of the Bible*, ed. G. W. H.] Lampe [(Cambridge 1969), vol. 2,] 384, "by the fourteenth century hearing without understanding latin services was accorded a sacramental value."

50. *Blunt* xl, 71.

51. *Bateson* xv; *Lampe* 414; *LP* 4, pt. 2, 1883–84, no. 4282.

52. Cf. above, 58.

53. *Bateson* ix, 244.

54. Ibid. ix; the brethren were older (at least 25) and better educated (often at Cambridge) than the sisters (cf. *RO3* 213).

55. *Aungier* 364–65; *Bateson* xiii–xv.

56. Cf. Index: Bridgettines; the vernacular.

57. Cf. Index: Bridgettines and *Aungier* 58.

58. Latin translations by Ficino, Trapezuntius, Argyropoulos, Theodore of Gaza, Hermolous Barbarus, Poggio and Erasmus (including his New Testament); original works by Salutati, Bruni, Poggio, Bessarion, Platina, Poliziano, Mafeo Vegio, Pico della Mirandola, Ficino, Petrarch (as devotional writer), Boccaccio, Savonarola, Lefevre d'Etaples, Reuchlin, Cusanus, More, Linacre, Colet and a good collection of classical Latin poetry (cf. *Bateson* viii–ix, C2, 3, 7, D118, G24, 32, H36, C9, 45, 11, B9, K61, H50–53, 56, 57, I6, 54, G12, C15, 26, 13, N37, D49, N3, 41, O49, S69, C5, B55, K37, S67, C4, O49, 41–42, B27, C2, N37, O48, C6, R51, M107, G24, A16, O17, G12, B10, N26, not an exhaustive list); cf. also *RO2* 343–44, 347–48.

59. *RO2* 347; *RO3* 213; cf. *Bateson* xxiii–vii for their donations.

60. Ibid. C2, 3, 6, 7, 13, 15, 18, B10, 49, 55 (not exhaustive).

61. Ibid., index and supplement.

62. *RO2* 219.

63. *Bateson* M27, 226, 258; *Allen* 49, 411–12.

64. Ibid. 412, 416, 528.

65. *Blunt* 3.

66. *Allen* 216; *Incendium Amoris* 78–83; Martin V's bull ratifying Syon's foundation had stated that Henry V wished to provide "opportunities for secular or regular priests, even of the Carthusian order, to minister to the enclosed at Syon" (ibid. 128); the Carthusians tended to attract mature men with formed dispositions, like the Bridgettine brethren (*RO2* 138; above, n. 54).

67. *Bonde* xiii^r; cf. xxvii^v; cf. above, 90–91, 93–94, below, 237, 239–45.

68. Cf. above, 185.

69. *The Folowyng of Christe* (but cf. *RO3* 221) and *Crossrowe* (ascribed to Bonaventure, but identical to the *Alphabetum Religiosorum* ascribed to Kempis in *Richardinus* 179ff. and in *T2* 686–89, where it is called *Alphabetum parvum monachi in schola Christi*); cf. *RO2* 347; *Bateson* A54 where *Opuscula felicis Hemmerlyn* is taken to refer to the Swiss historian Felix Haemmerlin (ibid. 252) in ignorance of the fact that Kempis was also known as Haemmerlein or Hemerken (the title page refers to *Crossrowe* as an "opuscule, sig. Iii^r).

70. Cf. *HI* 47^r; Index: John Climachus.

71. *Bateson* N87.

72. Cf. Index: Bridgettines; Franciscans, observant; mystical tradition, medieval; spiritual exercises, transmission of.

73. *RO2* 136–37, 223–24, 343–44; *Thompson* chaps. 9–10; for Bridget in Carthusian libraries, ibid. 326, 329, and for their interest in Rolle, ibid. 325, 329; *RO2* ibid.; *Incendium Amoris* 51–54; *Allen* 50.

74. *RO2* 223–26; the Windesheim Congregation was formed in 1394–95 (*Post* 310–11).

75. *RO2* 175, 223–26; J. H. Wylie, *The Reign of Henry the Fifth* (Cambridge 1914), vol. 1, 215–16.

76. D. & G. *Mathew*, 228–29.

77. Cf. also *RO2* 175, 180–81; *D. & G. Mathew* 227–28; both had foreign superiors and connections, and drew support from land and capital released by the recent suppression of the alien priories. Cf. further, *Aungier* 21, 533, 537–38; *Bateson* xxv; *Blunt* xxiii n. 1.

78. *Blunt* 59–60.

79. *Tyndale* 81; cf. *RO2* 181; *Wylie* 229; and for liturgical co–operation on the continent, cf. *D. & G. Mathew* 228–29. On the choreographical precision of Syon's observance, *Aungier* 320, "In the choir all shall be as angels inclining together, rising together, kneeling together, standing, turning and sitting together, all after one form going and coming together"; also 273–76, 323ff., 359; *Blunt* xxxviii.

80. *Thompson* 332; cf. *Bateson* M50, 100, R31, 219.

81. Cf. above, 186.

82. *Thompson* 332; cf. 337; *Bateson* M60–63: "an excellent example of the English mysticism of the late Middle Ages" (*Allen* 405–6).

83. *Blunt* 28; *HI* 46ᵛ.

84. Cf. above, 6; *Dibdin* 21–22; *Allen* 405–6.

85. Ibid. and Index: Holy Name, cult of; for MSS at Shene on the Name, *Thompson* 332.

86. *RO3* 207.

87. *Coulton* 729; Index: Bridgettines, Franciscans, observant.

88. *ER* sig. Aivᵛ.

89. *RO3* 212, 227 and n. 5; *D. & G. Mathew* 294 n. 124.

90. Cf. above, n. 19.

91. *Aungier* 430–33; *RO3* 220.

92. Cf. Index: "Jericho"; love; order; virtue; *W* sig. Avᵛ; *D* sigs. Cviiiʳ⁻ᵛ.

93. *Ward* 35 no. 3; cf. 10 no. 9, 143 no. 5; for Syon's relationship with the Desert Fathers (resembling the New Devotion's), *PP* ccxlviiᵛ–ixʳ, xxviᵛ.

94. Cf. Index: spiritual work.

95. [Richard of St. Victor,] *Benjamin Minor* [tr. S. V. Yankowski (Ansbach 1960)], 10–11.

96. Florence Radewijns, above, 82 and Index: devotion; cf. *William of St. Thierry* 19–20; *D* sig. Fiʳ.

97. *William of St. Thierry* 20; cf. *2 Tim.* 3:5 (Vulgate).

98. Perhaps written by Thomas Gascoign, the chaplain of Sir Hugh Fitzhugh and the biographer of Bridget, her confessor–amanuensis and daughter; published (*STC* 17542) at the wishes of Abbess Jordan and Confessor Fewterer (*Blunt* ix).

99. *Blunt* 21; cf. above, 195; *The Spiritual Exercises of St. Ignatius of Loyola*, ed. J. Rickaby (London 1915), "it is not in our power to bring on or maintain a flood of devotion, intense love, tears nor any other spiritual consolation; but that it is all a gift and grace of God our Lord," together with his definition of spiritual exercises as methods of "preparing and disposing the soul to remove from herself all disorderly attachments" (71, 73); cf. *Bonde* ixʳ; *Fewterer* fo. vᵛ; *Baxter* 118.

100. *PP* lxxiiʳ.

101. *Aungier* 19, 20, 22, 313, 525–27; *Blunt* 14, 5–6; H. Thurston in *The Month*, vol. 100, no. 458 (1902), 189–203; cf. *Coulton* 161.

102. Cf. *Blunt* 1, 6.

103. Ibid. 2, 4; cf. above, 61–72.

104. *Blunt* 1–2; cf. 147–48; and on the awakening of our faculties, cf. Index: sleep.

105. Ibid. 2–3; only a few of the Psalms are translated, for they already have them in Rolle's English and the vernacular scriptures, if they have a licence to read them.

106. Ibid. 49; "entendaunce," attending in the sense of hearing and understanding (*O.E.D.*); cf. below, n. 273 and Bernard quoted by R. Lawlor in *Parabola*, vol. 3, no. 1 (1978), 16: "in matters of faith, and in order to know the truth, the hearing is superior to vision. . . . You must know that the holy Spirit, in order to cause a soul to advance in spirituality . . . educates the hearing before coming to the vision. 'Listen, holy child,' he says,

'and see.' Why do you strain to see? It is necessary to lend the ear. The hearing, moreover, will restore vision to us, if our attention is pious, faithful and vigilant. Only the hearing attains to truth because it perceives the verb [Word]. And thus one must awaken the hearing and train it to receive the truth"; also Index: attention; listening, and Whytford's addition to the text in *HI* 73^V–74^r, "yet (in my opinion) the wit of hearing should be taken for the chief wit among Christians. . . . "

107. *Blunt* 8, "you that feel simply in your own wits & love to be informed."

108. Ibid. 23, 8, 40, 49, 73, 77, and for the *horarium*, 22, 51–54; cf. Index: food; scale; the soul; *lectio divina* and *D* sig. Ev^V; *Fewterer* fo. iiii^V.

109. *Blunt* 49; cf. 23, 39–40, 50 and 48, for the sleeping monk being led from the choir by an angel disguised as an old man, who asked him as he began to awaken, "whither comest thou to church, to sleep or to wake?"; for *The Meditations of Saint Bernard*'s usage, above, 125–26.

110. Cf. n. 106 above, and *Ward* 182 no. 107: "One day Abba Isaac was sitting beside Abba Poemen when they heard a cock crow. Abba Isaac said to him, 'Is it possible to hear that here, Abba?' He replied, 'Isaac, why do you make me talk? You and those like you hear those noises, but the vigilant man does not trouble about them.'"

111. Cf. ibid. 95 no. 46: "the brethren came to him to ask him about their thoughts. One of the elders said, 'John, you are like a courtesan who shows her beauty to increase the number of her lovers.' Abba John kissed him and said, 'You are quite right, Father.' One of his disciples said to him, 'Do you not mind that in your heart?' But he said, 'No, I am the same inside as I am outside'"; cf. Index: inner & outer life.

112. *Blunt* 5–6, 49; cf. 4, 22, 44, 46; *PP* clviii^V, clxviii^r; Augustine's Rule in *PL* 32:1379; *LER* sig. Dvii^V.

113. Cf. above, Index: attention, *LER* sig. Dvii$^{r–V}$; *Ward* 10 no. 9, "Strive with all your might to bring your interior activity into accord with God, and you will overcome exterior passions."

114. A traditional aphorism, often associated with Bernard; cf. Index: *orare est laborare*; *Notes and Queries*, 6th series, vol. 11 (1885), 477–78, where the following texts are given: "You beseech in prayer, you protect yourself and you work" (*Carminium Proverbialium Loci Communes*, London 1558), "'Let us raise our heart with our hands to God.' He who prays and works, raises his heart to God with his hands; he who truly prays and does not work, raises his heart to God and not his hands; he, however, who works and does not pray, raises his hands to God and not his heart. Therefore, . . . it is necessary to raise the heart to God in prayer, and to extend the hands in work to God" (Bernard on *Lam.* 3:41), "'and my prayer returned into mine own bosom,' and he who prays for another, works for himself" (Radulphus Ardens on *Ps.* 35:13); *Blunt* 90–91, 147–48 emphasises the balancing of action and contemplation.

115. *P* lxxix^V; cf. *Scala*, sig. aiiii^V "that the inner having of man's soul should be like to the outer"; *The Asian Journal of Thomas Merton*, ed. N. Burton, P. Hart and J. Laughlin (New York 1975), 64.

116. Cf. *Ward* 1–2 no. 1, 71 no. 6, 92 no. 32, 67 no. 8, 171 no. 27; Index: silence.

117. *Blunt* 42–43, 150; cf. *HI* 51^V–52^V.

118. *Blunt* 39; cf. 49 where four ways of strengthening attention are given, that is, to attend to the words without understanding, to attend to the literal sense, to "keep the mind" and attend to the inward understanding ("this is full hard to do continually . . . it gives great spiritual food to the soul if it be laboured discreetly in meek and clean conscience"), and lastly to attend to the correct form of the service (the easiest, hence "you are more bound thereto"); his main intention is to facilitate the third way (ibid. 49–50).

119. Cf. above, 128, 277 n. 14.

120. Cf. Index: attention, *PP* clx^{r}ff., "I shall declare . . . how many manner of attentions there be."

121. Blunt 40, citing Bernard and Isidore as sources.

122. Ibid. 41; cf. *LER* sig. Dvii$^{r–v}$; *HI* 47^V–8^r; *PP* clxii^r, clxiii^r, clxvi^r; *Blunt* 150, on dissensions among brethren "that be not in our power to escape always . . . yet it is in our power by grace not to consent wilfully to such stirrings," with which cf. Southwell quoted above, 207 and Index: perseverance; cf. also *Ward* 219 no. 38: "A brother asked Abba Sisoes, 'What shall I do, abba, for I have fallen?' The old man said to him, 'Get up again.' The brother said, 'I have got up again, but I have fallen again.' The old man said, 'Get up again and again.' So then the brother said, 'How many times?' The old man said, 'Until you are taken up either in virtue or in sin. For a man presents himself to judgement in the state in which he is found.'"

123. *Blunt* 45, 63; cf. 114–15 "work, so that that thing that the understanding knows [to be] evil and the will hates, be fled in deed . . . knowing of truth and right ruling of the will may not be but in a restful soul . . . good deeds may not be done without labour"; cf. Index: the Christian; liturgy; the mind; "violence."

124. G. Rupp, *Luther's Progress to the Diet of Worms* (New York 1964) 20, 29; cf. Index: "art is better than evil strength," "violence"; *Ward* 67 no. 1, "he is a monk who does violence to himself in everything," and 89 no. 18, *PP* cclxxxvii$^{r–v}$; there is a vivid example of this in Attar, *Muslim Saints and Mystics*, ed. A. J. Arberry (London 1979), 223.

125. On the 'first step,' cf. above, 126, 168–72, 221○22 and Index: religion.

126. *Blunt* 42, 50, 166; cf. *Bonde* v^r; *HI* 51^V–52^V.

127. *Blunt* 41; cf. *Bonde* xvi^V, xxiii^r; *PP* cxviii$^{r–v}$, clvii^{V}ff. identifying the dispersal of attention with the influence of the Devil.

128. *Blunt* 41–42; cf. Index: emotional life; prayer; sleep.

129. *Blunt* 42, 50; cf. *PP* clx^{r}–i^r, clxiii^r.

130. *Blunt* 50; cf. above, 183 and Index: grace.

131. *Blunt* 166, quoting Cassian; cf. Index: preparation; watching.

132. *HI* 51^V–2^V; cf. 56$^{r–v}$; *D* sig. Evii^V.

133. *Blunt* 42, "for evil custom, as Saint Augustine says, binds a man and as a burden bears him down"; cf. above, 119.

134. *Needleman* 138; *Ward* 249.

135. *Blunt* 43–44; above, n. 127; Bernard's exercise in this case, to "privily and continually" make the sign of the cross on one's breast, is given (cf. *PP* clviii^r, clxiii^r; above, 300 n. 95), evocative indeed for a man trying daily to meditate on the Passion, together with emphasising the need "perseverantly to labour to keep and to hold your mind upon our Lord and upon that [which] you say or sing"; for his influence; cf. *MBE* sigs. Cii^v–iii^r with *Blunt* 73–74; *MBE* Ciiii^v–Di^v with *Blunt* 39–50, 63–64; Dii^{r-v} and Cii^v–iii^r with 64–65 and 74; Diiii^{r-v} with 59–60; and cf. *Blunt* 27, 39–40, 44 and *Martz* passim.

136. Cf. *Blunt* 44, "Saint Bernard says the more effectual and speedful that prayer is, if it be done as it ought, the more fully and busily labours the malicious enemy to let [*i.e.* prevent] it"; and Index: The Devil.

Cf. *Eckhart* 73–74: "perfection in virtue comes from the struggle, as St. Paul says, 'Virtue is made perfect in weakness' (*2 Cor.* 12:9). The inclination to sin is not sin, but the will to sin is sin. . . . Indeed, if a man was well disposed and if he had the power to decide, he would not want the inclination to sin to die out in him, because without it man would be irresolute in every respect and in all his works"; cf. *Ward* 2 no. 5, "without temptations no–one can be saved," and 102 no. 3.

138. *Blunt* 63–64.

139. Cf. above, 146 and Index: order of daily life; and *Ecclus* 19:1, "he that despiseth small things shall fall by little and little" (Revised Version).

140. *DE* sig. Ciiii^v; Index: death, remembrance of.

141. *Blunt* 42–43; cf. above, 154–55, 221–22 and Index: conversion; *Golden Pystle*, sig. Bii^{r-v}; *PP* ccxxxv^r, ccxli^r; *Bonde* xx^{r-v}.

142. *Blunt* 43; cf. above, 145; *Ward* 230 no. 6, 210 no. 1.

143. Cf. *Blunt* 64–65.

144. Cf. *Matt.* 23:26, "cleanse first that which is within the cup and platter, that the outside of them may be clean also."

145. Cf. the very interesting story quoted in *Ward* 102 no. 3.

146. Cf. *Needleman*, passim, especially pt. 2, and below, 237–39.

147. Cf. *Ward* 161 no. 2, 186 no. 137, 2 no. 2, 178 no. 80, 210 no. 1; *Philokalia on Prayer of the Heart*, passim, especially 152–61: "he who does not have attention in himself and does not guard his mind, cannot become pure in heart and so cannot see God. He who does not have attention in himself cannot be pure in spirit, cannot weep and be contrite, nor be gentle and meek, nor hunger and thirst after righteousness, nor be merciful, nor a peacemaker, nor suffer persecution for righteousness' sake. Speaking generally, it is impossible to acquire virtue in any other way, except through this kind of attention" (St. Simeon the New Theologian, quoted at 158).

148. *Blunt* 64–65; Index: the heart.

149. *PL* 32:848–49: "Bodies move by their weight towards their own place: fire upwards, stone downwards. Our place is where we come to rest . . . my weight is my love: by it I am carried whithersoever it may be"; cf. *Burnaby* 106–7, *Przywara* 141; *PP* clxviii^r, "a man is more there, where his affection and love is, than where his body is."

150. *Philokalia on Prayer of the Heart*, 158–59: "Keep your mind there (in the heart), trying by every possible means to find the place where the heart is, in order that, having found it, your mind should constantly abide there. Wrestling thus, the mind will find the place of the heart" (St. Simeon).

151. *Blunt* 65; cf. *MBE* sigs. Dii^{r-v}, Cii^v–iii^r.

152. *PL* 32:661.

153. *Ward* 178 no. 80.

154. Cf. *Needleman* 186–87, 217, 222, 167–68, 176, 137–39.

155. *PL* 32:700; cf. 38:663, "For whatever you examine, is not examined totally," and above, 276 quoting *1 Cor.* 9:12; 'contemplation' is a translation of the word *gnosis* in the Greek Bible, which in turn translates the Hebrew *da'ath*, "an extremely intimate kind of knowledge involving the whole man, not just the mind" (*Needleman* 126–27).

156. *Blunt* 65.

157. Cf. ibid 62; above, n. 118.

158. Cf. above, 160–62 and Index: inner & outer life.

159. *Birget*, sig. Avii^r; *PP* cv^v; cf. cxvii^v.

160. *Ward* 67 no. 8, 193 no. 184, 217 no. 20 and 21, 225–26 no. 2 and 3, 102 no. 3; cf. Index: asceticism; body, the physical; will.

161. *Blunt* 62 and 46, where it is connected with being able to pay greater attention.

162. Ibid. 68–99.

163. Cf. Index: inner and outer life and *Blunt* 35, for example: "he takes more heed of the heart than of the voice. But when both accord in him, then is it best."

164. *Blunt* 4–5; *D* sigs. Bi^{v}ff.; Index: meditation.

165. *Blunt* 142–43; *Aungier* 245, 328; although it became institutionalised at Syon and among the Brethren by the end of the fifteenth century (*CF* 24), this remembering as a personal confrontation is preserved in earlier records (cf. *Jacob* 46–47; *Peters* 1; *Thomas* 244, 247; and Index: death, remembrance of; *Gem* 186–87; *Coulton* 93) and it was this which Whytford advocated (*DE* sigs Cviii^{r}ff., Fiii^r, *HI* 61^v, 67^r); More *English Works*, 358–59, 385, 374, 479–80; *Martz* 135–44; *Pourrat* 52–53.

166. *Aungier* 377–78; cf. *Blunt* 4–5; above, 204–8; for another Bridgettine practice which may have originated in spiritual exercise, cf. *Aungier* 346.

167. *Blunt* 50.

168. Ibid. 42.

169. Cf. above, 180.

170. *Early Fathers Philokalia* 124 (Evagrius).

171. Cf. *McConica* 56–57, 115–16, 123–24, 128–29, where Syon's literary production is seen as part of a campaign of Erasmian piety, an interpretation that is not followed here.

172. *RO3* 213; cf. Index: Fewterer, John.

173. *Aungier* 532–33; above, 214; John Trowell, the previous Confessor, is last heard of in

1518 (*Aungier* 82). Hussey was executed in 1537 for implication in the Lincolnshire risings; cf. *McConica* 132; *Fewterer* fo. +ii^r.

174. For 1536 letter, cf. *Aungier* 430–33; *LP* 8 no. 78 (calendered as 1535); above, 275. For 1535 letter, *Aungier* 435–38; *LP* 7 pt. 2 421–22, no. 1090.

175. *Aungier* 438–39.

176. *Bateson* appendix 1, xxiv–xxv, xxix–xxx: medical works B23, 32 and C43, Raulyn R61–64, Bernardino R65, Renaissance scholarship C18, G24, H36, 50–53 (Erasmus' Jerome), I51, N3, 4, Poggio S69, Bruni N3, Reuchlin G24, Ficino's Dionysius D118, the Victorines I34, N40, 86.

177. Cf. Index: mystical tradition, medieval.

178. Cf. Index: John Climachus.

179. *Bateson* O32, 92.

180. Ibid. H44; *Fewterer* fo. lvii^r admitting his material was "for the more part taken of Ludolph Carthusiense"; for Cisneros' influence, see Index: Cisneros.

181. *LP* 4 pt. 2, 1883–84 no. 4282; cf. 1877 no. 4260. The Abbess of Denny and an unnamed Greenwich Observant Friar also received these books; Bonde had written his *Consolatori* for the nuns of Denny Abbey, and the Observant Friars were associated with Syon through common outlook; cf. Index: Franciscans, observant.

182. *Fewterer* fos. +ii^r, +iii^r, "the exercises of all other spiritual meditations may be reduced and brought unto this . . . there is no kind of spiritual exercise but that it may be found in the Life and Passion of Christ"; cf. below, 294–95; *Longridge* 154–59; *PP* ccxcvi-ii^r–cccviii^r.

183. *Fewterer* fo. +iii^r.

184. Ibid. iiii^r; cf. *Ludolph* 1; Index: *imitatio Christi;* meditation.

185. Rupert of Deutz quoted in *Duby* 73: "The rites which are carried out during the divine service, according to a yearly cycle, are signs of the loftiest realities; they contain the greatest sacraments and the full majesty of the celestial mysteries. They were instituted for the glory of the head of the Church, our Lord Jesus Christ, by men who grasped the sublimity of those mysteries to the fullest extent and proclaimed it through the spoken and the written word and the rites. Among the spiritual treasures with which the Holy Ghost enriches its Church, we should lovingly cultivate the gift of fully understanding what we are actually saying when we pray and sing psalms."

186. *PP* ccli^r, cf. ccxxxiiii^{r-v}; cf. above, 184–94.

187. *Fewterer* fo. +ii^r; cf. Index: compunction; sin.

188. A Sufi saying quoted in *Needleman* 177.

189. *Fewterer* fo. +ii^v; cf. above, 117 and Index: self-knowledge; *Bonde* v^v, xvii^{r-v}, xxii^r.

190. Cf. Index: body, the physical; chaos in man; emotional life; self, man's lower.

191. Cf. Index: religion.

192. Cf. *HI* 60^v–65^v on what it is necessary to forget in order to remember differently, and also below, 235–36 and Index: "remembering."

193. [E.] Underhill [*Mysticism* (New York 1961)], 314–15; *Fewterer* fos. v^{r-v}: "cogitation has his signification and name of abiding. . . . Forasmuch as in such cogitations when reason and understanding has not that gift and grace of knowledge that it would have, it is constrained to abide . . . unto the time that he has got some perceiving thereof. And of this constraining speaks St. Bernard, saying: let the outward senses be gathered together in one, and constrained or subdued under the discipline and rule of the good will, and so kept under with the burden of good works and made obedient to the service of the spirit that in no means they be suffered to come at large at their sensual pleasure"; Bernard is often cited; cf. ii^v, iiii^r, vi^r, vii^r, viii^r (paginated as xii^r), viii^v for example.

194. Ibid. vi^{r-v}; cf. *Martz* 76 quoting Luis of Granada.

195. *Fewterer* fo. v^v; cf. above, 221–22 and Index: devotion.

196. *Martz* 115, quoting the Jesuit Puente.

197. *Fewterer* fo. iiii^v.

198. Cf. *PP* $clxxiiii^v$ speaking of different kinds of "bread" for the journey, $ccxxxii^v$, $ccxlvi^r$ and Index: food; scale; the soul.

199. *Wessel* 2 15; cf. Index: "remembering."

200. *Benjamin Minor* 88; cf. *William of St. Thierry* 9–10; Index: mountain; self-knowledge.

201. *Fewterer* fo. $+iii^v$; cf. $+iiii^r$.

202. Cf. Index: *imitatio Christi*.

203. *Fewterer* fo. $+ii^v$; cf. *PP* $cclv^v-vi^r$.

204. Cf. for example *Nasr* 37–38 on the *dhikr* (remembering or invocation): "the main method of Sufism, in fact, is to extend the prayers so that they become continuous, for as Hafiz says: 'How happy are those who are always praying,'" and *The Way of a Pilgrim*, ed. R. W. French (New York 1965), 198–99 and passim; for the uninterrupted invocation of the Jesus Prayer in the Orthodox Church, also above, 236, 315 n. 204 and Index: prayer; in both cases this exercise is linked with the body, the temple of the spirit (*Nasr* 38; above, n. 150 and Index: body, the physical).

205. *Peters* 71; cf. *Fewterer* fo. $+iii^r$: "if man desire that all his life be continual and perpetual prayer and that he would have his heart ever lifted up to God and his devotion or fervour ever renewed, he shall never get it more easily than by the remembrance of the Life and Passion of his Lord God, for there he may have in every word, act, behaviour and pain that Christ spoke, did, used and suffered, how to have compunction and sorrow in heart and how to be comforted in spirit. For in the consideration of them, now he may weep by compassion, now by giving thanks he may have sweet affections, now he may desire to be conformed unto Him and His will, now he may labour and wish to be wholly transformed into Him. Thus may man go from one exercise unto another to avoid tediousness and so ever to be in prayer"; cf. also Index: attention; Christ; prayer.

206. *Ps.* 105:4; cf. *1 Chron.* 16:11; *William of St. Thierry* 18–19; *Brown* 277.

207. *Fewterer* fo. $+iii^v$; *Cisneros Exercises* 253; cf. *Fewterer* fo. ix^v "the imitation and following of Christ is the most high and perfect religion and rule of a perfect person"; *Cisneros Exercises* 255, "the imitation of Christ in his Passion and death is the noblest rule and model of life and virtue"; *Ludolph* 23, "the imitation of Christ is the summary and the per-

fect religion of the perfect man . . . it is the rule and model of perfection of all life and virtue"; *Fewterer* fo. xiiii^{r-v}; and *Cisneros Exercises* 262.

208.   Ibid. 255–63; *Fewterer* fos. ix^{r}, x^{v}, xi^{v}, xii^{r}, xiii^{v}, xiiii^{r}; *Ludolph* 23.

209.   Cf. *Fewterer* fo. xi^{v}; *Cisneros Exercises* 258; *Longridge* 57–58; with Ignatius the centre of gravity has shifted uncompromisingly to the embattled exercitant.

210.   Cf. *McConica* 53, 56, 63; G. Mattingley, *Catherine of Aragon* (London 1942), 138; *Caraman* 6; and cf. above, 185, 218.

211.   Cf. above, 77.

212.   Cf. *Fewterer* fos. ii^{r-v}, iiii^{v}; *Cisneros Exercises* 255–56, 257–58.

213.   *Fewterer* fo. ii^{r}, iiii^{r}; cf. ii^{v}, i^{v} and *The Folowyng of Christe*, xxxvii^{r}, xxxvii^{v}.

214.   *Ludolph* 1; and on the "inward eye," *Fewterer* fo. +iii^{v}; above, 231.

215.   *The Spiritual Exercises of a Dominican Friar*, ed. C. Kirchberger (London 1957), 26; cf. M. Buber, *Tales of the Hasidim, The Later Masters* (New York 1970), 152, "The Unity of the Senses," preserving traditional Jewish teaching.

216.   *Ludolph* 26; *Cisneros Exercises* 261–62; cf. *PP* cclii^{v}; *Martz* 72, 71, 173–74; More, *English Works*, vol. 1, 358–59, 381–82, 388, 393; *Parkyn* 81–82; *Pourrat*, vol. 2, 319–22.

217.   *Fewterer* fos. +iiii^{r}, ii^{r}, iiii^{r-v}; cf. above, 13–15 and Index: *conformitas Christi*.

218.   Cf. above, 126–27 and Index: "remembering" and *D* sigs. Ei^{v}, Evii^{v}–viii^{r} on becoming able to see oneself; also Gregory the Great on true singers, who "when the Spirit speaks in them, hear themselves but not themselves, because they themselves are speaking, but in their speech they acknowledge with reverence the speaking of another" (quoted in *Material for Thought* 18).

219.   *Ward* 35, no. 1; Peryn quoted above, 105.

220.   *Philokalia on Prayer of the Heart*, 192–94; cf. 31–34; above, nn. 147, 150, 204, 205.

221.   Cf. Index: "the old man" and *PP* cviii^{r-v}, lx^{r}, cxvii^{v} on awakening from sleep.

222.   *Fewterer* fo. ii^{r}.

223.   Ibid. viii^{r}, cf. iiii^{r}.

224.   Ibid. xi^{r} citing Gerson, vii^{v}–viii^{r} (paginated as xii^{r}).

225.   Cf. Index: body, the physical; 'the flesh'; sensuality.

226.   Cf. Index: duality; inner & outer life; the soul; transformation.

227.   *Underhill* 220 (my italics); cf. Index: energies in man; 'the world.'

228.   *Fewterer* fo. iiii^{r}; *PP* ciiii^{r}, cxxi^{v}.

229.   Ibid. cclxxxvii^{v}ff.; *Fewterer* fo. iiii^{r-v}; cf. fos. +ii^{v}, +iii^{v}; *HI* 35^{v}; and, on the building of the inner temple within the monk, *Material for Thought*, 20.

230.   *Mark* 14:14–15; *Luke* 22:11–12; *Fewterer* fo. i^{r-v}; *PP* cclxxxix^{v}ff.; Index: the heart; the soul; *D* sigs. gviii^{v}–hi^{r}; *HI* 52^{v}.

231.   Cf. Index: the heart, 'the monastery within.'

232.   *Fewterer* fo. iiii^{r}; Gerard Groote suggested fasting on the three days of the week when

Christ was being betrayed in the concurrent meditation cycles, in order to deepen participation, to give the body its place (*T3* 35 and cf. above, n. 204).

233. *Cisneros Exercises* 31; cf. chaps. 4 and 5 passim and Index: spiritual exercises; *Zerbolt* 20–22.

234. Cf. *Aungier* 315; *DE* sig. Dviii^V; *P* ccxx^r, ccxxi^V; *PP* lix^r–x^r, ccxlvii^r, ccxlviiii^{r}ff., cclix^r–xi^V; *Bonde* vii^V.

235. Cf. *Fewterer* fo. +iii^V.

236. Cf. *On the Way to Self Knowledge*, ed. J. Needleman and D. Lewis (New York 1976), 13, 214–16.

237. Cf. [J.] Needleman [*A Sense of the*] *Cosmos* [(New York 1975)], 45–48.

238. Cf. *Fewterer* fo. i^{r-V} on the "two substances" in man, his failure to "nourish" what is higher in him and its consequent subordination to what is lower, despite momentary realisations of this through "inward inspirations"; also *D* sigs. cviii^{r-V}; *P* xli^{r-V}, cxcvi^V–viii^V, ccix^V–xi^V.

239. Needleman *Cosmos*, 46.

240. *Evagrius* lxxxii–viii, 14; cf. Index: *apalneia;* love; purification of emotion.

241. *Ward* 193 no. 184.

242. Ibid. 6 no. 22; cf. *P* ccix^V (paginated as ccxix^V)–xxi^V, quoted below, n. 265; *Evagrius* 4–10; Index: energies in man; inner & outer life.

243. Cf. above, nn. 204, 232 and Index: body, the physical; hence the association between meditation and *ars memorativa* in the use of the hand as a mnemotechnical device to magnify the force of 'remembering' (above, 204–8); Fewterer quotes extensively from Reynarde de Laudenberg, an Augustinian whose *Passio domini nostri Jesu Christi* (1501) incorporates an alphabetical memory system.

244. *PP* cxxi^V; it should be considered together with his *Consolatori* (1534?), a directory of conscience drawing on the same sources.

245. Cf. Index: *rapiaria.*

246. *PP* i^V; cf. clvi^V, ccxxxvi^r; above, 214–18, 223 and Index: the vernacular.

247. He quotes most often from Augustine, Aquinas, Bernard, Bonaventure, Gregory, Anselm, Gerson, Bridget, the Victorines, Chrysostom, Isidore, Origen, Cyprian, Alexander of Hales, Harpius (Henry of Herp, a fifteenth–century Brother of the Common Life who became an Observant Franciscan and whose writings were strongly influenced by Ruysbroeck) and from the Bible: on doctrine he tends to follow Aquinas, on the spiritual life, Augustine, Bernard, Bonaventure and Gerson.

248. *PP* lxxxvi^r quoting Gerard Zerbolt (cf. clxix^r); clxxiiii^r, ccxxxii^V and ccxlvi^r refer to mastication; cclxv^r and ccxlix^{r}ff. to Passion meditation.

249. Ibid. ccxlvii^V–ix^r, where Syon's service is said to be based on "the order of the old fathers of Egypt."

250. Cf. Needleman *Cosmos* 131–34, Index: The Trinity.

251. *PP* xxiii^V; on cleanness of heart, cf. clxvii^{r}ff., clxix^r, "in the cleanness of heart stands the end of our journey"; Index: the heart; purification of emotion.

252. *PP* i^{r-v}; cf. ii^r, lxxxv^r, cxiii^V, cxvii^V; *Bonde* xiii^r, xxvii^V, *HI* 71^r, "the examples of our foregoers be unto us documents, lessons and forms of living."

253. *PP* i^V, xix^{r}ff., xxiiii^r, lv^V, lxix^{r}ff.

254. Ibid. i^r; cf. xiiii^{r}ff.; above, 7–9; for Whytford's similar view, *P* xii^r–iii^r, xviii^V–xx^r; *LER* sig. Tiv^V; *HI* 24^V; and for Erasmus on the common obligation of all Christians, *Paraclesis* 7; *An exhortation to the diligent study of scripture* (Antwerp 1529), sig. (Av^V).

255. *PP* i^{r-v}, cf. ciiii^{r}ff.; the first five days relate to the active life of religion "otherwise called spiritual exercise" or mortification of the senses (cf. above, n. 2), the last two to the three parts of contemplation, prayer, reading and meditation.

256. Cf. Index: seven; three; The Trinity.

257. Cf. Index: influences.

258. *PP* ii^r, cxli^r.

259. Ibid. ii^r, viii^V.

260. The continuation or rediscovery of earlier teaching is not necessarily antipathetic to reform; Luther admired Bernard, whose writings on faith and works can be construed as a prototype of solifidianism (*Constable* XV:37–40) and Bonde's traditional remarks on the sufficiency of faith in knowing God (*PP* clxviii^V; cf. clxx^r, clxxxv^r, clxxxvi^V, clxxxvii^r) have been underlined in the edition used.

261. Cf. *PP* cclxxx^r, cclxxiii^V–iiii^r, cclxxii^r, cclxxxiiii^V–v^r, ccxcv^r, ccxcv^{V}ff.

262. Cf. *PP* clx^{r-v}, an example quoted below, 244.

263. *PP* xliiii^V–iiii^r; cf. ccxcv^r–vi^r; *D* sig. Cviii^r; Index: "Fall of Man'; "original justice" is a term much used by Zerbolt; Index: justice.

264. *PP* lx^r; cf. *Ps.* 121:4; "Israel" means "one who sees God" (cclxvii^V); he is indebted to Bonaventure and Richard of St. Victor in these passages.

265. Cf. *PP* cviii^{r-v}; also *P* ccxx^V–xi^r: "man's mind is as a rota or wheel in a wind that never does rest, but always turns and does renew cogitations and thoughts, both sleeping and waking. So that a person waking is sometimes ravished unto such matters in cogitations and thoughts as he never knew before, and so far does pass time therein that he knows not what he does, but [is] as though he were in a dream. . . . But when the person does well perceive wherewith the mind is occupied, then does begin the battle between the person and his thoughts, or rather between him and the authors or movers of those thoughts, that is, the Devil, the world and the flesh that does work in the sensuality according unto their properties. For then if the mind (at home with himself) be negligent and (for the pleasure moved in the sensuality) be loath to depart from those thoughts, and so do play with them, and suffer them to hang upon him (although they were not deadly), yet does the person put himself in jeopardy and . . . who loves peril, in peril shall fall. But when the person . . . does . . . rear or raise up the stomach & heart against those cogitations, with indignation and despite . . . and begin to fight strongly, and if he then with a good stomach and trust in our Lord, will thrust them unto the stone and knock their heads thereunto, he shall without any jeopardy or doubt have the victory. The stone is Christ, the heads of his thoughts

been their motions first . . . perceived" (pray not to be delivered, but for strength in battle); cf. above, 235, above n. and Index: Christ; energies in man; inner & outer life; meditation; for the relationship with the ascetical tradition of the Desert, *Evagrius* 29–30:50; *Ward* 102 no. 3; Index: Desert Fathers.

266. *PP* cclxvi^r–ii^v quoted at cclxvii^v, cf. ccxxxiii^v; the winning and keeping of "spiritual understanding" is the journey of the sixth day: just as oil is necessary for light, light is nourished by oil and clarifies it; "spiritual understanding" is the "bread of life," but may only be digested if a man has made perfectly the journey of the five preceding "days," for the light will not shine unless the heart be clean, and without light the mountain of contemplation cannot be climbed—it is vain to rise before the light (*Ps.* 126:2 Vulgate)—and climbing the mountain is to "lift our self above our self." This is an example of Bonde's conveyance of traditional symbolic thought.

267. Ibid. cclxxxvii^{r-v}; cf. cxlii^{r-v}.

268. Ibid. ccxxxv^r and cf. *Bonde* v^{r-v}, x^{r-v}, xiiii^v for the priest as doctor.

269. *PP* clii^r; cf. *Ward* 98 no. 2: "Prize the virtues and do not be the slave of glory; for the former are immortal, while the latter soon fades."

270. *PP* clxiii^r, clx^v; cf. *P* ccix^r (paginated as ccxix^r); "virtue" and *vir*, man, are etymologically cognate.

271. *PP* cxlviii^r–ix^r, citing Augustine, Gregory and Bonaventure; for Erasmus' treatment of this analogy, cf. *Dolan* 43; Index: listening.

272. *PP* clxiii^r; cf. above, n. 135; *P* ccxviii^v.

273. *Attendaunce, diligence, entencyon* and *intencyon* are often used synonymously in this material; cf. *PP* clix^{v}–x^r and above, n. 106 and Index: attention.

274. *PP* clx^r; cf. *Longridge* 163.

275. *PP* clx^r.

276. Ibid. clx^{r-v}.

277. Ibid. clx^v–xi^r, clxiii^r; cf. *LER* sig. Dvii^{r-v}; above, 225 and Index: attention; Brotherhood of the Common Life; spiritual exercises.

278. *PP* clx^v; cf. above, 55, 234.

279. *PP* cxxi^v, cxxii^v–iii^r; cf. cxxx^r–iiii^r, "the light of this gift of spiritual science, in the which, undoubtedly, if we be exercised, we shall see our self," and also *D* sig. Eiv^v.

280. *Ward* 98 no. 1.

281. *PP* cxvii^v.

282. *William of St. Thierry* 119–20 (cf. *Isa* 24:16 Vulgate), 51–52; cf. *PP* cxlviii^r, Index: consequence; inner & outer life; watching and the saying of Francis of Assissi, quoted in *William of St. Thierry* 51 n. 2, "Brother Body is our cell and the soul sits therein like a hermit and thinks on God and prays to Him"; in the symbolic thought of the Desert being in one's cell meant interior watchfulness, as in the advice given to a brother who complained of losing his peace when he left his cell, "Be watchful inwardly; be watchful outwardly" (*Ward* 186 no. 137; cf. 3 no. 10; also *Evagrius* xiii).

Bibliography

CONTEMPORARY SOURCES

Manuscripts

London, *BL* Sloane MS 1037 (1536).

Early Printed Books to 1700

Barcklay, R. *A Discourse of the Felicitie of Man* . . . (London 1603, W. Jaggard for W. Ponsonby, *STC* 1382, *BL* 721f40).

Baxter, R. *The Saint's Everlasting Rest* . . . (London 1653 4th ed., *BL* E704).

Bonde, W. *the consolatori of timorouse and fearefull consciencys* (London 1534?, M. Fawkes, *STC* 3276, *BL* 1A47940 [2]).

Bridget of Sweden. *Four revelations* . . . (London 1531?, T. Godfray, *STC* 1915, *BL* C37b12).

Colet, J. *A ryght frutefull monycion concernyng the ordre of a good chrysten mannes lyfe* . . . (London 1534, R. Copland for J. Bydell, *STC* 5547, *BL* C53i20).

Coverdale, M. *The Christen rule* . . . (London 1547?, *STC* 5789.7, *BL* C53gg8).

Dyall *A dyall of dayly contemplacyon or devine exercise of the mind* . . . (London 1578, Hugh Singleton, *STC* 5644, *BL* C122b11).

Dyurnall *A dyurnall for devoute soules to ordre themselfe therafter* (London 1530?, R. Wyer, *STC* 6928, *BL* C52d9).

Erasmus, Des. *Colloquiorum Familiarum opus* (Antwerp 1564, *BL* 012314de34); *De Contemptu Mundi*, tr. T. Paynell (London 1533, *STC* 10471, *BL* C110a5); *Enchiridion militis Christiani* . . . (London 1544, J. Bydell, *STC* 10484, *BL* 696a43 [2]), and anr. ed. (Antwerp 1523, *BL* C107aa7 [2]); *Paraclesis* . . . (Basle 1519, Froben, *BL* 1351f20 [2]), and anr. ed. *An exhortation to the diligent studye of scripture* (Antwerp 1529, "Luft Marburg," *STC* 10493, *BL* C37a25); *The Praise of Folie*, tr. T. Chaloner (London 1549, *STC* 10500, *BL* 90i24).

Fewterer, J. *The Myrrour or Glasse of Christes Passion* (London 1534, R. Redman, *STC* 14553, *BL* C53d16).

Foundacyon of Christendome, The (*incipit* of unidentified tract, *BL* C37a28 [2]).

Fox, R. *Contemplacyon of Synners* (London 1499, W. de Worde, *STC* 5643, *BL* 1A55215); *Rule of seynt Benet* (London 1516?, R. Pynson, *STC* 1859, *BL* G10245).

Hylton, W. . . . *medylde lyfe* (London 1516, R. Pynson, *STC* 4602, *BL* C24a7); *Scala Perfectionis* (London 1533, W. de Worde, *STC* 14045, *BL* C25d14).

Ignatius Loyola. *Exercitia Spiritualia* . . . (Antwerp 1689, *BL* 4406cc25).

Jesus. . . . *Iesus Psalter* (Antwerp 1575, J. Foulerem, *STC* 14563.5, *BL* C53a18).

John Climachus. *Scala Spiritualis* . . . (Toletana 1505, *BL* C29h7).

Latimer, H. *The fyrste sermon* . . . (London 1549, J. Daye, *STC* 15272, *BL* C53a11).

Luis of Granada. *Of Prayer and Meditation* . . . [*and*] *An excellent Treatise of Consideration and Prayer* (London 1599, P. Short for W. Wood, *STC* 16910, *BL* 4410e23).

Manual. *A Manuall of praiers* . . . (Rouen 1583, *STC* 17263, Bodleian 8°M58Th, and anr. ed. (Calice 1599, *STC* 17266, *BL* 3455df27); *A Manuall for meditation* . . . , by I. R. (*STC* 17278.5, Bodleian 8°M37Th).

Mombaer, J. *Rosetum exercitiorum spiritualium et sacrum meditationum* (Paris 1510, I. Petit, *BL* Hirsch iv 1517).

More, T. *The Workes of Sir Thomas More* . . . , ed. W. Rastell, 2 vols. (London 1557, J. Cawood, J. Walley and R. Tottle, *STC* 18076, *BL* C11b14 and 15).

Peryn, W. *Spirituall Exercyses* . . . (London 1557, J. Walley, *STC* 19784, *BL* 4404c57).

Petrarch, F. *Opera* . . . , 4 vols. (Basle 1581, S. Henricpetri, *BL* 639m8).

Primer. *This prymer of Salysbury use* . . . (Paris 1534, F. Regnault, *STC* 15985a5, *BL* C107aa5), and anr. ed. (Paris 1538, Regnault, *STC* 16001, *BL* C53c14).

Psalter. *The Psalter of Sainct Hierome* . . . (Antwerp 1576, J. Foulerum, *STC* 14506, *BL* C53a18 [2]).

Rhegius, U. *The olde Learnyng and the new* . . . (London 1548, R. Stoughton, *STC* 20842, *BL* 1020b3).

Rich, E. *The Myrrour of the chyrche* (London 1527, W. de Worde, *STC* 966, *BL* C25k19).

Ryckes, J. *Ymage of love* (London 1532?, W. de Worde, *STC* 21472, Bodleian Crynes 846).

Sampson, T. *A Warning to take heed of Fowlers Psalter* (London 1578, T. Vautrollier for G. Bishoppe, *STC* 21685, *BL* 3936a31); *A Sermō* . . . *of pacience* (London 1550, N. Hyll for J. Shefelde, *STC* 14638, *BL* C143a27).

Southwell, R. *A Short Rule of Good Life* (London 1622, S. Omers and J. Heigham, *STC* 22970, *BL* C26k22 [1]).

Symon Anker. *The fruyte of redempcyon* (London 1532, W. de Worde, *STC* 22560, *BL* C53k12).

Wessel Gansfort *De Oratione et Modo Orandi* (Zwolle 1520?, *BL* 477a41 [3]).

Whytford, R. *Crossrowe* (London 1537, J. Waylande, *STC* 25413.5, *BL* 4402aaa58 [1]); *The folowyng of Christe* (London 1535?, R. Redman, *STC* 23964.7, *BL* IX Eng 128 [1]); *Golden Pystle* (London 1530, W. de Worde, *STC* 1912, *BL* C40c17); *The Martiloge* (London 1526, W. de Worde, *STC* 17532, *BL* C25k18); *A Werke* . . . (London 1537, R. Redman, *STC* 25425, *BL* C111aa34).

Editions, Translations and Selections

Allen, W. *A Briefe Historie* . . . , ed. J. H. Pollen (London 1908).

Attar, Farid al–Din. *Muslim Saints and Mystics*, tr. A. J. Arberry (Persian Heritage Series no. 1, London 1966, 1979 ed.).

Augustine. *An Augustine Synthesis*, ed. E. Przywara (London 1936).

Becon, T. *Prayers* . . . , ed. J. Ayre (Parker Society, Cambridge 1844).

Benedict. *The Rule of Saint Benedict*, ed. J. McCann (London 1952).

Bonaventure. *Itinerarium mentis in Deum* . . . , ed. Father James (London 1937).

Boorde, A. *The Fyrst Boke of the Introduction of Knowledge* . . . , ed. F. J. Furnivall (*EETS* extra series 10, London 1870).

Bradford, J. *The Writings* . . . , ed. A. Townsend, 2 vols. (Parker Society, Cambridge 1848–53).

Bruni, L. *Humanistisch–philosophische Schriften*, ed. H. Baron (Leipzig 1928).

Cisneros de, G. J. *Obras Completas*, 2 vols. (Montserrat 1965); *Book of Exercises for the Spiritual Life*, ed. E. Allison Peers (Montserrat 1929); *A Book of Spiritual Exercises and a Directory for the Canonical Hours*, ed. a monk of St. Augustine's monastery, Ramsgate (Monastic Gleanings 11, London 1876).

Cloud of Unknowing, The, ed. E. Underhill (London 1912, 6th ed. 1956).

Eckhart, Meister. *Meister Eckehart, Deutsche Predigten und Traktate*, ed. J. Quint (3rd ed., Munich 1969); *Selected Treatises and Sermons*, ed. J. M.Clark and J. V. Skinner (Classics of the Contemplative Life, ed. J. M. Hussey, London 1958); *Tractates from Meister Eckhart* (privately printed at the press of Pembridge Design Studio, London 1982).

Erasmus, Des. *Opus Epistolarum* . . . , ed. P. S. Allen, 12 vols. (Oxford 1906–); *Christian Humanism and the Reformation, Selected Writings* . . . , ed. J. C. Olin (New York/London 1965); *Erasmus on his Times* . . . *the Adages*, ed. M. M. Philips (Cambridge 1967); *The Essential Erasmus*, ed. J. P. Dolan (New York 1964); *The Lives of Jehan Vitrier and John Colet*, tr. J. H. Lupton (London 1883).

Elyot, T. *The Governor*, ed. S. E. Lehmberg (Everyman Library 227, London 1907, 1962 ed.).

Evagrius Ponticus. *The Praktikos and Chapters on Prayer*, tr. J. E. Bamberger (Cistercian Studies Series no. 4, Kalamazoo 1981).

Ficino, M. *The Letters*, ed. School of Economic Science, vol. 1 (London 1975); *Theologie Platonicienne* . . . , ed. R. Marcel, 2 vols. (Paris 1964).

Florence Radewijns. *Tractatulus* . . . *(Multum Valet)*, ed. H. Nolte (Friburg 1862).

Fox, R. *Letters* . . . , ed. P. S. and H. M. Allen (Oxford 1929).

Gardner, E. G. (ed.). *The Cell of Self Knowledge* . . . (The Medieval Library 9, London 1925).

Gerard Groote. *Gerardi Magni Epistolae*, ed. W. Mulder (Tekstuitgaven van ons geestelijk erf. dl. 3, Antwerp 1933); *Tractatus de quatuor generibus meditationum*, ed. A. Hyma (Archief voor geschiedenis van het Aartbisdom Utrecht 49, Utrecht 1924).

Gerard Zerbolt. *The Spiritual Ascent*, tr. J. P. Arthur (London 1908); *De Reformatione virium animae*, ed. M. De La Bigne in *Magna Bibliotheca Veterum Patrum* . . . , 17 vols. (Paris 1654), vol. 5, cols. 839–80.

Holinshed, R. *Holinshed's Chronicles* . . . , 6 vols. (London 1807).

Hylton, W. *The Scale of Perfection*, ed. G. Sitwell (London 1953); *Minor Works*, ed. D. M. Jones (Orchard Books 17, London 1929).

Ignatius Loyola. *The Spiritual Exercises* . . . , ed. W. H. Longridge (London 1919, 1950 ed.) and anr. ed., J. Rickaby (London 1915).

Jacobus de Voragine. *The Golden Legend*, ed. F. S. Ellis, 3 vols. (London 1892).

Latimer, H. *The Works* . . . , ed. G. E. Corrie, 2 vols. (Parker Society, Cambridge 1844–45).

Ludolph of Saxony. *The Hours of the Passion* . . . , ed. H. J. C. (London 1887).

Merton, T. *The Asian Journal*, ed. N. Burton, P. Hart and J. Laughlin (New York 1973, 1975 ed.).

More, T. *The Complete Works* . . . (Yale edition, New Haven 1963–); *The English Works* . . . , ed. W. E. Campbell and A. W. Reed, 2 vols. (London 1927–31); *Selected Letters*, ed. E. F. Rogers (New Haven 1961); *Lives* . . . *by W. Roper and N. Harpsfield*, ed. E. E. Reynolds (Everyman Library 19, London 1963).

Myrc *Instructions* . . . , ed. F. Peacock (*EETS* old series 31, London 1868).

Nugent, E. M. (ed.). *The Thought and Culture of the English Renaissance* (Cambridge 1956).

Obermann, H. A. (ed.). *Forerunners of the Reformation* . . . (London 1967).

Osuna de, F. *The Third Spiritual Alphabet*, tr. A Stanbrook Benedictine (London 1931).

Pantin, W. A. (ed.). *Documents illustrating the* . . . *English Black Monks 1215–1540*, 3 vols. (Camden Third Series 45, 47, 54, London 1931–37).

Parkyn, R. *Tudor Treatises*, ed. A. G. Dickens (YARS 125, Wakefield 1959).

Peryn, W. *The Spiritual Exercises* . . . , ed. C. Kirchberger (London 1957).

Peters, G. *The Divine Soliloquies* . . . , tr. "Monialis" (London 1920).

Petry, R. C. (ed.). *Late Medieval Mysticism* (Library of Christian Classics, London 1957).

Philokalia. *Writings from the Philokalia on Prayer of the Heart* and *Early Fathers from the Philokalia*, ed. E. Kadloubovsky and G. E. H. Palmer (London 1951, 1954).

Pico della Mirandola. *On the Dignity of Man, On Being and the One, Heptaplus*, ed. C. G. Wallis, P. J. W. Miller and D. Carmichael (Library of Liberal Arts, New York 1965).

Renaissance Philosophy of Man, The, ed. E. Cassirer, P. O. Kristeller, and J. H. Randall Jr. (Chicago 1948, 1956).

Richard of St. Victor. *Benjamin Minor*, tr. S. V. Yankowski (Ansbach 1960).

Richardinus, R. *Commentary on the Rule of St. Augustine*, ed. G. G. Coulton (Scottish Historical Society, 3rd series 26, Edinburgh 1935).

Rolle, R. *English Writings...*, ed. H. E. Allen (Oxford 1931); *The Melos Amoris...*, ed. E. J. F. Arnould (Oxford 1957); *The Incendium Amoris...*, ed. M. Deanesley (University of Manchester Historical Series 26, Manchester 1915); *Some Minor Works...*, ed. G. E. Hodgson (London 1923); *Yorkshire Writers...*, ed. C. Horstmann, 2 vols. (Library of Early English Writers, London/Leipzig 1895).

Santillana, G. (ed.). *The Age of Adventure* (New American Library, New York 1956).

Starkey, T. *A Dialogue between... Pole and... Lupset*, ed. K. M. Burton (London 1948).

Thomas Aquinas. *Summa Theologica*, tr. English Dominican Fathers (London 1911–22) and anr. ed. tr. T. Gilby and others (London/New York 1964–).

Thomas a Kempis. *The Founders of the New Devotion*, tr. J. P. Arthur (London 1905); *The Imitation of Christ*, tr. B. I. Knott (London 1963) and anr. ed. anon. (Everyman Library 484, London 1960).

Tractatus de cotidiano holocausto spiritualis exercitii, ed. C. Hirsche in *Prolegomena zu einer neuen Ausgabe der Imitatio Christi*, 3 vols. (Berlin 1873).

Tyndale, W. *Expositions and notes...*, ed. H. Walter (Parker Society, Cambridge 1849).

Wace, H. and P. Schaff (eds.). *Select Library of Nicene and Post Nicene Fathers...*, 14 vols. (Oxford 1890–1900).

Way of a Pilgrim, The, tr. R. M. French (New York 1965).

Whytford, R. *The Martiloge...*, ed. F. Proctor and F. S. Dewick (Henry Bradshaw Society pub. 3, London 1893).

William of St. Thierry. *The Golden Epistle*, tr. W. Shewring (London 1930, 1980 ed.).

Wilkins, D. (ed.). *Concilia Magnae Brittaniae et Hiberniae*, 4 vols. (London 1737).

MODERN SOURCES

Adamson, J. W. "The extent of literacy in England in the fifteenth and sixteenth century," *Transactions of the Bibliographical Society*, 2nd. series 10, 1930; *The Library*, 4th series, vol. 10, 163–93.

Allison, A. F. and D. M. Rogers. *A Catalogue of Catholic Books in English... 1558–1640* (Biographical Studies vol. 3, no. 4, Bognor Regis 1956).

Aston, M. *The Fifteenth Century* (Library of European Civilisation, ed. G. Barraclough, London 1968).

Axon, W. E. "The Lady Margaret as a lover of literature," *The Library*, new series, vol. 8, 1907, 34–41.

Bainton, R. *Here I Stand* (New York 1950); *Studies on the Reformation* (London 1964).

Bamford, C. Review article of *The Plan of St. Gall...*, W. Horn and E. Born, 3 vols. (Berkeley 1979). *Parabola*, vol. 7, no. 2 (May 1982), 96–99.

Brown, P. *Augustine of Hippo* (London 1967, 1969 ed.).

Buber, M. *Tales of the Hasidim, the Later Masters* (New York 1948, reprinted 1970).

Burckhardt, J. *The Civilisation of the Renaissance in Italy*, tr. S. G. C. Middlemore (Basle 1860, 1965 London Phaidon ed.).

Burnaby, J. *Amor Dei* . . . (The Hulsean Lectures 1938, London 1938).

Bush, D. *The Renaissance and English Humanism* (Toronto 1939).

Cambridge History of the Bible, The. 3 vols., vol. 2 ed. G. W. H. Lampe (Cambridge 1969).

Caraman, P. J. "An English monastic reformer of the sixteenth century," *The Clergy Review*, vol. 28, no. 1 (July 1947), 1–16.

Chambers, R. W. *Thomas More* (London 1935, 1963 ed.).

Chitty, D. *The Desert a City* (Oxford 1966).

Clay, R. M. *The Hermits and Anchorites of England* (London 1914).

Cohn, N. *The Pursuit of the Millennium* (London 1957, 1962 ed.).

Comper, F. M. *The Life of Richard Rolle* (London/Toronto 1928).

Connolly, J. L. *John Gerson: Reformer and Mystic* (Université de Louvain, Recueil de travaux publiés par les membres des Conferences d'Histoire et de Philologie, 2nd series, fasc. 12, Louvain 1928).

Constable, G. *Religious Life and Thought (11th and 12th Centuries)* (Variorum Reprints CS 89, London 1979).

Coulton, G. G. *Five Centuries of Religion*, 4 vols., vol. 4: *The Last Days of Medieval Monachism* (Cambridge Studies in Medieval Life and Thought, Cambridge 1950); *Ten Medieval Studies* (Cambridge 1930).

Crehan, J. "Saint Ignatius and Cardinal Pole," *AHSI*, anno 25, fasc. 49 (Jan.–June 1956), 72–98.

Davis, R. H. C. *A History of Medieval Europe* (London 1957, 1963 ed.).

Denifle, H. *Luther et le Lutheranisme*, tr. J. Pacquier, 4 vols., vol. 2 (Paris 1914).

Dibdin, T. F. *Typographical Antiquities*, 4 vols. (London 1810–19).

Dickens, A. G. *The Counter Reformation* (Library of European Civilisation, ed. G. Barraclough, London 1968); *The English Reformation* (London 1964, 1967 ed.); "The Last Medieval Englishman," in *Christian Spirituality, Essays presented to G. Rupp*, ed. P. N. Brooks (London 1975), 141–83.

Dictionary of National Biography, ed. S. Lee and L. Stephen, 63 vols. (London 1885–).

Douie, D. L. *Archbishop Pecham* (Oxford 1952).

Duby, G. *The Age of the Cathedrals* . . . , tr. E. Levieux and B. Thompson (Geneva 1966–67, 1981 London ed.).

Evenett, H. O. and J. Bossy. *The Spirit of the Counter Reformation* (The Birkbeck Lectures in Ecclesiastical History 1951, Cambridge 1968).

Ferguson, W. "Renaissance tendencies in the religious thought of Erasmus," *JHI*, vol. 15, no. 4 (Oct. 1954), 499–508.

Fosbroke, T. D. *British Monachism* (London 1802, 1843 ed.).

Foss, M. *The Founding of the Jesuits* (London 1969).

Freeman, R. *English Emblem Books* (London 1948).

Gage, A. *The One Work* (London 1961).

Gardner, H. "Walter Hilton and the mystical tradition in England," in *Essays and Studies*, vol. 22 (English Association, Oxford 1937).

Garin, E. *Science and Civic Life in the Italian Renaissance*, tr. P. Munz (New York 1969).

Gasquet, F. *The Eve of the Reformation* (London 1900, 1919 ed.).

Goldschmidt, E. P. *Gothic and Renaissance Bookbindings*, 2 vols. (London 1928).

Grundmann, H. *Religiose Bewegungen im Mittelalter* (Historische Studien Hft. 267, Berlin 1935).

Haller, W. *The Rise of Puritanism* (Columbia 1938, 1957 ed. New York).

Heath, P. E. *English Parish Clergy* . . . (Studies in Social History, London 1969).

Hill, C. *Society and Puritanism* . . . (London 1964, 1969 ed.).

Holmes, G. *The Florentine Enlightenment* (London 1969).

Huizinga, J. *The Waning of the Middle Ages* (London 1924, 1965 ed.).

Hyma, A. *The Christian Renaissance* . . . (New York/London 1925); *The Youth of Erasmus* (University of Michigan pub., History and Political Science, vol. 10, Ann Arbor, Michigan 1930).

Jacob, E. F. *Essays in the Conciliar Epoch* (Manchester 1953); "Gerard Groote and the beginnings of the New Devotion in the Low Countries," *JEH*, vol. 3, no. 1 (Jan.–April 1952), 40–57.

Janelle, P. *Robert Southwell, the Writer* (London 1935).

Jedin, H. *A History of the Council of Trent*, tr. E. Graf, vol. 1 (London 1957).

Jones, R. *The Flowering of Mysticism* (New York 1939).

Jung, E. M. "On the nature of evangelism in sixteenth–century Italy," *JHI*, vol. 14, no. 4 (Oct. 1953), 511–27.

Jungmann, J. A. *The Mass of the Roman Rite*, 2 vols. (New York 1951–55).

Knappen, M. M. *Tudor Puritanism* (Chicago/London 1939, 1965 ed.).

Knowles, D. *The English Mystical Tradition* (London 1960); *The Monastic Order in England 940–1216* (Cambridge 1943, 1963 ed.); *The Evolution of Medieval Thought* (London 1962, 1965 ed.).

Kristeller, P. O. *Eight Philosophers of the Italian Renaissance* (Stanford 1964); "Lay religious traditions and Florentine Platonism," in *Studies in Renaissance Thought and Letters* (Edizioni di Storia e Letteratura, vol. 54, Rome 1956), 99–121; *The Philosophy of Marsilio Ficino*, tr. V. Conant (Columbia Studies in Philosophy 6, New York 1943); "Giovanni Pico della Mirandola and his sources," in *L'Opera e il Pensiero di Giovanni Pico della Mirandola nella Storia dell' Umanesimo* (Florence 1965), 35–142; *Renaissance Essays from the Journal of the History of Ideas*, ed. with P. P. Wiener

(New York 1968); *Renaissance Thought . . .* (Harvard 1955, 1961 ed.); *Renaissance Thought II . . .* (New York 1965).

Kurtz, L. P. *The Dance of Death and the Macabre Spirit in European Literature* (Institute of French Studies, Columbia University, New York 1934).

Lacarriere, J. *The God Possessed* (Paris 1961, London 1963 ed.).

Lawlor, R. "Geometry in the Service of Prayer," *Parabola*, vol. 3, no. 1 (Feb. 1978), 12–19.

Lawson, J. *A Town Grammar School through Six Centuries* (London 1963).

Leff, G. *Heresy in the Later Middle Ages . . .* , 2 vols. (Manchester 1967).

Lewis, C. S. *The Allegory of Love . . .* (Oxford 1936, 1958 ed.).

Little, A. G. "The introduction of the Observant Friars into England," *PBA* vol. 10 (London 1923), 455–71, and vol. 27 (1927), 155–61.

Louth, A. *The Origins of the Christian Mystical Tradition* (Oxford 1981, 1983 ed.).

Lupton, J. H. *A Life of Dean Colet* (London 1909).

McCann, J. and C. Cary Elwes. *Ampleforth and its Origins . . .* (London 1952).

McConica, J. K. *English Humanists and Reformation Politics . . .* (Oxford 1965).

Male, E. *The Gothic Image . . .* , tr. D. Nussey (Paris 1908, 1961 ed.).

Material for Thought, no. 13 (Far West Editions, San Francisco 1992).

Mathew, D. and G. *The Reformation and the Contemplative Life* (London 1934).

Martz, L. L. *The Poetry of Meditation* (Yale Studies in English, vol. 125, New Haven 1954).

Mattingley, G. *Catherine of Aragon* (London 1942).

Miles, L. *John Colet and the Platonic Tradition* (London 1962).

Mullins, P. J. *The Spiritual Life according to St. Isidore of Seville* (Catholic University of America Studies in Medieval and Renaissance Latin Language and Literature 13, Washington, D.C. 1940).

Nasr, S. H. *Living Sufism* (London 1972, 1980 ed.).

Needleman, J. *Lost Christianity* (New York 1980); *A Sense of the Cosmos* (New York 1975); *The New Religions* (New York 1970, 1977 ed.); *Consciousness and Tradition* (New York 1982).

New Catholic Encyclopaedia, 15 vols. (New York 1967).

Nicoll, M. *The New Man* (London 1950, 1967 ed.).

Notes and Queries, 6th series, vol. 11 (London Jan.–June 1885).

Nuttall, G. F. *The Puritan Spirit* (London 1957).

Obermann, H. A. *The Harvest of Medieval Theology* (Cambridge Mass. 1963).

O'Connor, M. *The Art of Dying Well . . .* (Columbia University Studies in English and Comparative Literature 156, New York 1942).

Owst, G. R. *Literature and Pulpit in Medieval England* (Oxford 1933, 1961 ed.); *Preaching in Medieval England* (Cambridge Studies in Medieval Life and Thought, Cambridge 1926).

Panofsky, E. *Renaissance and Renascences in Western Art* (London 1970).

Pantin, W. A. "Some medieval English treatises on the origins of monasticism," in *Medieval Studies presented to Rose Graham*, ed. V. Ruffer and A. J. Taylor (Oxford 1950), 189–215; "Two treatises of Uthred of Bolden on the monastic life," in *Studies in Medieval History presented to F. M. Powicke*, ed. R. W. Hunt, W. A. Pantin and R. W. Southern (Oxford 1948), 363–85.

Peters, W. A. M. "Richard Whytford and St. Ignatius' visit to England," *AHSI, anno* 25, *fasc.* 49 (Jan.–June 1956), 328–50.

Phillips, M. M. *Erasmus and the Northern Renaissance* (London 1949).

Pourrat, P. *Christian Spirituality*, tr. W. H. Mitchell and S. P. Jacques, 3 vols. (London 1922–27).

Reed, A. W. *Early Tudor Drama* (London 1926).

Rice, E. F. Jr. *The Renaissance Idea of Wisdom* (Harvard Historical Monographs 37, Cambridge Mass. 1958).

Rieger, J. H. "Erasmus, Colet and the schoolboy Jesus," in *Studies in the Renaissance*, no. 9 (Renaissance Society of America, New York 1962), 187–94.

Robb, N. *Neoplatonism of the Italian Renaissance* (London 1935).

Robin Skynner, A. C. "The relationship of psychotherapy to sacred tradition," in *On the Way to Self Knowledge*, ed. J. Needleman and D. Lewis (New York 1976), 204–39.

Rupp, G. *Luther's Progress to the Diet of Worms* (London 1951, 1964 ed.).

Schuon, F. "No activity without Truth," in *The Sword of Gnosis*, ed. J. Needleman (Baltimore 1974), 27–39.

Seebohm, F. *The Oxford Reformers* (Everyman Library 665, London 1914).

Simon, J. *Education and Society in Tudor England* (Cambrdge 1966).

Sole, S. H. *Jesus Psalter . . .* (London 1888).

Southern, A. C. *Elizabethan Recusant Prose* (London 1950).

Southern, R. W. *The Making of the Middle Ages* (London 1953, 1959 ed.).

Spitz, L. *The Religious Renaissance of the German Humanists* (Cambridge, Mass. 1963).

Squire, A. "Aelred of Rievaulx and the monastic tradition concerning action and contemplation," in *Downside Review,* no. 72 (1954), 289–303.

Thompson, E. M. *The Carthusian Order in England* (Church Historical Society pub. new series 3, London 1930).

Thrupp, S. *The Merchant Class of Medieval London* (Chicago 1948).

Thurston, H. "The so–called Bridgettine Rosary," in *The Month*, vol. 100, no. 458 (Aug. 1902), 189–203; "The first Englishman to make the Spiritual Exercises," in *The Month*, vol. 142, no. 712 (Oct. 1923), 336–47.

Tuveson, E. L. *Millennium and Utopia . . .* (Berkeley/Los Angeles 1949).

Underhill, E. *Mysticism . . .* (London 1911, 1961 ed.).

Villari, P. *The Life and Times of Girolamo Savonarola*, tr. L. Villari, 2 vols. (London 1888–9).

Walker, D. P. *The Ancient Theology* . . . (London 1972).

Walker, K. *The Conscious Mind* (London 1962).

Watrigant, H. "La méditation méthodique et l'école des frères de la vie commune" and "La méditation méthodique et Jean Mauburnus," in *Revue d'ascétique et de mystique,* vols. 3 (Toulouse 1922), 134–35, and 4 (1923), 13–29.

Weis, F, L. *The Life, Teachings and Works of Johannes Denck* (Strasbourg 1924).

White, H. C. *Social Criticism in Popular Religious Literature of the Sixteenth Century* (New York 1944); *The Tudor Books of Private Devotion* (Madison, Wisc. 1951).

Wind, E. *Pagan Mysteries in the Renaissance* (London 1958, 1967 ed.).

Workman, H. B. *The Evolution of the Monastic Ideal* (London 1913).

Wright, L. B. *Middle Class Culture in Elizabethan England* (Huntingdon Library pub., Chapel Hill, University of North Carolina 1935).

Wylie, J. H. *The Reign of Henry the Fifth*, 3 vols. (Cambridge 1914).

Yates, F. *Giordano Bruno and the Hermetic Tradition* (London 1964); *The Art of Memory* (London 1966, 1969 ed.).

Zeeveld, W. Gordon. *Foundations of Tudor Policy* (Harvard 1948, 1969 ed.).

Zijl, T. P. Van. *Gerard Groote, Ascetic and Reformer* (Catholic University of America Studies in Medieval History, new series 18, Washington, D.C. 1963).

Index

Abba Alonius, 220

Abbaye of the Holy Ghoste, 6

abbot, the representative of Christ, xv

abgeschiedenheit. See Meister Eckhart

academic study: and experience, xiv, xxi, 87, 122, 141, 153, 177, 228, 237, 242, 244; limitations of, ix, 83–84, 111, 115–16, 134–35, 137, 138, 148–49, 150. *See also* self-knowledge

accidie, 225

action & 'active life', 1–19, 149, 197, 245, 305 n. 2. *See also* contemplation & 'contemplative life'; Martha & Mary; 'mixed life'; Renaissance, Italian

activation, ix, 97, 118, 126

"actual attention." *See* "angels, attention of"

adiaphora, 260 n. 130, 292 n. 162

Adrian IV (Pope), 195

agape, 239. *See also* love

Alberti, Leon Battista, 25–26

alchemy, 148

Alcock, John (bishop of Ely), 3–4

Alexandria, legend of the cobbler of, 50, 52

Ambrose, Saint, 90

analogical thought, 1, 166, 243, 319 n. 266, 320 n. 282; in Bridget, 72–74; in Hylton, 14–15; and *lectio divina,* 3; in New Devotion, 71, 94, 97; in William of St.Thierry, x, 245; in *Ymage of love,* 59–72, 78. *See also* The Bible; meditation

anchorites, medieval, xviii

Andreae, J. V., 51

"angels, attention of," 243–44. *See also* attention

Anglican church, 198, 240

Anglo-Saxon monasticism, 213

Anselm, Saint (archbishop of Canterbury), 93, 135

Anthony the Great, Saint, 237; and angel, 137; and cobbler of Alexandria, 50; 'first monk', 50, 239; on pleasing God, 305. n. 6; on sleep, 300 n. 101

anticlericalism in 16th cent. *See* Erastianism

Antonio da Barga, 122

apatheia, 49, 220, 239, 302 n. 125. *See also* asceticism; purification of emotion

Apophthegmata Patrum, 220, 226–27. *See also* Desert Fathers

Aristotle, in Renaissance thought, 25

Arnold of Schoonhoven, 304 n. 196

ars memorativa, 59, 165, 317 n. 243. *See also* meditation; "remembering"

ars moriendi, 191–92, 214. *See also* death

"art is better than evil strength," 18, 167–68, 206. *See also* craft; "violence"

art, traditional Christian, ix; imagery of, 78; meditation on, 71

"as above-so below," 14. *See also* order; unity

asceticism, xviii-xix, 32, 69, 236–39, 305 n. 2; and balance, 47–50, 137, 238; Gans-

ties
Epistle of Prayer, 49–50
Erasmus, Desiderius: on baptismal vow,
36, 51; Christian humanism of, 26, 32,
51–52, 53, 56–57; on Christian warfare,
35–36; on circles of humanity in body of
Christ, 15; on city as monastery, 5,
51–52, 56; and Luther, 26, 31, 51–52;
and mixed life, 36, 41, 44, 50–52, 56–57,
104; on monastic life, 40, 43, 50–51, 57,
64, 102; and New Devotion, 5, 32,
51–52, 53, 56–57, 93; and personal freedom, 40, 43, 102; *philosophia Christi,* 15,
32, 52, 93; on 'regeneration of man', 52;
and restoration of theology, 51–52, 53,
56–57; his search, 53, 56–7. Works: *De
Contemptu Mundi,* 40; *Enchiridion,* 15,
25, 35, 41, 51–52, 230; *Paraclesis,* 52. *See
also* Colet, John; Luther, Martin; Ryckes,
John; Whytford, Richard
Erastianism, 5, 58
"estrangement, land of," (*regio dissimilitudinis*), 115–17, 120, 122
Evangelicals, Italian. *See* Ochino,
Bernardino
evil, 56, 79, 118. *See also* good & evil

fac quod in se est, 55, 156, 159–60, 193,
222, 226
faith, 83; 'the age of', xiii, 42; man's lack of,
ix, 32, 115; medieval ideals of, xix; "in
search of understanding," xiii, 16, 32,
46, 73, 107, 125, 133, 135, 181–82; and
submission, 37, 103, 220. *See also* hope;
love
'Fall of man', 211, 223; and New Devotion,
78, 116–22, 168, 180, 242; in *Regula
Benedicti,* xvii. *See also* duality; justice;
sin
family, 193. *See also* 'common life, the';
matrimony
fear: of God, 70, 73, 93, 86, 138, 191;
morality of, 36, 39, 70, 155, 191, 238;
and wisdom, 276 n. 51
Feckenham, Abbot John, 3

Fewterer, John, 217–18, 220, 296 n. 55. *See
also The Glasse of Christes Passion*
Ficino, Marsilio: on action & contemplation, 27–29; on chaos in man, 29, 33–34;
on living in present, 33–34; and New
Devotion, 29–34; on remembering ones
death, 34; his search, 32–33; on self-
knowledge, 29, 32–33, 70; on sleep of
man, 29, 32; on the soul, 29, 31–34; and
Syon, 229; on unity of religion and philosophy, 31–33. *See also* contemplation
& 'contemplative life'; guilds, lay religious; Platonists, Renaissance
fire, 73–74. *See also* duality; Spirit, The Holy
Fish, Simon, 42, 136
Fisher, John (Archbishop of Canterbury),
12, 214, 229
Fitzhugh, Sir Hugh, 213
Flanders, intellectual and spiritual life of,
75
'the flesh': disorganised appetites of, 69,
84–85, 150, 208, 227, 236–38, 243, 293
n. 171; opposes the spirit, 46, 73. *See
also* body, the physical; The Devil; self,
man's lower; 'the world'
Florence Radewijns, 121, 147, 172, 204; on
being a brother, 81, 136; and Desert
Fathers, 91, 97, 137, 149; on devotion,
82; on disorder of the three forces, 117;
on habits, 284 n. 53; on holy work, 137,
164; on imagination, 136; his indifference to reputation, 89; his methods,
146; on monastic vow, 108; and nucleus
of Brotherhood, 76, 81, 88–90, 134, 145;
on paying for ones livelihood, 136.
Works: *Multum Valet,* 91; *Omnes Inquit
Artes,* 91
The Floure of godlye prayers (Thomas
Becon), 197
Fontius, 31
food: analogy of, 47–49, 97, 107–8,
147–48, 150–51, 183, 200–201, 203, 223;
of impressions, 48, 107, 150–51, 163,
200, 233, 238; for mind, ix, 93. *See also
masticatio;* prayer; scale; the soul

Hylton, Walter *(continued)*
Christ', 14–15, 50, 60; on self-observa-
tion, 17–18. Works: *Medylde lyfe,* 10–19;
Scala Perfectionis, 9, 218. *See also* Rolle,
Richard

"I am": Christ's saying, 107; in prayer, x,
105–6, 126, 206; and the 'upper chamber', 157. *See also* the heart
ideals, religious: medieval, 22, 120, 167,
172, 189; in 16th century, 50, 180. *See
also* balance; faith; order; service
idleness, 1, 135–36, 137, 164, 205
Ignatius Loyola, 182; and Montserrat, 106,
120–21, 234; and New Devotion, 71,
106, 112, 120–21, 153, 162; and Syon,
185, 218, 234–35, 309 n. 99. Works:
Confessions, 49; *Spiritual Exercises,* 36,
49, 70–71, 73, 112, 120, 129, 156, 165,
176, 183–85, 203, 206, 222, 230, 234–35,
239. *See also* Jesuits
'Image of God', man as: teaching of, 59, 77,
79–80, 120–29, 154, 157, 176, 190, 203,
211, 236, 240, 243; deformation of, xviii,
68–69, 78, 101, 116–29, 199; and "image
of love," 68–69, 74, 78; and work of
Brethren, 82, 88. *See also* justice; order;
scale; the soul; The Trinity
imagination (fantasy), 135–36, 139, 168
imitatio Christi: and Bridgettines, 66, 230,
233–35; and Carthusians, 100; Colet on,
56; and humanism, 154, 251 n. 21; in
Isidore of Seville, 192–93; and New
Devotion, 2, 56, 106, 146, 153–54,
156–59; and *vita apostolica,* 2, 11, 106.
See also Christ, Presence of; *conformitas
Christi;* Gerard Groote; Peryn, William;
Thomas à Kempis
Imitatione Christi, De. See Thomas à Kempis
impressions. *See* food
influences, 98, 128–29, 139, 166–67,
209–10, 231–32, 241. *See also* Christianity; religion; search; spiritual exercises;
'the world'

inner & outer life of man: analogy of
monastery, 6; analogy of workshop, 12;
'Bernard' on, 123; in humanist thought,
31, 39; and "image of love," 74; and
mixed life, 13, 15, 17–18, 55, 72, 78, 164,
172, 180, 195, 198, 201, 205–6, 236,
241–42; separation of, x, 29, 65, 69,
78–79, 130, 138, 249–50 n. 22; and 'spiritual Christianity', 63–65, 79; unifying
of, 65, 72, 223, 228, 245; William of St
Thierry on, x, 245; and work of Brotherhood, 82, 130, 138, 141, 159, 160–61,
228; *See also* energies in man; the soul
instinct, 183
intentio: Bridget on, 72–4; Brotherhood's
renewal of, 55, 70, 109, 111, 133, 140,
141–44, 149, 161, 167, 171–72, 178, 302
n. 141; discovery of, 128, 134, 139, 166;
in *Dyurnall,* 178, 183; false, 148; and
monastic vow, 111, 204; Peryn on, 195;
in Southwell, 204, 205, 206; 'wish' &
'attention', 18. *See also* spiritual work
Isidore of Seville, 90, 192–93

Jacob's ladder, 23
"Jericho," city of the moon: Cisneros on,
120–21; and compunction, 128; explo-
ration of, 121, 133–34, 139, 166–67;
Mombaer on, 121; Zerbolt on, 115–16,
119, 156, 220. *See also* self-knowledge
Jerome, Saint, 4, 60, 90, 92
"Jerusalem," city of peace, 116, 120, 121,
167
Jesuits: asceticism of, 49; and Calvinists,
70; influence of, 176, 201, 203–9; and
New Devotion, xx, 99, 176, 183, 203,
209, 232–33; *Regulae* of, 203. *See also*
Ignatius Loyola; psychology, traditional
'Jesus Prayer', 236, 312 n. 147, 313 n. 150,
315 n. 204. *See also* Holy Name
John the Baptist, 206
John Cassian: *Collations* of, 91; and Gerard
Groote, 90–94; and intentio, 111, 149;
on manual work, 137; on three ways of
spiritual life, 1. *See also* asceticism;

Desert Fathers; Gerard Groote; *intentio;* manual work
John Climachus, Saint: and Syon, 92, 218, 229, 296 n. 55; and Brotherhood, 82, 90–93. *See also* Desert Fathers
John Hatten, 92, 112, 146–47
John Ketel, 87, 134; his exercise, 140, 142, 144–47, 154, 164. *See also The Devout Exercises;* nullity, human; order of daily life
John of Leeuwen, 87
John of Leiden, 51
John Vos of Heusden, 76, 85, 146, 163, 212
Judgement, The Last, 226
justice, 175, 190; "original justice," 78, 117, 121, 128, 242–43; *Regula Benedicti* on, xvi-xvii. *See also* energies in man
'justification', 155, 222. *See also* liberation

Keating, Thomas, 65, 197–98
Kingdom of Heaven, The, 107
knowledge & being: and love, 221; and spiritual exercise, 239; and understanding, xiv, 28, 96, 116, 151–52, 166–67, 171–72. *See also* being; self-knowledge; understanding; wisdom
Knowles, David, 218

Lacke, Richard, 217
Lamentable annotations taken forth of our Rule, 45–46
Landino, Cristofero, 26–27, 42
Last Supper, The, 14
Latimer, Hugh, 43, 50, 164
latin, 143, 215–16, 230. *See also* philology; the vernacular
lay brethren, 110, 214–15
lay devotion: Erasmus on, 36, 41, 51–52, 56–57; and humanist thought, 21–46, 50–52, 77, 104, 288 n. 102; and mixed life, xx, 4–5, 50, 55–56, 72–73, 104, 107–8, 176–210, 212, 241; in Rolle and Hylton, 5–19; and Third Rule of St. Francis, 76. *See also* Bridgettines; Brotherhood; devotion; 'mixed life'; the

monk; order of daily life; Platonists, Renaissance; spiritual exercises, transmission of; Windesheim; Zerbolt, Gerard
Lazarus, 119
lectio divina: Bernard on, 97; and listening, 65, 197, 201; in *Regula Benedicti,* xv. *See also* analogical thought; Brotherhood, study of; food; Gregory the Great; listening; The Word
Lefevre d'Etaples, Jacques, 21
liberation (salvation), 101, 115–16, 128, 166; Colet on, 56; the 'first death', 191. *See also* 'regeneration of man'
'light', 94, 120, 127, 242
Lily, John, 55
listening, 123, 142–43, 160–61, 310 n. 106, 316 n. 218; and prayer, 125–26, 223, 243. *See also* the heart; lectio divina; silence; The Word
literacy, 5, 71, 178, 187, 200. *See also* printing presses
liturgy, ix, xxi, 221, 241; participation in, 106–107, 152, 162, 167–73, 189, 190–92, 222–23, 225, 231; at Syon, 219, 222–29. *See also* attention; *opus dei;* participation; "remembering"
Lollards, 5, 168; writings of, published in early sixteenth century 47, 57, 165, 217. *See also* Beguines; heresy
love: Christian search for, 59–74, 126–27, 145, 220–21; as consciousness of heart, 18, 232–33, 258 n. 72; and duality of human psyche, 15, 71–72; lack of in man, ix, 115; of neighbour as oneself, 126–27, 136, 170, 179, 189; non-egoistic, 60, 68–70, 107, 208; ordering of, 68–74, 119, 120–21, 125, 178, 180, 220–21, 272 n. 74; in Renaissance thought, 27, 30, 33; self-love, 66, 126, 157–58; "true image of," 67–72; as warfare, 156. *See also* Brotherhood; Christianity; emotional life; faith; the heart; hope; magic; Rolle, Richard; Ruysbroeck, John; the the soul

purification of emotion: and contemplation, 10–11; work of the monastery, xv, xviii, 220–21, 226–27, 232, 240; and Ignatian Exercises, 184; and New Devotion, 34, 146, 151. *See also apatheia;* asceticism; emotional life; Presence of God; spiritual exercises; Way of the monk
Puritanism, 9, 187, 189, 295 n. 35
Pythagoras, 1, 21

Quentin, Johan, 186
questioning. *See* search; self-examination

Radical Reformation, 65, 75, 85, 161, 164. *See also* Denck, Hans
rapiaria, 89, 105, 149, 200, 239–40
Ravenna, ix
Rawlyns, Nicholas, 45
reason: "head of the the soul," 29, 79; light of, 190; and love, 70; subserves physical body, 16, 29, 78–79, 117–19. *See also* body, the physical; mind; the the soul
"recollection": exercise of, 16, 107, 130–31, 142, 152, 183, 191, 198; of oneself, 105–6, 129–31, 183, 195, 209, 232–33, 236. *See also* meditation; "remembering"
Recusant lists, 214
redemption ("spiritual creation"), 237. *See also* 'regeneration of man'
Reformation, 3; contradictions of, 102; wish for freedom in, 64, 102, 112–13. *See also* lay devotion; 'mixed life'; Protestant reformers
'regeneration of man', 130, 211–12; and Bridgettines, 236–37, 241; Erasmus on, 52; Peryn on, 196; in Renaissance thought, 22–23; and work of Brotherhood, 82, 88, 121, 130, 139, 154, 212. *See also* attention; liberation; transformation
regio dissimilitudinis. See "estrangement, land of"
Regula Benedicti, xv-xix, 24, 43, 62, 203. *See also* death; Desert Fathers; 'Fall of man'; habits; humility; justice; *lectio div-*

ina; monastic rules; self-denial; self, man's lower; spiritual work; Way of the monk
religion: begins above level of life, 55, 125, 127–28, 135–39, 150–51, 156, 166–67, 170, 180–81, 185, 201, 208, 220–22, 224, 228, 232, 242, 245; "of the heart," 6, 209; humanist redefinition of, 24–34, 80, 92–93; monasticism as, xiv, 3–4; *re-ligio,* xiv, 14–15, 28, 116, 152, 212, 225; 16th century reorientation of, x-xi, xiii, xx, 3, 98, 99. *See also* Christianity; 'mixed life'; monastery, the medieval; Platonists, Renaissance; practicality in religion; religious method; Ways, the traditional; 'the world'
religious method: 'how' of religion, 97, 116, 138, 150, 152, 165–73; Ignatian, 156; monastic knowledge of, 16, 36, 106–8, 121–22, 159. *See also* craft; monastery, the medieval; practicality in religion; psychology, traditional; spiritual exercises; spiritual work; Way of the monk
"remembering": and forgetting, xvi, 144, 167, 177, 204, 232, 235–36; and mixed life, 107–8, 139, 141, 143–44, 148, 179–81, 233; oneself, x, xi, xix, 14–15, 33, 79, 105–6, 122, 123, 125–28, 135, 171–72, 175, 182–83, 195–96, 223. *See also* attention; liturgy; meditation; "recollection"; *ruminatio;* self-knowledge; spiritual exercises
remorse. *See* conscience
Renaissance, Italian, 2; and ancient wisdom, 21–34, 80; and 'active life', 24–28, 34, 172; and origins of modern science, 24, 32; and Protestantism, 11, 74; and 'three lives', 25–34. *See also* freedom; Humanism; Petrarch; Platonists, Renaissance; urban culture
renewal: and New Devotion, 53, 97, 99–100, 111, 134–35; of tradition, xiv, 99–100, 106. *See also* attention; Christian tradition; *intentio*

vice, 11
Victorine school: and Brotherhood, 90;
and medieval mystical tradition, 90,
217–18, 240; and Syon, 62, 217, 218,
229. See also Hugh of St. Victor; Richard
of St. Victor
"violence," 113, 193, 206, 224
Virgin Mary, 9, 156, 222–29. See also The
Myroure of Oure ladye; Ymage of love
"virtual attention," 244. See also attention
virtue, 148, 220, 243, 278 n. 18; in Renaissance thought, 25, 26
vita apostolica, 1–2, 11–12, 104, 106, 236.
See also 'being in, but not of, the world';
Christianity, early; 'mixed life'
Vita Christi (Ludolph of Saxony), 186,
229–30
Vitis Sanctorum Patrum, De, 90–91. See
also Desert Fathers

warfare, inner. See psychomachia
watching: and Desert Fathers, xxi, 320 n.
282; in Ficino, 32; and prayer, xxi,
17–18, 69, 78, 133, 139, 147, 168–72,
190; in Southwell, 175, 205–8; and Syon,
78, 190, 225–27, 242; and work of
Brotherhood, 133, 139, 141, 147,
168–72, 178. See also "remembering";
self-observation; sleep
'the way in life', 4, 43–44, 55; and New
Devotion, 98, 162, 164, 245; and Renaissance Platonists, 34. See also 'being in,
but not of, the world'; craft; Gerard
Groote; 'mixed life'; the New Devotion;
order of daily life
Way of the monk, 4, 185, 211–12; Gerard
Groote on, 100–102, 109; and mixed
life, xiii, xv, xx, 17–18, 128, 135, 146,
176, 177–78, 211–12; against nature,
xvii, xix, 46, 103, 224, 305 n. 204; and
Regula Benedicti, xvii, 211. See also
Desert Fathers; faith; the monk; 'mixed
life'; psychology, traditional; religious
method; sleep; spiritual work
Ways, the traditional, 101–2, 135; disci-

plines of, 103–104, 141, 158; and mixed
life, 139, 166; and philosophy, 23–24,
32–33; Plotinus on, 258 n. 71. See also
'the way in life'; Way of the monk
Wessel Gansfort, 71, 148, 150; and Brotherhood, 83, 130; on meditation, 48, 130,
142, 155–56, 170–71. Works: De Oratione, 130; De Sacramento Eucharistiae,
47–48, 107–8, 159, 162, 233; Scala Meditationis, 172; Tractatus de cohibendis cogitationibus, 130. See also attention; food;
meditation; "recollection"; "remembering"; The Word
'who am I?', ix, xvi, 123, 140, 151, 160
Whytford, Richard, 223, 225, 235; and
Christian humanism, 187; and Colet's
circle, 55; and Counter-Reformation,
187, 191, 235; and Erasmus, 77, 102,
192; and Ignatius, 185, 188, 191; on
mixed life, 12, 50, 57, 179, 189; and New
Devotion, 187–89, 190–92, 204, 229,
301 n. 118; and Observance, 4, 71, 77,
187, 199, 220; on sleep, 78; and transmission of spiritual exercises, 36, 77, 92,
179, 186, 187–93, 196, 199, 209–10, 218.
Works: Dayly exercyse, 187, 188, 191–92,
215, 226; Dialoge, 63, 73, 162, 187, 188,
189–91, 200, 215; The folowyng of
Christe, 66, 218; Jesu Psalter, 9, 75;
Pacience, 187, 192–93; Pype of Perfection,
187, 240; Saynt Augustyn's Rule, 215,
229; Werke, 36, 179, 187–89, 190, 204,
215. See also Bridgettines; craft; Holy
Name; lay devotion; monastic vow
will: corruption of (see 'Fall of man'); free-
will, 55, 184, 193, 220, 225, 228; and the
involuntary, xvi, xvii; in Renaissance
thought, 28–31, 92; and monastic vow,
102–103; self-will, 141, 184, 200; and
understanding, 129, 232–33. See also
intentio; justice; love
William of St. Thierry, x, 46, 245
Windesheim: and study of ancient texts,
92; decline of, 108, 162–63; foundation,
76, 81, 85, 108; and lay devotion,

IE